I08195335

WATERFALLS OF MICHIGAN

GUIDEBOOK SERIES

PHIL STAGG

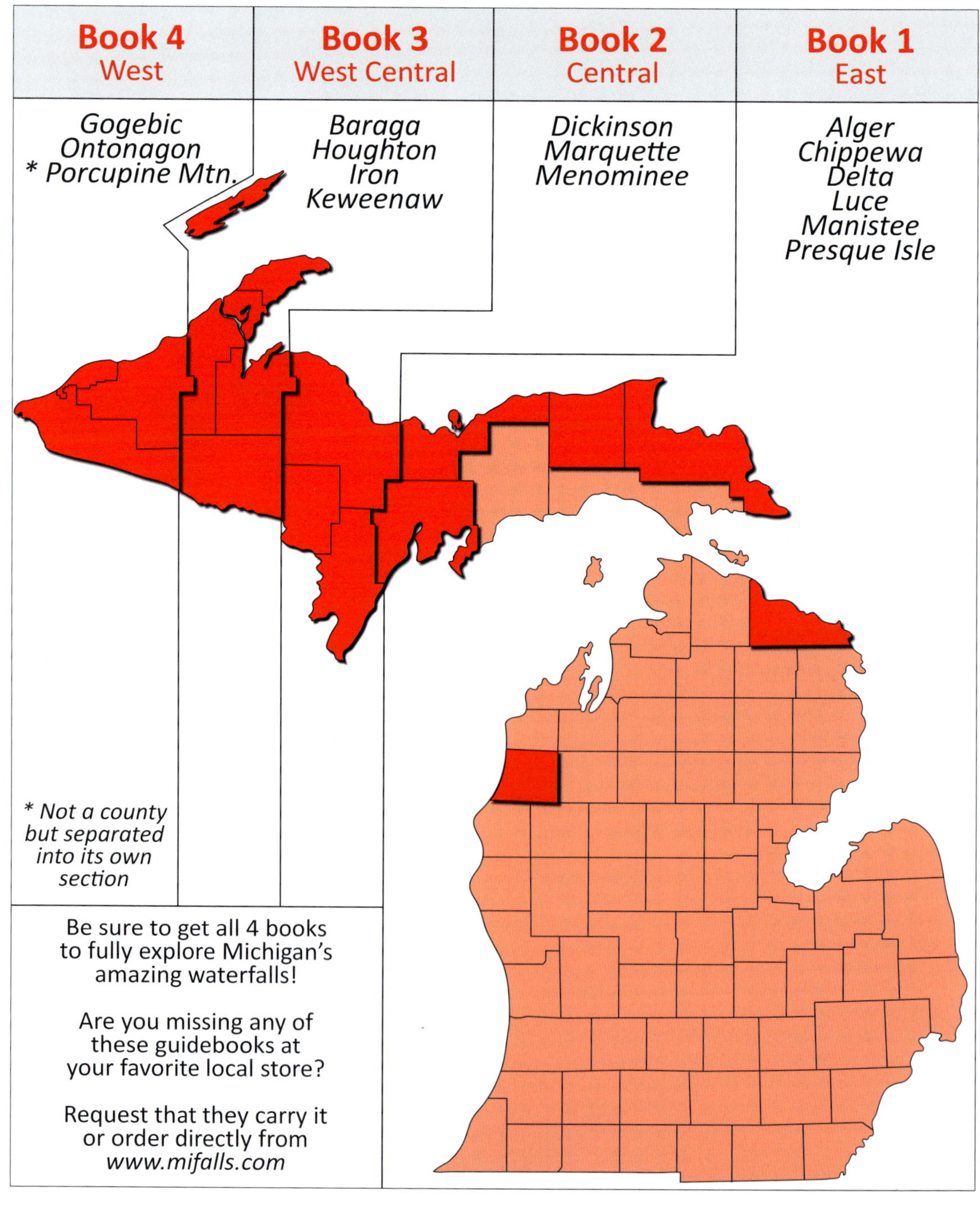

Be sure to get all 4 books to fully explore Michigan's amazing waterfalls!

Are you missing any of these guidebooks at your favorite local store?

Request that they carry it or order directly from *www.mifalls.com*

Waterfalls of Michigan

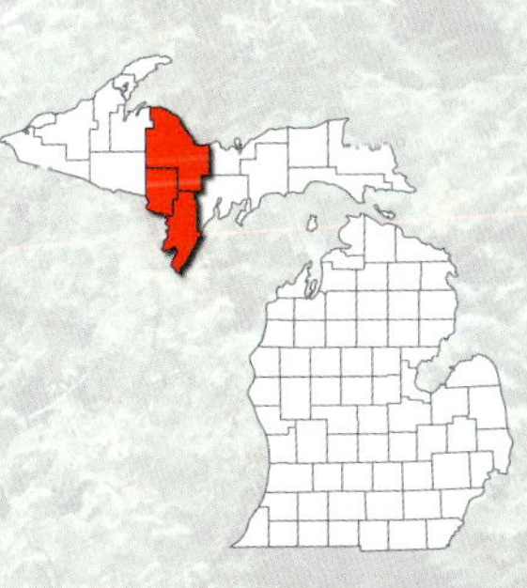

The Definitive Guide to the Waterfalls of Michigan

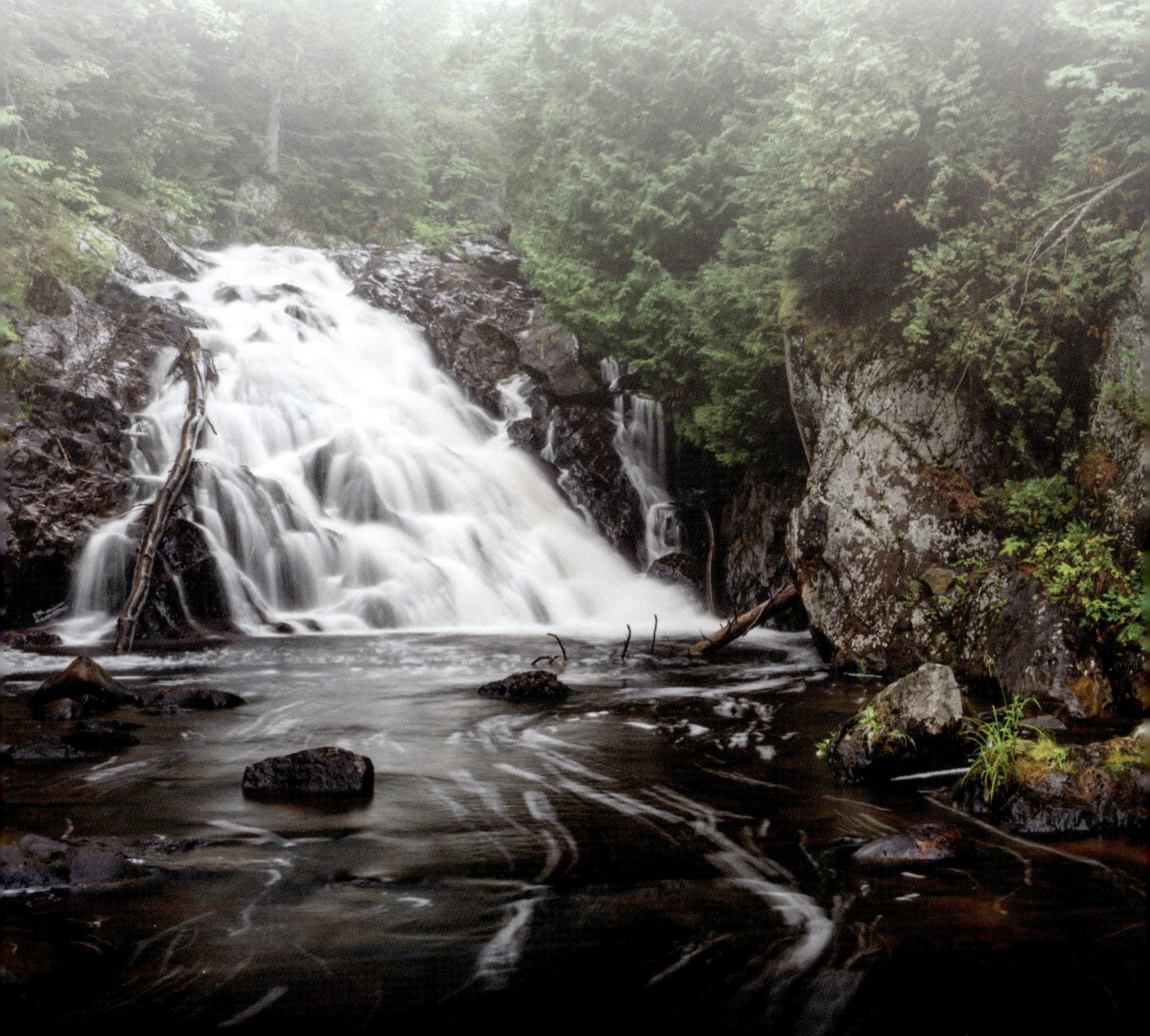

Book 2 - Central

Dickinson • Marquette
Menominee Counties

Phil Stagg

Waterfalls of Michigan
Book 2 - Central

Published by:

MI Falls Publishing
11765 West Cadillac Rd.
Cadillac, MI 49601
231•920•8416

www.mifalls.com

ISBN: 978-0-9971346-2-9
LCCN: 2016900613

Photography: Phil Stagg
Text: Phil Stagg
Design: Phil Stagg

Printed in the United States of America

First Printing: March 2017

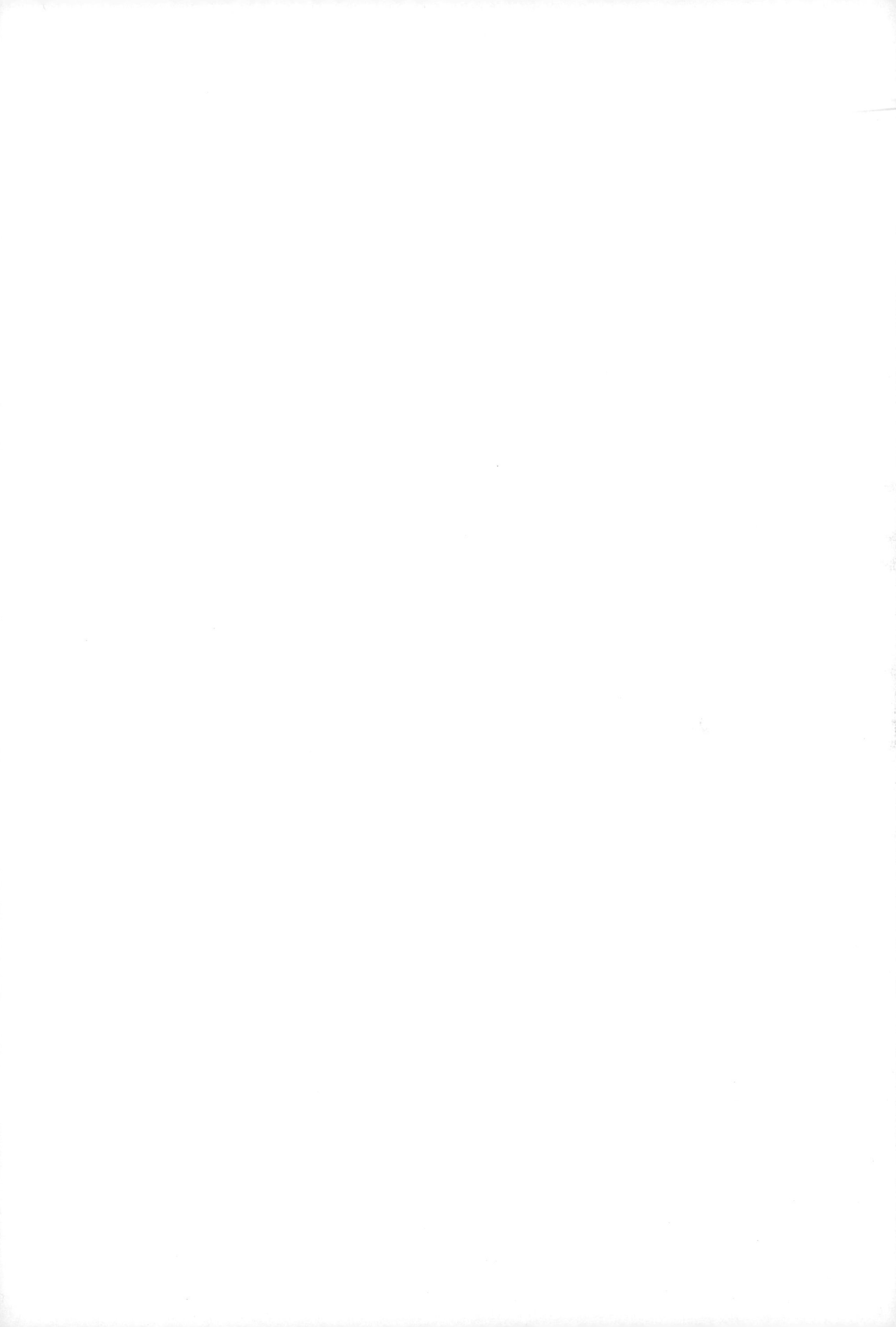

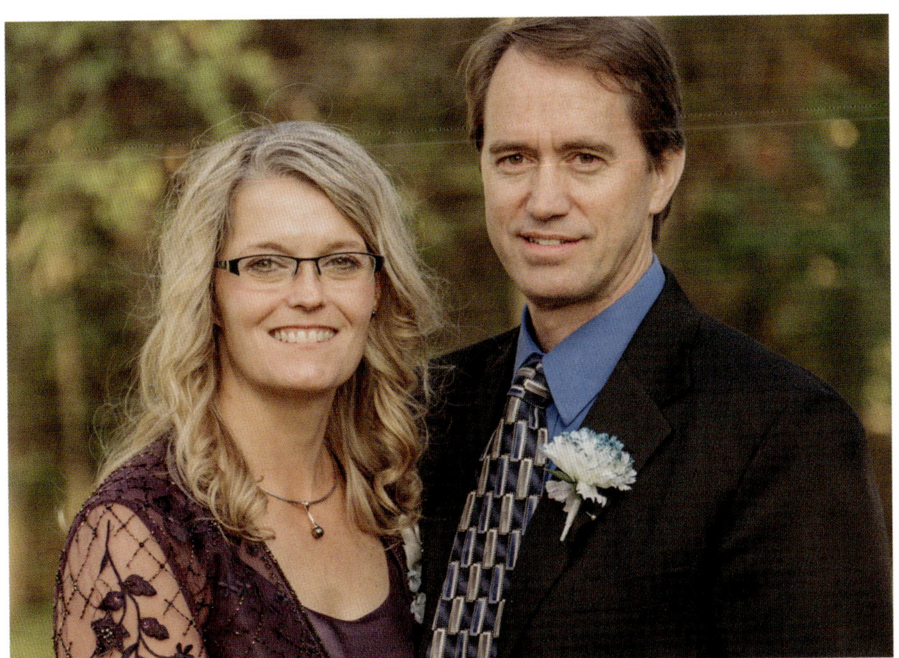

Phil Stagg

The heavens are telling the glory of God; and their expanse is declaring the work of His hands. Day to day pours forth speech, and night to night reveals knowledge. There is no speech, nor are there words; their voice is not heard. Their line has gone out through all the earth, and their utterances to the end of the world. In them He has placed a tent for the sun, which is as a bridegroom coming out of his chamber; it rejoices as a strong man to run his course. Its rising is from one end of the heavens, and its circuit to the other end of them; and there is nothing hidden from its heat.
- Psalm 19:1-6

It has been a joy to explore the waterfalls of the great state of Michigan. The beauty that is found while hiking through the wilds of the Upper Peninsula is sometimes truly breathtaking. I would recommend that you take time to follow some of my footsteps and see for yourself. And as you go, take time to see the little things. Feel the delicate touch-me-nots that are clustered by so many streams. Watch a little chipmunk as it stares at you with its glassy eyes and nervous tail. Smell the earthy scent of freshly fallen leaves. Listen to the rhythmic crash of Lake Superior onto a rocky shore. Taste a recently ripened thimbleberry plucked from its hiding place beneath oversized deep green leaves. As you experience the countless thrills of being out in nature, remember to thank nature's Creator.

I would like thank my wife, Cindy (pictured above with me), once again. She has done an immense amount of work to help me with this many yeared project. From proof reading the manuscripts, to keeping the house running smoothly, to managing our books, and so much more, she has been invaluable. Thanks so much, my love!

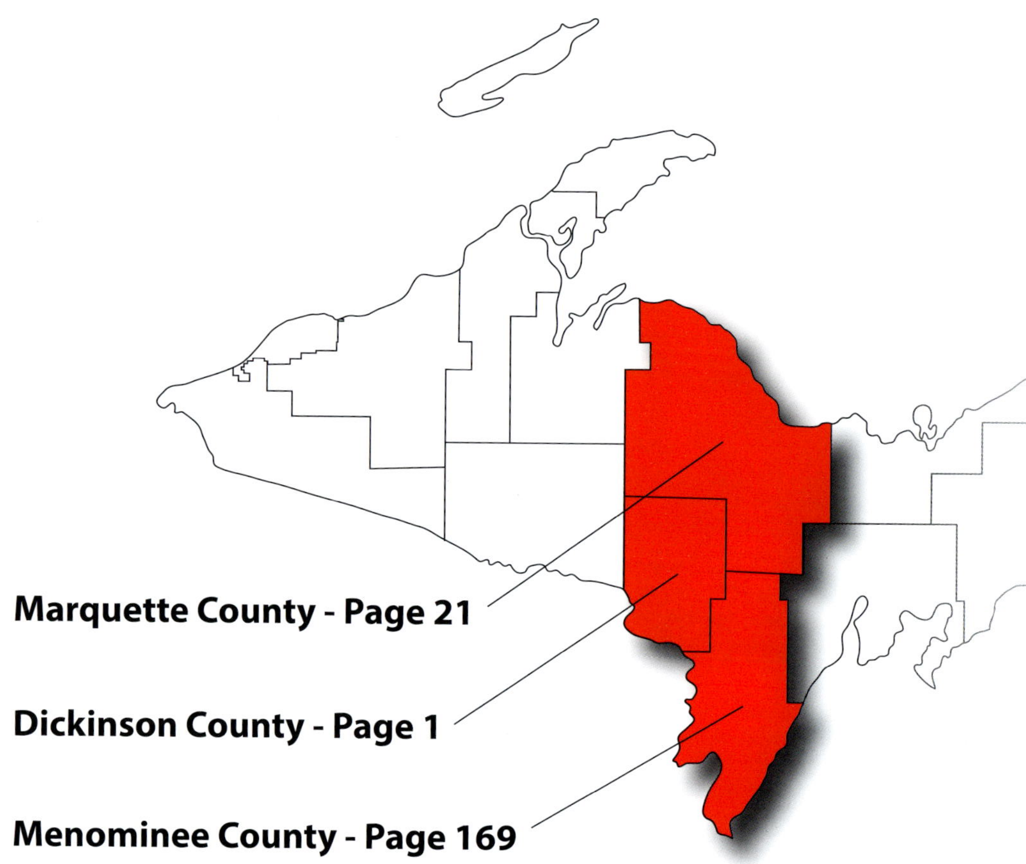
Marquette County - Page 21
Dickinson County - Page 1
Menominee County - Page 169

TABLE OF CONTENTS

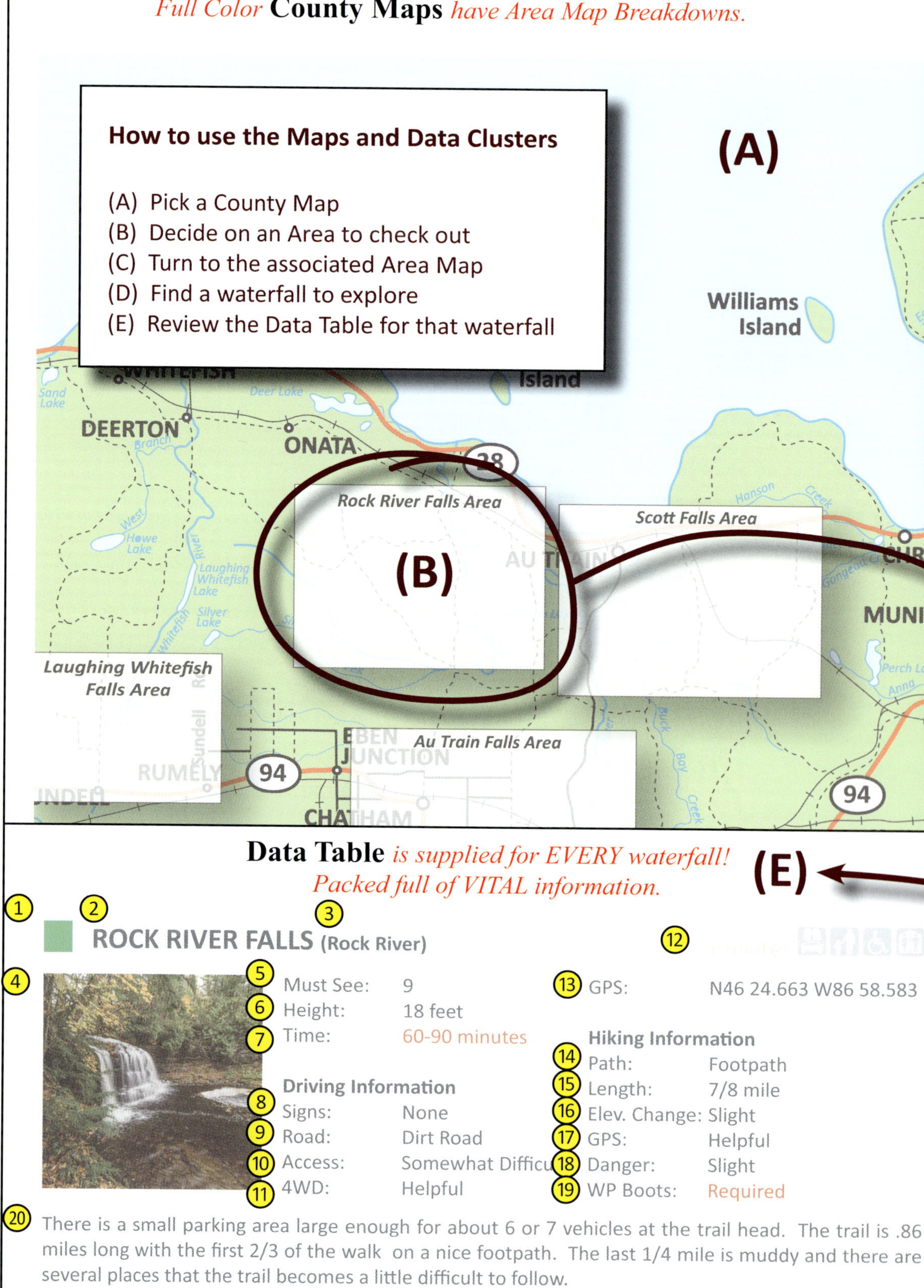
Full Color County Maps have Area Map Breakdowns.
How to use the Maps and Data Clusters
(A) Pick a County Map
(B) Decide on an Area to check out
(C) Turn to the associated Area Map
(D) Find a waterfall to explore
(E) Review the Data Table for that waterfall
(A)
Williams Island
Island
DEERTON
ONATA
28
Rock River Falls Area
(B)
Scott Falls Area
MUNIS
Laughing Whitefish Falls Area
RUMELY
94
EBEN JUNCTION
Au Train Falls Area
CHATHAM
94
Data Table is supplied for EVERY waterfall!
Packed full of VITAL information.
(E)
1
2
ROCK RIVER FALLS (Rock River)
3
12
4
5 Must See: 9
6 Height: 18 feet
7 Time: 60-90 minutes
Driving Information
8 Signs: None
9 Road: Dirt Road
10 Access: Somewhat Difficu
11 4WD: Helpful
13 GPS: N46 24.663 W86 58.583
Hiking Information
14 Path: Footpath
15 Length: 7/8 mile
16 Elev. Change: Slight
17 GPS: Helpful
18 Danger: Slight
19 WP Boots: Required
20 There is a small parking area large enough for about 6 or 7 vehicles at the trail head. The trail is .86 miles long with the first 2/3 of the walk on a nice footpath. The last 1/4 mile is muddy and there are several places that the trail becomes a little difficult to follow.

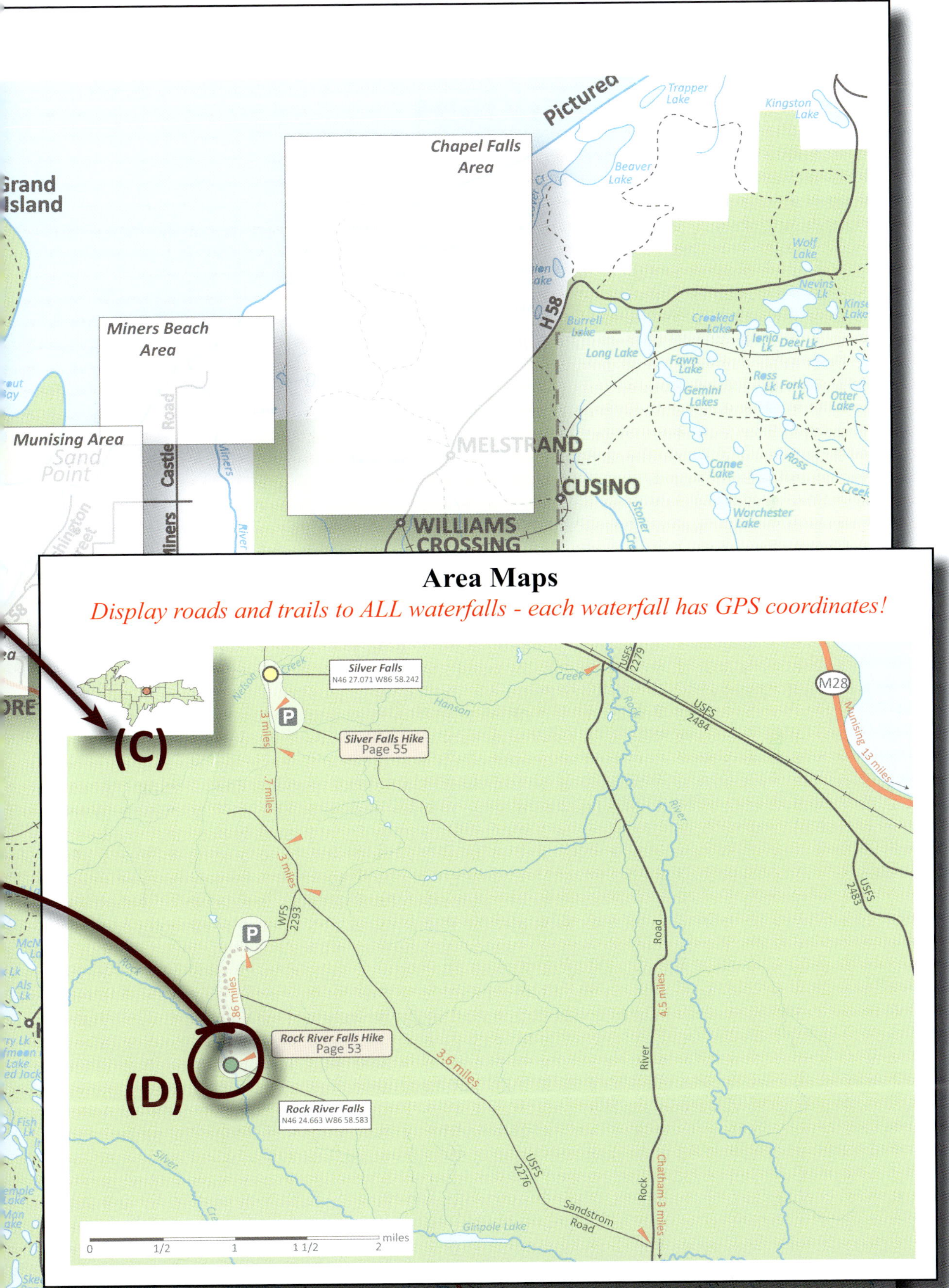
Chapel Falls Area
Miners Beach Area
Munising Area
Grand Island
Pictured
MELSTRAND
CUSINO
WILLIAMS CROSSING
Area Maps
Display roads and trails to ALL waterfalls - each waterfall has GPS coordinates!
(C)
(D)
Silver Falls
N46 27.071 W86 58.242
Silver Falls Hike
Page 55
Rock River Falls Hike
Page 53
Rock River Falls
N46 24.663 W86 58.583
M28
Munising 13 miles
USFS 2484
USFS 2483
USFS 2276
WFS 2293
Sandstrom Road
Rock River Road
Chatham 3 miles
3.6 miles
4.5 miles
Ginpole Lake
miles

Data Table
Definitions

Must See Swatch (1) The colored square in the upper, left corner of the Waterfall Data Tables corresponds with the color in the Waterfall Area Map for each particular waterfall and is derived from the "Must See" rating. Those waterfalls with a "Must See" rating of 1-3 are "Red" waterfalls. "Yellow" waterfalls have ratings of 4-6, and "Green" waterfalls are rated 7-10. Think of the "Must See Colors" as you would a standard traffic light.

Green: GO!! You've got to check these out!
Yellow: SLOW DOWN!! These are OK waterfalls, perhaps it'll be nice to visit once or twice.
Red: STOP!! These are waterfalls, or at least considered waterfalls by some, but unless you are a die-hard waterfall fan, you probably won't enjoy them.

Waterfall Name (2) "Where did you get the names from?" Good question! Most waterfalls were named many years ago and those names were incorporated into the USGS maps which are the basis for most of the maps that we have today. These resultant maps bear those names which are now commonly recognized. In the cases where waterfalls were not named on the USGS maps, the naming of the falls becomes more interesting. I typically have named "unnamed" waterfalls by the area of the river or creek on which they are found. An example of this would be "Carp River Falls - Upper #3". Also, just because a waterfall doesn't have a published name doesn't mean that the residents of an area don't have a name for it. I have tried to use the locally accepted names whenever possible.

You will also find that I rarely start a waterfall name with "Upper", "Middle", or "Lower". For ease of indexing, the name of the fall typically comes first, followed by the locational modifier and/or number if applicable.

③ *Waterway Name*

Most of the waterways on which waterfalls are found have long established names. Just like waterfalls, there are some small creeks that have no published names, but do have locally accepted names. I have used these names whenever known.

④ *Waterfall Picture*

A small picture of each waterfall is attached. Some waterfalls are on posted, private land. If I wasn't able to receive permission to photograph the waterfall, there is obviously no picture.

⑤ *Must See Rating*

Each waterfall is rated on a 1-10 scale, with one being the least desirable and 10 being the most. The following is the guideline I use:

10. Gorgeous! Great eye appeal! Inspiring! One of the best waterfalls in Michigan.
9. Excellent waterfall! You will want to make many repeat visits.
8. Very nice waterfall! Very popular!
7. Nice waterfall. Worth coming back to see several times.
6. An above average waterfall. Might want to see it again.
5. A nice all-around waterfall. Perhaps worth a repeat visit.
4. An OK waterfall. Probably not worth coming back to.
3. Don't have your hopes too high - it's not that good.
2. Avid waterfall enthusiasts may want to check it out just to say that they did.
1. It's water. It's falling. Who cares?

The "Must See" rating is my attempt at describing only the visual desirability of each waterfall. It doesn't take into account the difficulty in getting to the waterfall. There are some very nice waterfalls that require a substantial hike over rough terrain. The difficulty in reaching the waterfall doesn't figure into "Must See" rating.

Everyone has their own taste in waterfalls. What I am looking for in a waterfall is a visually pleasing setting combined with water that is falling at angles and with rates in keeping with the overall genre of the waterfall. Consistency and lack of obvious flaws is also important.

There may be times when you disagree with my rating. Keep in mind that water level, season, temperature, weather conditions, sun position, and even frame of mind affect the visual desirability of any waterfall at any point in time.

I have included the "Must See" rating to offer you a standardized method of comparing waterfalls so that you have some idea of which waterfalls you may wish to view.

Waterfall Height ⑥ This is an estimate of the height of the waterfall in feet. This is a potentially poor piece of information. Let me explain. If a waterfall has a free drop of 20 feet, flattens out for 20 to 30 feet of river length and then it has small cascading drops of 4 to 6 inches per drop for another 20 feet of accumulated drop, there would be a total drop of 40 feet. When viewing the waterfall, some people may consider just the free drop as the waterfall height, while others may include the additional 20 feet of cascades downstream. I tried to include the "normal" waterfall portion of the falls in my height estimates. I think of most waterfalls as viewable from one location. If a portion of the waterfall is not photogenic, then I may not have included that part in the overall height of the waterfall.

Hike Time ⑦ How much time should you plan for a hike? I have included an estimated amount of minutes or hours to plan for a hike. I am assuming that a hike entails a leisurely walk to and from the waterfall and includes an "appropriate" amount of time for viewing the waterfall.

Is there a Sign? ⑧ Most waterfalls have no signs announcing their presence. The waterfalls that do, have signs that are made by the Federal Government, the State of Michigan, counties, and some by private individuals.

Worst Road Type ⑨ In the process of driving to a waterfall the roads typically go from good to worse. So the road that a waterfall is accessed from will tell you what to expect for the worst driving conditions on your waterfall quest.

Accessibility ⑩ There is a wide variety of difficulty when it comes to finding a particular waterfall. A waterfall on a main road with signs announcing its presence is very easy to find. The more turns that are required off of a main road, the more difficult or complicated it becomes to find.

Is a 4WD needed? ⑪ You will find it easier to drive to some waterfalls with a 4WD vehicle. High clearance vehicles are sometimes needed.

⑫ *Quick Reference*

Ghosted Symbols

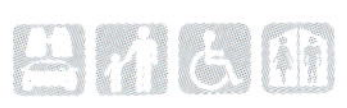

Activated Symbols

Private

The "activated symbols" are the ones (if any) that apply to this particular waterfall.

Private This waterfall is on private land and more often than not the land is posted and the waterfall is not accessible to the public. *Note that this information is to the best of my knowledge. There very well may be more waterfalls on private land, but since it was not posted I was unaware. Be respectful of property owners and follow their wishes.*

- The waterfall can be viewed from a vehicle.
- A particularly kid-friendly waterfall.
- Wheelchair accessible
- Bathroom facilities are available, normally at the beginning of the hike. There will be flush, composting, or vault toilets.

⑬ *GPS Coordinate*

The GPS coordinate for the waterfall is written in degrees and minutes.

⑭ *Type of Path*

There are a variety of hiking trails that you will encounter. Expect everything from graded and paved trails to narrow dirt footpaths to no paths at all! Note that sometimes there will be one type of path at the beginning of the hike and another one entirely by the end. The worst type of path to the waterfall is listed here.

⑮ *Hike Length*

This is the length of the hike to the falls. Remember to double the length for a round trip estimate. Some hikes have a number of waterfalls along the route. The length for any particular waterfall along that hike is the distance from the vehicle to that waterfall, typically including the previous waterfalls found along the way.

⑯ *Elevation Change*

Many waterfalls involve a change in elevation, either along the hike or climbing down into a ravine to the waterfall.

⑰ *GPS Needed?*

Do you need a handheld GPS to find this waterfall? If so, make sure that you are using a reliable GPS and are familiar with its functions and use. Don't forget to take spare batteries. Having a compass with you is a great backup as well.

Danger (18) Viewing waterfalls has some inherit danger; walking along potentially wet or icy paths or boardwalks, hiking over uneven ground and climbing into and out of ravines and gorges, standing at the brink of a fifty foot waterfall, navigating moss covered rocks near swift moving waters. Yes, caution is always important. But some waterfalls are more difficult to view or get to, so I trust this "Danger" category will help you to decide which waterfalls are right for you to view.

Waterproof Boots? (19) I prefer to keep my feet dry on waterfall hikes. If there are muddy trails or rivers or creeks that need to be forded I recommend wearing waterproof boots. I wear calf high boots when needing something more than my waterproof hiking shoes that are only ankle high.

Description (20) Find out a little more about the waterfall or hike in this brief description.

Waterfall Etiquette

Proper waterfall etiquette begins with a proper attitude toward people and the environment. Many waterfalls in the Upper Peninsula are on private land. Fortunately for us, many of the land owners allow individuals to drive on their property, park on it, and hike across it.

1) NEVER trespass on posted property. Obey all signs. The private property rights of all land owners must be respected.

2) Don't invade someone's personal space. Just because there isn't a "No Trespassing" sign doesn't mean that you can drive up next to their house, park your vehicle, and walk across their back yard to a waterfall just behind their house. Use common sense. Have proper waterfall etiquette. Do unto others as you would want them to do unto you. This timeless principle always holds true.

There are some waterfalls that are "OK" to view, but they are also quite close to residences. Be quiet and considerate. Be courteous and respectful.

3) Clean up after yourself. I know of a land owner that doesn't allow waterfall enthusiasts onto his land because every year he removes several bags of garbage from around the waterfall on his property. We must do better. Don't leave anything behind on your hikes. In fact, help clean up after others. If we all would do our part, I believe that more land owners would allow us to view the beauty that resides within their estates.

Respecting land owners and the environment in which the wonderful waterfalls of Michigan reside must be our top priority. Forsaking these principles will result in the loss of access to more and more waterfall locations. We must not let that happen.

CHAPTER 1
DICKINSON COUNTY

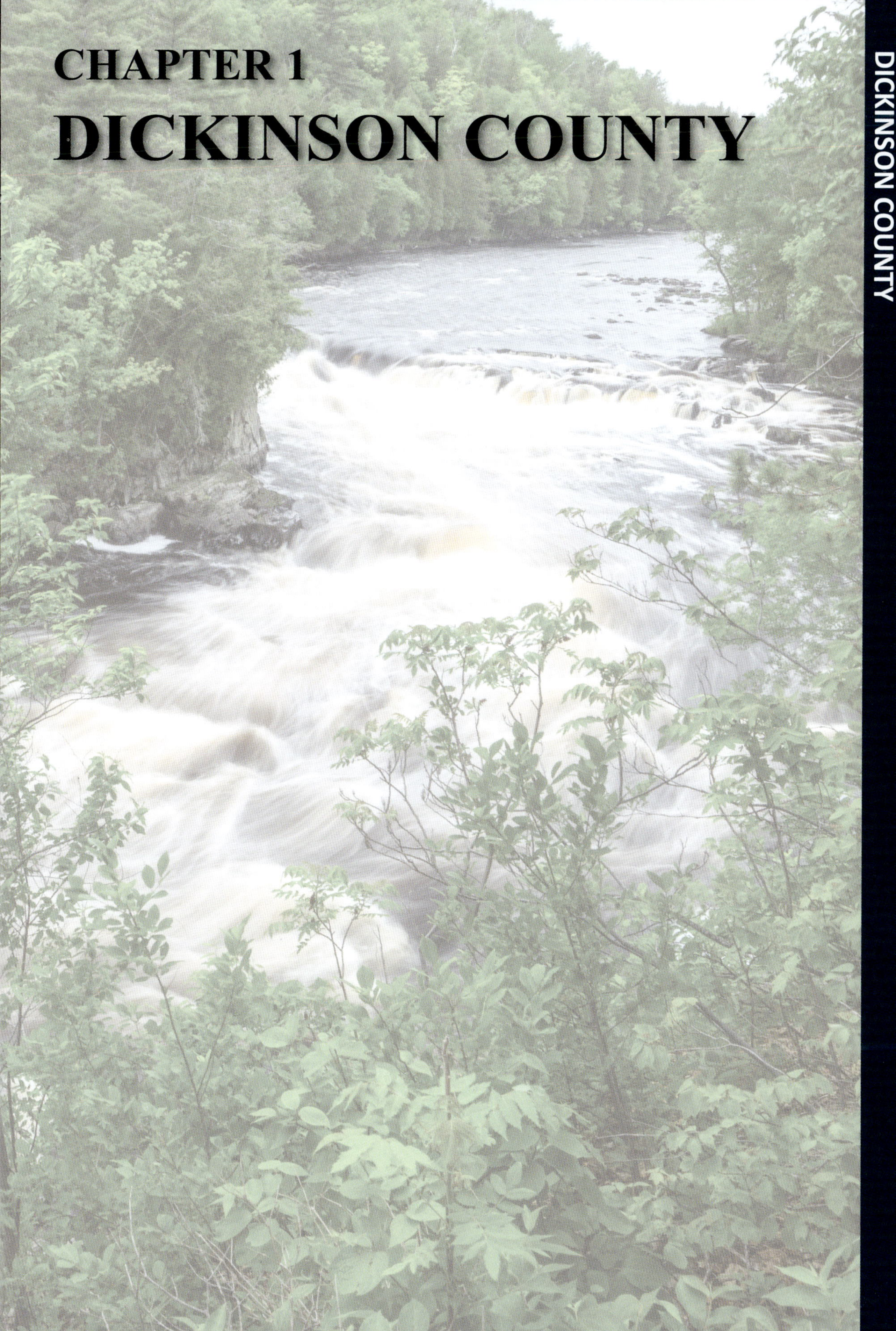

DICKINSON COUNTY CONTENTS

MAPS..........
HIKES..........
WATERFALLS..........

TABLE OF CONTENT KEY

DICKINSON COUNTY FACTS

Founded:	1891
Size:	761 square miles
Population (2010):	26,168
County Seat:	Iron Mountain

Dickinson County is Michigan's newest county, being drawn up in 1891. The county was named after Donald M. Dickinson, a Michigan lawyer that became the United States Postmaster General from 1888 to 1889. After serving as the Postmaster General he returned to Michigan. Two years later, when this new county was split off from Marquette, Menominee, and Iron Counties, it was decided to name the county in Mr. Dickinson's honor.

The city of Iron Mountain, the county seat, also has the largest population in Dickinson County. It contains nearly 1/4 of the residents in the county. The city is named after the iron ore that was mined nearby from the late 1800s and well into the 1900s. After disappointing early searches, iron ore was discovered beneath a swampy, wet portion of land. In order to effectively work underground, this water had to be constantly removed. A massive steam pump was built for this purpose. The pump, which can be seen today in Iron Mountain at the Cornish Pumping Engine & Mining Museum, weighed an estimated 725 tons and was capable of removing 5,000,000 gallons of water per day! It is considered one of the world's biggest machines.

While in Iron Mountain you may want to check out the Millie Mine Bat Cave. It's technically not a cave, but an abandoned iron mine shaft. Now it contains one of the largest bat colonies in North America. It is estimated that around 1 million bats live in the shaft. It is an official Michigan Wildlife Viewing Area and visitors are welcome. Check out www.michigan.org/property/millie-mine-bat-cave for more information.

Iron Mountain also sports one of the world's highest artificially made ski jumps. Pine Mountain Jump rises 176 feet above Pine Mountain. It is the largest ski jump in the United States (not including ski flying hills). Tournaments are often scheduled at the site, and it is considered by many to be the most difficult jump in the world.

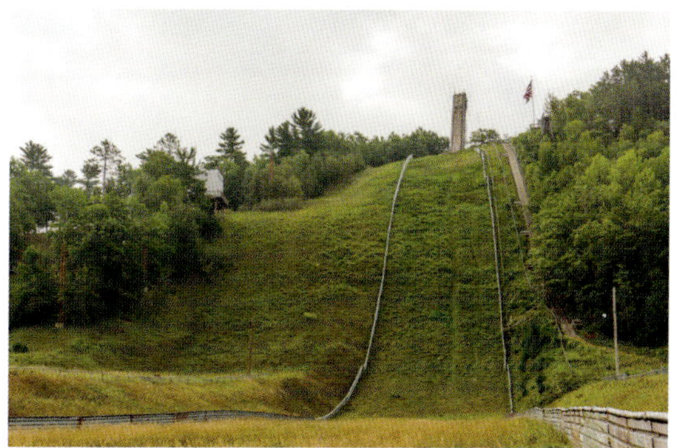

Visit the Iron Mountain Iron Mine that is about halfway between Iron Mountain and Escanaba. It is located right off of US-2 and has a large image of "Big John" standing along the side of the good sized parking lot. Underground tours are seasonally available. Check their website for more informations: www.ironmountainironmine.wixsite.com/ironmine

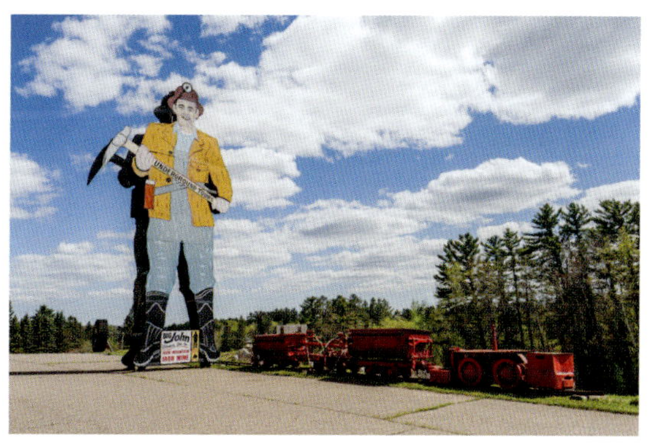

Dickinson County Map

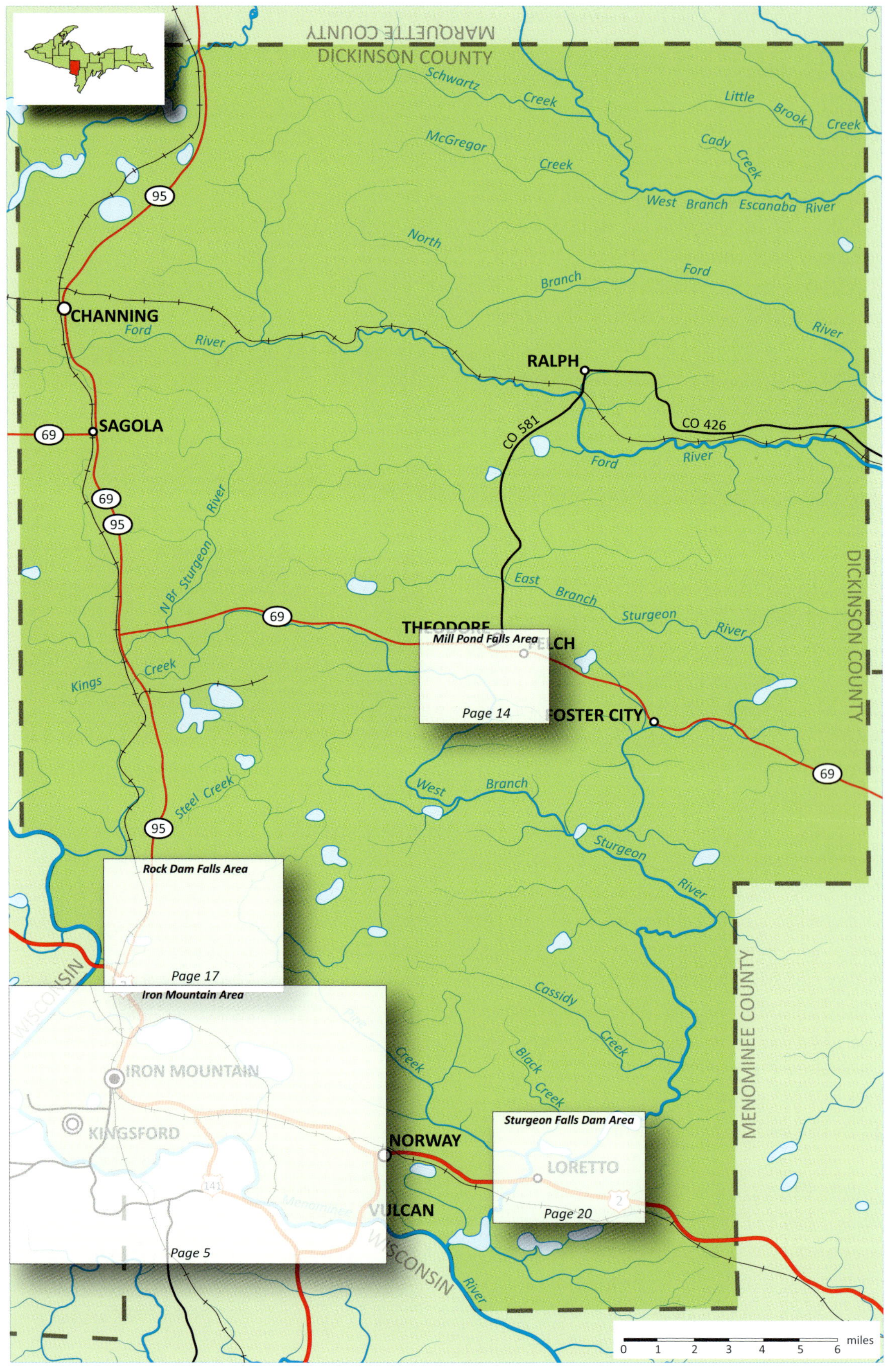

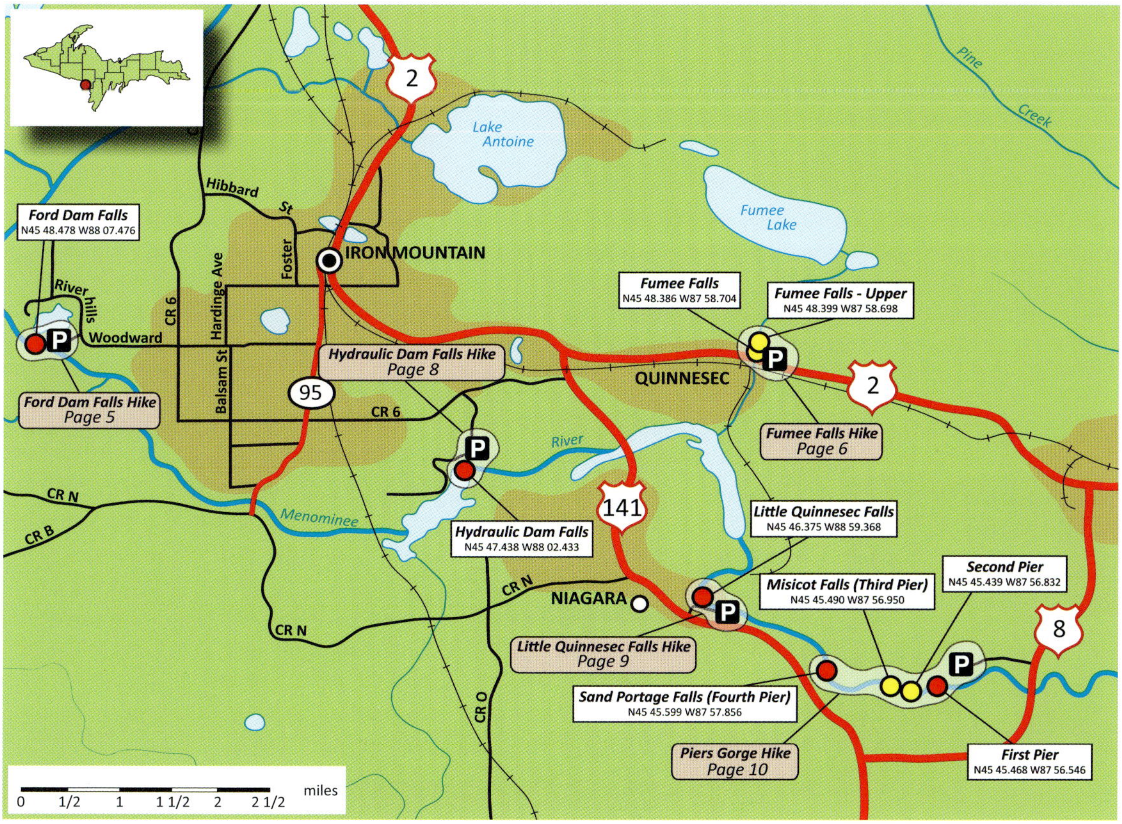

Ford Dam Falls Hike

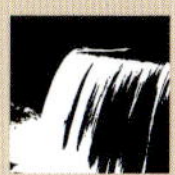

Ford Dam Falls: A nice paved parking lot accommodates a large number of vehicles. Cowboy Lake Park has a pit toilet, picnic tables, a playground, grills and a pavilion. This is a very nicely landscaped park. The parking lot is located at N45 48.479 W88 07.379

Directions: Turn west onto M-95 off of US-2 in downtown Iron Mountain. M-95 turns left (south) after 2 blocks. Follow M-95 for another .9 miles. Turn right (west) onto Woodward Avenue. Follow it for nearly 2.5 miles. The road will make a sweeping bend to the right (north). Halfway around the bend turn left (west) onto Cowboy Lake Road. Continue to the end (about .3 miles). Cowboy Lake Park is situated here with Cowboy Lake to the north and the Menominee River to the south. The Henry Ford Dam is to the west of the parking lot.

FORD DAM FALLS (Menominee River)

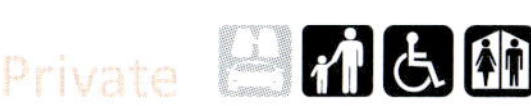

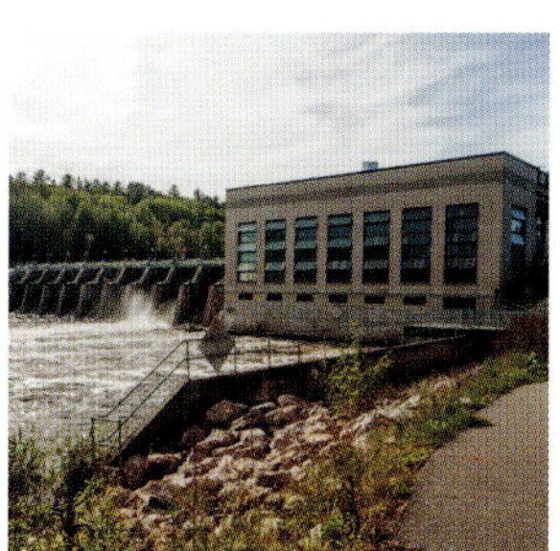

Must See:	2	GPS:	N45 48.478 W88 07.476
Height:	12 feet		
Time:	5-15 minutes	Hiking Information	
		Path:	Paved sidewalk
Driving Information		Length:	150 yards
Signs:	None	Elev. Change:	Slight
Road:	Secondary	GPS:	None
Access:	Somewhat easy	Danger:	Slight
4WD:	N/A	WP Boots:	N/A

There are ten sections in this dam, which is one of the nicer looking dams in the U.P. A paved walkway from the parking lot leads to the dam viewing area. This is a wheel chair accessible destination.

Fumee Falls Hike

Fumee Falls: The small creek cascades down about 20 feet in full view of US-2.

Fumee Falls - Upper: Climb to the top of the stairs to view the two short drops that make up the upper falls.

Directions: About 4 miles east of Iron Mountain and 4 miles west of Norway on US-2 is the unincorporated community of Quinnesec. The Helen Z. Lien Roadside Park is found on the north side of the road where Fumee Creek flows beneath the road. Park here. Fumee Falls can be seen from the vehicle. There is also a footbridge that crosses the creek. A stairway on the right side of the creek leads to the upper falls.

FUMEE FALLS (FUMEE CREEK)

Private 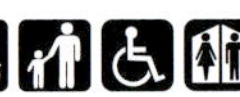

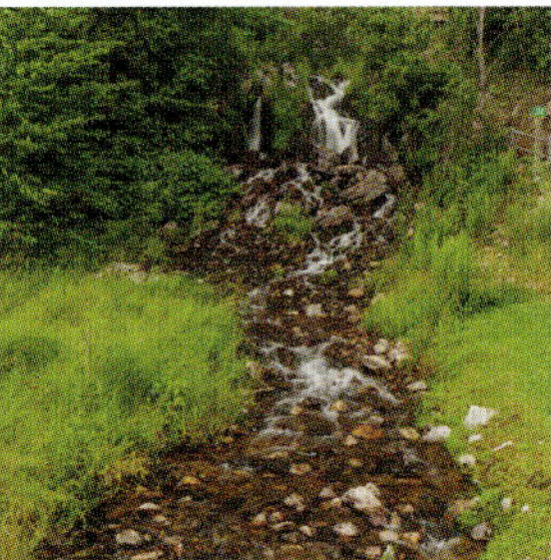

Must See:	6	GPS:	N45 48.386 W87 58.704
Height:	20 feet		
Time:	5-15 minutes	Hiking Information	
		Path:	N/A
Driving Information		Length:	N/A
Signs:	Good sign	Elev. Change:	Slight
Road:	Main	GPS:	None
Access:	Very easy	Danger:	N/A
4WD:	N/A	WP Boots:	N/A

The roadside park located below the falls is a popular picnic area and a great place for families. The bridge over the creek is wheelchair accessible.

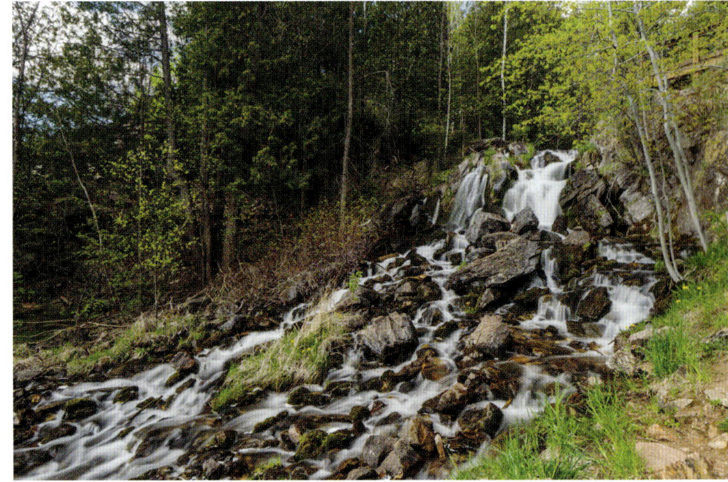

The footbridge over Fumee Creek below the falls

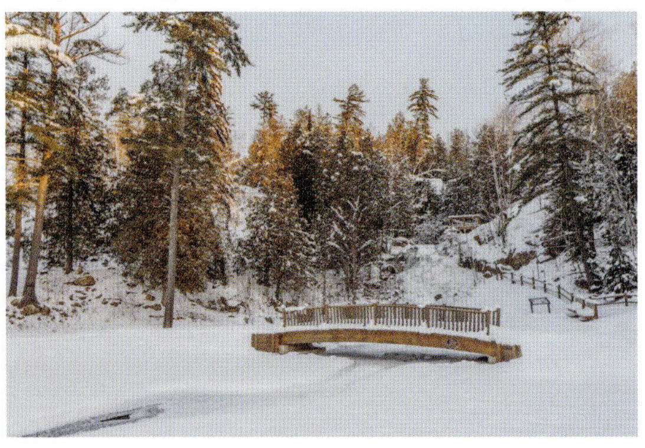

Some of the park facilities right next to US-2

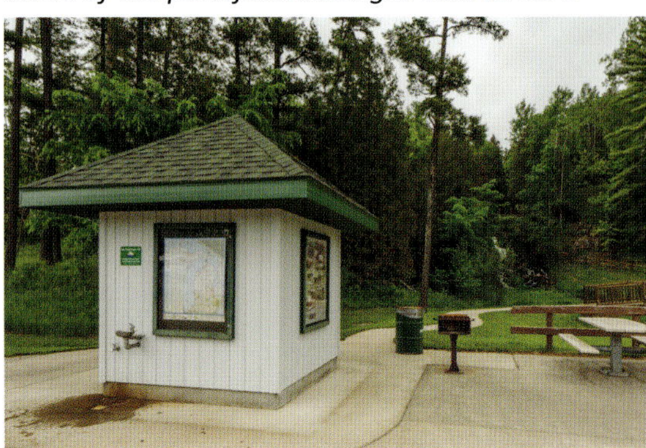

FUMEE FALLS - UPPER (FUMEE CREEK)

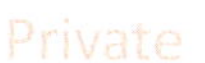
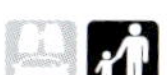
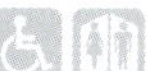
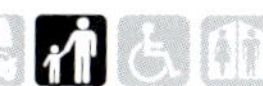

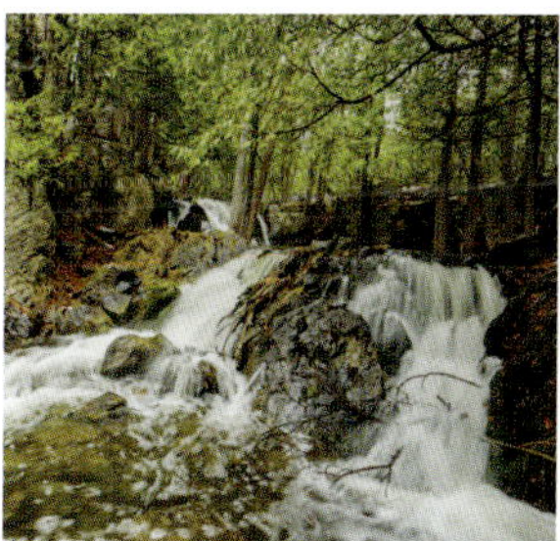

Must See:	5
Height:	9 feet
Time:	10-20 minutes

Driving Information

Signs:	Good sign
Road:	Main
Access:	Very easy
4WD:	N/A

GPS:	N45 48.399 W87 58.698

Hiking Information

Path:	N/A
Length:	N/A
Elev. Change:	Minor
GPS:	None
Danger:	N/A
WP Boots:	N/A

Stairs lead up to this upper set of drops. Be on the lookout for poison ivy in the area. As close to US-2 as this waterfall is, it has the "feeling" of being somehow a more secret location - perhaps because it is up the stairway and around a small bend.

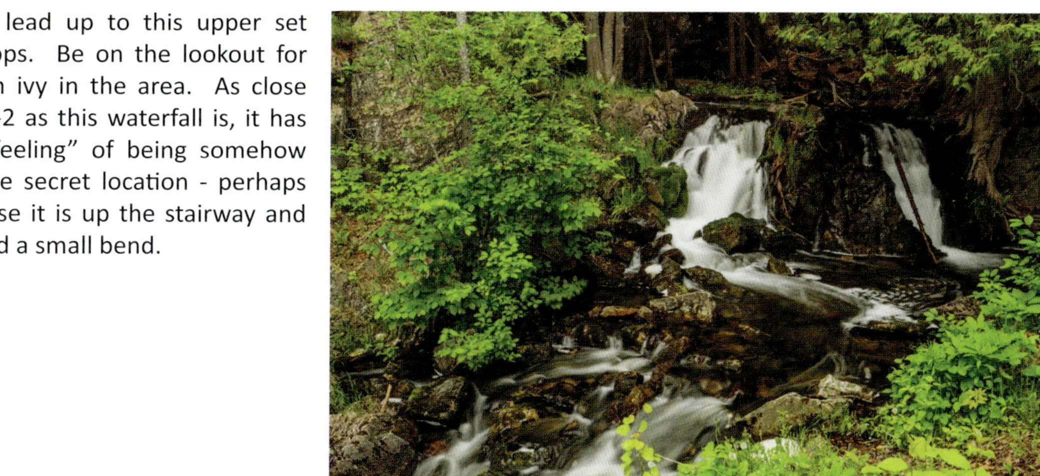

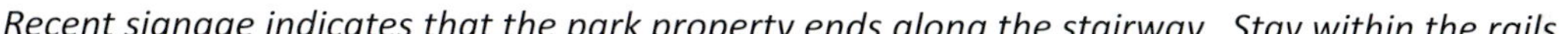

Recent signage indicates that the park property ends along the stairway. Stay within the rails.

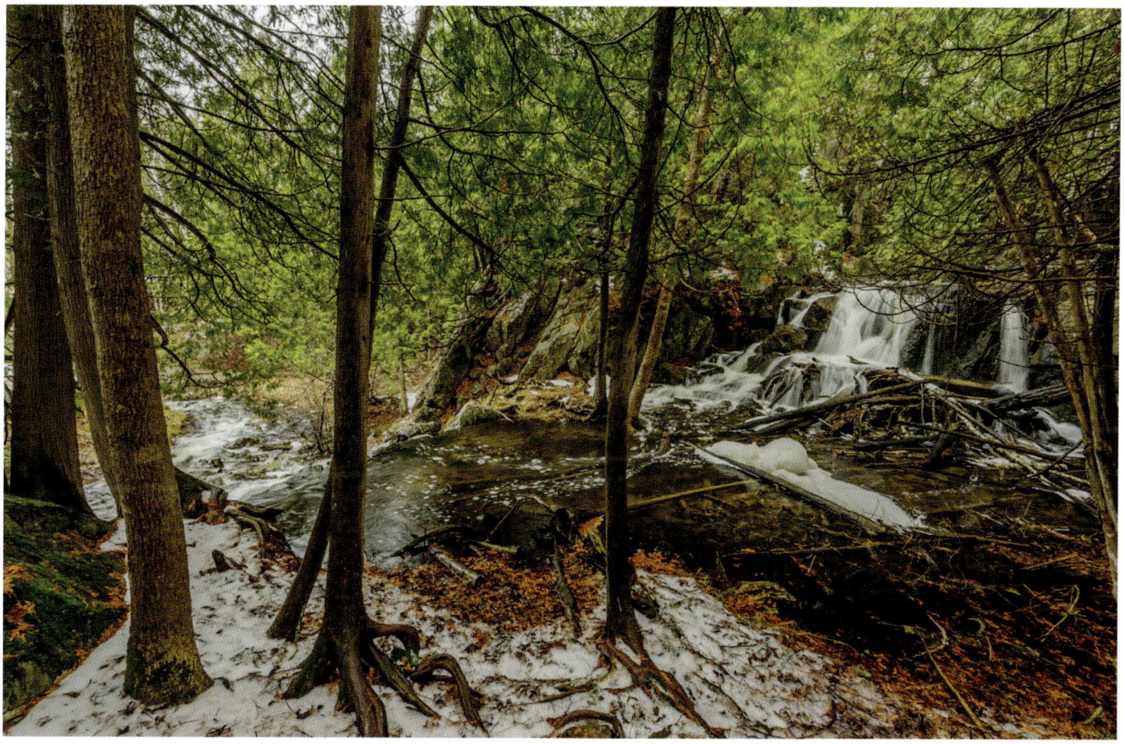

Hydraulic Dam Falls Hike

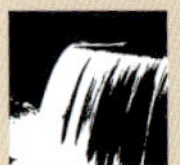

Hydraulic Dam Falls: The Menominee River here is again dammed up for creating hydroelectric power. Some bedrock can be seen on the far side of the river below the dam.

Directions: Turn south off of US-2 onto Hydraulic Falls Road at N45 48.488 W88 02.852 (1.5 miles west of the intersection of US-141). Follow the winding road for about 1.5 miles to a roadside dirt parking lot. Park. Hike down the fisherman's trail to the river.

HYDRAULIC DAM FALLS (MENOMINEE RIVER)

Private 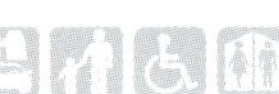

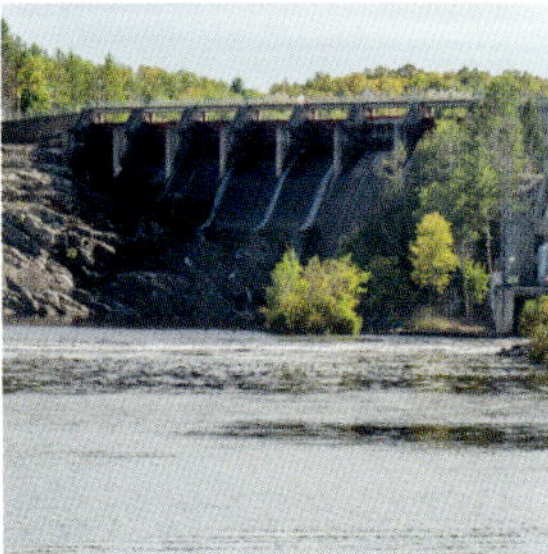

Must See:	2	GPS:	N45 47.438 W88 02.433
Height:	25 feet		
Time:	10-15 minutes	Hiking Information	
		Path:	Fisherman's footpath
Driving Information		Length:	200 yards
Signs:	None	Elev. Change:	Moderate
Road:	Secondary	GPS:	Helpful
Access:	Somewhat easy	Danger:	Slight
4WD:	N/A	WP Boots:	N/A

I don't recommend parking near the dam itself. The overflow area isn't visible from there. Instead, park off of Hydraulic Falls Road in a little circular dirt parking area just before the access road to the dam. Hike down the fisherman's trail through a small field and then down a fairly steep hillside into the river gorge to see the spill area next to the dam.

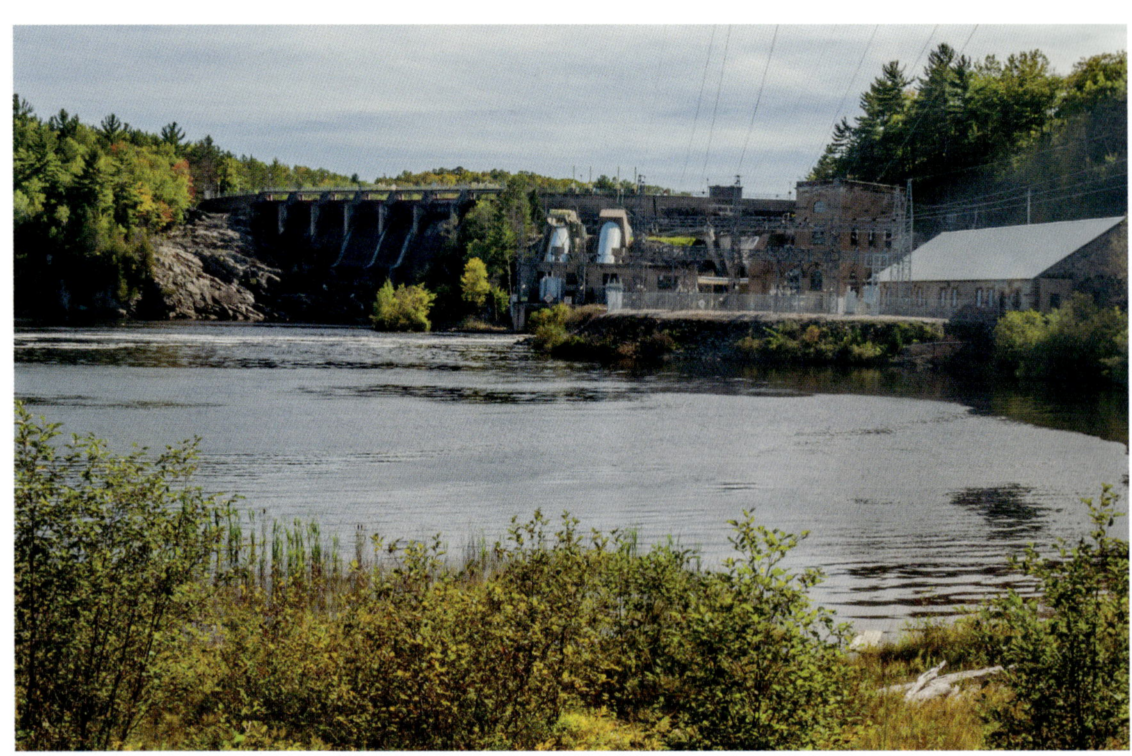

Little Quinnesec Falls Hike

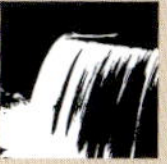

Little Quinnesec Falls: This hydroelectric plant channels water from what once was a beautiful waterfall, if the bedrock that is exposed around the sides of the dam is any indicator. Now the sprawling concrete complex and adjoining businesses restrict access to the immediate area.

Directions: Turn south onto US-141 (halfway between Iron Mountain and Quinnesec). Follow the road for about 3.3 miles to Clark Street. Turn left (north). The street bends to the right (east) after about 400 feet and becomes Mill Street. Continue about .1 miles to a small parking area on the left (north) that was installed by the power company. There is a boat launch here. Walk back west on the side of the street (Mill Street). The street turns abruptly left (Clark Street) at a security fence. Near the turn is a trail that heads to the right (north). Follow the trail down to the river. The waterfall can be vaguely viewed across the river and upstream from here.

LITTLE QUINNESEC FALLS (MENOMINEE RIVER)

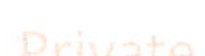

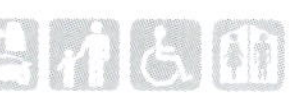

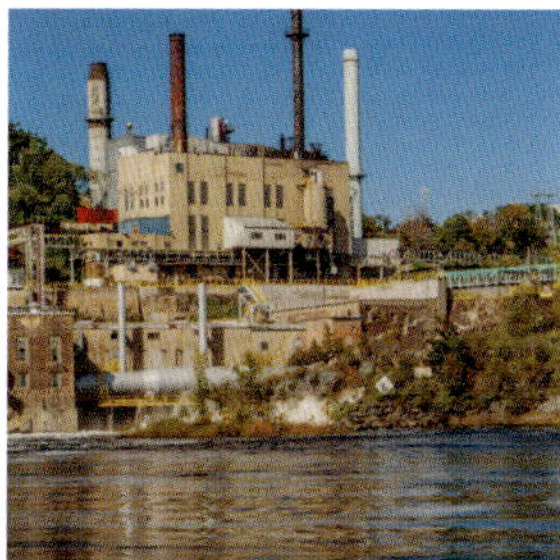

Must See:	3	GPS:	N45 46.375 W87 59.368
Height:	30 feet		
Time:	10-15 minutes	Hiking Information	
		Path:	Footpath
Driving Information		Length:	.2 miles
Signs:	None	Elev. Change:	Slight
Road:	Secondary	GPS:	Helpful
Access:	Somewhat easy	Danger:	Slight
4WD:	N/A	WP Boots:	N/A

The falls are inaccessible to the general public. You may be able to get closer to the falls from a boat. The water only flows when there is excess water from the power plant. The power plant is built right up to the waterfall. The left side of the waterfall is now concrete, as is the top of the falls.

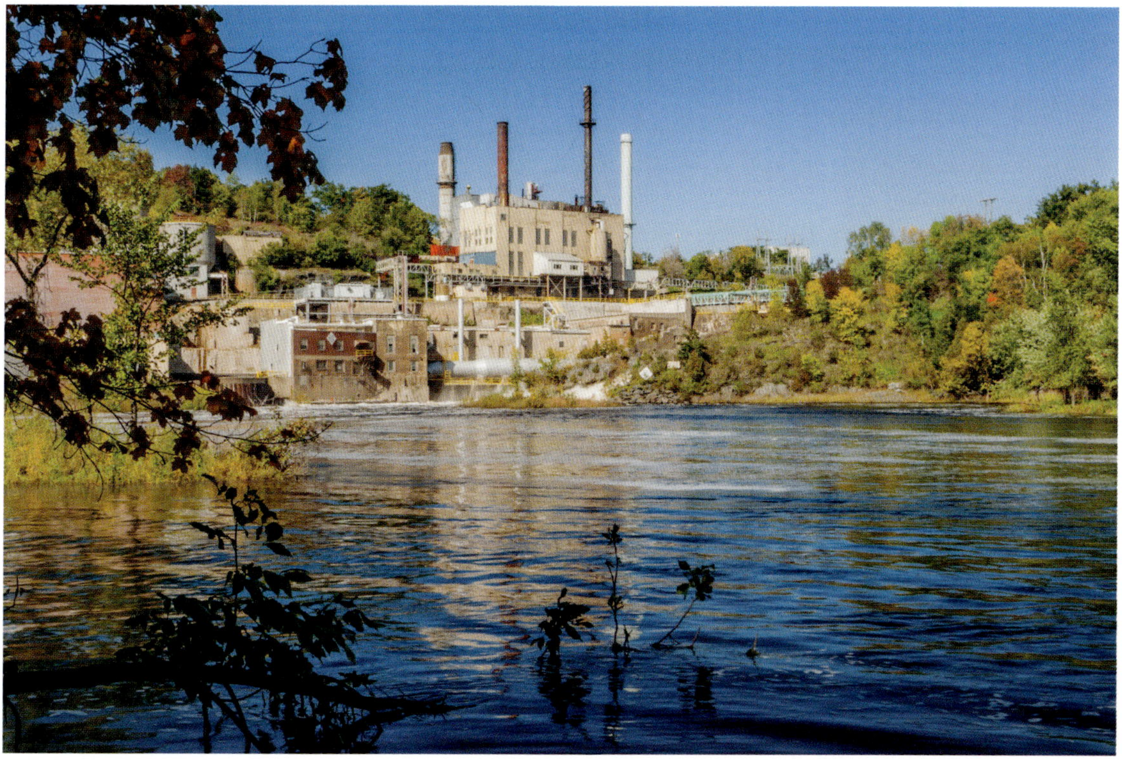

Piers Gorge Hike

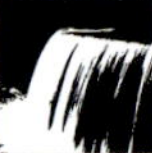

Winding along next to the Menominee River is a trail through the Piers Gorge. It is not a difficult hike since it is relatively flat and well groomed. And as a bonus, there are some interesting rock formations to enjoy during the hike. Along the trail are signs labeled "Pier 1", "Pier 2", "Pier 3" and "Pier 4". These "piers" refer to rocky formations that give a semblance of a pier. The first three are within 1/2 mile of the trailhead, while Pier 4 is about 1 mile further down the trail. Although these drops have been labeled as waterfalls, they are basically aggressive rapids, with none of the pizzazz of a "typical" waterfall. This is one of the more used trails in the Upper Peninsula. It is common to see a number of individuals, of all ages, taking advantage of the nicely shaded walk. There are several locations along the path that are used to "put in" for white water rafting.

Pier 1: A rocky, shallow rapids can be viewed from bedrock that is more interesting than the river.

Pier 2: This drop is also known as "The Sisters" or "Twin Sisters" by those who enjoy white water rafting or kayaking. This is the second best drop in the gorge with interesting splays of water falling around jagged, rocky fingers.

Misicot Falls (Pier 3): The best of the drops on this stretch of river, the 8 foot Misicot Falls is best viewed from a small hill that rises along the riverbank.

Sand Portage Falls (Pier 4): Sand Portage Falls is found below an island situated in a bend in the river. As the river comes back together, a small rapids is formed. There is an outcropping of rocks that can be clambered over next to the river for a diversion at the end of the 1.5 mile hike.

Directions: In Norway, head south on US-8 from US-2 for 2 miles. Turn right (west) onto Piers Gorge Road. Drive to the end of the road (about 1 mile). The trailhead for the Piers Gorge Trail will be obvious. Park and hike down the well maintained trail to the Piers.

FIRST PIER (MENOMINEE RIVER)

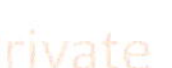

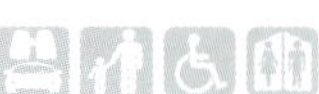

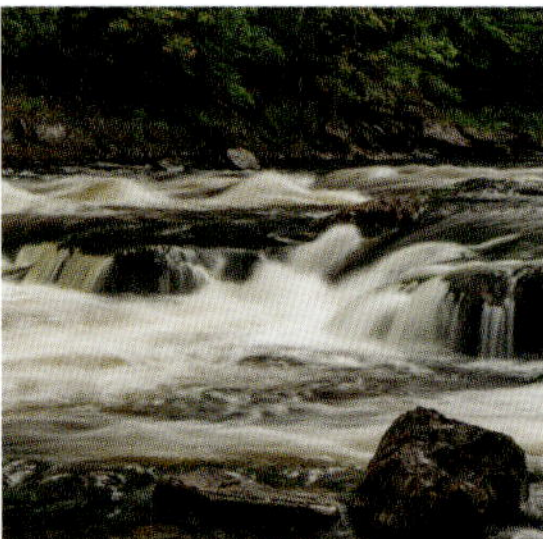

Must See:	3	GPS:	N45 45.468 W87 56.546
Height:	2 feet		
Time:	15-25 minutes	Hiking Information	
		Path:	Improved path
Driving Information		Length:	200 yards
Signs:	"Piers Gorge"	Elev. Change:	Minor
Road:	Dirt	GPS:	Helpful
Access:	Somewhat easy	Danger:	Slight
4WD:	N/A	WP Boots:	N/A

A rocky expanse borders the river. Eye catching water-filled holes provide interest that the river may lack. The heavily pocked black bedrock with striations running in line with the river looks like ribs from an ancient creature when viewed from the "Pier".

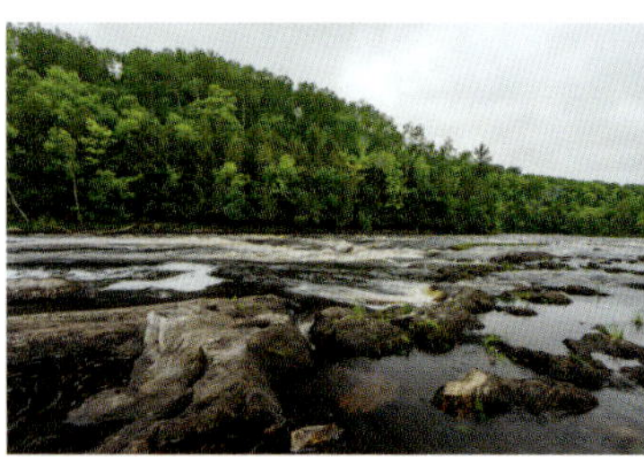

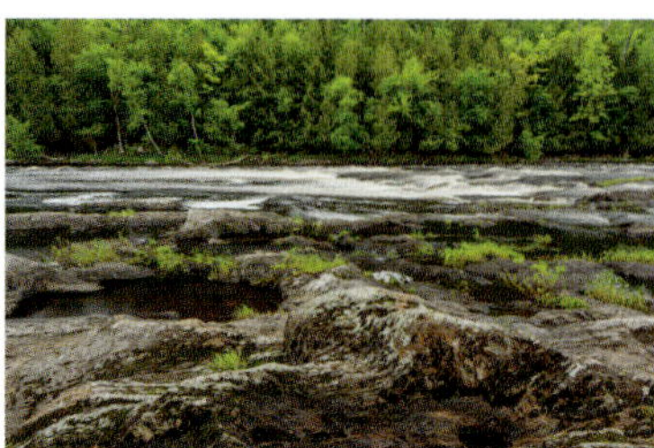

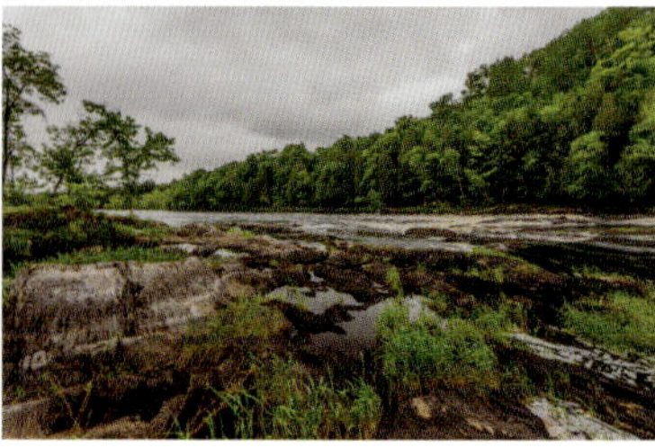

SECOND PIER (MENOMINEE RIVER)

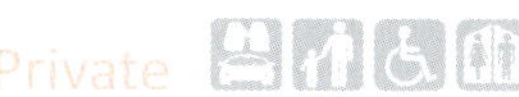

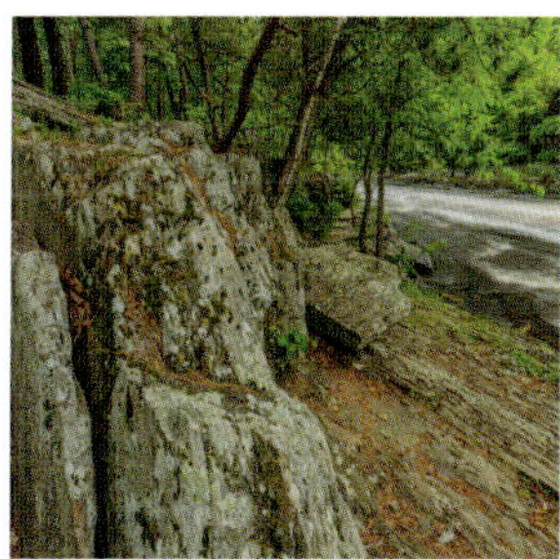

Must See:	4	GPS:	N45 45.439 W87 56.832
Height:	2 feet		
Time:	30-45 minutes	Hiking Information	
		Path:	Improved path
Driving Information		Length:	.3 miles
Signs:	"Piers Gorge"	Elev. Change:	Minor
Road:	Dirt	GPS:	Helpful
Access:	Somewhat easy	Danger:	Slight
4WD:	N/A	WP Boots:	N/A

Also known as "The Sisters", it is a short drop, only a couple of feet, but it has interesting character with sharp rock fingers slicing through the falling river.

A shallow gorge ends at this point. As the river bends 50 yards downstream from the waterfall, the rocky bedrock walls drop down to the river's edge.

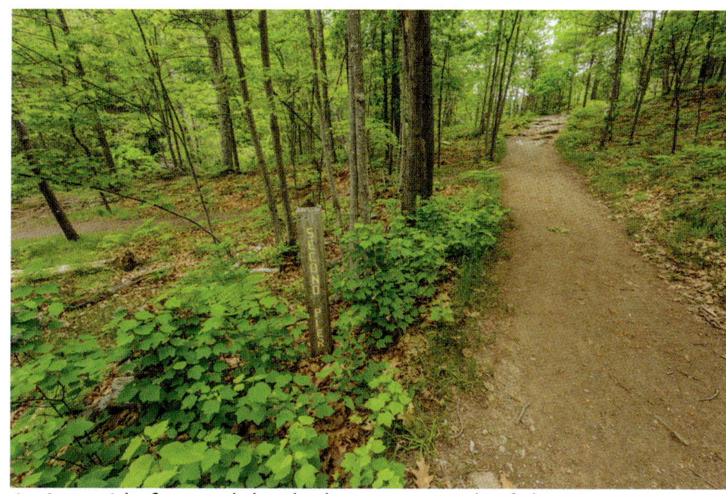

A nice, wide footpath leads the way to each of the Piers

The rocky side of the gorge that runs down to the river

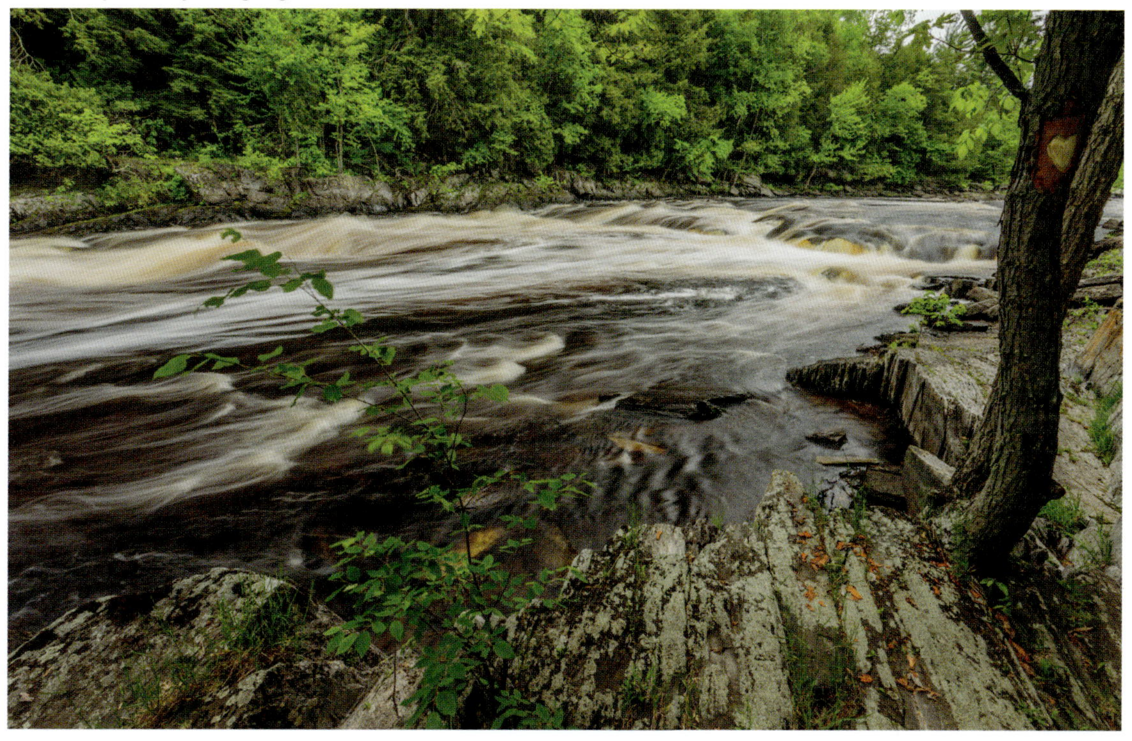

MISICOT FALLS AKA: THIRD PIER (MENOMINEE RIVER)

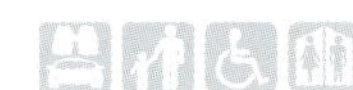

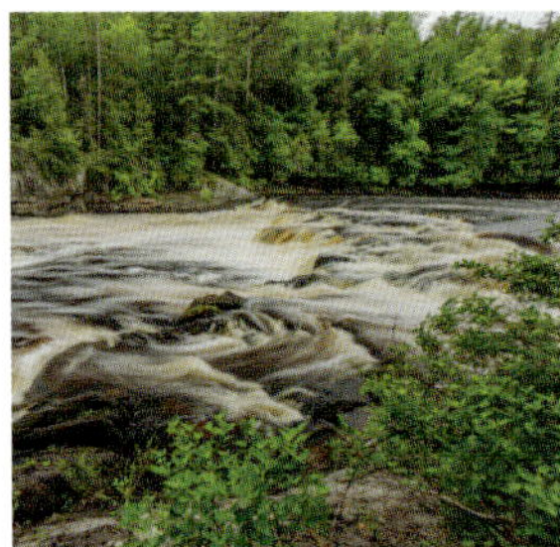

Must See:	6
Height:	8 feet
Time:	45-60 minutes

Driving Information

Signs:	"Piers Gorge"
Road:	Dirt
Access:	Somewhat easy
4WD:	N/A

GPS: N45 45.490 W87 56.950

Hiking Information

Path:	Improved path
Length:	.5 miles
Elev. Change:	Moderate
GPS:	Helpful
Danger:	Slight
WP Boots:	N/A

Misicot Falls is laid out nicely, as seen from the top of a cliff that borders the river's edge. It can also be viewed from water level downstream of the overlook. The river makes an "S" curve with the waterfall marking its start.

The river falls over jagged mounds of bedrock as the river bends around a sheer wall of rock on the Wisconsin side of the river.

The footpath wanders close to the river at this point

Looking down into the gorge not far from the "Third Pier" sign

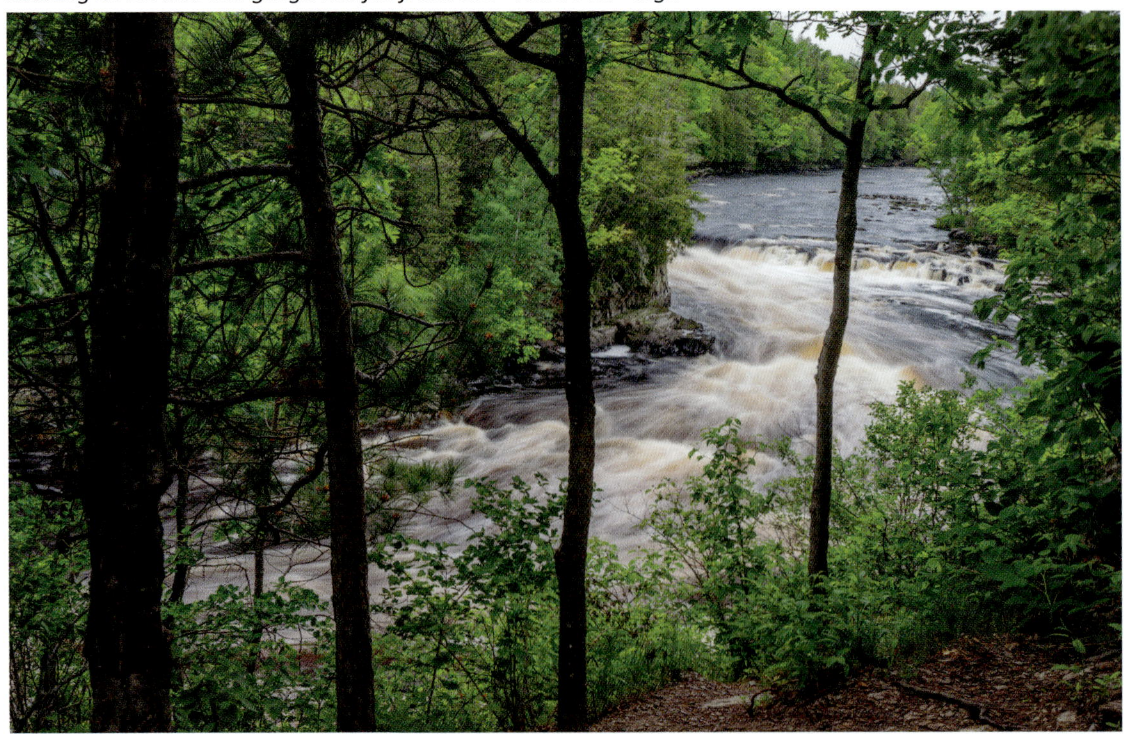

SAND PORTAGE FALLS AKA: FOURTH PIER (MENOMINEE RIVER) Private

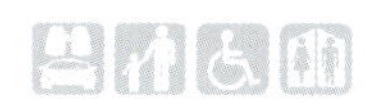

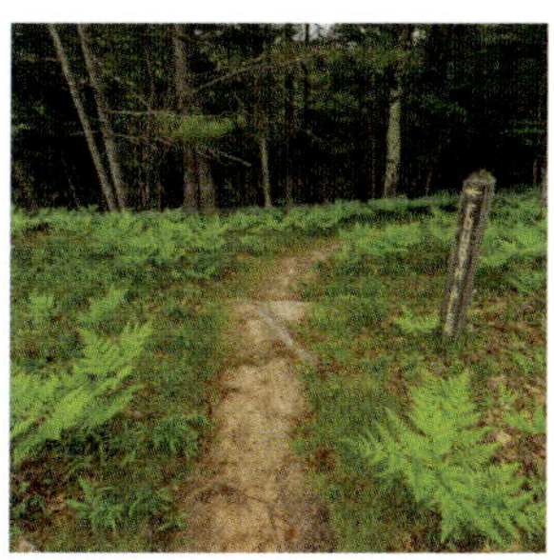

Must See:	3	GPS:	N45 45.599 W87 57.856
Height:	3 feet		
Time:	75-90 minutes	**Hiking Information**	
		Path:	Improved path
Driving Information		Length:	1.5 miles
Signs:	"Piers Gorge"	Elev. Change:	Moderate
Road:	Dirt	GPS:	Helpful
Access:	Somewhat easy	Danger:	Slight
4WD:	N/A	WP Boots:	N/A

Part of an intriguing rock outcropping can be seen in the foreground. A couple of rocky islands stand in the center of the river.

There are heavy rapids at the Fourth Pier. Rocks are submerged just below the water level at this wide portion of the river. There is a nice outcropping of rock from which to view the small falls. It's a nice long walk. I wish that there was a better waterfall at the end of it, though. Watch out for downed trees along the hike.

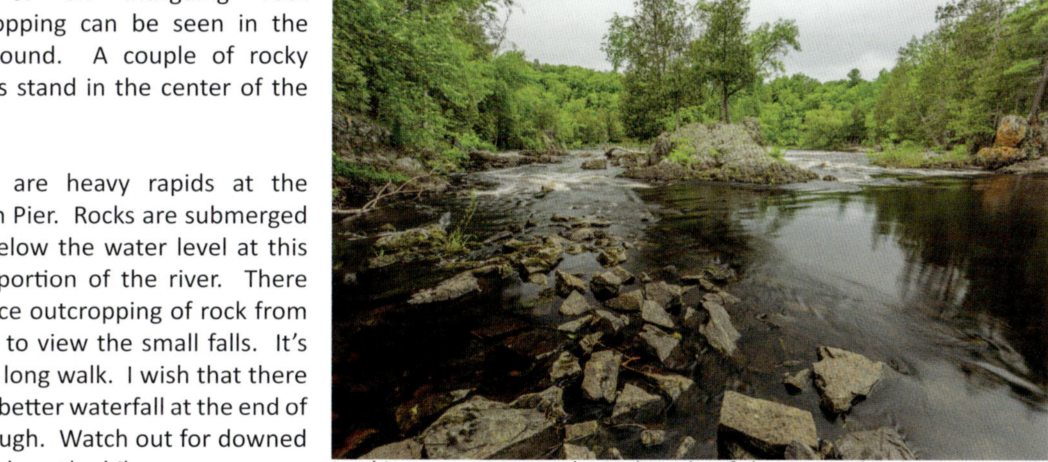

Looking upstream to the right side of the main island

The main section of the river (looking toward Wisconsin) - and the rapids in that stretch

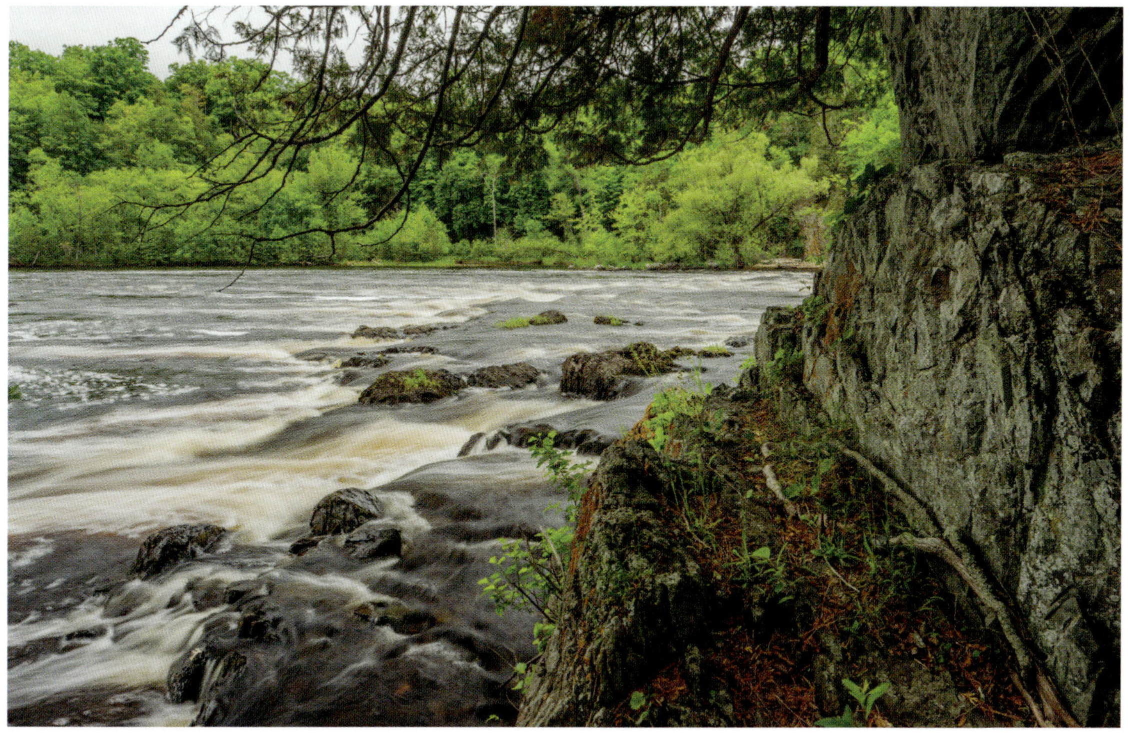

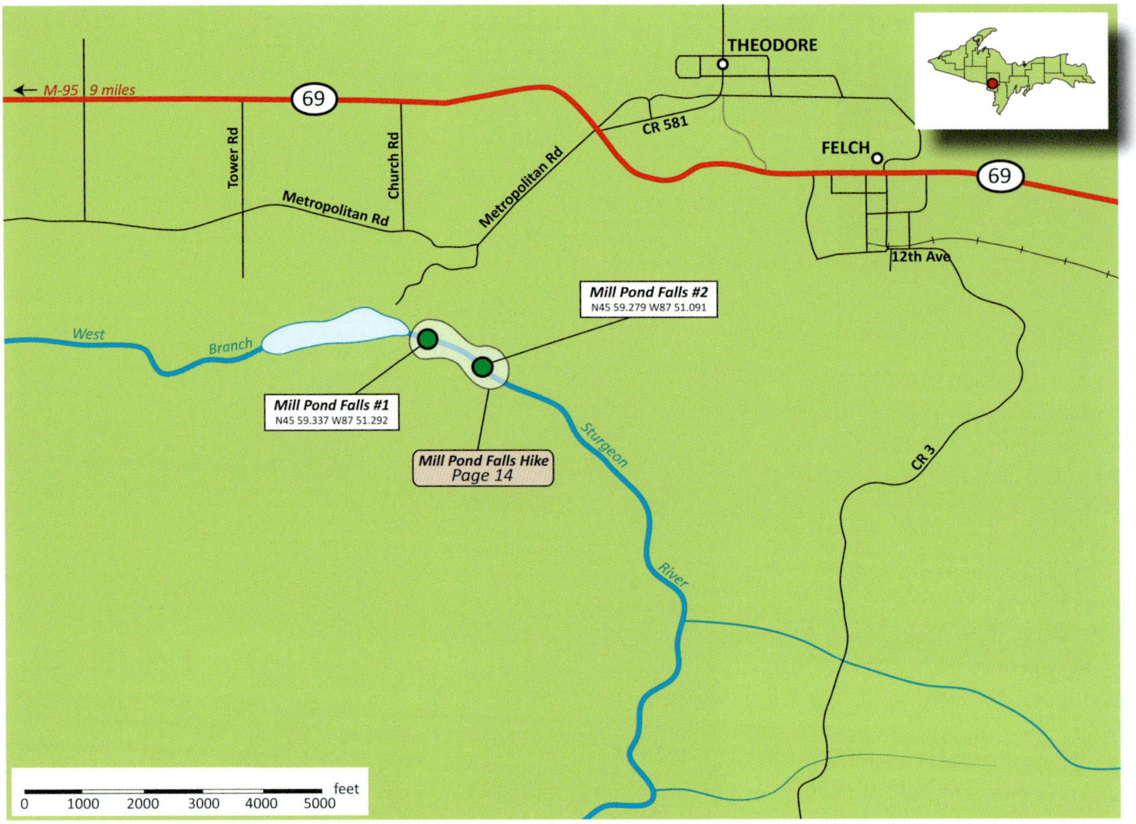

Mill Pond Falls Hike

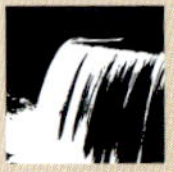

Mill Pond Falls #2: Viewing of this waterfall is ideally from the steep sloping rock bedrock that slants down toward the waterfall. Be careful not to slip and slide into the river.

Mill Pond Falls #1: This unique waterfall is secreted in a sheltered stretch of river. Overhanging branches and a thicker forest surround the river and playful waterfall.

Directions: Thirteen miles north of Iron Mountain, M-69 roughly parallels US-2 starting at M-95 then heading to the east before gently swinging southeasterly. Twelve miles to the east of M-95 on M-69 is the village of Felch. A little over 1 mile to the southwest are the Mill Pond waterfalls. According to the local residents that I spoke to, the waterfalls are on public land, but the obvious hiking route runs right past someone's house. They gave me directions for an alternate route, but after hiking to the falls and back I am not sure that I wasn't infringing on private property. I was also informed that there was another way in to the falls - down a series of trails, but I wasn't able to figure out their directions. Perhaps hiking in from CR-3 would work.

MILL POND FALLS #2 (WEST BRANCH STURGEON RIVER)

Private 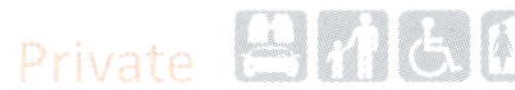

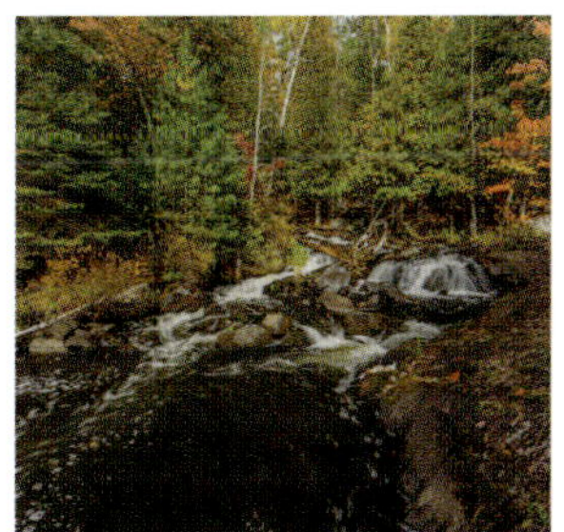

Must See:	7	GPS:	N45 59.279 W87 51.091
Height:	15 feet		
Time:	50-90 minutes	Hiking Information	
		Path:	N/A
Driving Information		Length:	Variable
Signs:	None	Elev. Change:	Moderate
Road:	Secondary	GPS:	Required
Access:	Difficult	Danger:	Increased
4WD:	Helpful	WP Boots:	Recommended

The river was extremely high when I visited the falls (as seen in the shot to the right). The viewing area slants down steeply to the river. Be careful as the terrain is rugged, with undergrowth and rocky ledges creating a difficult hike.

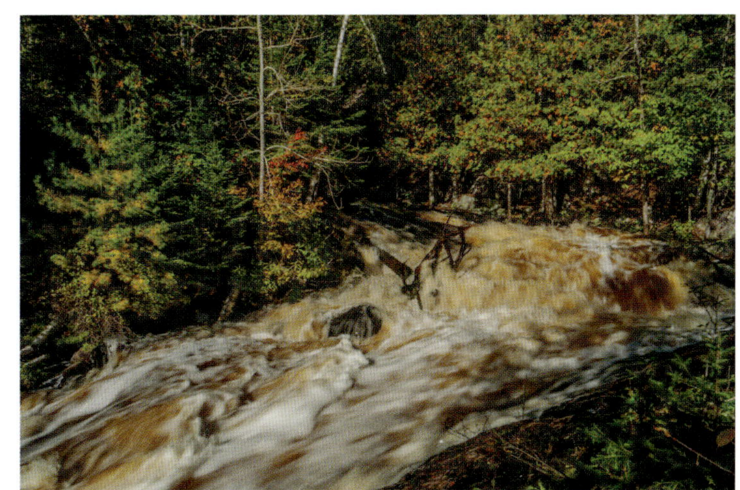

Roaring river after heavy rains.

The waterfall is the top half on a large "S" curve. Water gushes from the heavily wooded area at the top of the falls. A large rock promontory turns the river quickly to the right halfway down the rushing waterfall. There is a large pool below the falls that meanders back to the left, completing the "S".

A more "typical" look at the river where an abundance of the bedrock is showing

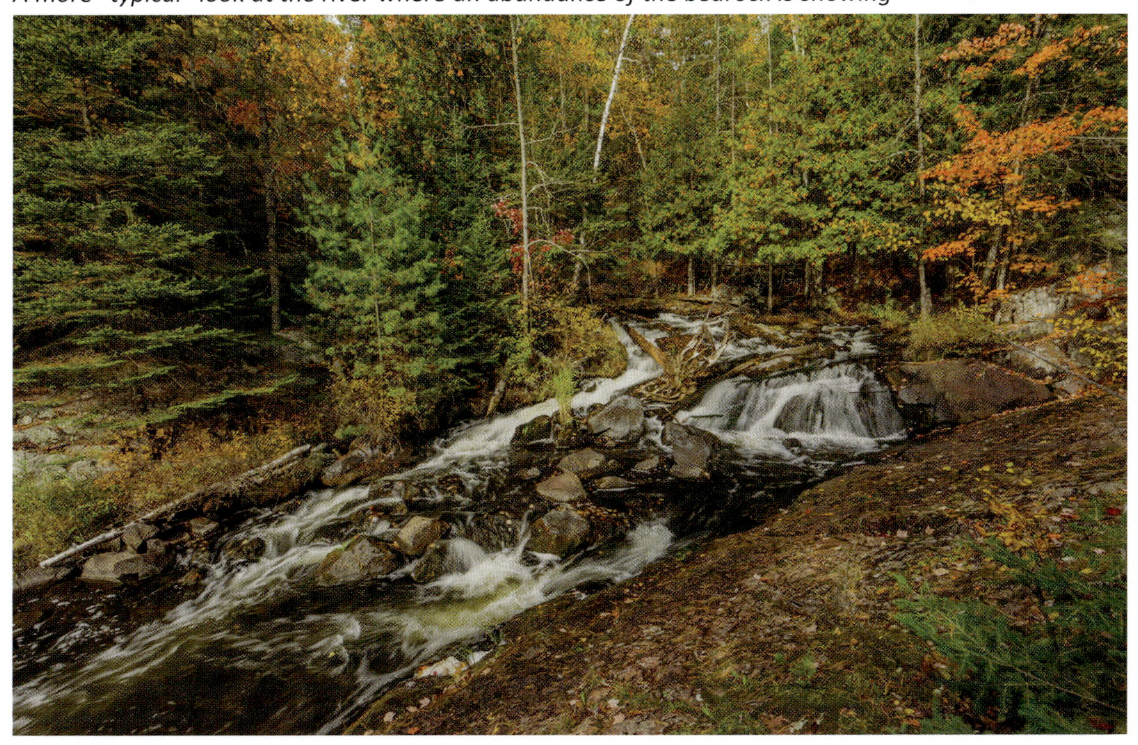

MILL POND FALLS #1 (WEST BRANCH STURGEON RIVER)

Private 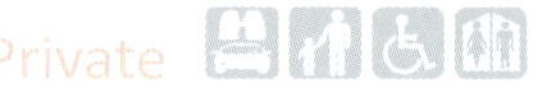

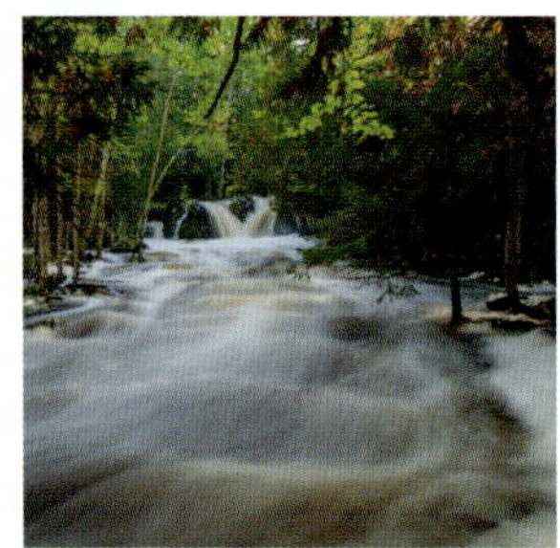

Must See:	8	GPS:	N45 59.337 W87 51.292
Height:	10 feet		
Time:	50-90 minutes	**Hiking Information**	
		Path:	N/A
Driving Information		Length:	Variable
Signs:	None	Elev. Change:	Moderate
Road:	Secondary	GPS:	Required
Access:	Difficult	Danger:	Increased
4WD:	Helpful	WP Boots:	Recommended

A rock in the middle of the falls splits the river in half and then another rock divides the river again. The second split dumps a small waterfall on the far side of the river, while the front side of the second split sends water shooting back toward the water that was diverted from the first rock. This takes place at the top of the waterfall, so the river that is divided at the top of the near drop is reunited halfway down to the spill pool. This makes for a very unique and interesting waterfall! Large moss covered bedrock is found on both sides of the river.

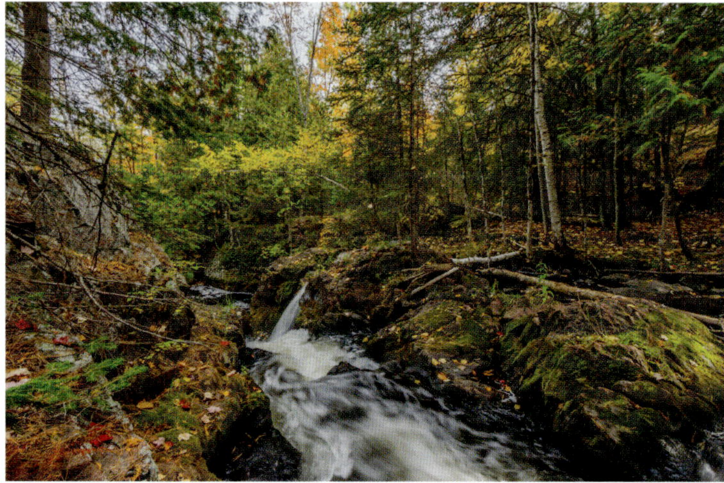

Looking down from the top of the waterfall

Notice the difference between the water level in this shot and the thumbnail above

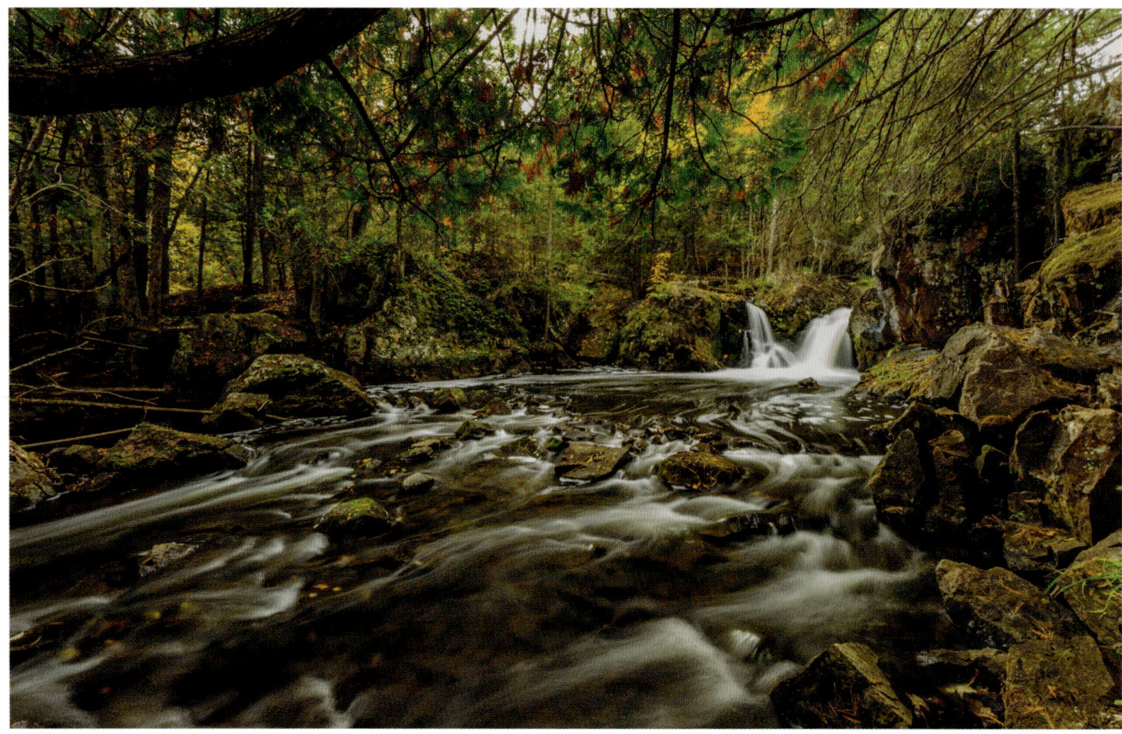

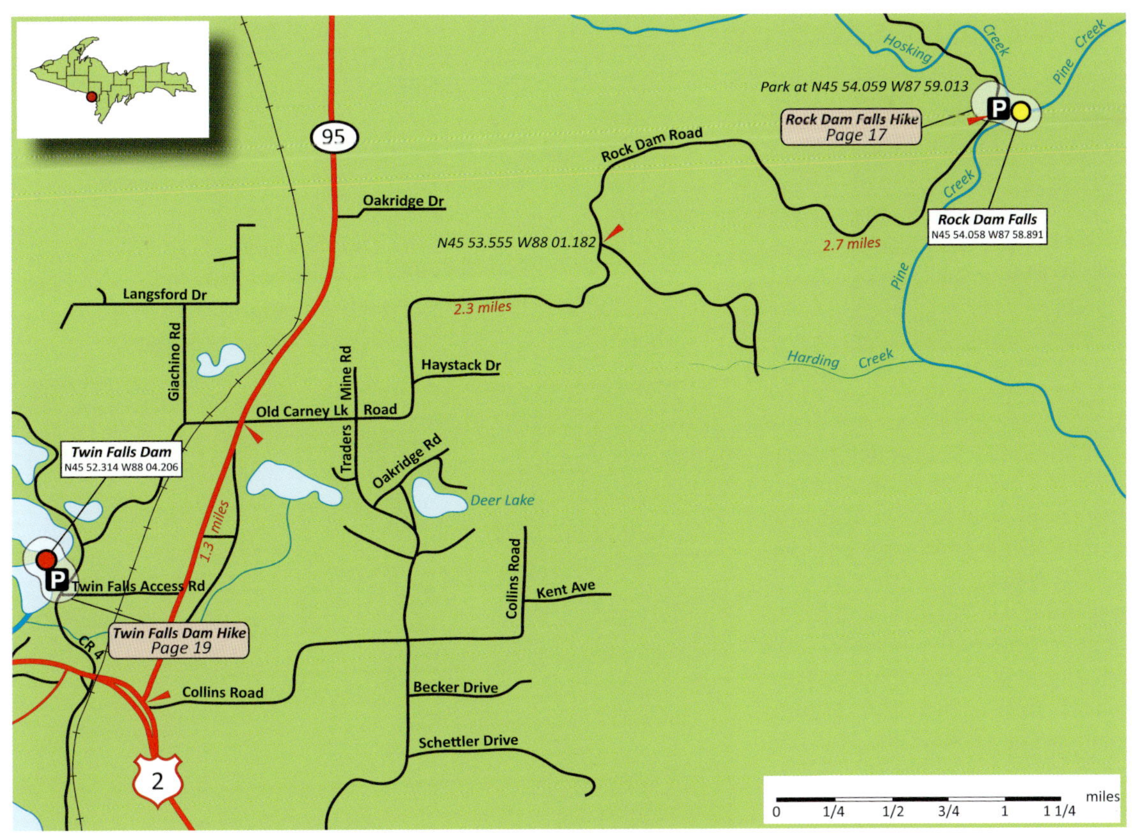

Rock Dam Falls Hike

Rock Dam Falls: A heavily travelled narrow footpath leads to the base of the falls and beyond. Ladder bridges span the creek at several points. The creek tumbles in cascades around moss encrusted boulders before ending in a 30 foot wide spill pool. A 70 foot cliff to the right overlooks the falls. A large amount of deciduous trees makes this a beautiful fall destination. Follow the trail that leads to the top of the falls to the view the upper cascades. Continue up the trail to see what appears to be a mass of gray-white marble infused with flecks of burnt red.

Directions: Travel north from US-2 on M-95 for 1.3 miles. Turn right on Old Carney Lake Road (east) for 2.3 miles (the pavement ends after about 1 mile - stay on the main road). Stay left @ N45 53.555 W88 01.182 for 2.7 miles (ignore the numerous side trails). Turn into the circle drive @ N45 54.059 W87 59.013 for 75 yards. Park. An obvious, though narrow footpath heads through the undergrowth from the far end of the circle. The falls can be heard from the parking area.

ROCK DAM FALLS (PINE CREEK)

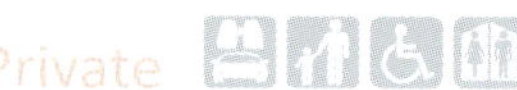

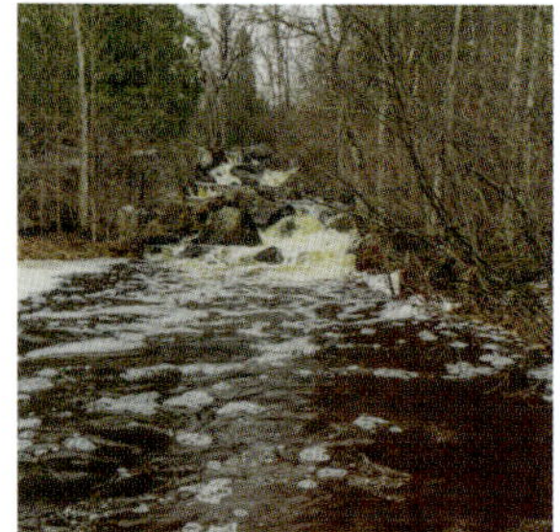

Must See:	6	GPS:	N45 54.058 W87 58.891
Height:	12 feet		
Time:	20-40 minutes	**Hiking Information**	
		Path:	Narrow Footpath
Driving Information		Length:	150 yards
Signs:	None	Elev. Change:	Slight
Road:	Dirt	GPS:	Helpful
Access:	Somewhat Difficult	Danger:	Slight
4WD:	Helpful	WP Boots:	Recommended

A heavily travelled narrow footpath leads to the base of the falls and beyond. Ladder bridges span the creek at several points. The creek tumbles in cascades around moss encrusted boulders before ending in a 30 foot wide spill pool. A 70 foot cliff to the right overlooks the falls. A large amount of deciduous trees makes this a beautiful autumn destination. Follow the trail that leads to the top of the falls to view the upper cascades. Continue up the trail to see what appears to be a mass of gray-white marble infused with flecks of burnt red.

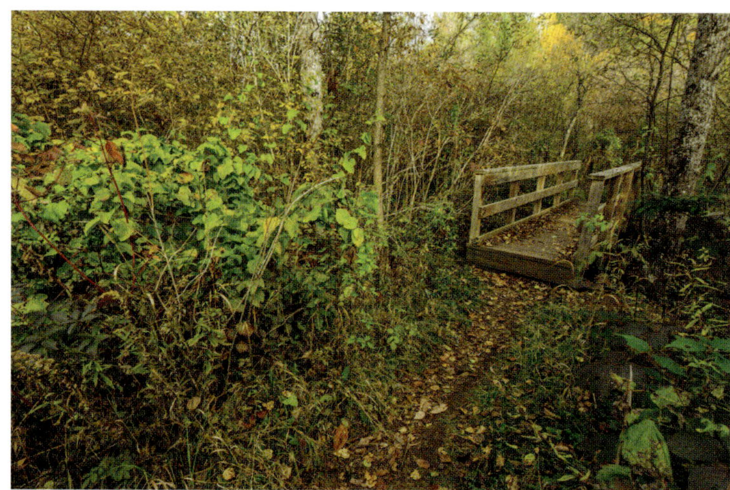

A portion of the footpath and one of the bridges

The top cascade up near the "white bedrock"

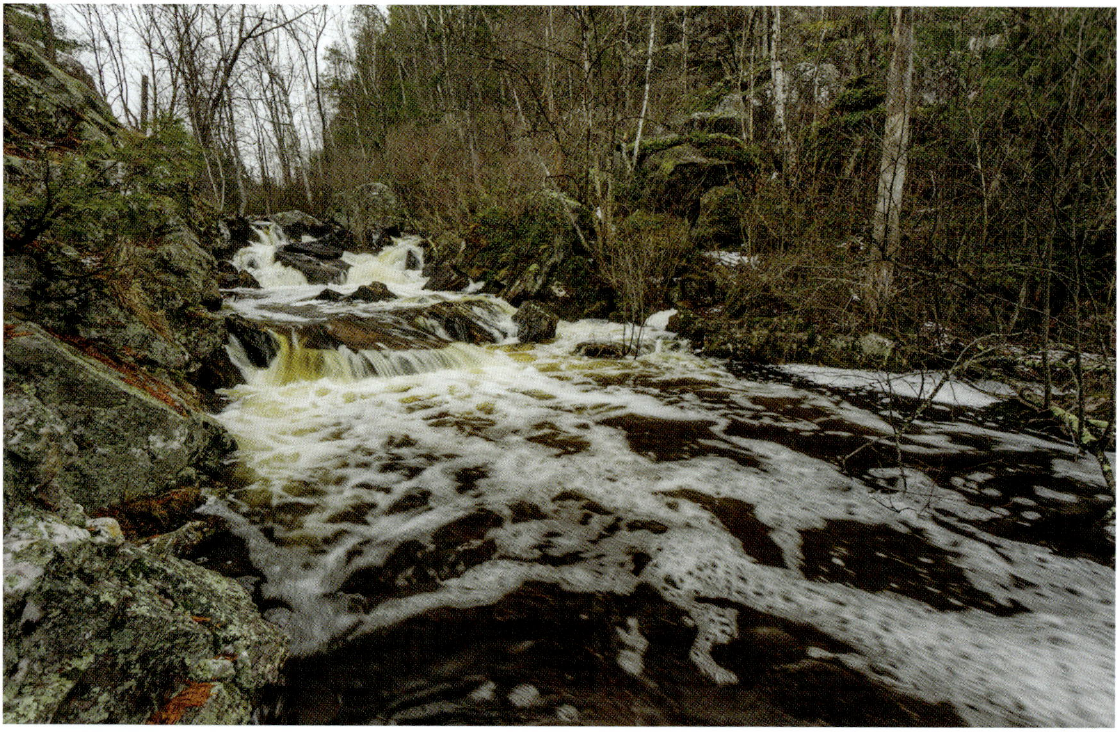

Twin Falls Dam Hike

Twin Falls Dam: There is no viewing of the spillway from the dam parking area.

Directions: Head north on M-95 from US-2 for .5 miles to Twin Falls Access Road. Turn left (west). In .5 miles cross Bass Lake Road and continue for another 200 yards on the short road to the dam.

TWIN FALLS DAM (MENOMINEE RIVER)

Private 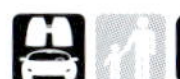 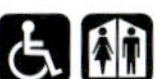

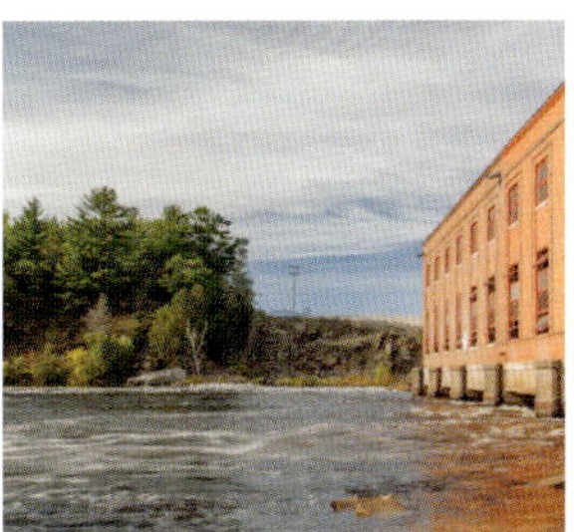

Must See:	1	GPS:	N45 52.314 W88 04.206
Height:	10 feet		
Time:	5-10 minutes	**Hiking Information**	
		Path:	N/A
Driving Information		Length:	100 feet
Signs:	None	Elev. Change:	Slight
Road:	Secondary	GPS:	N/A
Access:	Fairly Easy	Danger:	Slight
4WD:	N/A	WP Boots:	N/A

There is a pit toilet near the parking lot. Nearby is Twin Falls Flowage and Badwater Lake. Over 600 acres of fishing is accessible. Blue gill, bass, perch, crappie, and northern pike are commonly caught.

Upstream from here is the historic Upper Twin Falls Bridge. It was rebuilt in 1911 because the dam was under construction at that time and the old bridge would be flooded in the backwaters. A lovely waterfall flows beneath it. Unfortunately, it is now buried in the backwaters and is no longer visible.

The dam was completed in 1912 and renovated in 2016.

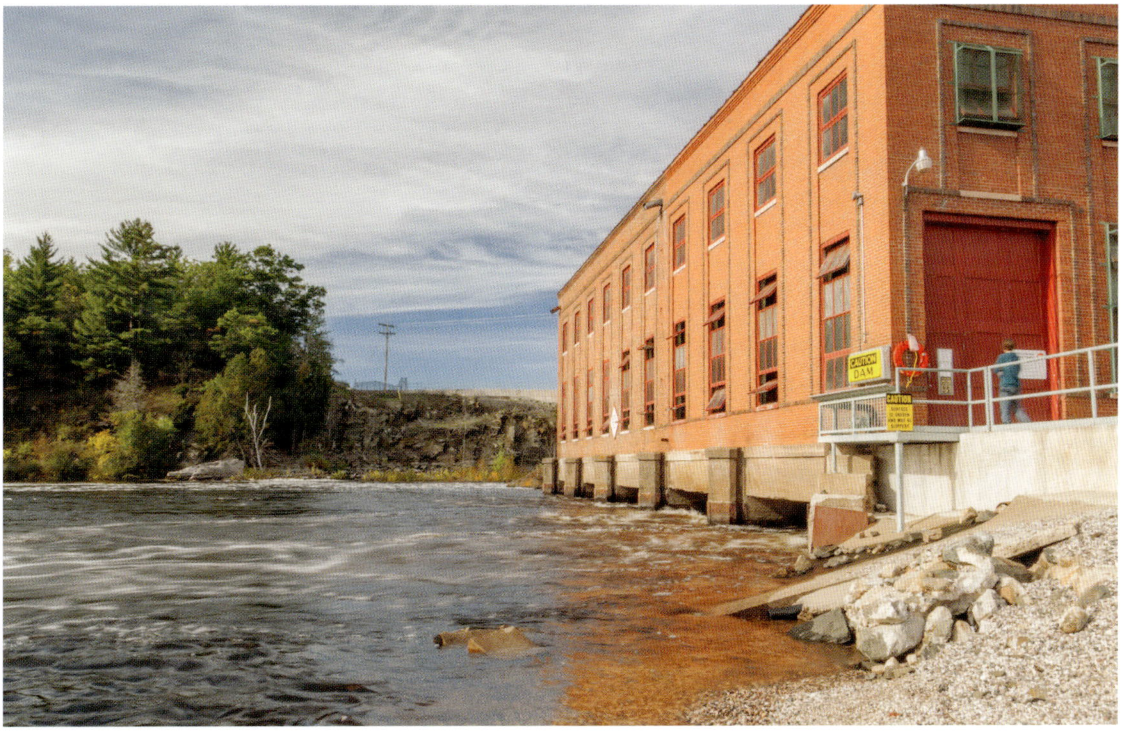

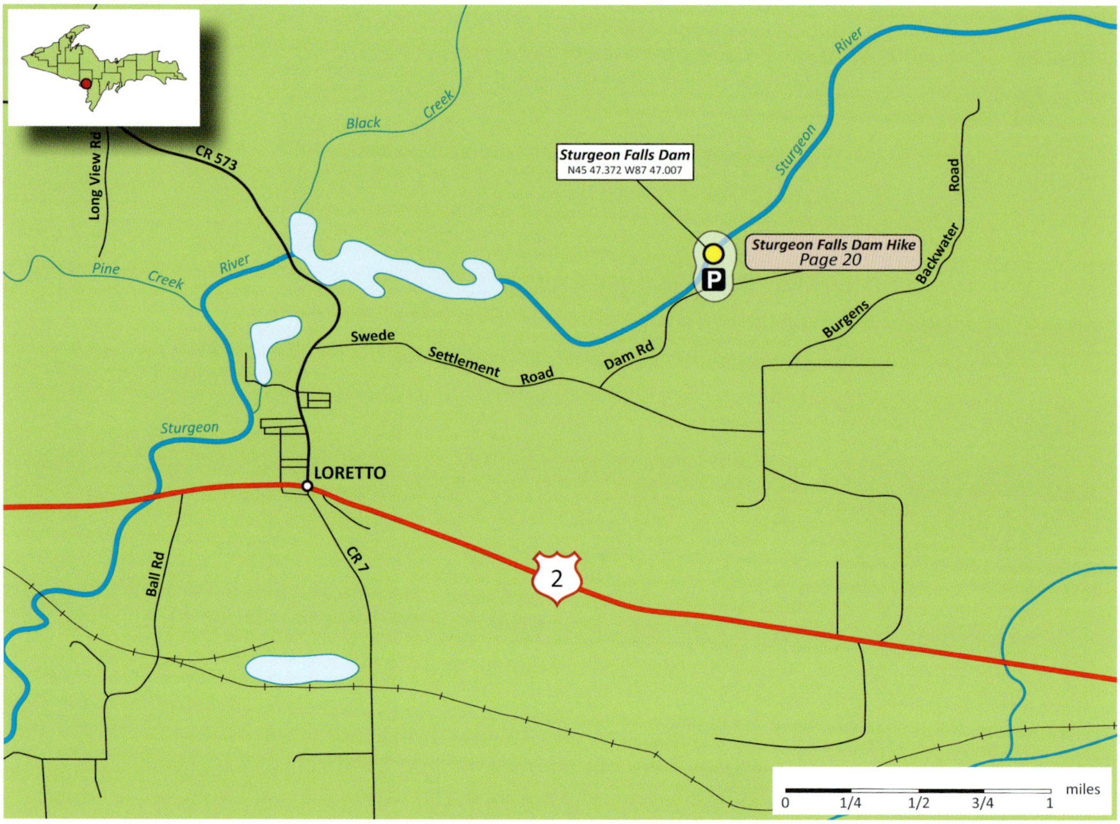

Sturgeon Falls Dam Hike

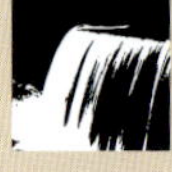

Sturgeon Falls Dam: The Sturgeon Dam was constructed in 1919. It was removed in stages between 2003 and 2005 at a cost of about $2 million. As a result, there is now about 1/4 mile of fast rapids along the Sturgeon River. I have documented one of the drops as a point of reference.

Directions: In Loretto, turn north on State Street off of US-2. In .5 miles turn right (east) onto Swede Settlement Rd. Turn left (northeast) in 1.2 miles onto Sturgeon Dam Road (dirt road). It dead ends at a gate. If the gate is open, it is possible to drive down to a larger "parking area" where 4-wheelers run up some fairly steep hills. Otherwise, walk down the 2-track that almost immediately parallels the river.

STURGEON FALLS DAM (STURGEON RIVER)

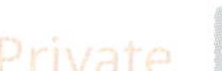

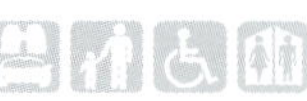

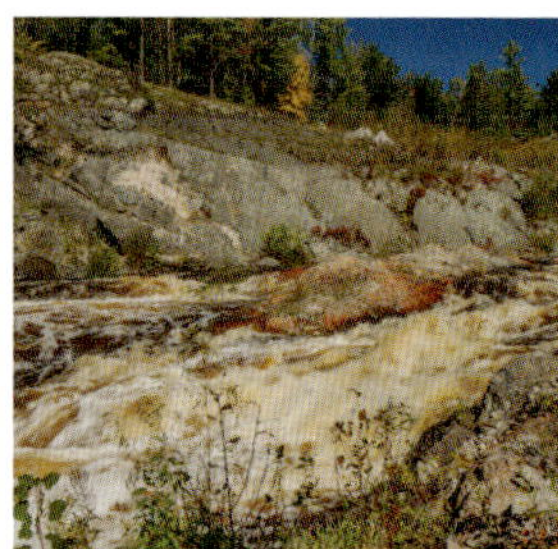

Must See:	4	GPS:	N45 47.372 W87 47.007
Height:	4 feet		
Time:	30-45 minutes	Hiking Information	
		Path:	Slight Footpath
Driving Information		Length:	1/4 mile
Signs:	None	Elev. Change:	Slight
Road:	Dirt	GPS:	Recommended
Access:	Fairly Easy	Danger:	Slight
4WD:	N/A	WP Boots:	None

An island of red rock is surrounded by gently falling rapids just down river from this point. The 2-track that follows the Sturgeon River through hardwoods and conifers is a very picturesque walk, especially in the fall.

CHAPTER 2
MARQUETTE COUNTY

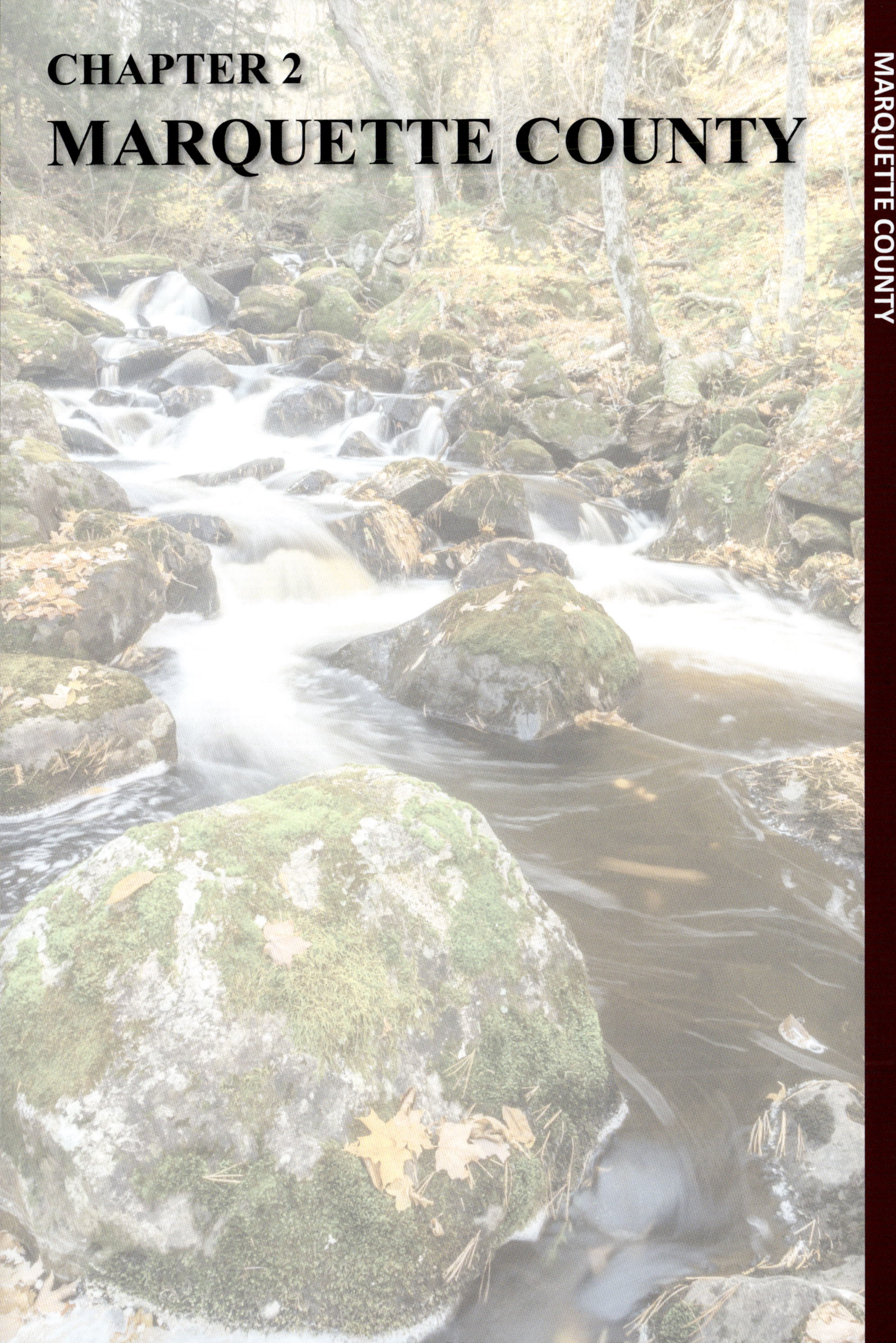

MARQUETTE COUNTY CONTENTS

MAPS.....................................
HIKES.....................................
WATERFALLS..........................

TABLE OF CONTENT KEY

MAPS...
HIKES...
WATERFALLS.........................

TABLE OF CONTENT KEY

MAPS..
HIKES..
WATERFALLS..........................

TABLE OF CONTENT KEY

WARNER FALLS AREA 140

YELLOW DOG FALLS AREA 148

MAPS..........
HIKES..........
WATERFALLS..........

TABLE OF CONTENT KEY

MARQUETTE COUNTY FACTS

Founded:	1861
Size:	1,808 square miles
Population (2010):	67,077
County Seat:	Marquette

The county was named after Jacques Marquette, a Jesuit priest and an early explorer in the area. While the borders for the county were set in 1843, they were modified over nine times through 1891.

Marquette County dwarfs the rest of the counties in Michigan by its shear size. In fact, comprising 1,873 square miles of rugged Upper Peninsula land area, Marquette County is larger than the state of Rhode Island, and is only slightly smaller than Delaware! Marquette County ranks as the 17th largest county east of the Mississippi.

The Huron Mountains are located in Marquette and Baraga Counties. They contain the highest and most rugged terrain found in Michigan. However, a large portion of the mountain range located within Marquette county is inaccessible since it is privately owned by the ultra-elite Huron Mountain Club. Although the club is research friendly, the public is strictly prohibited from crossing its borders.

A couple of lighthouses grace the Lake Superior Shoreline in Marquette County. Marquette Harbor Light is easily seen from a number of locations near downtown Marquette. It's bright red structure is easily recognized. Just outside of Big Bay, further up the coast from Marquette, is Big Bay Point Lighthouse, now a lovely bed and breakfast. www.bigbaylighthouse.com

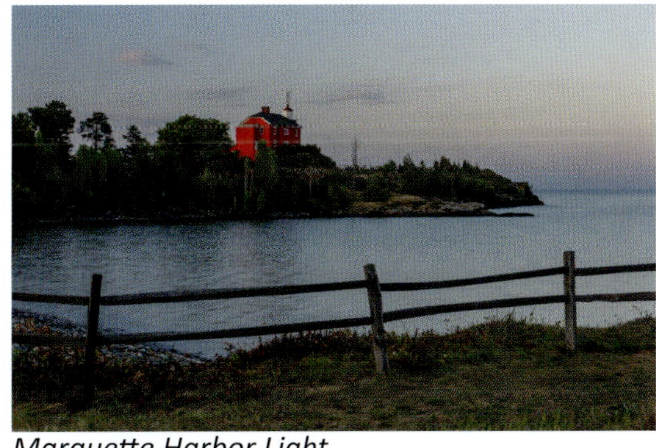

Marquette Harbor Light

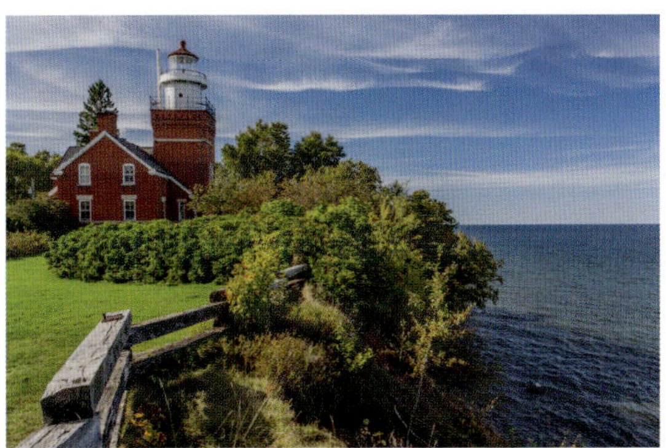

Big Bay Point Lighthouse Bed & Breakfast

Little Presque Isle, meaning "false island" in French, is found just north of Marquette. The island at one time could be accessed by a narrow strip of land. Now it takes wading 150 yards through water that may be up to hip deep to get to the rocky island that from the air resembles a the body of a dragon staring back at the mainland.

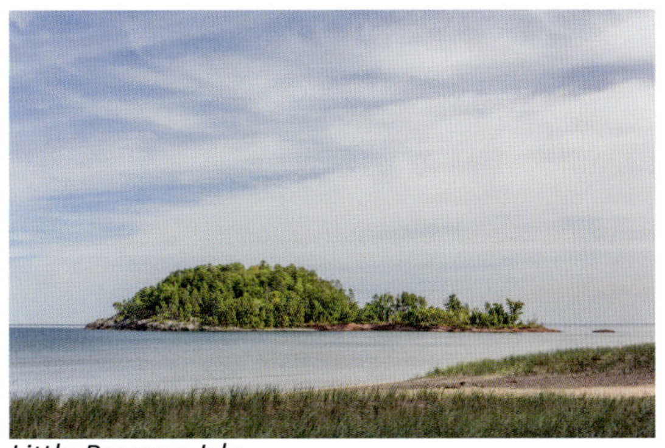

Little Presque Isle

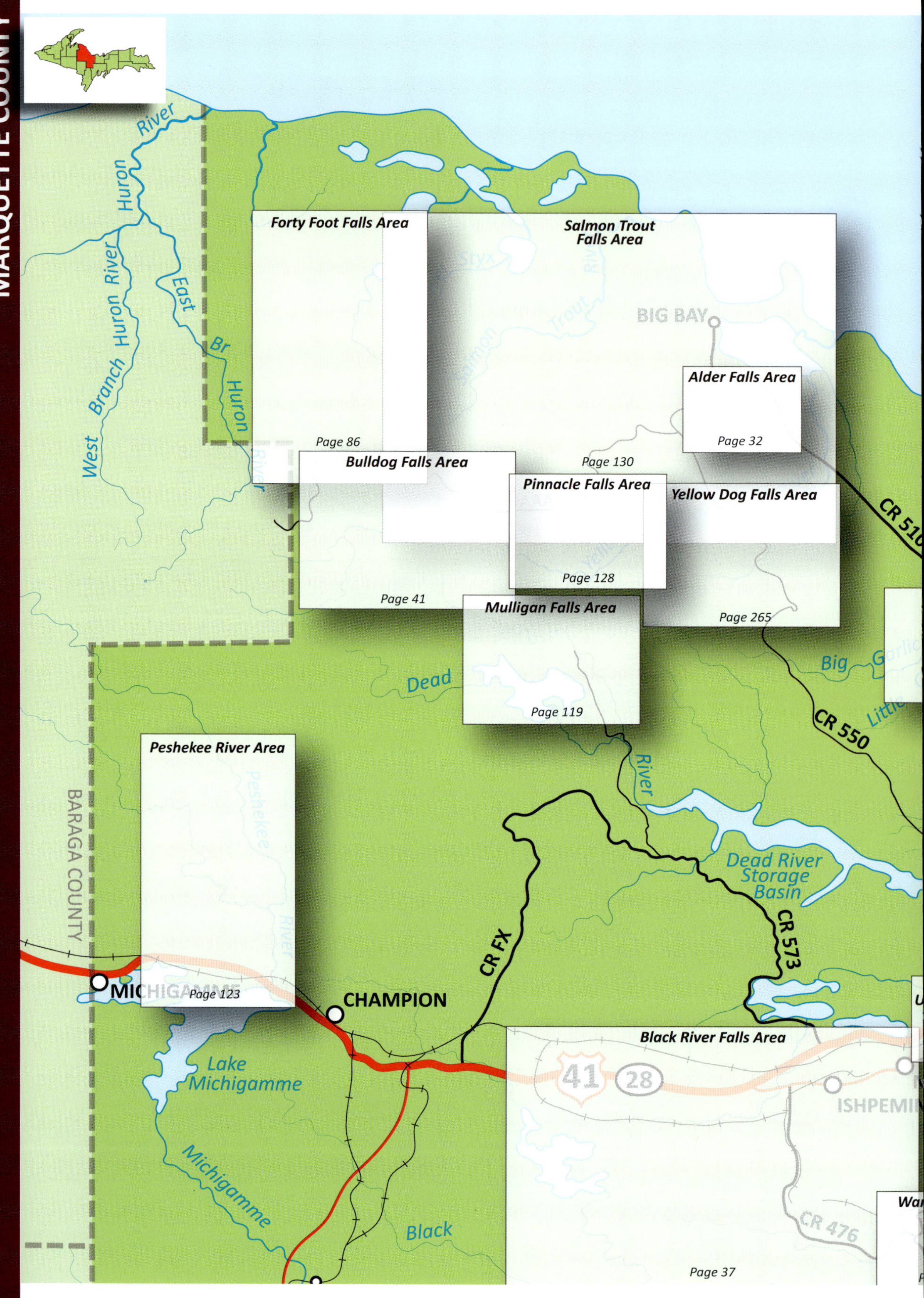

Forty Foot Falls Area
Page 86
Salmon Trout Falls Area
Page 130
BIG BAY
Alder Falls Area
Page 32
Bulldog Falls Area
Page 41
Pinnacle Falls Area
Page 128
Yellow Dog Falls Area
Page 265
Mulligan Falls Area
Page 119
Peshekee River Area
Page 123
Black River Falls Area
Page 37
River
Huron
West Branch Huron River
East Br Huron
BARAGA COUNTY
Dead
River
Big
CR 550
CR 510
Dead River Storage Basin
CR 573
CR FX
MICHIGAMME
CHAMPION
Lake Michigamme
Michigamme
Black
41
28
ISHPEMI
CR 476

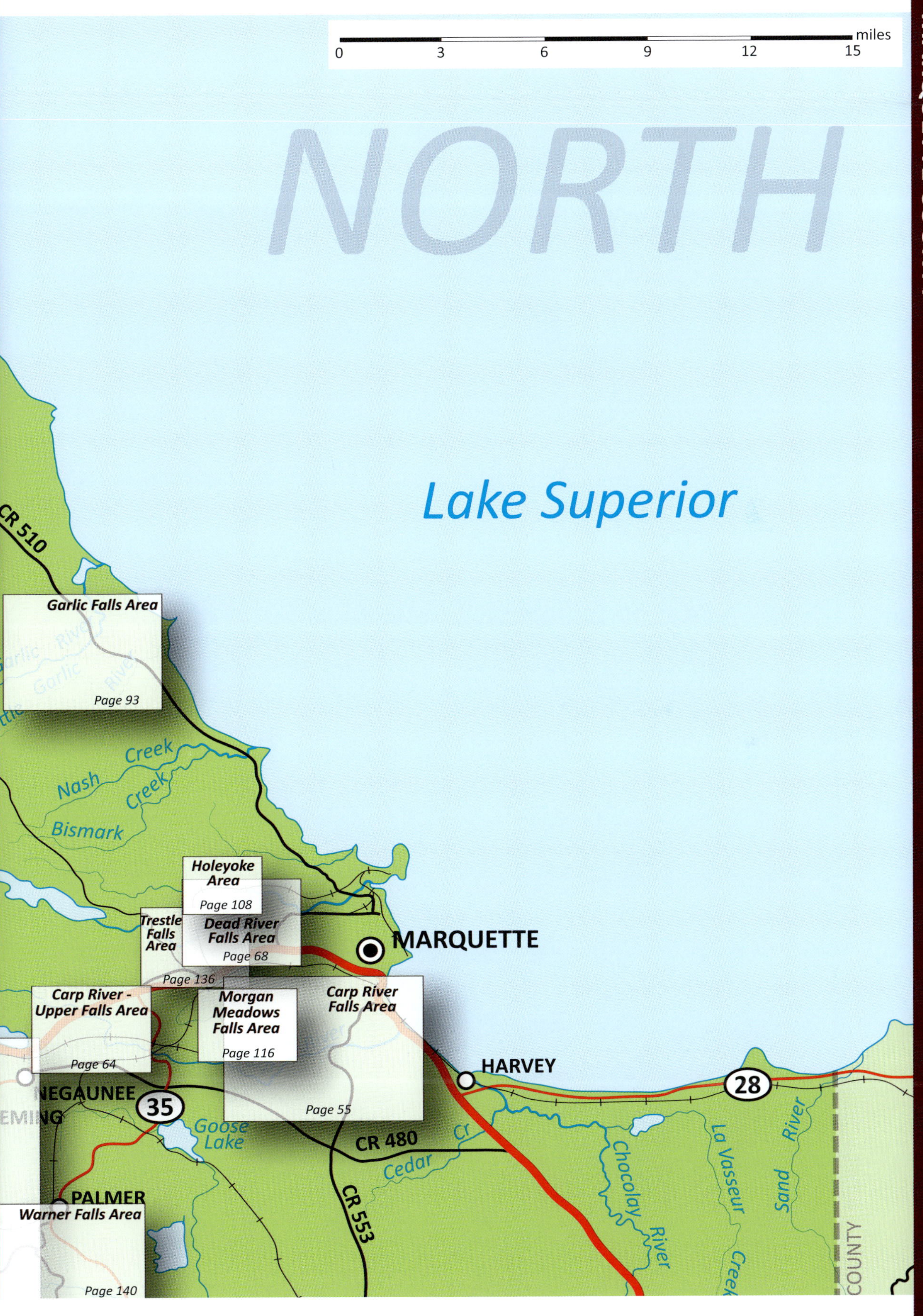

miles
0
3
6
9
12
15
NORTH
Lake Superior
CR 510
Garlic Falls Area
Page 93
Nash
Creek
Creek
Bismark
Holeyoke Area
Page 108
Trestle Falls Area
Dead River Falls Area
Page 68
Page 136
MARQUETTE
Carp River - Upper Falls Area
Page 64
Morgan Meadows Falls Area
Page 116
Carp River Falls Area
Page 55
HARVEY
28
NEGAUNEE
35
Goose Lake
CR 480
Cedar
Cr
CR 553
PALMER
Warner Falls Area
Page 140
Chocolay
River
La Vasseur
Creek
Sand
River
COUNTY

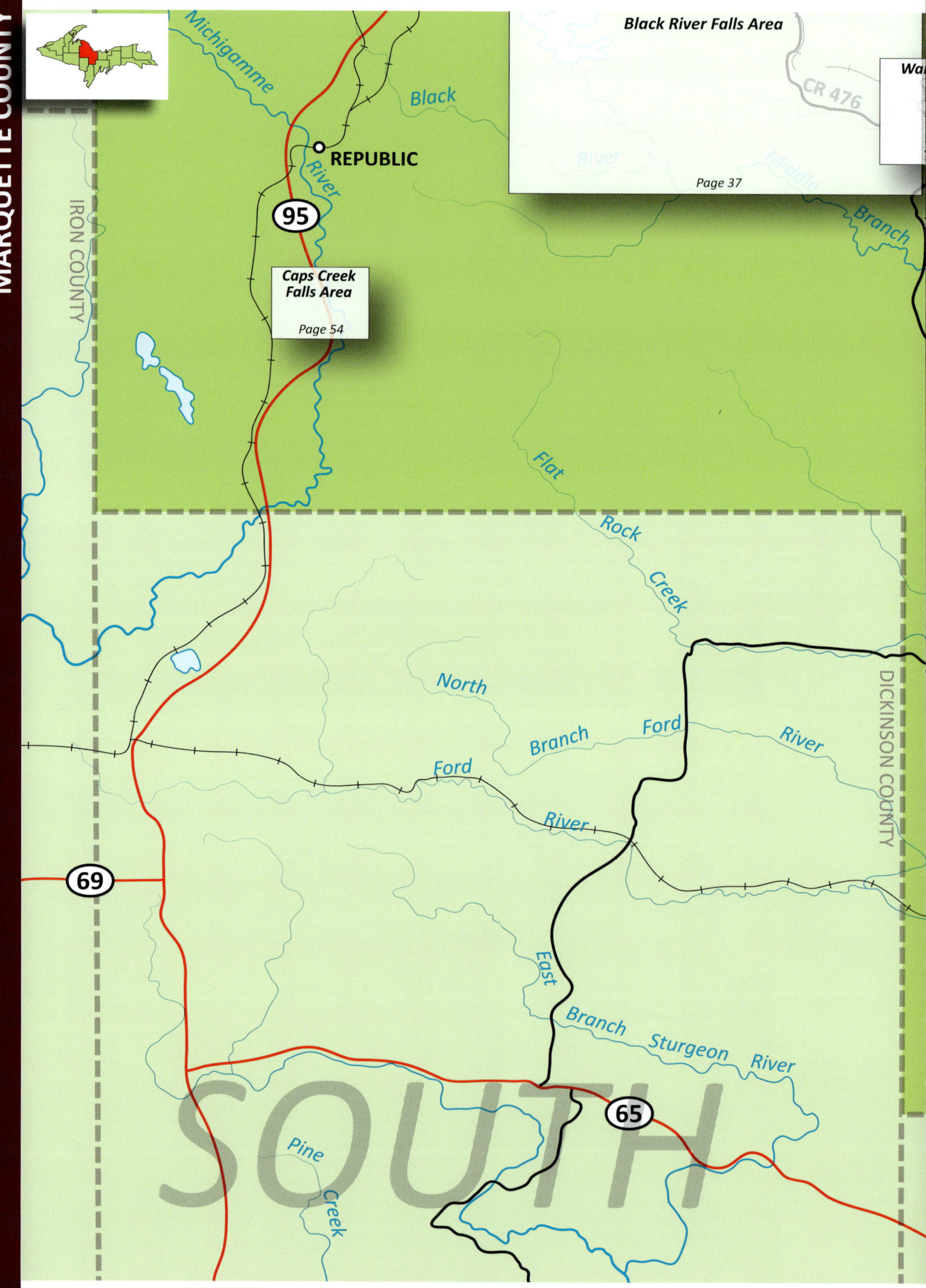
Michigamme
Black
REPUBLIC
River
95
Black River Falls Area
CR 476
Page 37
Middle
Branch
IRON COUNTY
Caps Creek Falls Area
Page 54
Flat
Rock
Creek
North
Branch
Ford
River
Ford
River
DICKINSON COUNTY
69
East
Branch
Sturgeon
River
65
SOUTH
Pine
Creek

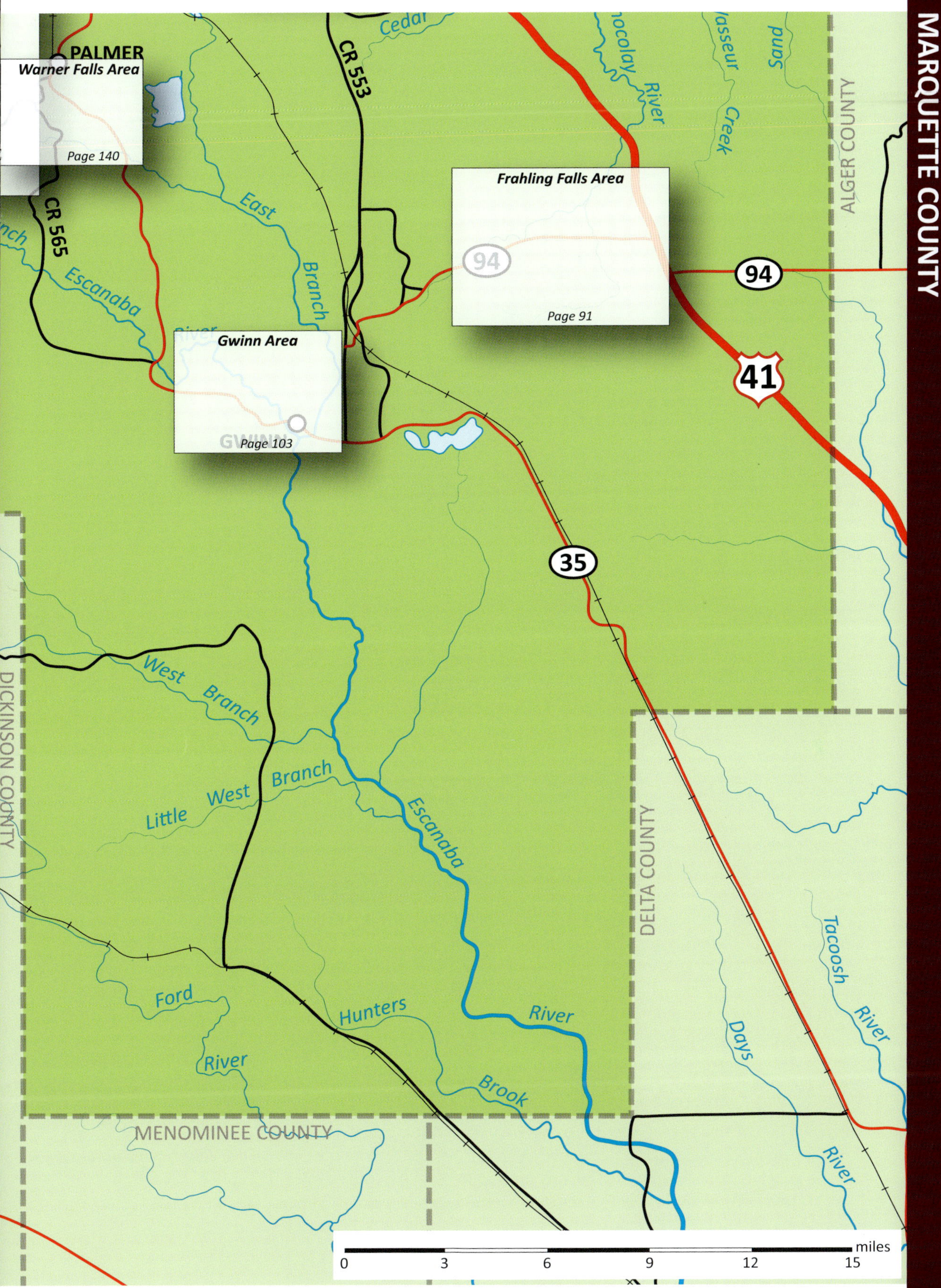
PALMER
Warner Falls Area
Page 140
Frahling Falls Area
Page 91
Gwinn Area
Page 103
CR 553
CR 565
94
41
35
East Branch
Escanaba River
West Branch
Little West Branch
Escanaba River
Ford River
Hunters Brook
Days River
Tacoosh River
Creek
Sand
ALGER COUNTY
DICKINSON COUNTY
DELTA COUNTY
MENOMINEE COUNTY
miles
0
3
6
9
12
15

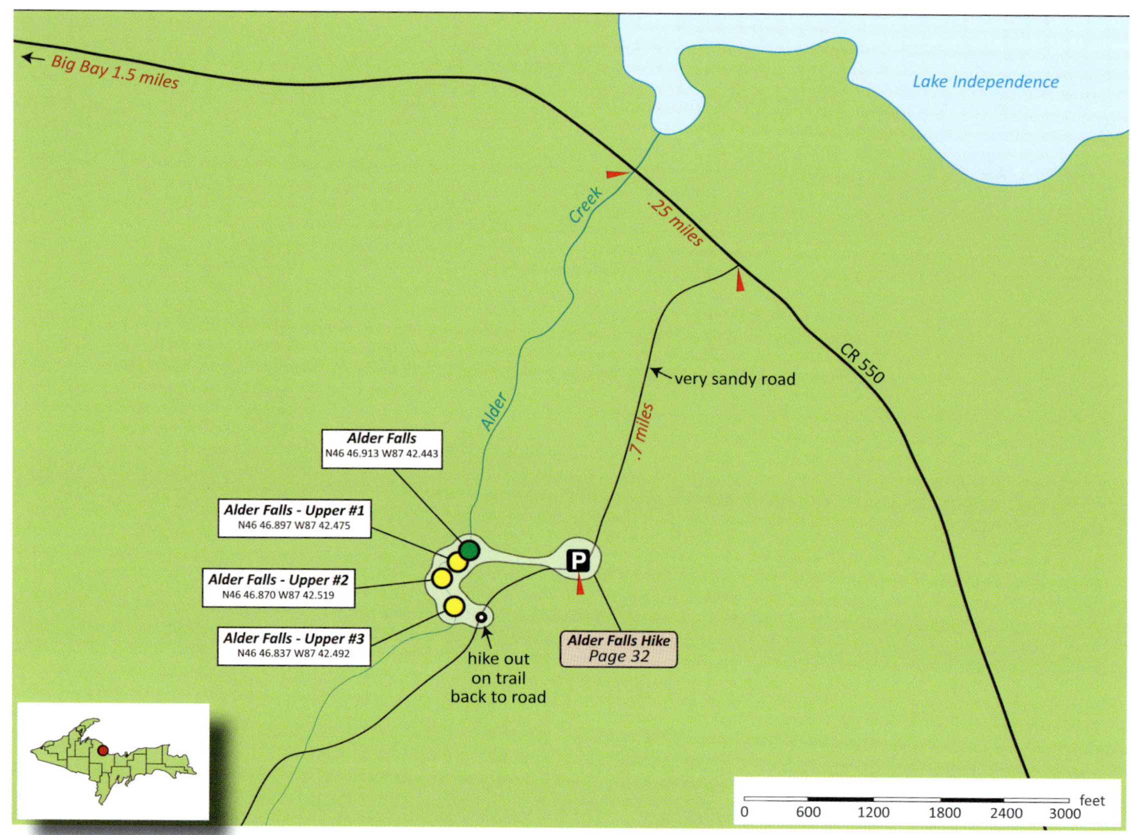

Alder Falls Hike

Alder Falls should be on the list of all waterfall enthusiasts. Just southeast of the quaint little town of Big Bay, Alder Falls is somewhat difficult to find. These waterfalls are on private property. However, a sign at the parking area implies that visitors are welcome but must not leave traces of having been there. As always, access to waterfalls can change over time. Obey the wishes of land owners and be considerate.

Directions: Drive on CR-550 from Marquette toward Big Bay. Approximately 2.5 miles before entering Big Bay, Alder Creek Truck Trail (no road sign) is on the left (west) at N46 47.366 W87 41.860. This is the last road before crossing Alder Creek. The road immediately forks. Stay to the left. The "road" to the right is a long driveway to a residence. Alder Creek Truck Trail is a very sandy 2-track. (A 4WD vehicle is helpful, but not normally required.) Follow the road for .7 miles to the parking area. There is room for a couple of vehicles on either side of the trail. Park. Hike down the nice footpath that ends with a somewhat precarious hillside approaching the river. The falls are just upstream from where the trail deposits you on the riverbank and can be viewed from both sides of the river, if you dare to cross on the rocks and fallen trees that present themselves for the more adventurous among us! Continue upstream for three more waterfalls. As much as possible stay on the east side of the river. This is my recommended path for viewing all the falls. Cross the river below Alder Falls. View #1 from the west (far) side of the river. Cross the river again. Follow the river to #2 which is in a gorge. Wade up the river to get a closer view of #2. Backtrack the short distance out of the gorge. Climb up the east (near) side to the top of the gorge. Follow up river until it's possible to climb back down to the river's edge. Follow the river to #3. Climb back up out of the gorge after viewing #3. This can be a VERY STEEP climb. Continue on the trail up river. It quickly leaves the river and cuts back over to the sandy 2-track (head to N46 46.833 W87 42.423), intersecting it about 250 yards south of the parking area.

ALDER FALLS (ALDER CREEK)

Private 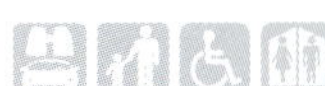

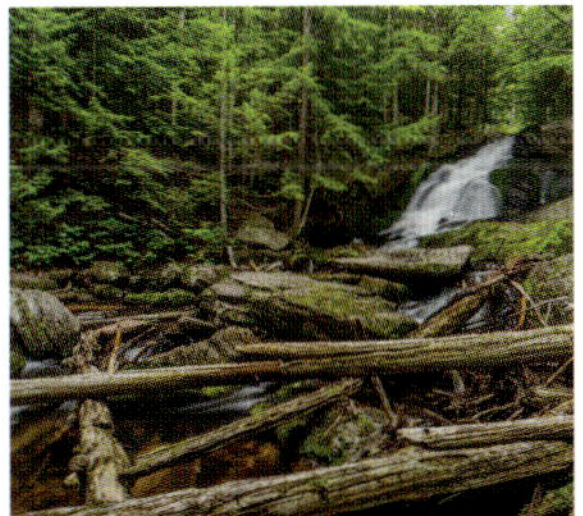

Must See:	8	GPS:	N46 46.913 W87 42.443
Height:	20 feet		
Time:	15-30 minutes	**Hiking Information**	
		Path:	Unimproved footpath
Driving Information		Length:	.13 miles
Signs:	None	Elev. Change:	Moderate
Road:	Sandy 2-track	GPS:	Helpful
Access:	Somewhat difficult	Danger:	Moderate
4WD:	Helpful	WP Boots:	Helpful

A 3 foot wide channel at the top of the falls widens out to a veil about 15 feet wide as it slides over the bedrock. Black rocks backdrop the 20 foot falls that end in the shallow 30 foot wide river that is strewn with boulders and tree trunks. In the U.P. it is rare to meet fellow waterfall adventurers at all but the most popular waterfalls. So it was surprising to run across Douglas Feltman here as he was also photographing the falls. Check out his videos on the internet at *https://vimeo.com/feltphoto1*.

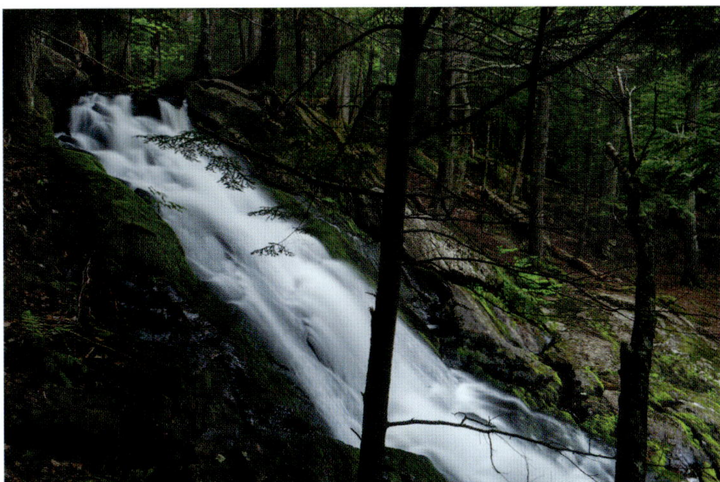

The steep side of the waterfall can be a little treacherous to climb

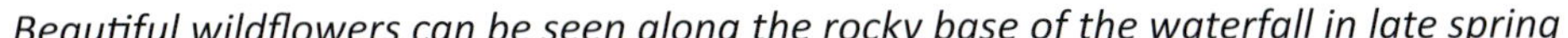

Beautiful wildflowers can be seen along the rocky base of the waterfall in late spring

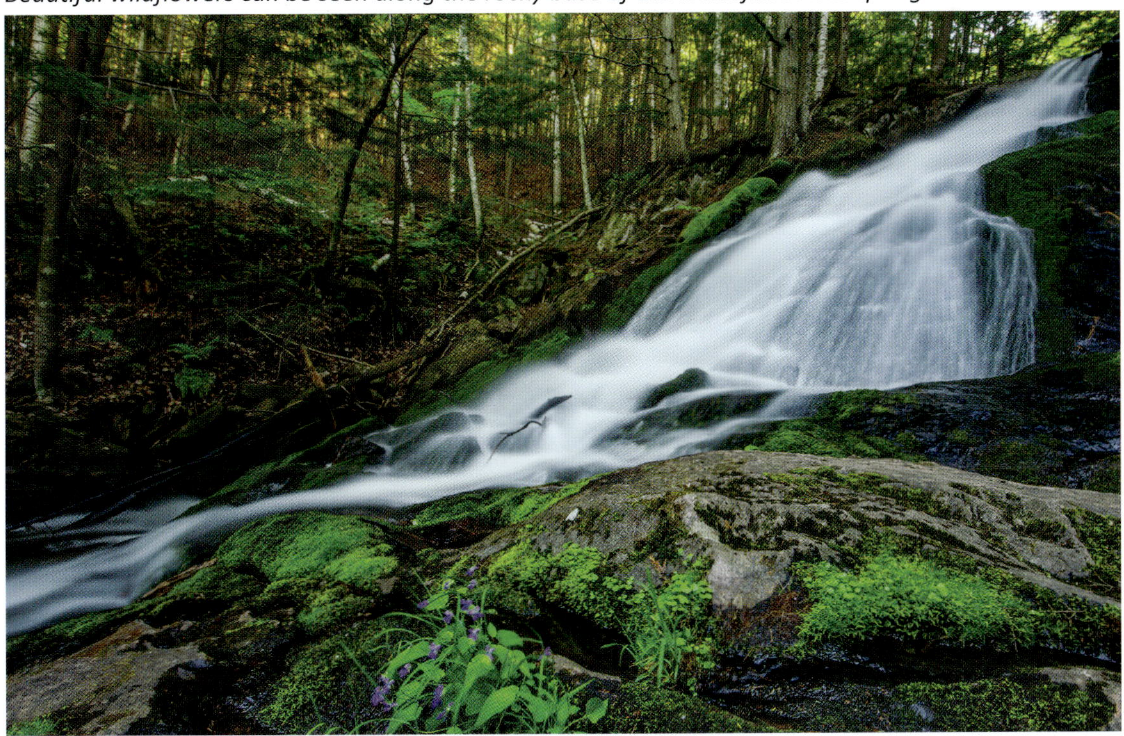

ALDER FALLS - UPPER #1 (ALDER CREEK)

Private 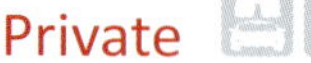 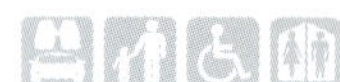

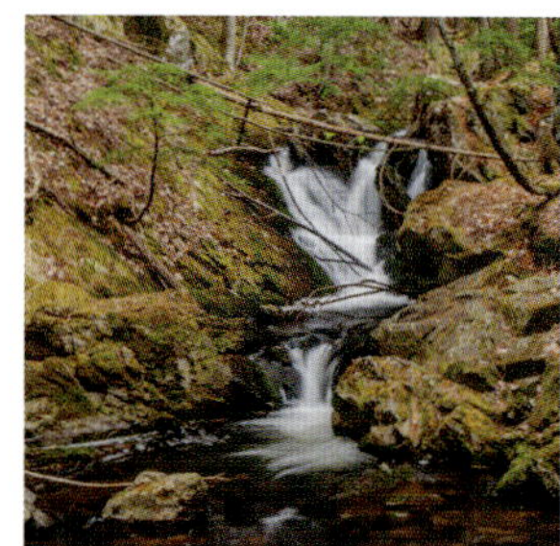

Must See:	5	GPS:	N46 46.897 W87 42.475
Height:	8 feet		
Time:	25-45 minutes	Hiking Information	
		Path:	Unimproved footpath
Driving Information		Length:	.16 miles
Signs:	None	Elev. Change:	Moderate
Road:	Sandy 2-track	GPS:	Recommended
Access:	Somewhat Difficult	Danger:	Moderate
4WD:	Helpful	WP Boots:	Recommended

Large, irregular shaped slabs of rock are heaved up at a sharp angle. The creek tumbles around the lower ones into a narrow crevasse - as narrow as 1 foot at a lower drop 20 feet downstream from the main drop. High winds have recently downed a number of trees in the area. Several of these fell across the creek just below the falls. They will be there for some time without human intervention.

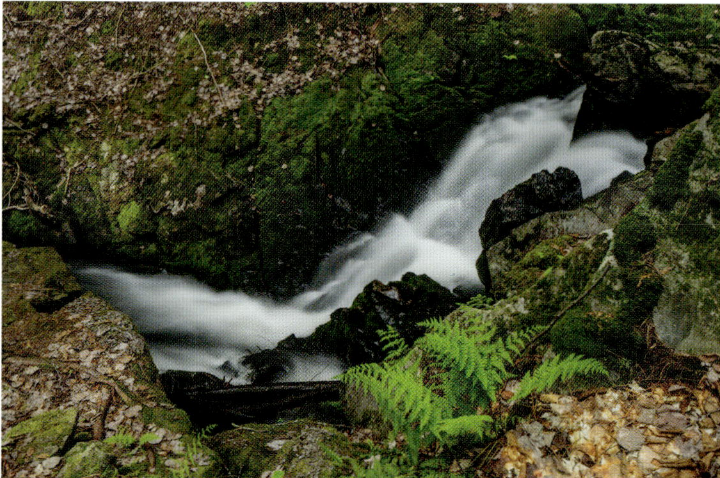

The waterfall rests down in a narrow crevasse.

Very little soil sits on the bedrock here. It makes it difficult for plants to grow.

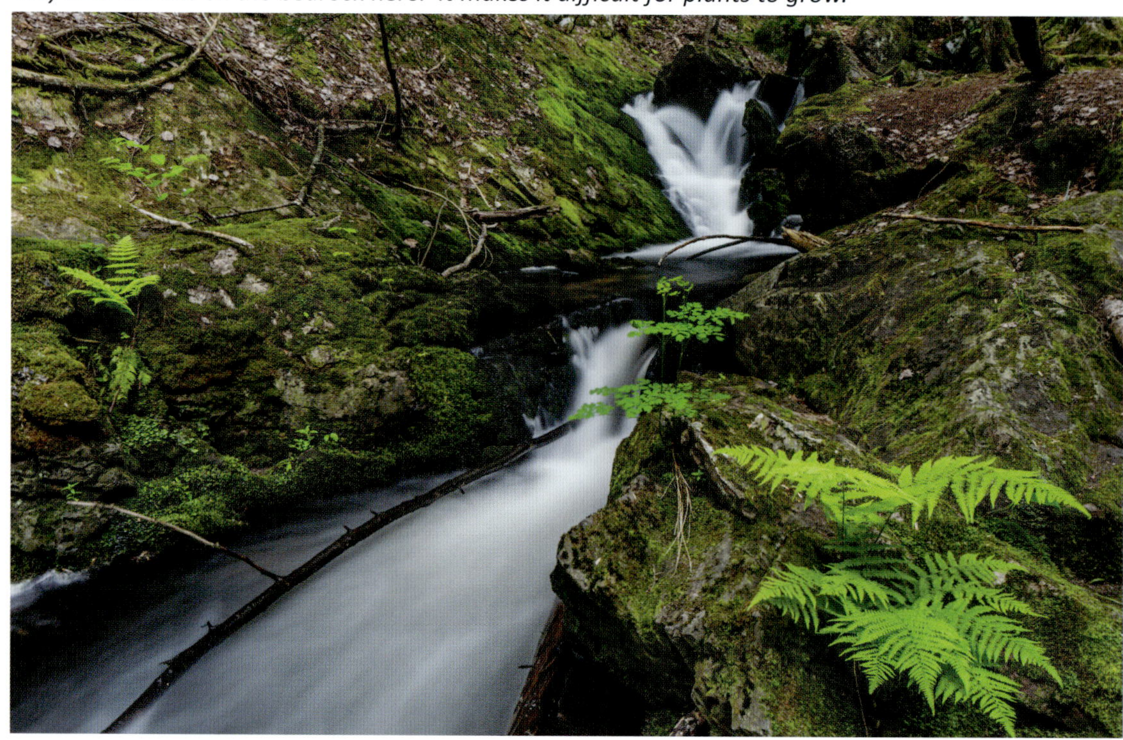

ALDER FALLS - UPPER #2 (ALDER CREEK)

Private  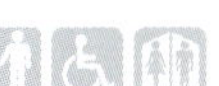

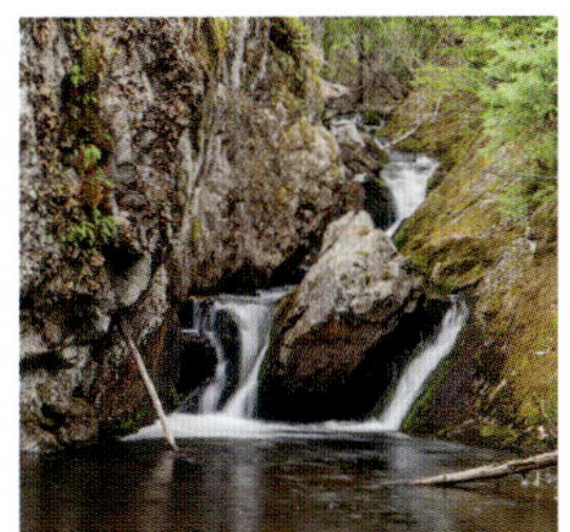

Must See:	6	GPS:	N46 46.870 W87 42.519
Height:	9 feet		
Time:	35-55 minutes	**Hiking Information**	
		Path:	Unimproved footpath
Driving Information		Length:	.22 miles
Signs:	None	Elev. Change:	Elevated
Road:	Sandy 2-track	GPS:	Recommended
Access:	Somewhat difficult	Danger:	Elevated
4WD:	Helpful	WP Boots:	Required

Twenty foot high rock walls guard both sides of the creek with a deep spill pool reaching from wall to wall. The falls arc in a strange backward "C" shape as they fall toward the right side of the gorge and then are shoved back to the left.

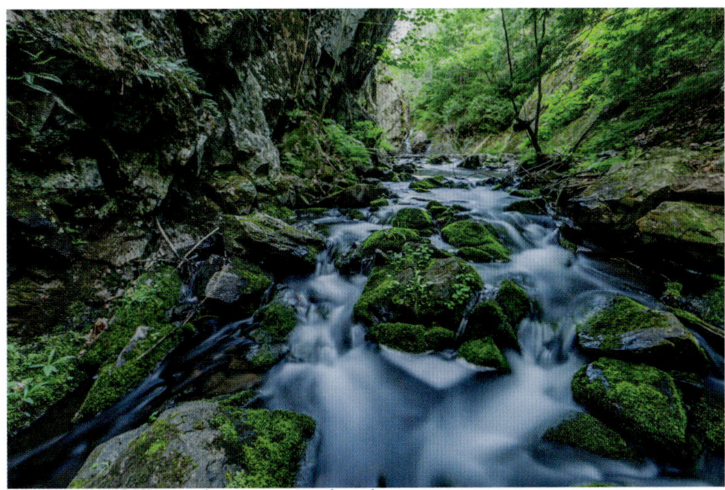

The waterfall can be seen in the distance upstream

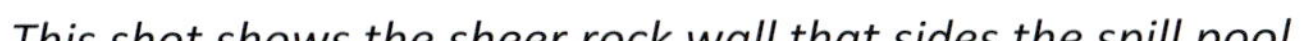

This shot shows the sheer rock wall that sides the spill pool

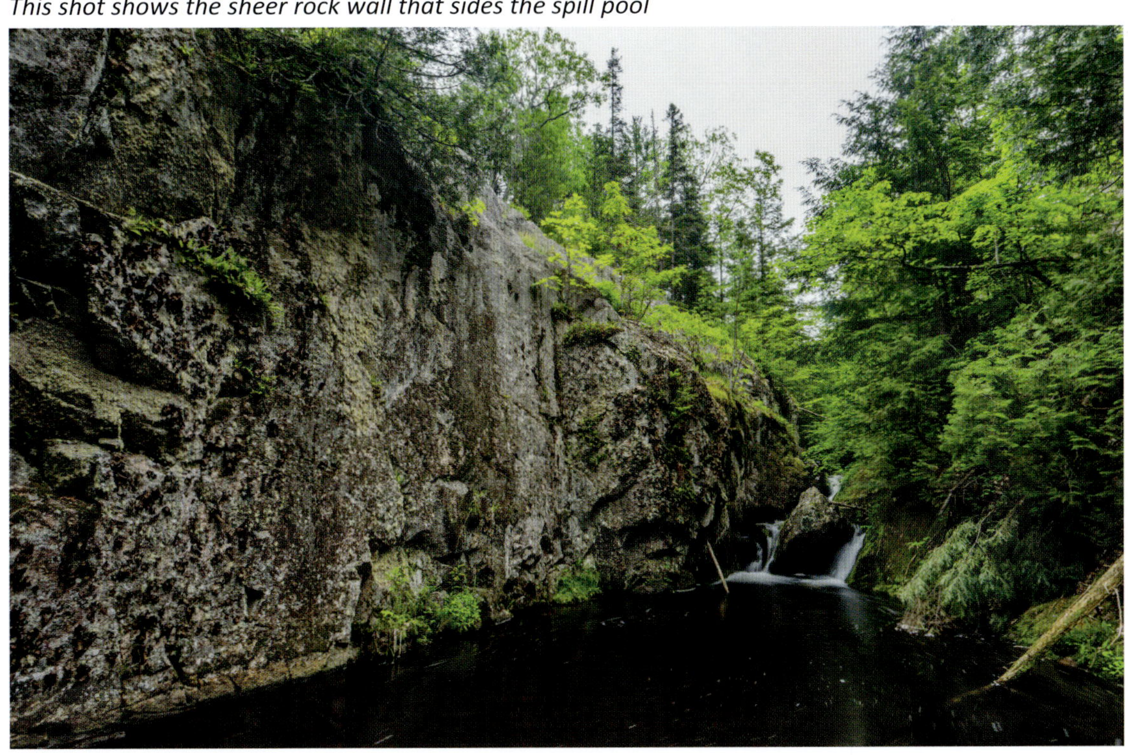

ALDER FALLS - UPPER #3 (ALDER CREEK)

Private 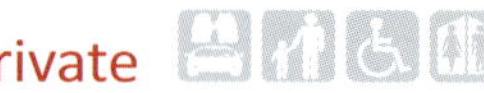

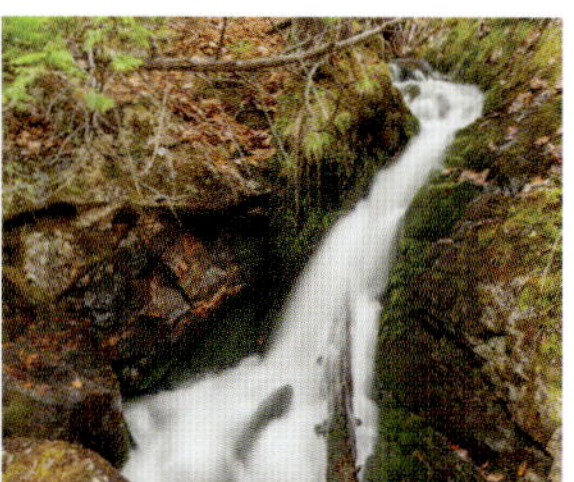

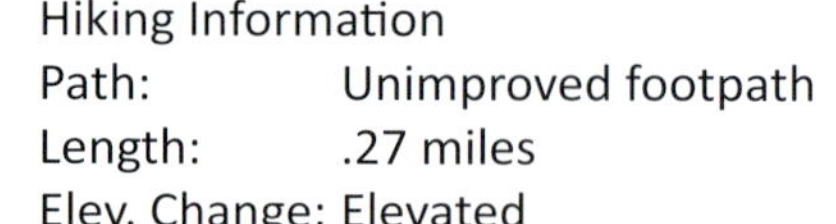

Must See:	4	GPS:	N46 46.837 W87 42.492
Height:	8 feet		
Time:	50-75 minutes	Hiking Information	
		Path:	Unimproved footpath
Driving Information		Length:	.27 miles
Signs:	None	Elev. Change:	Elevated
Road:	Sandy 2-track	GPS:	Recommended
Access:	Somewhat difficult	Danger:	Elevated
4WD:	Helpful	WP Boots:	Required

Massive boulders, one as large as a truck, have fallen into the gorge - at one point completely blocking it. The Upper #3 waterfall runs around the top side of this rock, sliding down the moss covered gorge wall. The rugged boulders and rock walls can elicit claustrophobic feelings.

I recommend taking a shortcut back to the sandy road and then to the vehicle. There is a faint trail that marks this route.

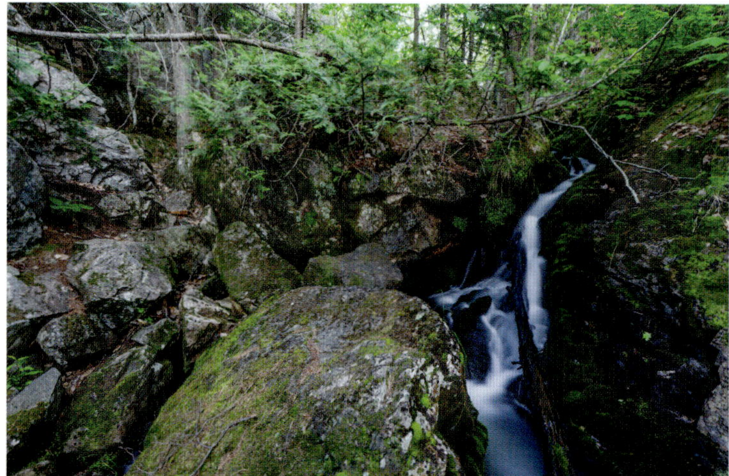

There are not many flat places to plant your feet around here!

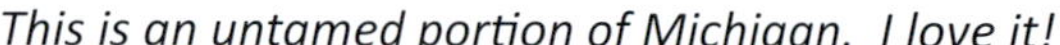

This is an untamed portion of Michigan. I love it!

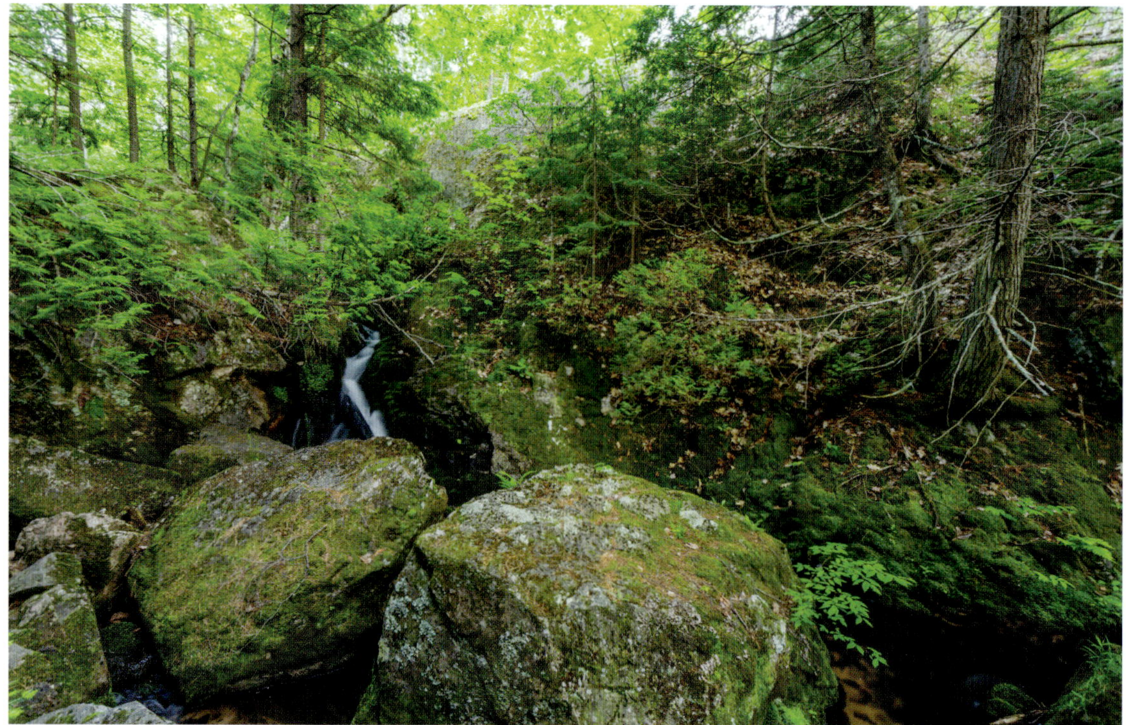

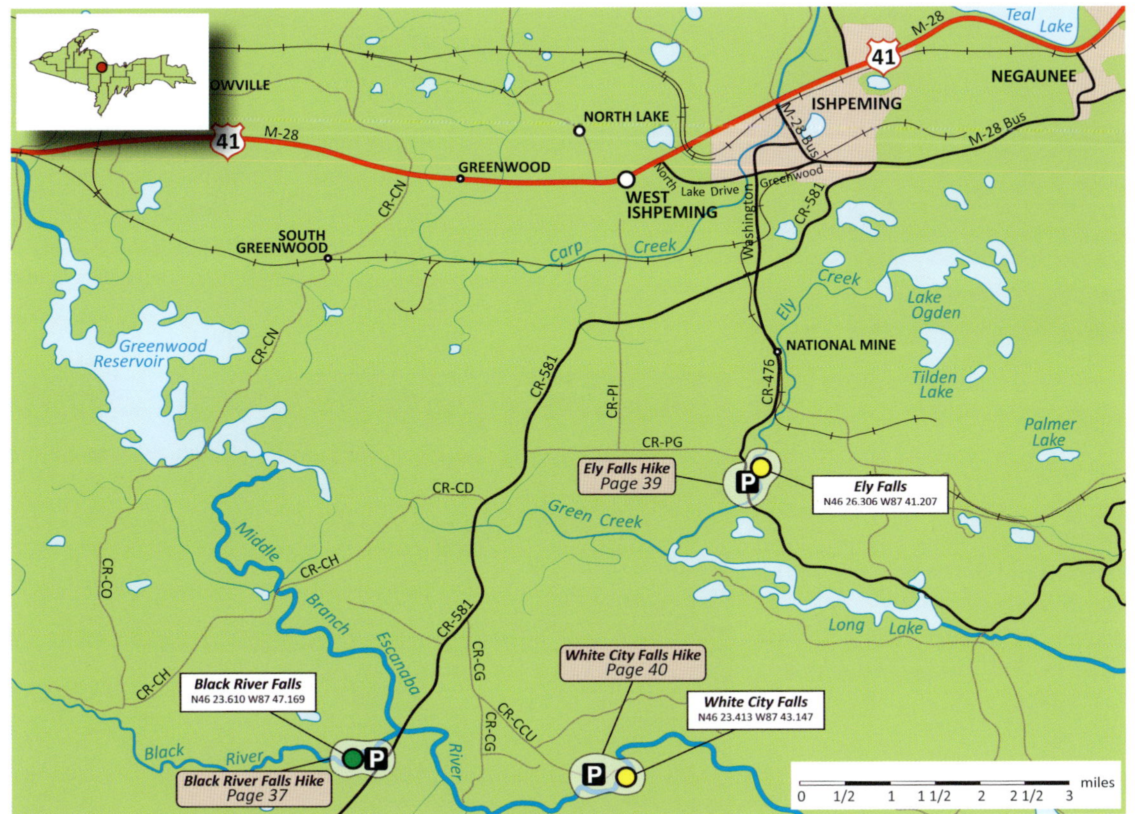

Black River Falls Hike

Black River Falls: The Black River runs through a narrow, shallow canyon; vertical walls rising on either side of the raging river. The trail from the parking area leads to the top of the cliff on the south side of the river. There is an old wooden footbridge that crosses the river to get down to the river level below the falls.

Directions: Off of US-41 in Ishpeming, turn southeast onto the western end of Business M-28 Loop which heads easterly through downtown Ishpeming. In 1 mile after turning onto the Business Loop, turn right (south) onto CR-581 (South Pine Street). In about 9.9 miles turn right (west) onto an unimproved dirt road (N46 23.264 W87 46.784). Drive .6 miles to N46 23.134 W87 47.508. Turn right (north) and drive .2 miles. Turn right (northeast) @ N46 23.321 W87 47.653 and drive for .4 miles to a circular parking area on the left (north). Park @ N46 23.536 W87 47.218. Hike 200 yards down a well-worn footpath to the falls.

BLACK RIVER FALLS (BLACK RIVER)

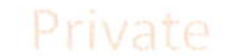

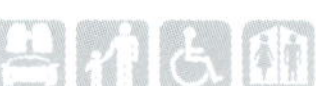

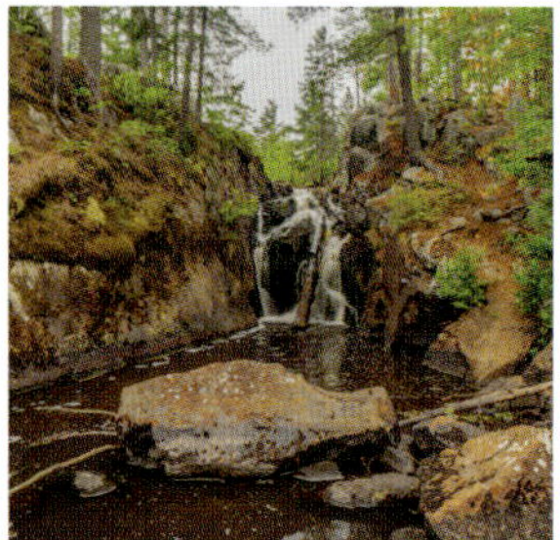

Must See:	7	GPS:	N46 23.610 W87 47.169
Height:	20 feet		
Time:	15-30 minutes	Hiking Information	
		Path:	Unimproved footpath
Driving Information		Length:	200 yards
Signs:	Small - well marked	Elev. Change:	Moderate
Road:	Unimproved dirt	GPS:	N/A
Access:	Somewhat difficult	Danger:	Slight
4WD:	Helpful	WP Boots:	Helpful

This is a popular picnic and camping area. There is evidence of campfires between the trailhead and the rocky knoll overlooking the falls. White bubbles churned up from the falls sit in vivid contrast to the black waters of the river. Wearing waterproof boots allows for some wading in the river to find new vantage points for viewing the waterfall.

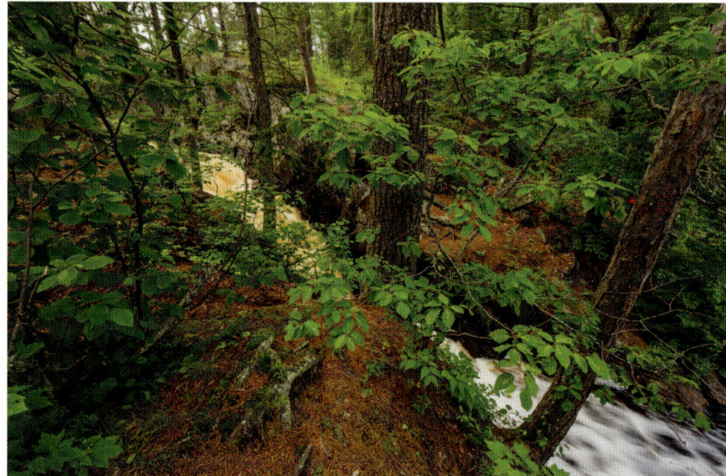
Looking through the trees at the drop from the cliff edge.

The river rapidly widens out directly below the waterfall. However, the pool is filled with boulders.

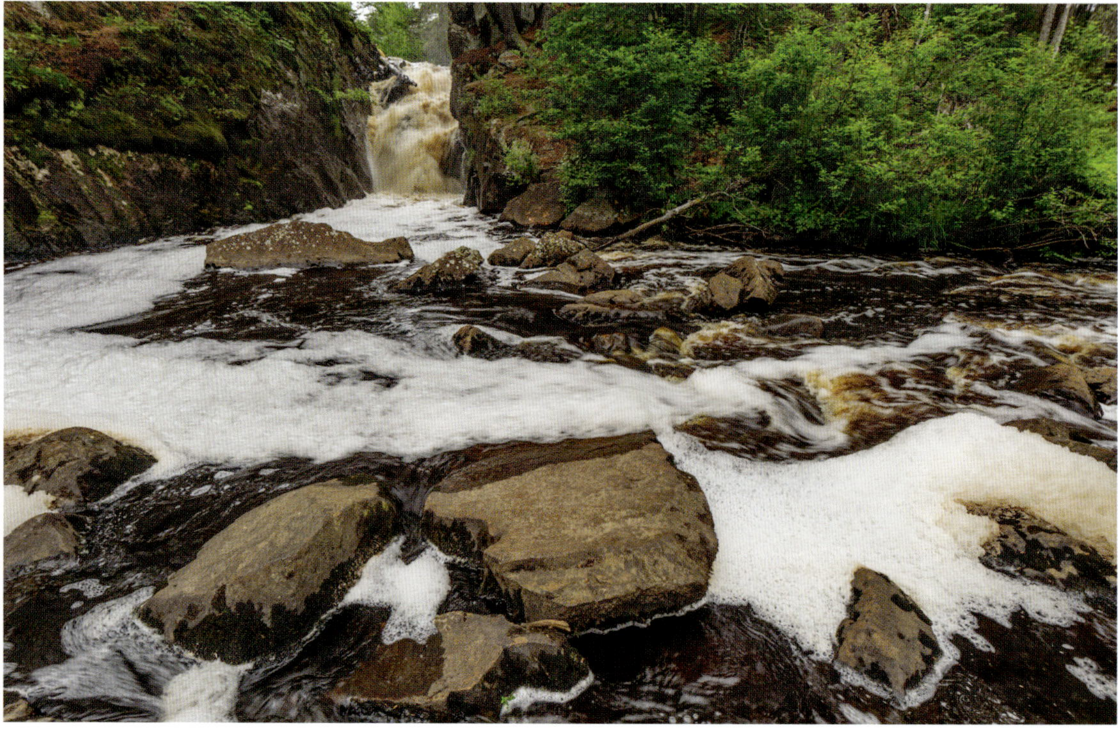

Ely Falls Hike

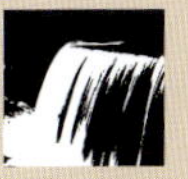

Ely Falls: An ATV trail parallels CR-476 for a short distance then cuts over to Ely Creek, cresting a rocky outcropping. The creek and falls are down below. The falls are centered in the narrow creek bed. Boulders line the sides of the bed, further diminishing the overall effect of the creek's size.

Directions: Turn west onto Washington Street off of Business M-28 in Ishpeming (in about .4 miles it will turn to the south). In about 4.4 miles, park on the side of the road. Several footpaths lead from the road up to an ATV trail that leads to the falls.

ELY FALLS (ELY CREEK)

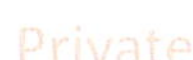

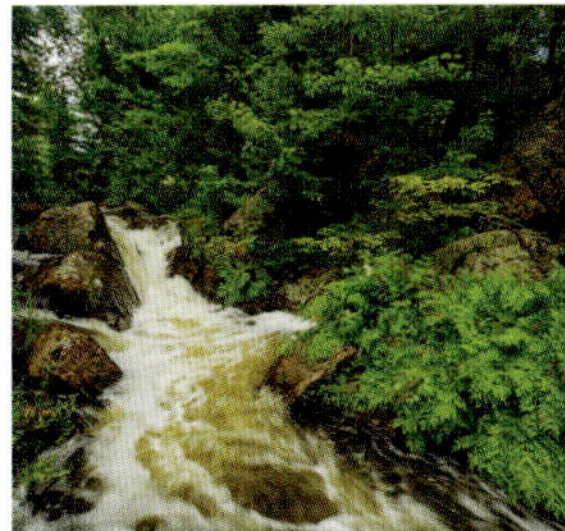

Must See:	5	GPS:	N46 26.306 W87 41.207
Height:	18 feet		
Time:	20-40 minutes	Hiking Information	
		Path:	Unimproved footpath
Driving Information		Length:	.20 miles
Signs:	None	Elev. Change:	Moderate
Road:	Secondary	GPS:	Helpful
Access:	Somewhat difficult	Danger:	Slight
4WD:	N/A	WP Boots:	Helpful

A pair of coyotes crossed the road and entered the woods ahead of me the first time I ventured to Ely Falls. I recall the concern I had taking my youngest son with me on the short hike since he was just 5 at the time. And, of course, I had bad directions and was about 1/2 mile away from the falls, trying to work my way across a swamp! Other than a cut thumb, we returned unscathed and eventually found the lovely waterfall after driving further down the road.

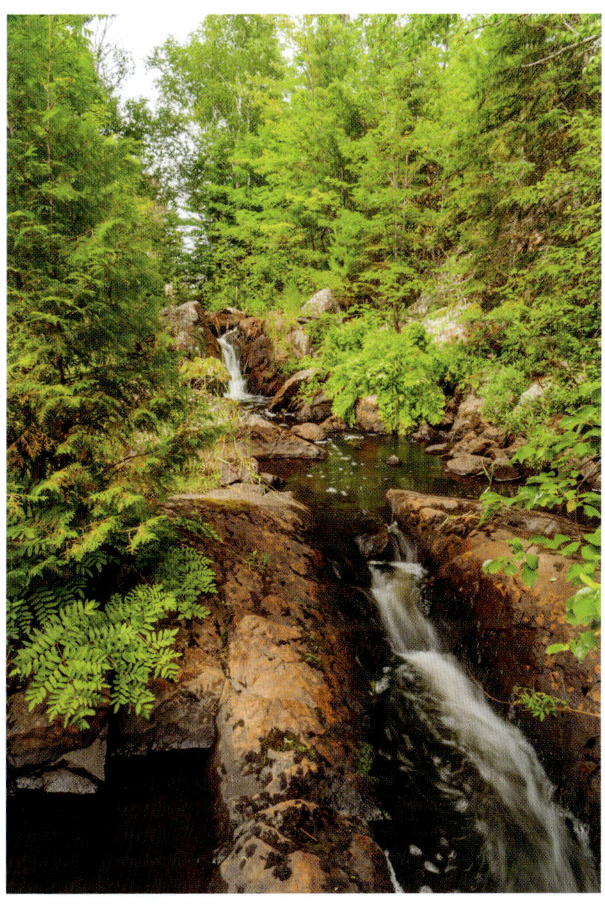

Enjoy the rocky river with this nice, small waterfall that includes 3 drops as it runs in a semi-circle around a rocky knob. It first cascades down a 10 foot chute. Then the river widens and pours through teeth-like rocks in a 4 foot drop. Twenty yards later it encircles an island and falls over a final 4 feet on either side of the island. The river slows and widens even further in a marshy spill pool featuring a collection of lily pads with a flat hewn rock backdrop.

The rocky outcropping above the waterfall

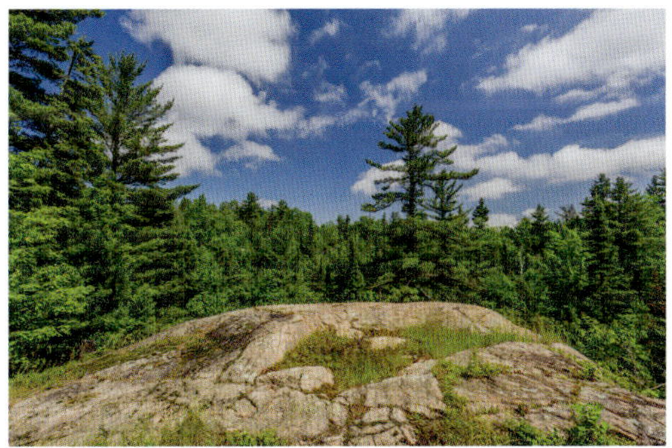

White City Falls Hike

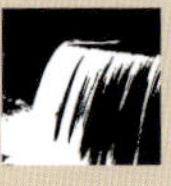

White City Falls: A flat ledge waterfall snuggles up next to a mound of mottled tan and brown granite. The sheer drop into a large pool widens out and gently flows around an island. A nice cottage commands a view of the island and waterfall. This is on private property.

Directions: These directions start the same as the Black River Falls Hike- Off of US-41 in Ishpeming, turn southeast onto the western end of Business M-28 Loop which heads easterly through downtown Ishpeming. In 1 mile after turning onto the Business Loop, turn right (south) onto CR-581 (South Pine Street). After 7.5 miles, turn left (south) onto CR-CG. In .8 miles the road veers to the left. The road immediately "V's". Take the left fork. The road is now CR-CCU. In .8 miles the road changes to CR-PPE. In 1 mile there is a gate across the road. The rest of the road is on private property, which ends at the cottage that overlooks the falls. Do not enter without prior permission.

WHITE CITY FALLS (ESCANABA RIVER - MIDDLE BRANCH) Private

Must See:	6	GPS:	N46 23.413 W87 43.147
Height:	5 feet		
Time:	15-30 minutes	Hiking Information	
		Path:	Dirt Road
Driving Information		Length:	About 1/2 mile
Signs:	None	Elev. Change:	Slight
Road:	Dirt	GPS:	N/A
Access:	Somewhat difficult	Danger:	Slight
4WD:	Helpful	WP Boots:	Helpful

The spill pool below the falls widens out and surrounds an island just down river from the falls. A small wooden bridge spans from the near bank to the island. The waterfall is directly up river from the grass covered end of the island. Remember, this is on private property. Do not enter without permission.

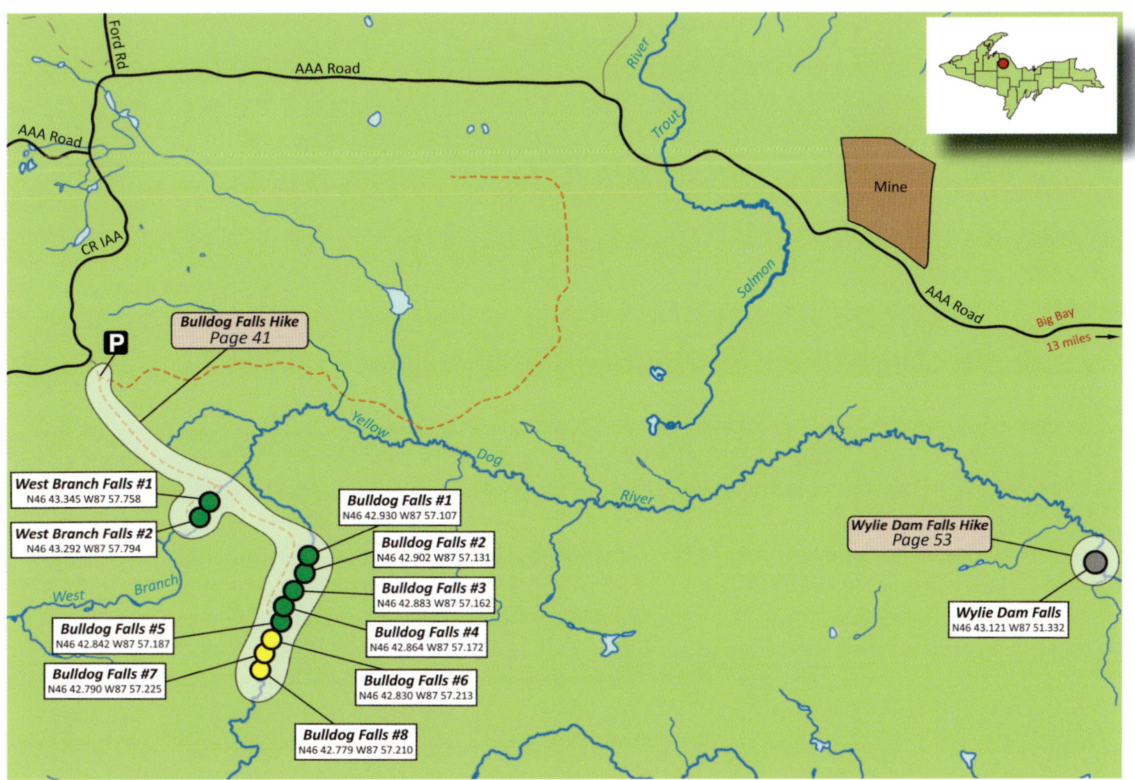

Bulldog Falls Hike

I will never forget my experience finding the Bulldog falls. It was the afternoon of October 12, 2009, and after cataloging 12 waterfalls that day, I was trying to get in one last batch of falls before heading home. Unfortunately, every attempt at locating the falls was coming up fruitless. I was driving down CR-AAA and ckecking out every 2-track that looked promising, only to find each of them ending 2 to 3 miles from the waterfalls (assuming that the GPS coordinates that I was using were correct). I continued heading west on CR-AAA with my GPS telling me that the waterfalls were getting further away and my hopes of finding them were diminishing as well. Suddenly, the road turned south and the waterfalls once again were getting closer. I found what must have been the only house within a 10 mile radius with a gentleman working outside and asked him if he knew where the Bulldog Falls were. To my surprise, he told me that I was close to the trail head!

Following the rough two-track that he had told me about, I found the trail head and quickly started down the nearly 2 mile hike to the falls. This late in the fall the sun was setting at 7:08 PM and I was just getting underway at 3:40 PM. Since I had never been to these waterfalls and didn't know what kind of terrain to expect, I hoped that I had enough time to explore the waterfalls, photograph and write down my observations, and make it back to the truck before the sun went down.

The hike was golden! The entire landscape took on a yellowish hue with beautiful autumn leaves dropping all around. In contrast with the gorgeous walk, what a disappointment it was to finally make it to the river, only to discover that the first two "drops" that I encountered were both small rapids and certainly not worth the long walk.

After the initial disappointment, I continued upstream with some trepidation. Fortunately, I was greeted with a magnificent sight! Bulldog Falls #1 appeared as a tumbling cascade of white water flowing over and around black rocks that were topped with green moss and newly fallen golden leaves. The sight was awe-inspiring! I clambered up to the top of the steep hill and found Bulldog Falls #2 hiding over the crest. It was one glorious sight after another.

If only I would have had more time to explore I would have discovered that there were many more falls up river. But the relentless hands of time were swiftly bringing an end to the day, and I had 2 miles to hike back to my truck. To complicate matters, the slight mist that had accompanied me on my walk to the falls turned into an October snowstorm. What a relief to see the truck through the trees at 6:35 PM, having beaten the elements and the clock once again!

Directions: From Big Bay, drive south on CR-550 for about 2 miles to CR-510. Turn right (CR-510 only goes to the right). After about 2.6 miles, stay to the right to merge onto CR-AAA. Drive 12.9 miles (this will take you past the mine after which CR-AAA turns into a dirt road). At this point, turn left (N46 45.507 W87 58.442) and head south. CR-AAA has merged with Ford Road (CR-IAA). In another 1/2 mile, CR-AAA turns to the right. DON'T TURN! Continue on straight for another .4 miles. The road will fork here (N46 44.827 W87 58.342). Go straight. Keep going for another 1.2 miles. There will be a 2-track to the left (N46 44.094 W87 58.559). Follow the 2-track until it ends. There is a display board with a small roof over it that gives information regarding the wilderness area that you are about to enter. There is also a locked box that is for contact information and anticipated dates for entering and exiting the forest in case of emergency situations. Hike to the West Branch at 1.1 miles. The two West Branch falls are only a short distance up river from the trail. After viewing these two falls, come back to the original trail. Ford the West Branch River. Continue another .7 miles to the Yellow Dog River. The trail becomes very faint. Follow the river upstream. An ancient bridge spans the river near the base of the 1st falls. An island stands in the middle of the river. A second bridge runs from the island to the far side of the river. The terrain gets very steep at this point. Both sides of the river rise rapidly. The 2nd falls occur in a bend in the river just above #1 falls. Continue climbing up to the top of the gorge. Follow a raised aquaduct-like bedrock channel to view the next four waterfalls. The final two waterfalls are in a flatter space with larger spill pools around which wild grasses grow profusely.

BULLDOG FALLS #1 (YELLOW DOG RIVER)

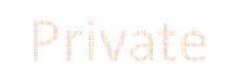

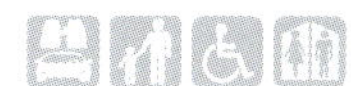

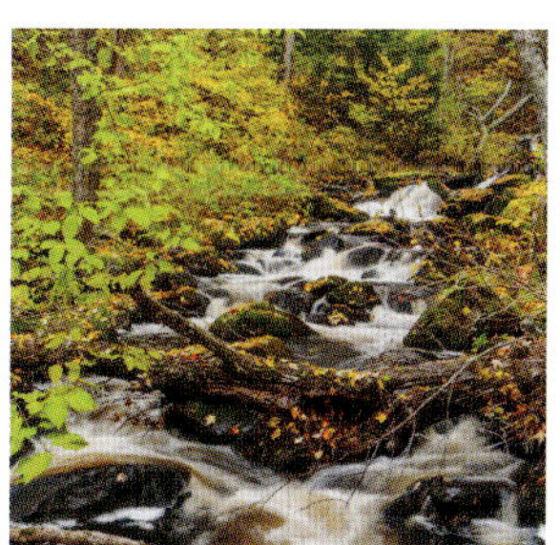

Must See:	8	GPS:	N46 42.930 W87 57.107
Height:	35 feet		
Time:	2.5-3.5 hours	Hiking Information	
		Path:	Footpath then none
Driving Information		Length:	1.8 miles
Signs:	None	Elev. Change:	Elevated
Road:	2-track	GPS:	Required
Access:	Very difficult	Danger:	Elevated
4WD:	Helpful	WP Boots:	Required

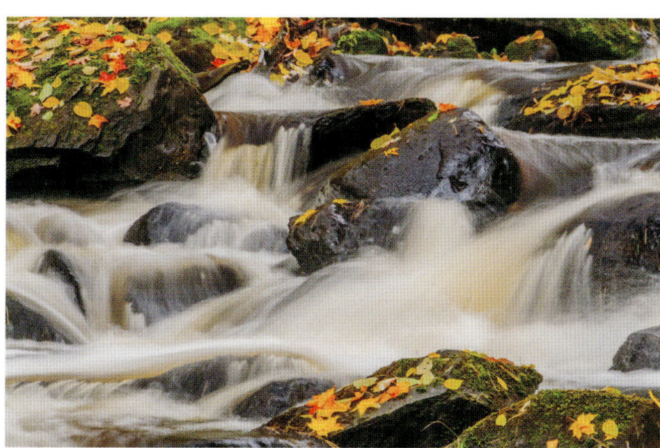

A multitude of moss covered rocks fill the riverbed. Be careful as you climb around on the hill that is the foundation for this waterfall. The steep and sometimes slippery sides can be dangerous.

There is about a 35 foot total drop as the river cascades over green, mossy rocks. When those mossy rocks are covered in red and yellow leaves, so much the better! The river comes tumbling down amongst 2 to 4 foot diameter rounded boulders. The base of the waterfall ends by splitting around an elongated island. There are very old bridges dating back to the original McCormick owners. These bridges span both sides of the river onto the island. Passing over these bridges is the easiest way to cross the river at this point. The far side of the bridge is at N46 42.969 W87 57.088.

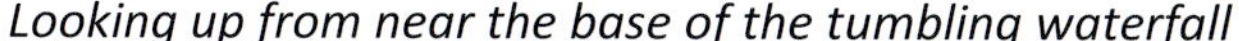

Looking up from near the base of the tumbling waterfall

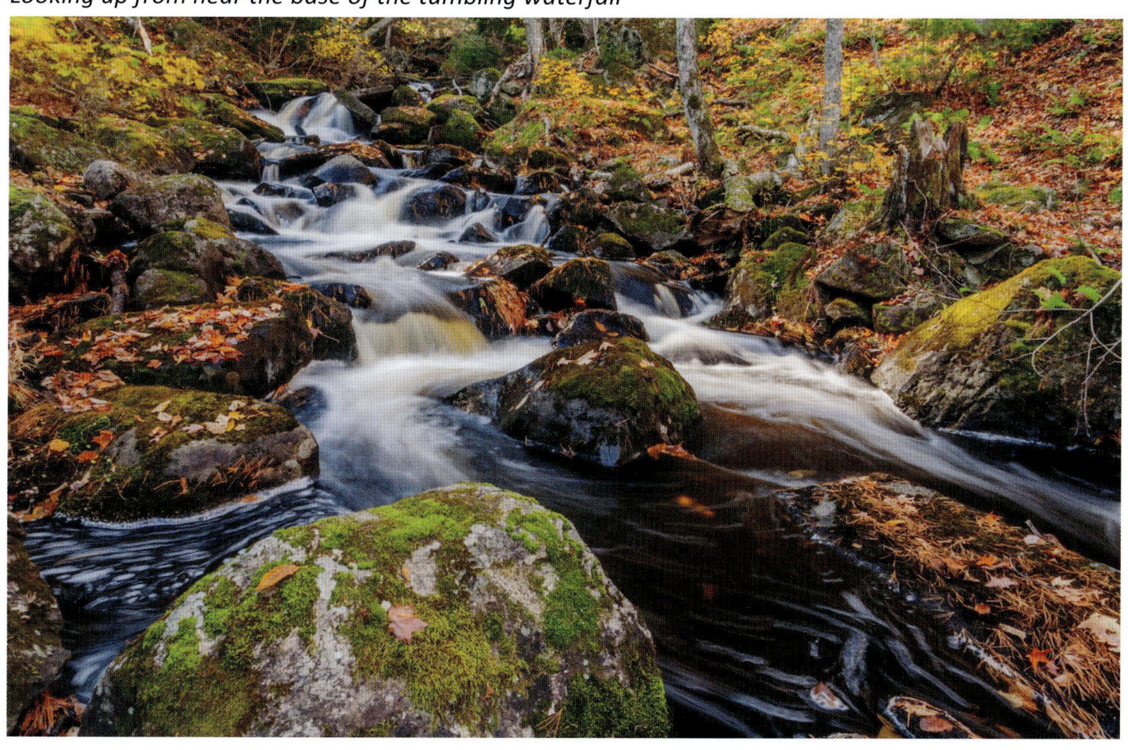

BULLDOG FALLS #2 (YELLOW DOG RIVER)

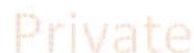
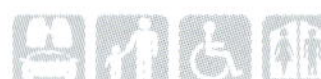

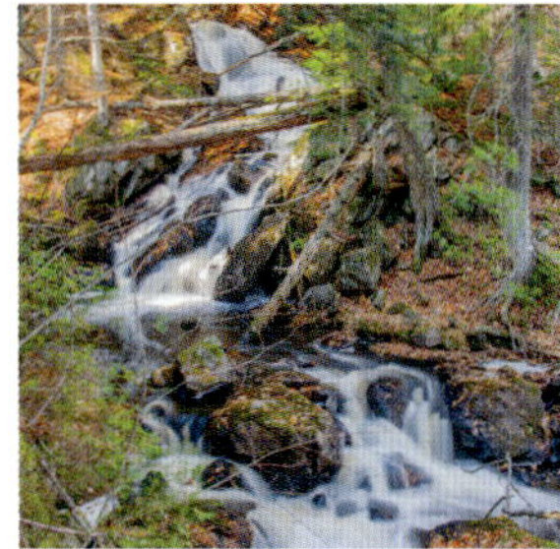

Must See:	8	GPS:	N46 42.902 W87 57.131
Height:	20 feet		
Time:	2.5-3.5 hours	Hiking Information	
		Path:	Footpath then none
Driving Information		Length:	1.8 miles
Signs:	None	Elev. Change:	Elevated
Road:	2-track	GPS:	Required
Access:	Very difficult	Danger:	Elevated
4WD:	Helpful	WP Boots:	Required

Climb to the top of the hill that Bulldog Falls #1 tumbles down and you will be greeted by this wonderful waterfall. Unfortunately, Bulldog Falls #2 is not easily viewed. You will find yourself perched on the edge of a cliff as you gaze over and down into this beauty. Cross the river down below Falls #1 and climb up the far side of the ravine. Follow the steep incline up around the bend in the river to where the #2 falls start. It's possible to view the waterfall more closely from here.

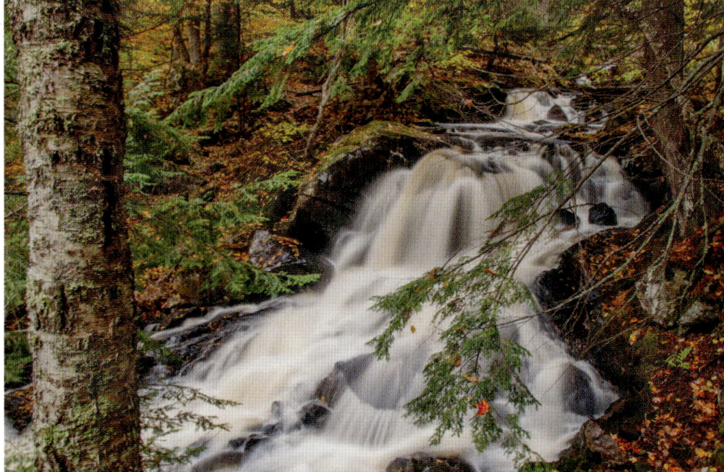

Peering down into gorge from the east side

Up near the top of the waterfall on the western side with lovely wildflowers in bloom

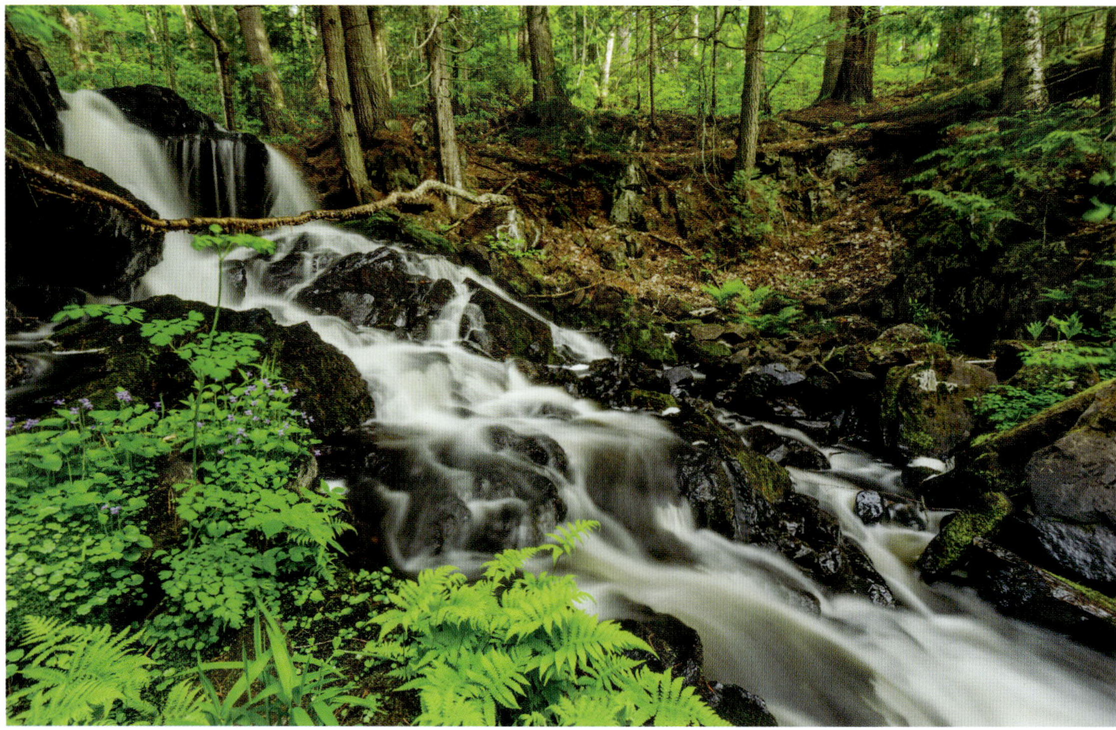

BULLDOG FALLS #3 (YELLOW DOG RIVER)

Private 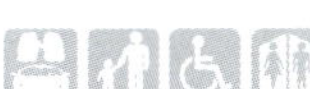 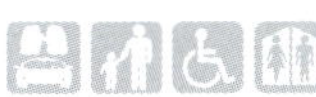

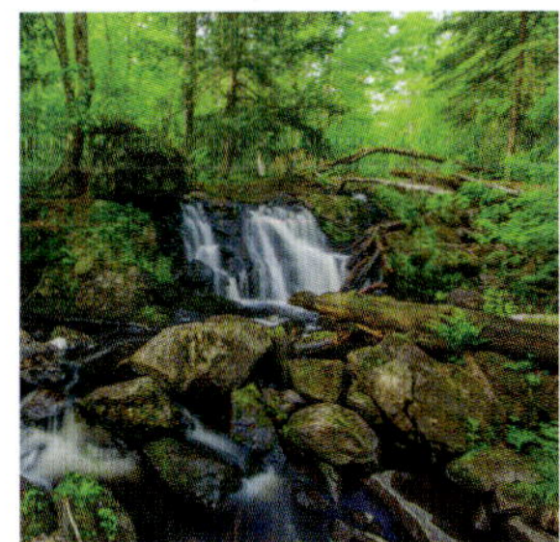

Must See:	7
Height:	12 feet
Time:	2.75-4.0 hours

Driving Information

Signs:	None
Road:	2-track
Access:	Very difficult
4WD:	Helpful

GPS: N46 42.883 W87 57.162

Hiking Information

Path:	Footpath then none
Length:	1.9 miles
Elev. Change:	Elevated
GPS:	Required
Danger:	Elevated
WP Boots:	Required

The wide angular drop is best viewed from the west side of the river. A large fern covered boulder sits above the left side of the falls.

Bulldog Falls #3 is a fast cascade with a mostly vertical drop of 5 feet before the river turns to the left and cascades eight more times over flat rock shelves. The river then flattens out.

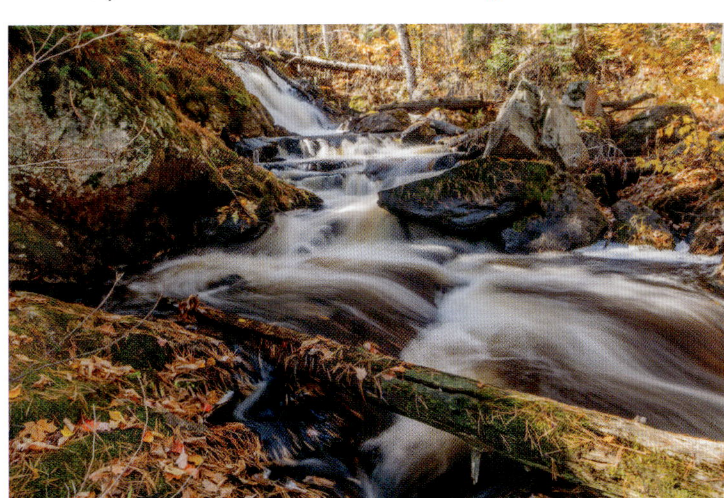

What a strange rock perched up above the waterfall!

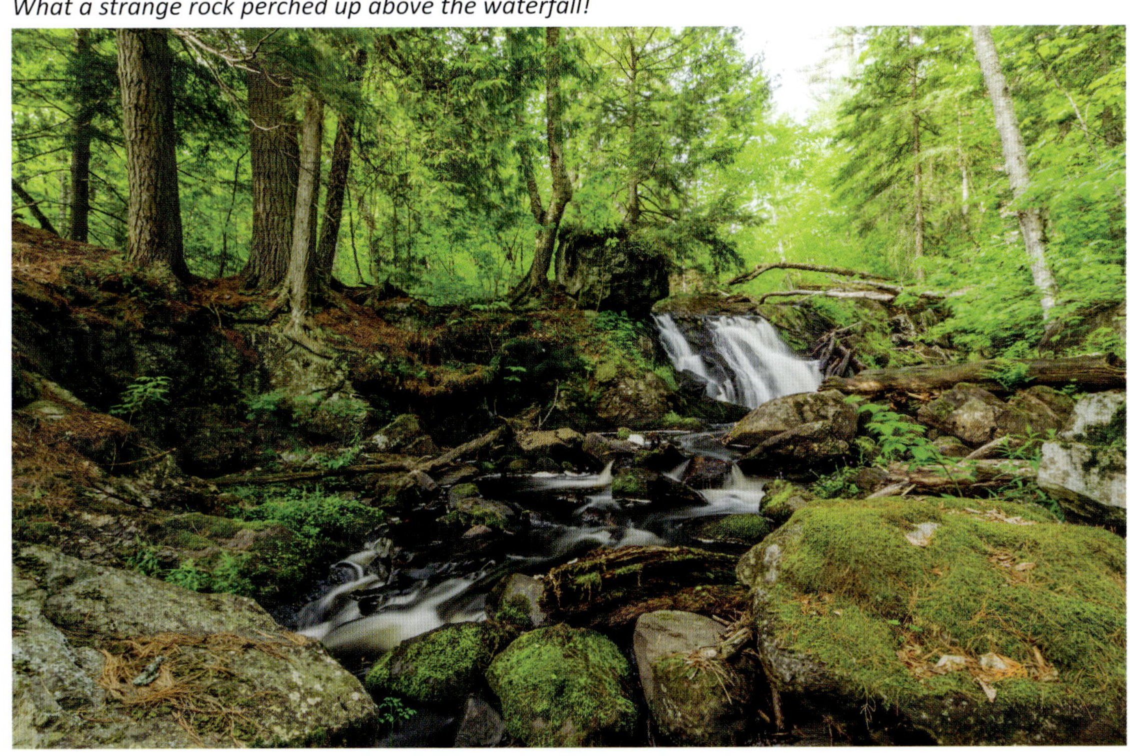

BULLDOG FALLS #4 (YELLOW DOG RIVER)

Private

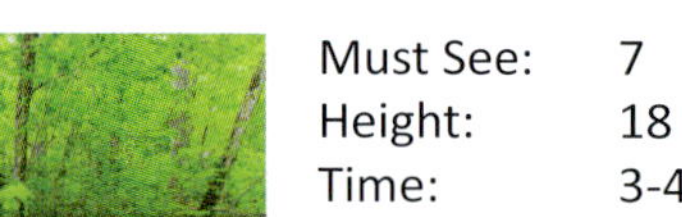

Must See: 7
Height: 18 feet
Time: 3-4 hours

Driving Information
Signs: None
Road: 2-track
Access: Very difficult
4WD: Helpful

GPS: N46 42.864 W87 57.172

Hiking Information
Path: Footpath then none
Length: 1.9 miles
Elev. Change: Elevated
GPS: Required
Danger: Elevated
WP Boots: Required

Just up above #3 the Yellow Dog River slides down rapidly along an angled rock that tips the river back toward tilted bedrock that creates a trough.

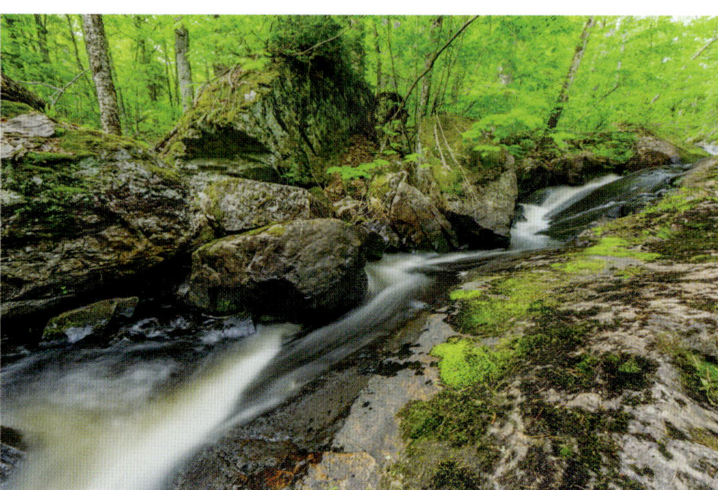

This is a LONG slide with exposed rock all around. Angled bedrock forces the river through an elevated channel of rock. It seemingly defies gravity as the river is actually above the surrounding valleys.

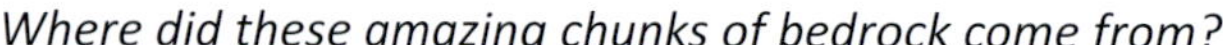

Where did these amazing chunks of bedrock come from?

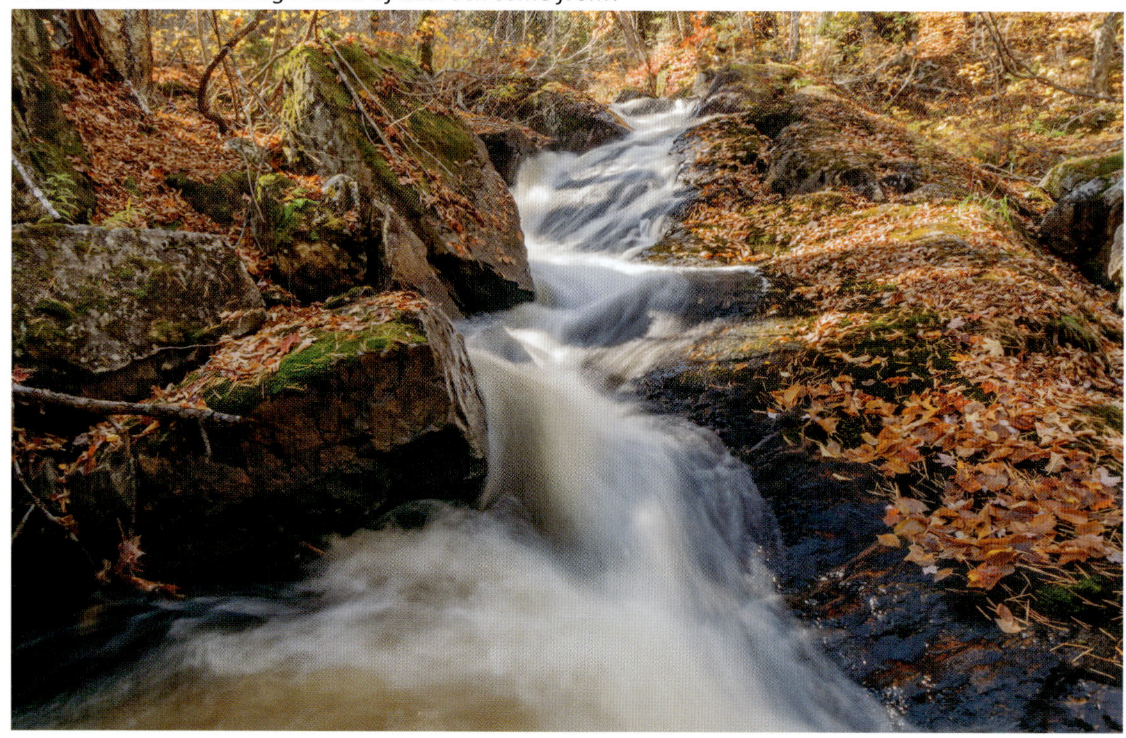

BULLDOG FALLS #5 (YELLOW DOG RIVER)

Private 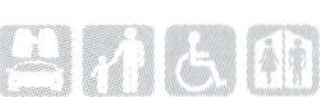

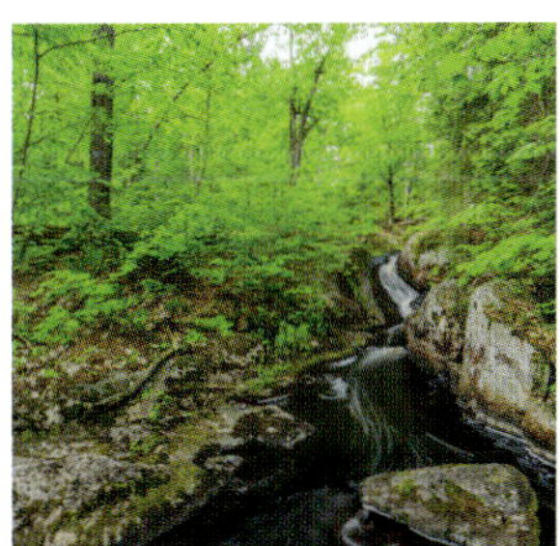

Must See: 7
Height: 10 feet
Time: 3-4 hours

Driving Information
Signs: None
Road: 2-track
Access: Very difficult
4WD: Helpful

GPS: N46 42.842 W87 57.187

Hiking Information
Path: Footpath then none
Length: 2.0 miles
Elev. Change: Elevated
GPS: Required
Danger: Elevated
WP Boots: Required

Rusty brown, gray and black boulders sit next to a severely angled smooth layer of bedrock. The river flows through a backward "C" shaped trough that results from their intersection. More of the boulders are set along the side of the river as it continues through a deep spill pool.

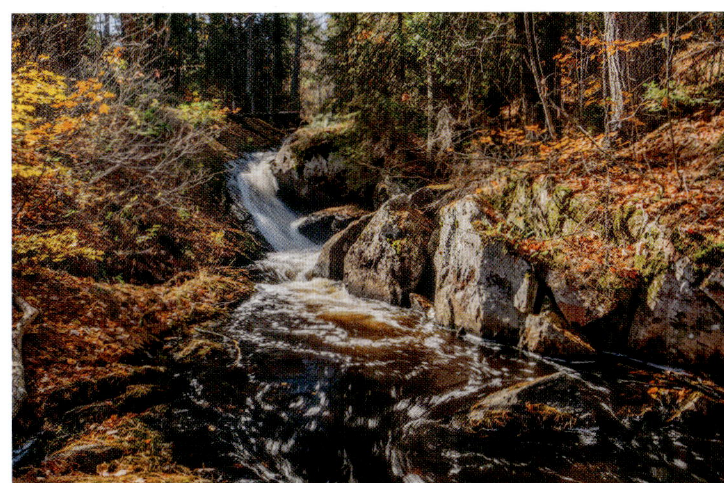

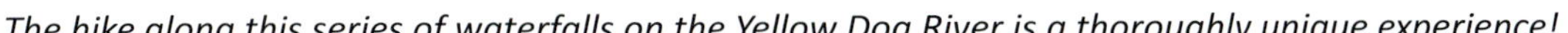

The hike along this series of waterfalls on the Yellow Dog River is a thoroughly unique experience!

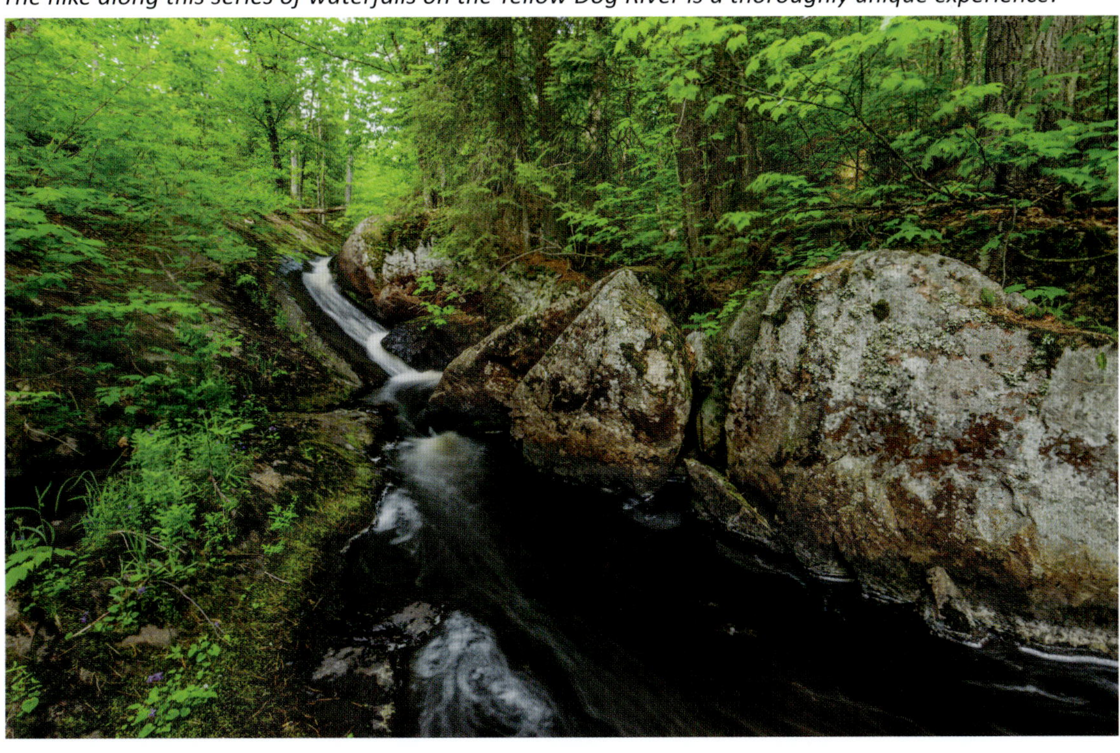

BULLDOG FALLS #6 (YELLOW DOG RIVER)

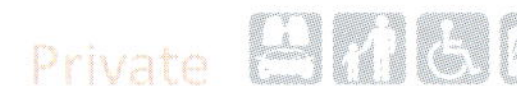

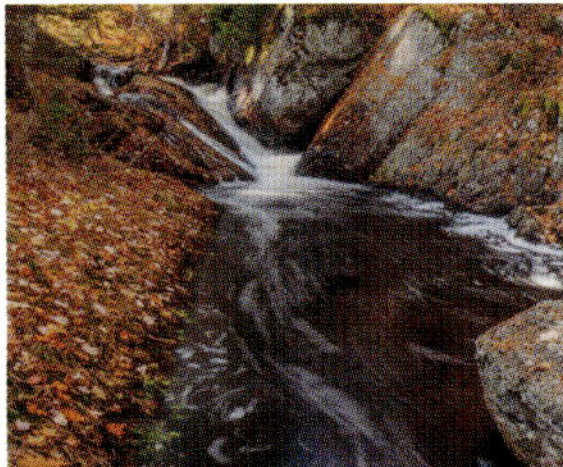

Must See:	6
Height:	8 feet
Time:	3.25-4.25 hours

Driving Information	
Signs:	None
Road:	2-track
Access:	Very difficult
4WD:	Helpful

GPS:	N46 42.830 W87 57.213

Hiking Information	
Path:	Footpath then none
Length:	2.0 miles
Elev. Change:	Elevated
GPS:	Required
Danger:	Elevated
WP Boots:	Required

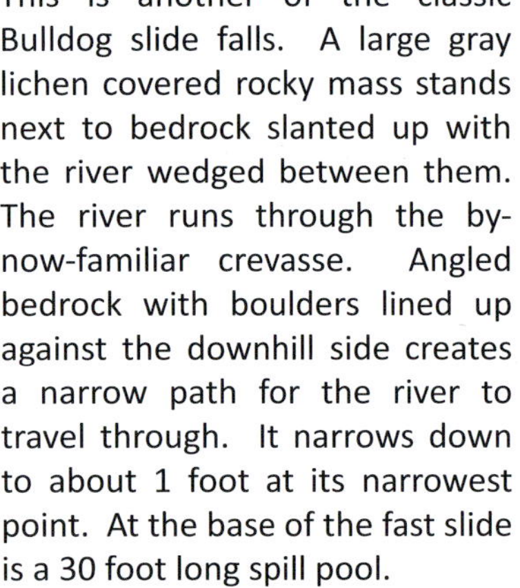

This is another of the classic Bulldog slide falls. A large gray lichen covered rocky mass stands next to bedrock slanted up with the river wedged between them. The river runs through the by-now-familiar crevasse. Angled bedrock with boulders lined up against the downhill side creates a narrow path for the river to travel through. It narrows down to about 1 foot at its narrowest point. At the base of the fast slide is a 30 foot long spill pool.

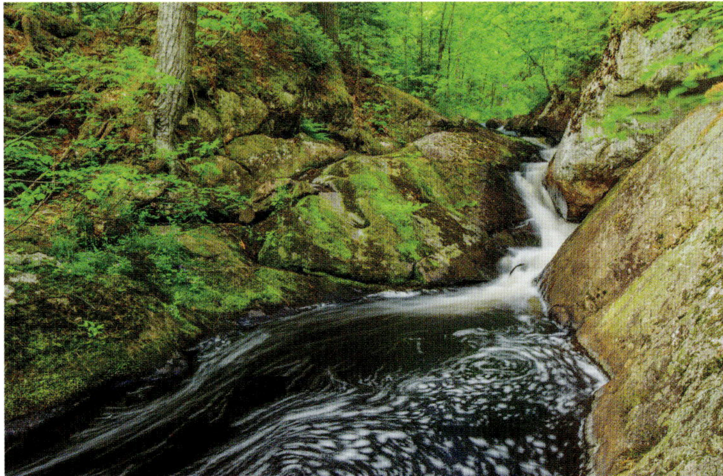

I love the peanut shaped boulder that lies planted in the center of the narrow river.

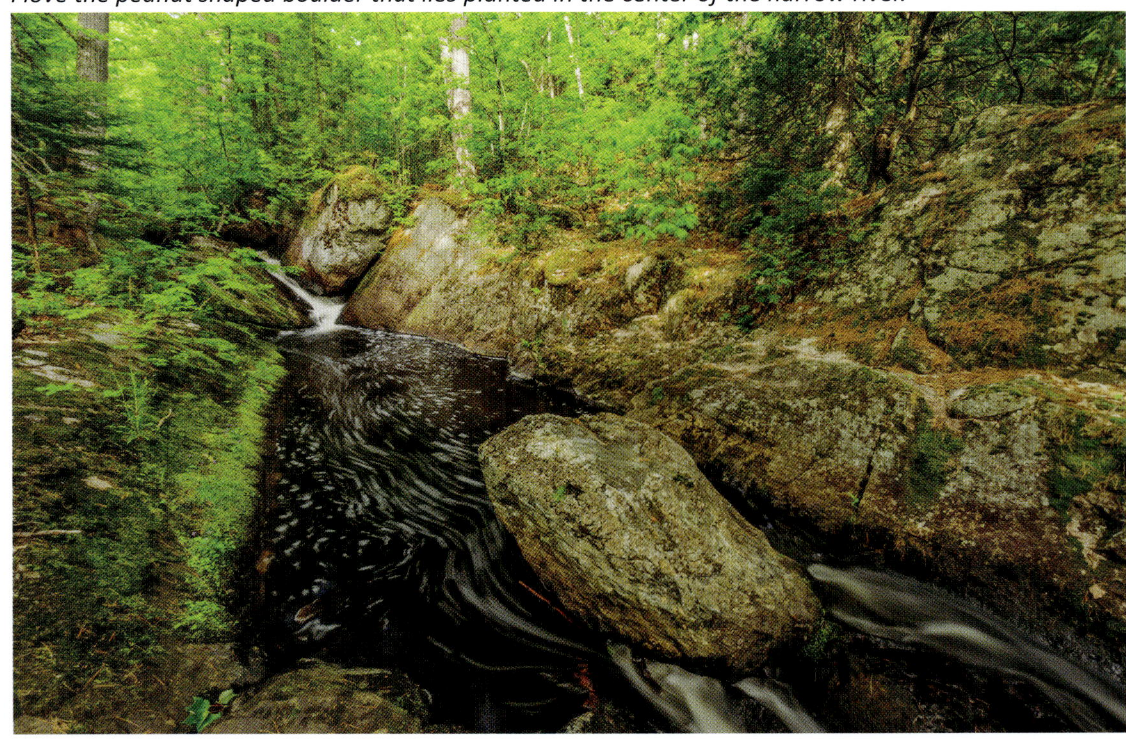

BULLDOG FALLS #7 (YELLOW DOG RIVER)

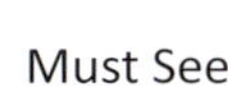

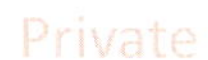

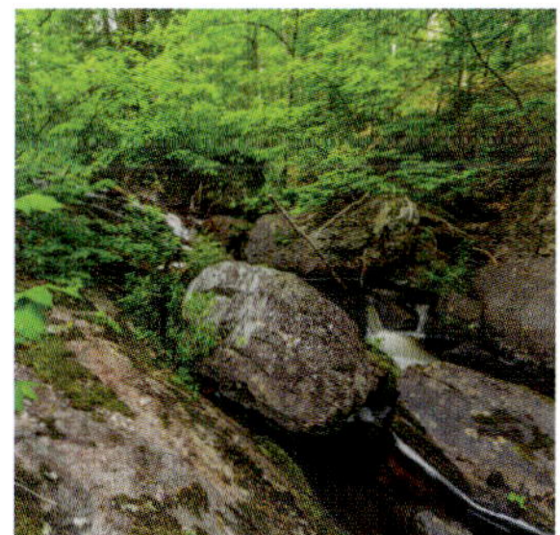

Must See:	4	GPS:	N46 42.790 W87 57.225
Height:	9 feet		
Time:	3.25-4.25 hours	**Hiking Information**	
		Path:	Footpath then none
Driving Information		Length:	2.1 miles
Signs:	None	Elev. Change:	Elevated
Road:	2-track	GPS:	Required
Access:	Very difficult	Danger:	Elevated
4WD:	Helpful	WP Boots:	Required

Water flows over uneven surface, narrowing from 15 feet wide at the top to just 4 feet across as it approaches the base of the slide. Boulders below the slide narrow the river further, until it's down to 1 foot wide like a long funnel. More nice rocks below the falls support large ferns, other grasses and even a small cedar tree.

During the summer, undergrowth starts to dominate the area, making it difficult to appreciate the waterfall.

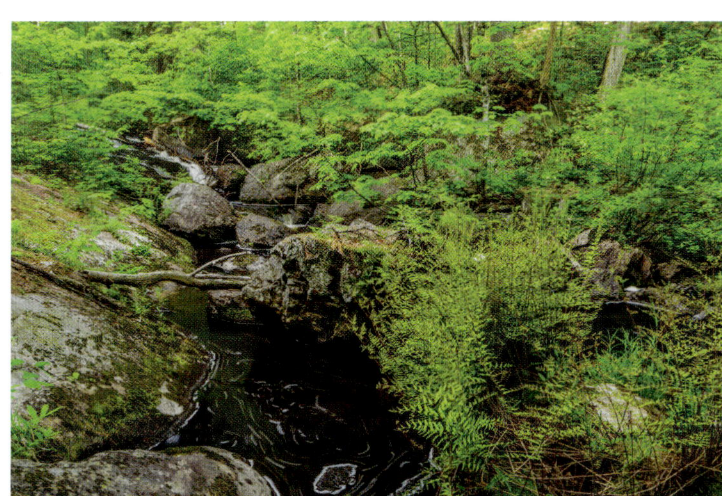

This is getting close to the plateau, where the terrain flattens out a bit.

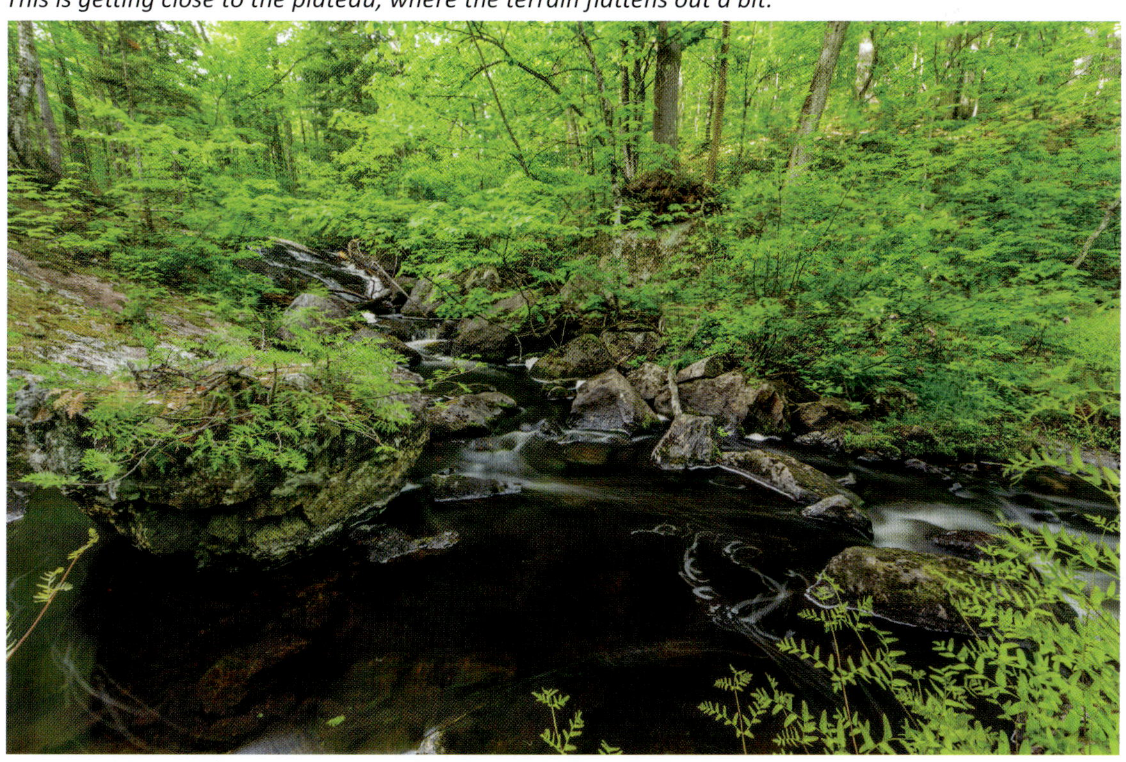

BULLDOG FALLS #8 (YELLOW DOG RIVER)

Private

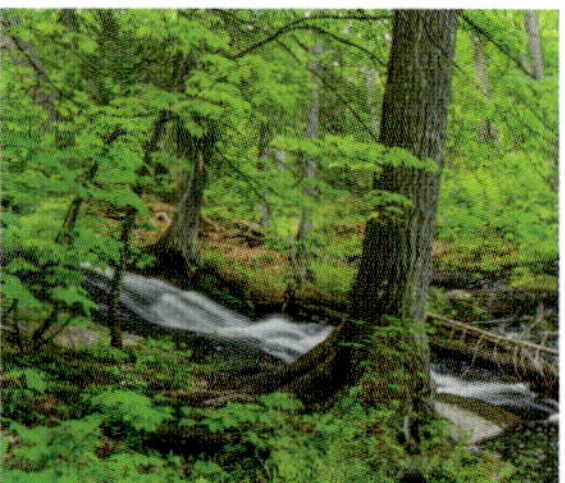

Must See:	6	GPS:	N46 42.779 W87 57.210
Height:	8 feet		
Time:	3.25-4.25 hours	Hiking Information	
		Path:	Footpath then none
Driving Information		Length:	2.1 miles
Signs:	None	Elev. Change:	Elevated
Road:	2-track	GPS:	Required
Access:	Very difficult	Danger:	Elevated
4WD:	Helpful	WP Boots:	Required

The Yellow Dog River divides around a pine covered island, sliding over black basalt to a deep dark pool to form the furthest of the falls on this river. In drier times the right fork of the river may dry up.

This is the top of the Bulldog waterfall series. The terrain is now quite leveled out and the river runs slowly up above this drop.

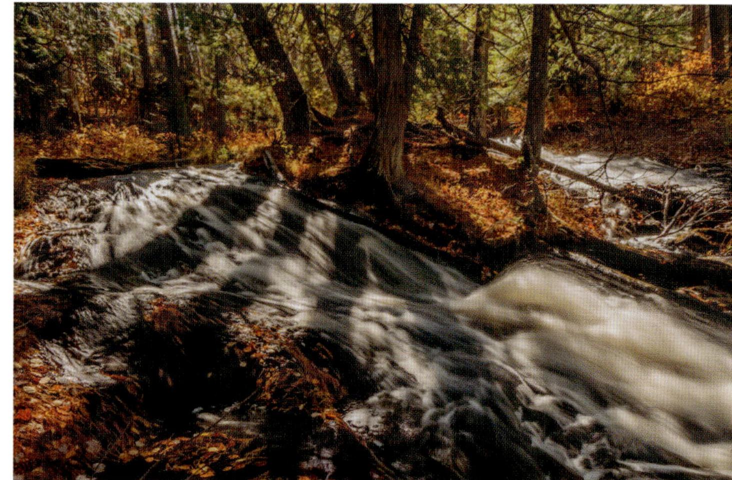

The large calm spill pool below the waterfall slide is good sized and ringed by large delicate fern.

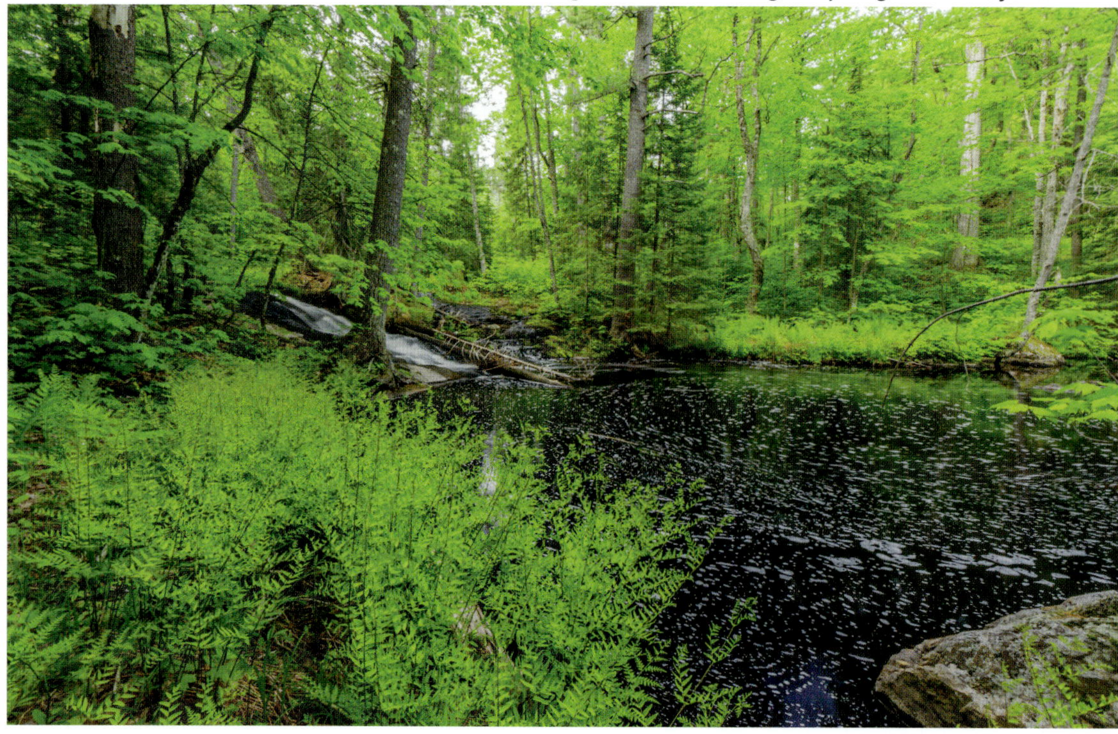

WEST BRANCH FALLS #1 (YELLOW DOG RIVER - WEST BRANCH) Private

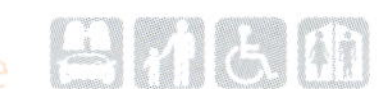

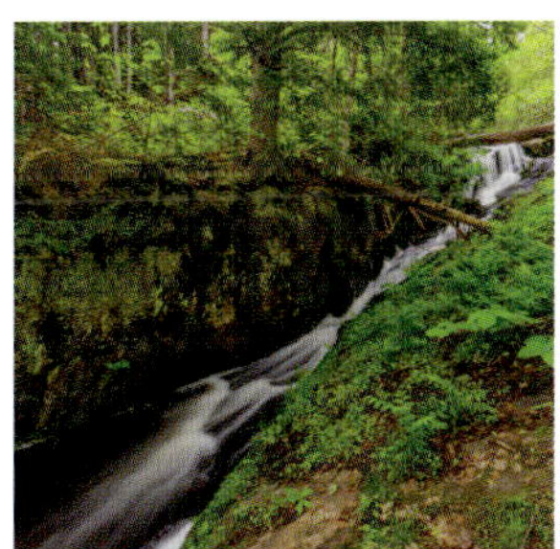

Must See:	8	GPS:	N46 43.345 W87 57.758
Height:	30 feet		
Time:	1.5-2.25 hours	Hiking Information	
		Path:	Footpath
Driving Information		Length:	1.0 miles
Signs:	None	Elev. Change:	Moderate
Road:	2-track	GPS:	Required
Access:	Very difficult	Danger:	Elevated
4WD:	Helpful	WP Boots:	Required

The main falls tucked along a high rock wall are shaped in a half moon configuration. The waterfall starts at the top, cascading down and running over bedrock. Halfway down the arc it drops in terraces about 6 feet into a channel that funnels down along a face of bedrock that is about 10 feet high. The wall is pinkish-brown with lichen and moss growing on the side of it. It narrows down into a slot that at one point is about only 1 foot wide.

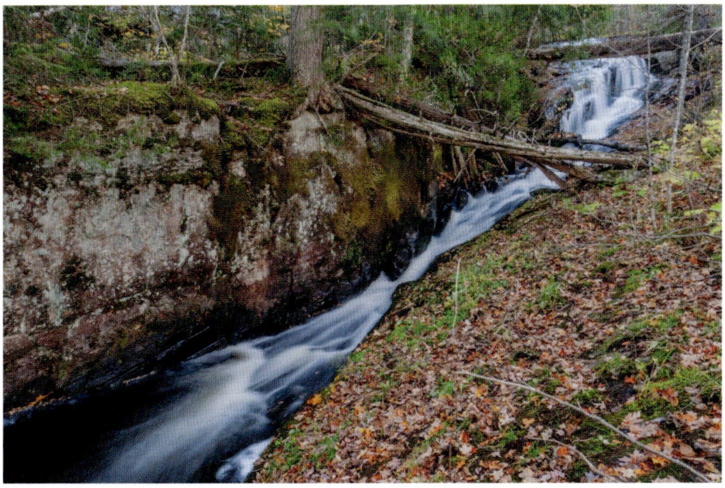

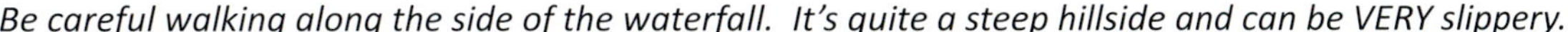

Be careful walking along the side of the waterfall. It's quite a steep hillside and can be VERY slippery.

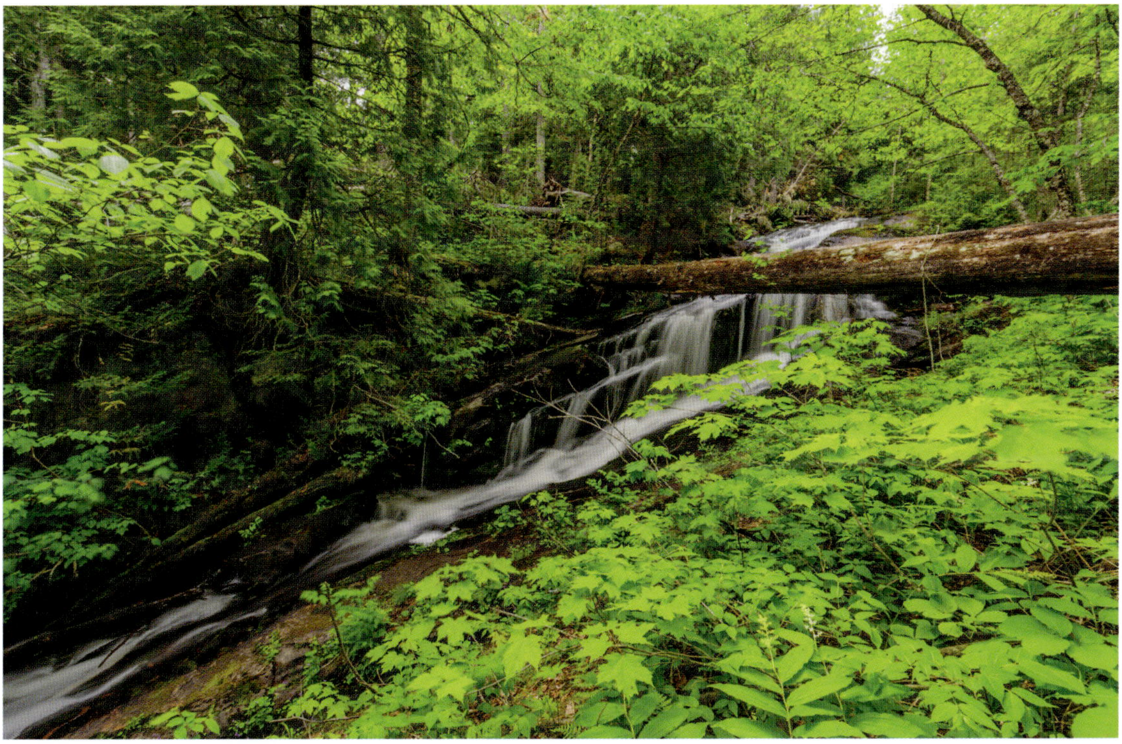

WEST BRANCH FALLS #2 (YELLOW DOG RIVER - WEST BRANCH) Private

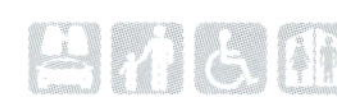

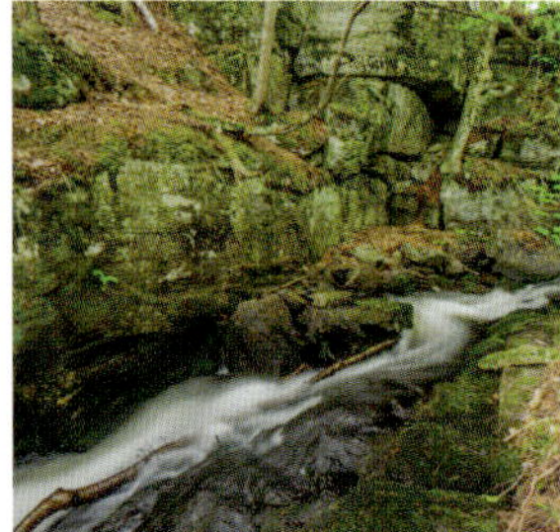

Must See:	7	GPS:	N46 43.292 W87 57.794
Height:	20 feet		
Time:	1.5-2.25 hours	**Hiking Information**	
		Path:	Footpath then none
Driving Information		Length:	1.0 miles
Signs:	None	Elev. Change:	Moderate
Road:	2-track	GPS:	Required
Access:	Very difficult	Danger:	Moderate
4WD:	Helpful	WP Boots:	Required

This is a winding "S" curving waterfall. Large squared off blocks of basalt rise 30 feet from the opposite side of the river. The riverbed angles toward the rock wall, keeping the river wedged in a narrow channel 2 to 4 feet wide. It tumbles and slides over a 70 yard stretch of river. Pines overlook both side of the river. There is no free drop on these falls - rather they slide and cascade in a fast elevation change. The waterfall area is surrounded with cedar trees that stand like sentinels amongst the rocks on the far side of the river.

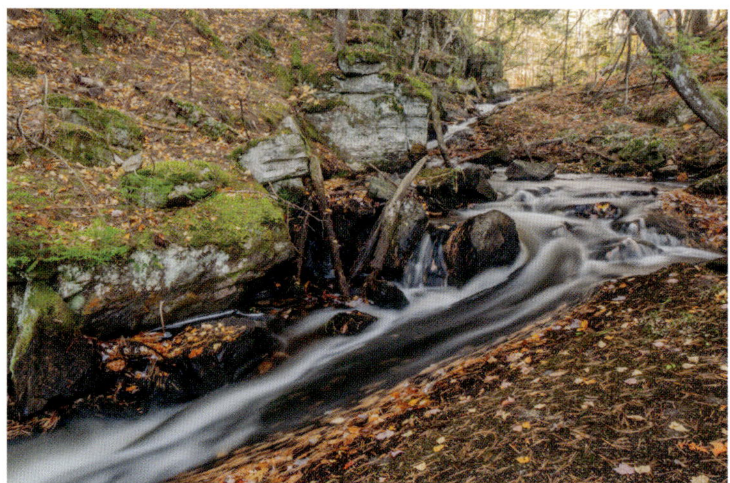

Look for beautiful greenery in spring and early summer

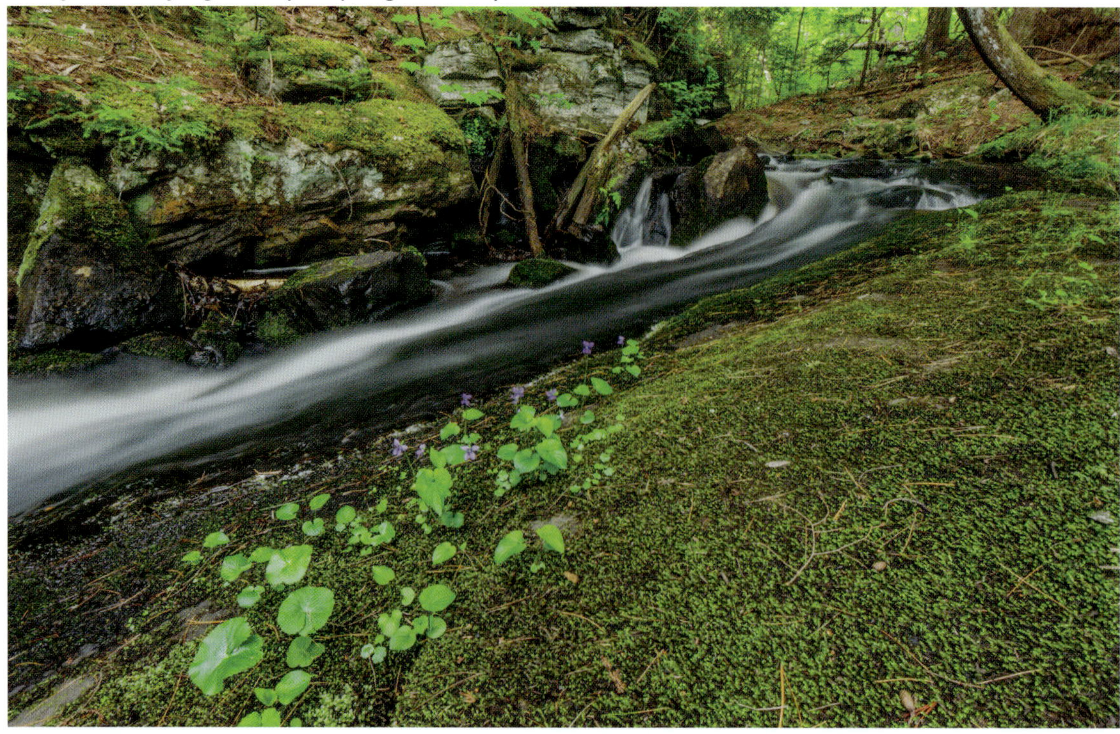

Wylie Dam Falls Hike

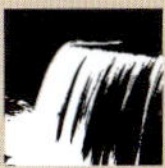

Wylie Dam Falls is on private property and off limits to viewing. Stay off posted private property without permission.

Directions: Wylie Dam Falls is found on the Yellow Dog River about halfway between the Bulldog Falls and Pinnacle Falls. The dirt road to it off of CR-AAA Road is gated, with several hunting cabins located near the river.

WYLIE DAM FALLS (YELLOW DOG RIVER)

Private

Must See:	N/A
Height:	?
Time:	?

Driving Information

Signs:	None
Road:	Dirt
Access:	Difficult
4WD:	Helpful

GPS: N46 43.121 W87 51.332

Hiking Information

Path:	?
Length:	?
Elev. Change:	Elevated
GPS:	Helpful
Danger:	?
WP Boots:	?

The waterfall is probably the remains of rocky bedrock where a dam once aided lumbering activity in the Yellow Dog Plains. It looks to be an oversized set of rapids on the historic river.

This is on private land and there is no public access to the waterfall.

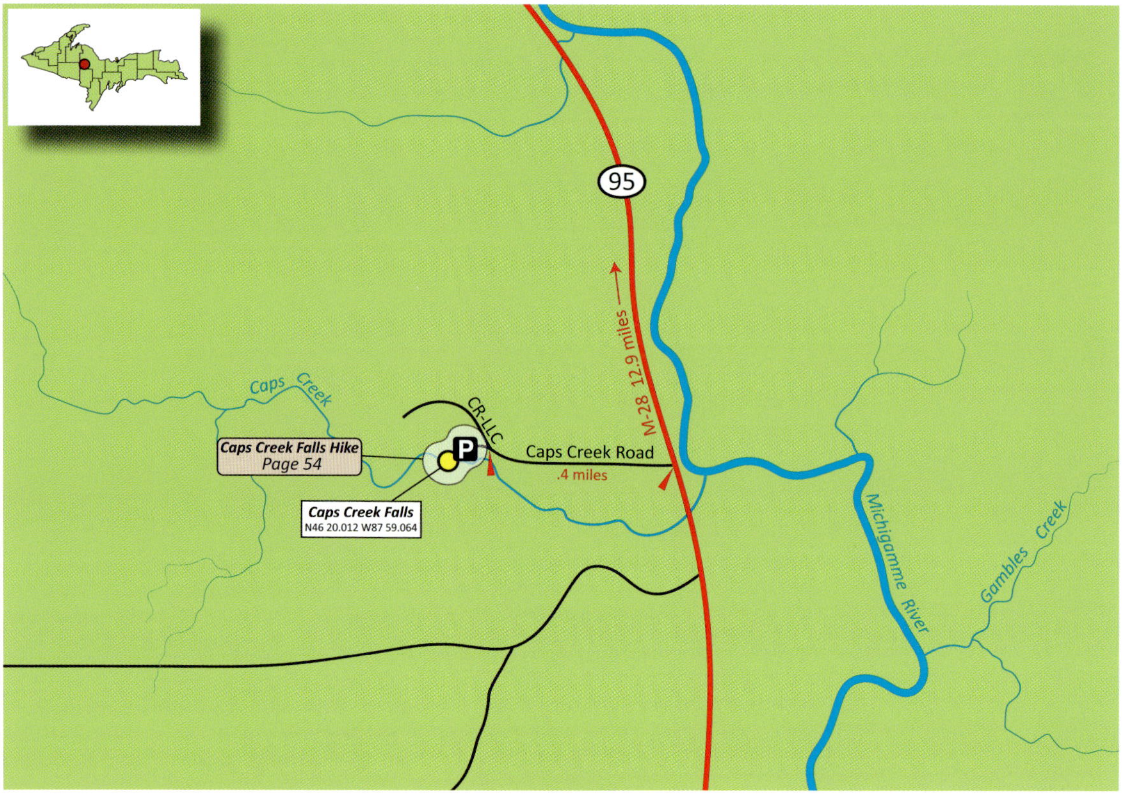

95
M-28 12.9 miles
Caps Creek
CR-LLC
Caps Creek Road
.4 miles
Caps Creek Falls Hike
Page 54
Caps Creek Falls
N46 20.012 W87 59.064
Michigamme River
Gambles Creek

Caps Creek Falls Hike

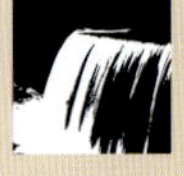

Caps Creek Falls is one of the few waterfalls found in the southern portion of Marquette County. It is on private property, situated right behind a residence. Do not attempt to view without permission.

Directions: Drive 12.9 miles south on M-95 from M-28. Turn right (west) onto Caps Creek Road (.4 miles south of the Leif Erickson Memorial Roadside Park). Follow the road for .4 miles. Then stay on the blacktop driveway to the left for .1 miles to a house. The waterfall is behind the house.

CAPS CREEK FALLS (CAPS CREEK)

Private 

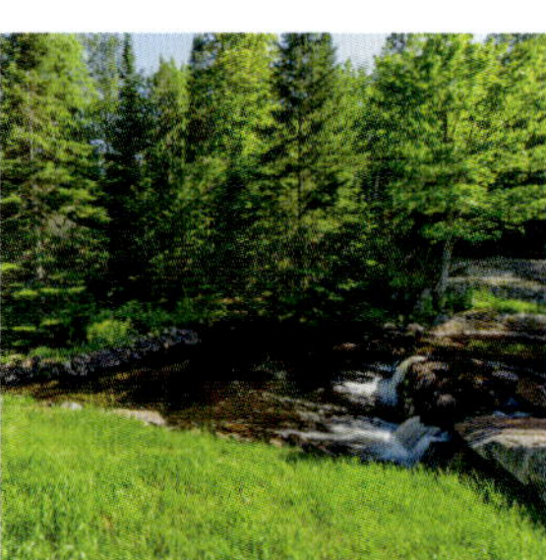

Must See:	4	GPS:	N46 20.012 W87 59.064
Height:	3 feet		
Time:	5-10 minutes	Hiking Information	
		Path:	N/A
Driving Information		Length:	100 yards
Signs:	None	Elev. Change:	Slight
Road:	Side road	GPS:	N/A
Access:	Somewhat easy	Danger:	Slight
4WD:	N/A	WP Boots:	N/A

A quaint house with a nicely manicured lawn overlooks the Caps Creek Falls. Igneous bedrock rises from the earth on either side of the falls, providing solid, bare viewing platforms. A deep spill pool butts up to the rock lined walls. A wooden foot bridge spans the creek just above the waterfall. This is on private property. Get permission before viewing.

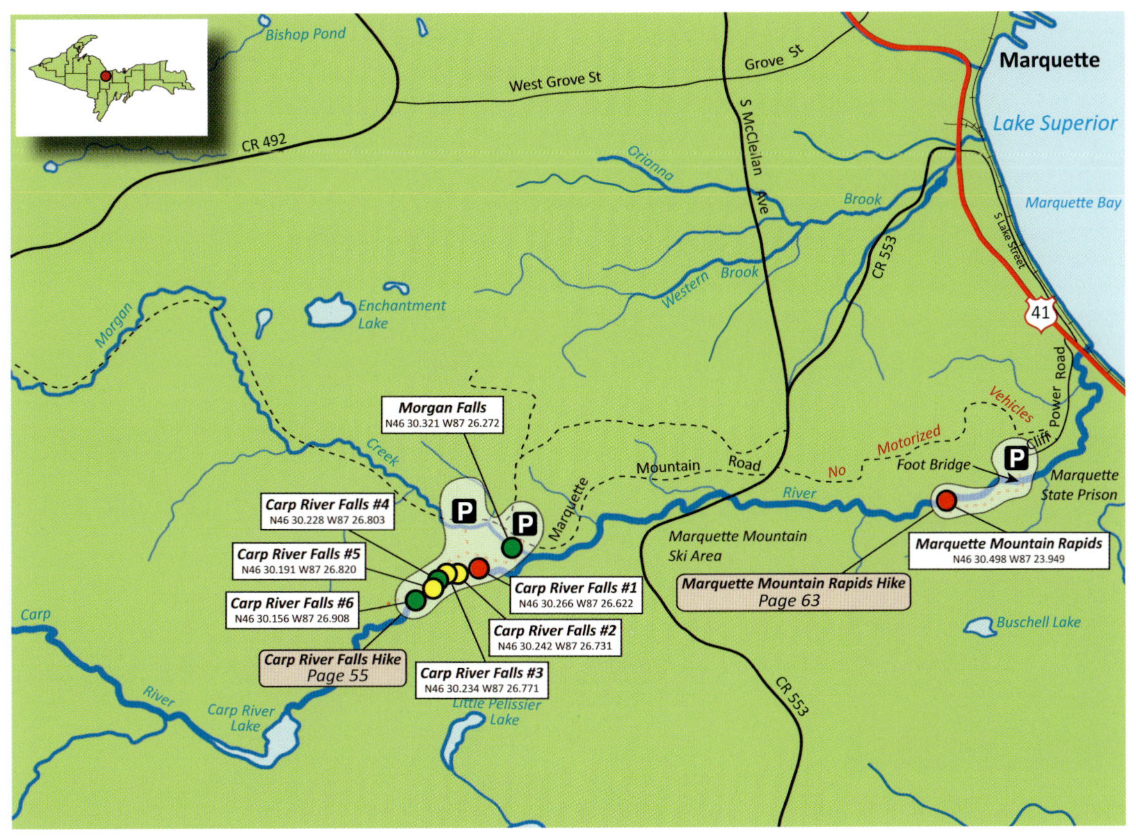

Carp River Falls Hike

The Carp River Falls Area is an interesting study in contrasts. Marquette is a thriving college city with bustling streets and large box stores. And yet just a couple of miles south from the heart of the city is the Carp River, sporting beautiful waterfalls and rugged terrain. Morgan Falls, one of my favorites, is easily accessed and very photogenic (in fact, I met a photographer and model setting up for a shoot on one of my many trips to Morgan Falls). For those desiring longer and more daring hikes, following the Carp River upstream provides added adventure.

Directions: The key feature to look for is Marquette Mountain, a ski area that has been in operation since 1957. It is located on M-553 about 4 miles south of Marquette and 10 miles north of Sawyer International Airport. Running to the north of Marquette Mountain is the Carp River. Follow M-553 north, crossing the bridge over the river. Look to the left. Almost immediately past the bridge is a dirt road that cuts back hard to the west. Turn left and follow the dirt road for 1.3 miles. There is space for a couple of vehicles to pull off to the left (south) between sandy banks. The trail to Morgan Falls drops off quickly down to the creek. In the past couple of years a set of stairs have been constructed to make the climb safer and easier. At the creek, either walk across logs that span the creek, or wade through the knee deep waters. Climb down the 15 feet high hill to the base of the falls, a plateau between Morgan Creek and Carp River. This flat area is perfect for viewing the falls and having a picnic!

There are two ways to get to the Carp River Falls. The most obvious is also the longest and more difficult. From Morgan Falls follow the creek to Carp River, a short 100 yards or so. Then hike along Carp River back up river along steep hillsides, climbing down whenever possible to view the falls. There is a labyrinth of narrow footpaths along the river, most likely made by college students. This route is 1.4 miles round trip. The other hike is shorter (1 mile), but has more involved directions.

This shorter, 1 mile round trip hike starts by driving from the Morgan Falls parking area further west (away from M-553) for about .2 miles. Park off of the road at a sandy area on the right. Hike to the left (southwest) atop a half-buried large water pipe that is used to transport water from the dam up river to the power generation plant miles from here. Follow the "pipe" for .4 miles. Along the way it will cross Morgan Creek with a minimal handrail added for protection along this span. At N46 30.268 W87 26.898 there is a 2-track that turns to the left. A concrete and steel ramp may be seen at this juncture. This 2-track ends in about 700 feet at Carp River Falls #6. From here, follow the river down river for .28 miles along the narrow footpaths that follow the top and side of the ravine. This stretch of river houses the six waterfalls described here. After getting to the #1 falls, cut back north for about 700 feet to get back to the buried water pipe. Follow the pipe to the northeast back to the vehicle.

MORGAN FALLS (MORGAN CREEK)

Private  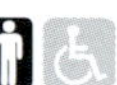 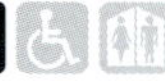

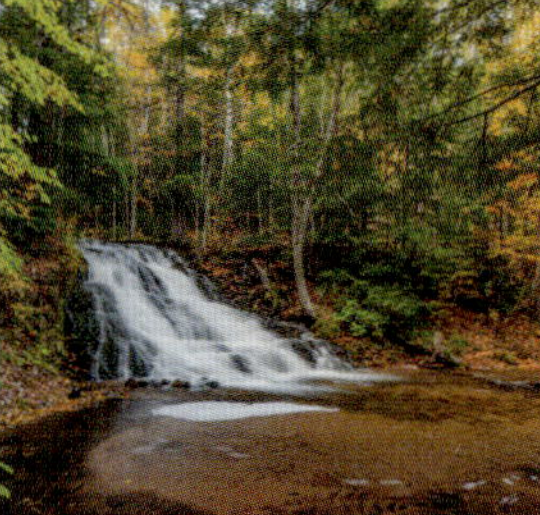

Must See:	9	GPS:	N46 30.321 W87 26.272
Height:	20 feet		
Time:	10-30 minutes	Hiking Information	
		Path:	Footpath
Driving Information		Length:	100 yards
Signs:	None	Elev. Change:	Moderate
Road:	Dirt road	GPS:	Helpful
Access:	Somewhat difficult	Danger:	Moderate
4WD:	Helpful	WP Boots:	Helpful

I rate this as "kid-friendly". It can be tricky getting young children across the creek, but once to the base of the falls, they will have a great time wading in the sandy shallow spill pool and creek or playing in the flat, somewhat open area between the creek and the river.

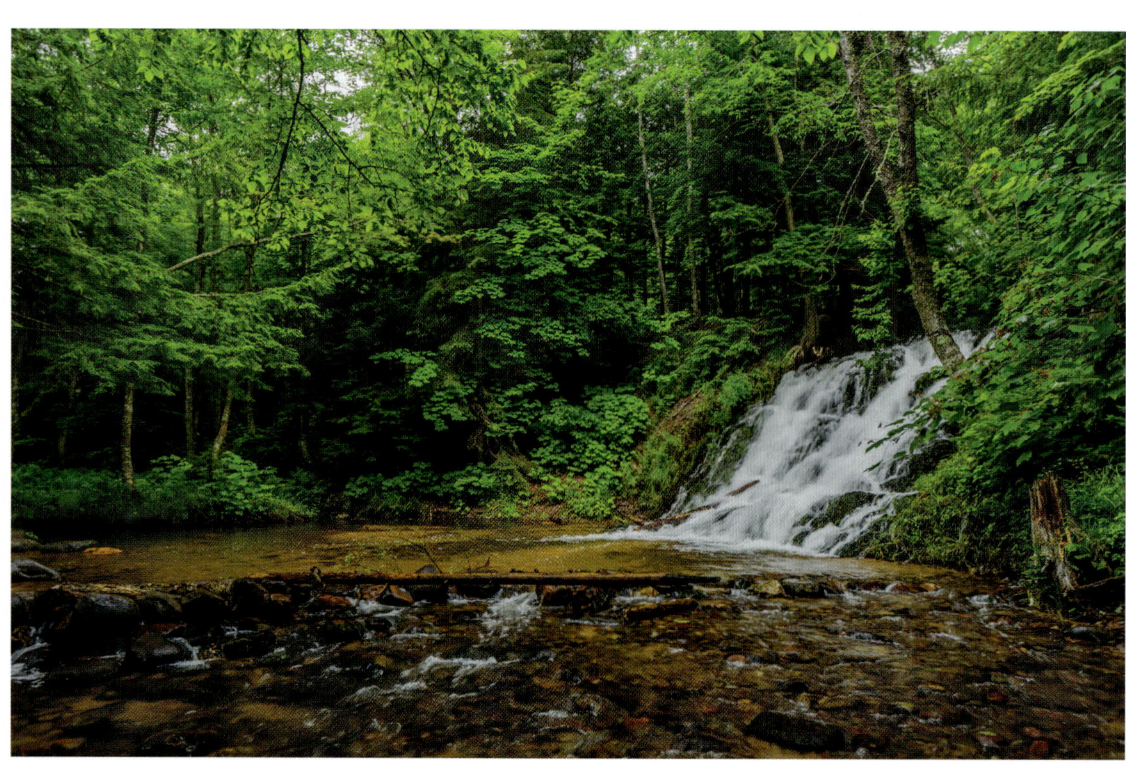

CARP RIVER FALLS #1 (CARP RIVER)

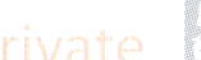

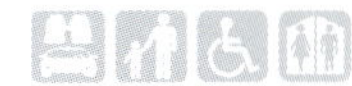

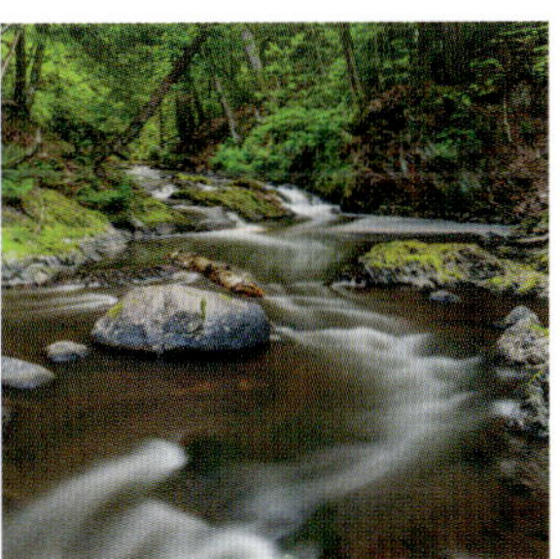

Must See:	3
Height:	4 feet
Time:	30-60 minutes

Driving Information

Signs:	None
Road:	Dirt road
Access:	Somewhat difficult
4WD:	Helpful

GPS:	N46 30.266 W87 26.622

Hiking Information

Path:	Unimproved footpath
Length:	.34 miles
Elev. Change:	Moderate
GPS:	Recommended
Danger:	Elevated
WP Boots:	Helpful

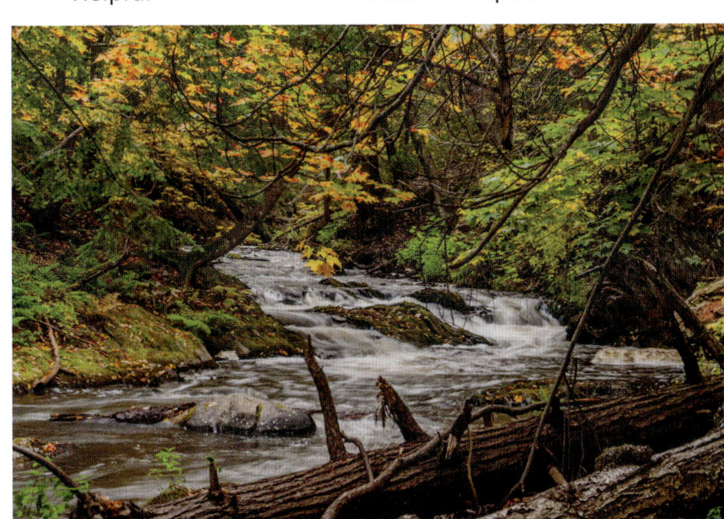

After hiking past nearly continuous rapids from downstream where Morgan Falls joins the Carp River, the first of the Carp River Falls offers a little taste of what's to come.

The river runs through a shallow gorge, flaking pink-gray bedrock lying exposed on either side. Pinching down a bit, the river turns in a subtle "S" curve, the main portion of the waterfall found at the second curve. Here, the turbulent river surges down 3 feet over moss covered rounded boulders. Then the river turns to the left, flowing around several rocks, narrows down and then drops another foot. Cedar, birch, poplar, and maple comprise the bulk of the trees that hug up close to the river.

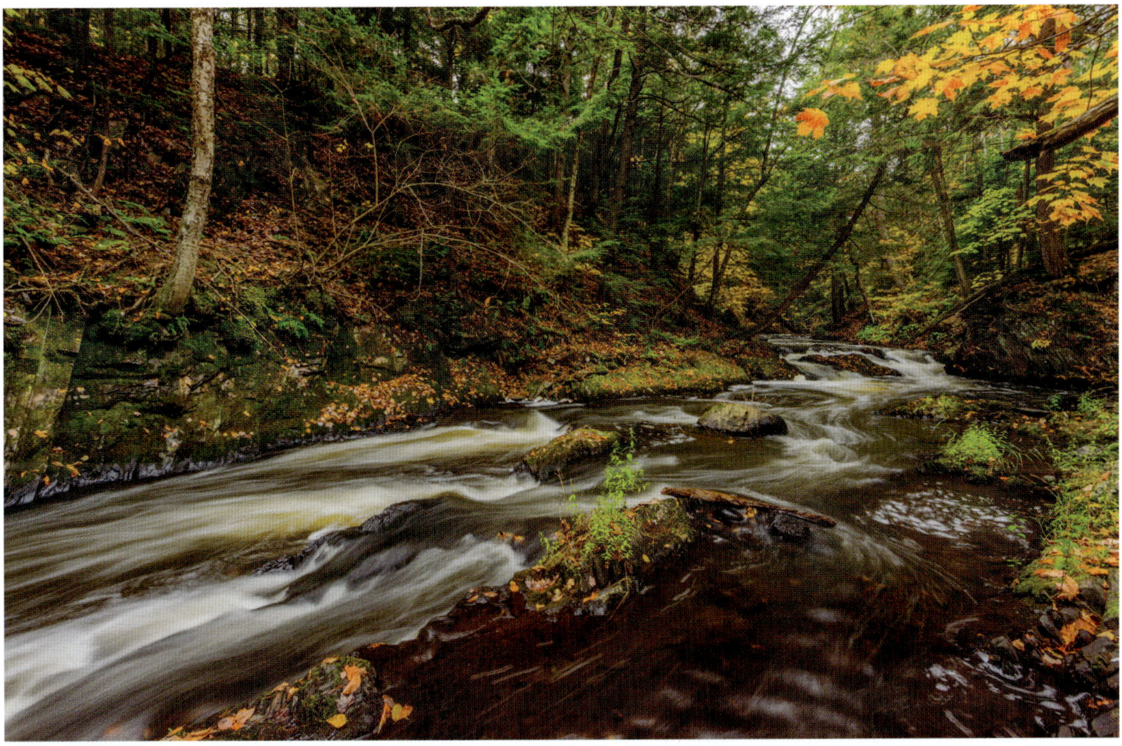

CARP RIVER FALLS #2 (CARP RIVER)

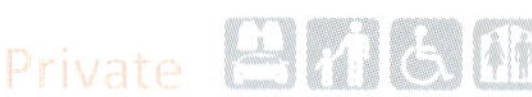

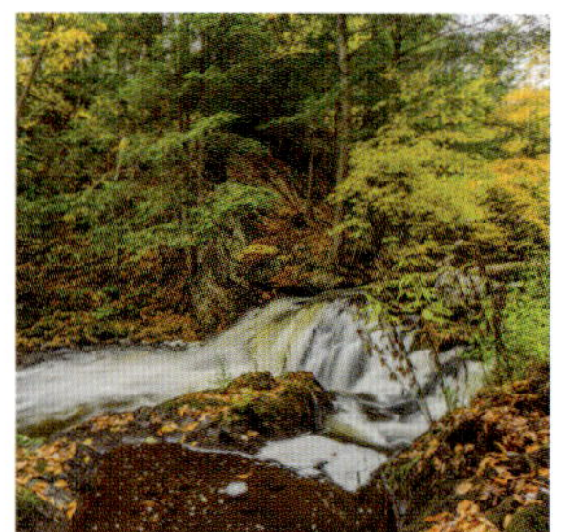

Must See:	5	GPS:	N46 30.242 W87 26.731
Height:	5 feet		
Time:	40-60 minutes	**Hiking Information**	
		Path:	Unimproved footpath
Driving Information		Length:	.44 miles
Signs:	None	Elev. Change:	Moderate
Road:	Dirt road	GPS:	Recommended
Access:	Somewhat difficult	Danger:	Elevated
4WD:	Helpful	WP Boots:	Helpful

The trail between #1 and #2 rises rapidly. It drops back down at the waterfall to only about 15 feet above the river. The far side, however, is 50 to 60 feet high. This horseshoe shaped waterfall is nearly a vertical plunge, with overflow water running through a maze of black basalt on the near side of the river. A large smooth-ish boulder, nearly 5 feet high, sits in the viewing area below the waterfall. Several more, smaller but of similar build, are found around the waterfall. Where did they come from? They look nothing like the bedrock.

This classic cascading waterfall can be viewed from river level. A small strip of land juts out into the river, giving just enough room for several people to stand along its edge, looking out past a small rise to view the left side of the falls. This waterfall would be best viewed from the other side of the river but there is no good way to get there.

The tight, horseshoe shape is evident in the bedrock. Above shot: the far side of the river rises sharply!

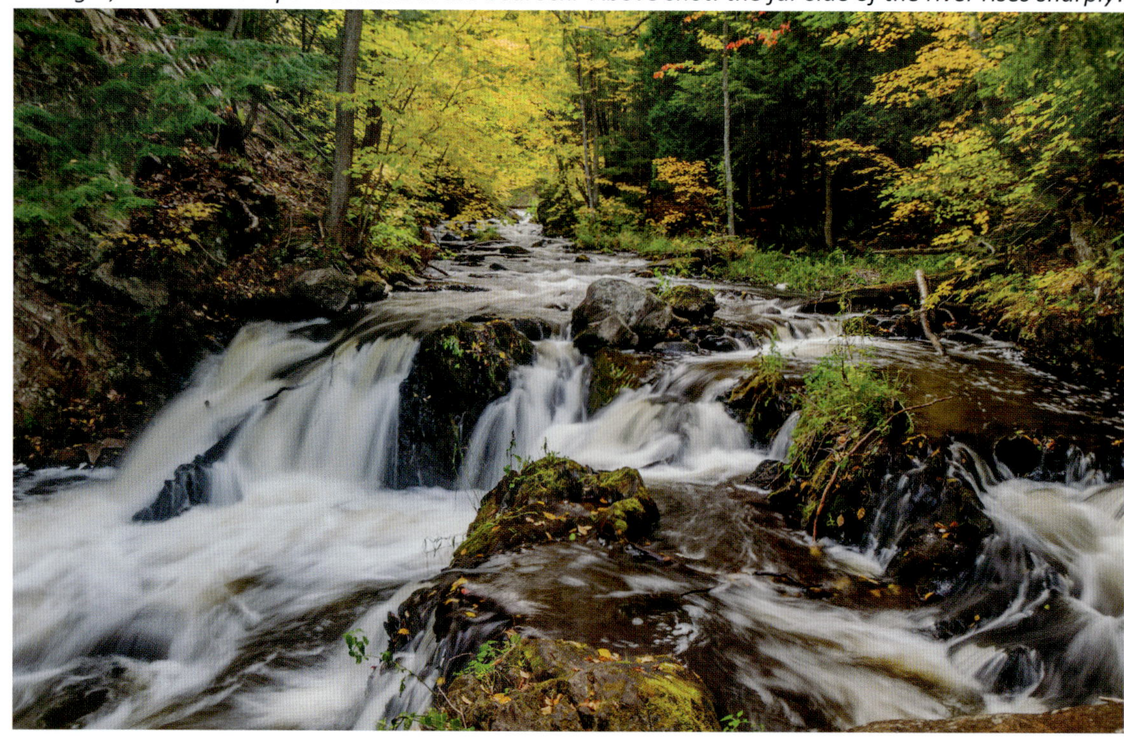

CARP RIVER FALLS #3 (CARP RIVER)

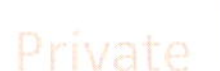
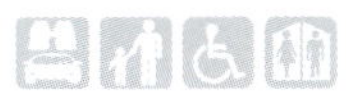

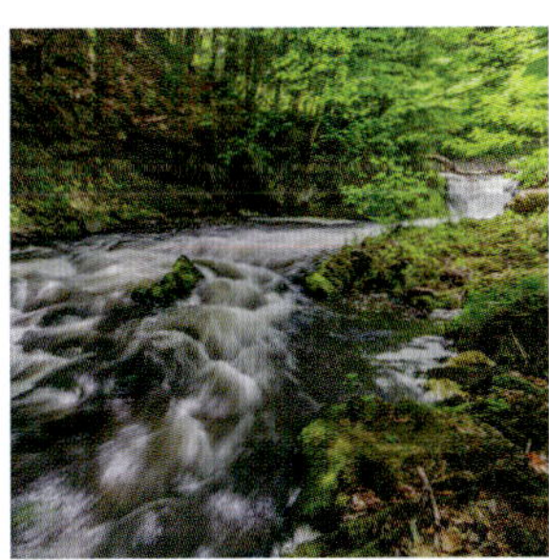

Must See:	4	GPS:	N46 30.234 W87 26.771
Height:	4 feet		
Time:	50-75 minutes	**Hiking Information**	
		Path:	Unimproved footpath
Driving Information		Length:	.47 miles
Signs:	None	Elev. Change:	Moderate
Road:	Dirt road	GPS:	Recommended
Access:	Somewhat difficult	Danger:	Elevated
4WD:	Helpful	WP Boots:	Helpful

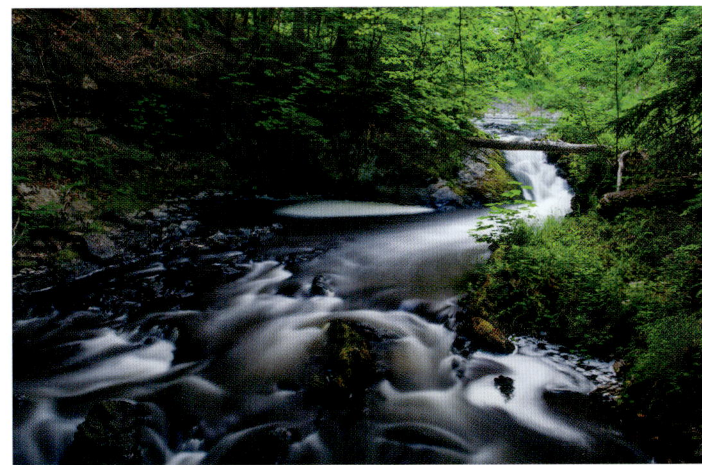

It's any easy hike along the river's edge between #2 and #3. The gorge walls on either side rise 40 feet, towering over the river. Fierce rapids mark its course to the next waterfall. A narrow footpath leads along the river's edge, providing close access to the waterfall.

Walking along the river and seeing the water channelled down to only 2 to 3 feet across, rushing down the short causeway and tumbling over lovely rapids is a beautiful sight! This drop is just below #4. That waterfall is so magnificent, it would be easy for this unique little waterfall to get lost in what's just around the corner.

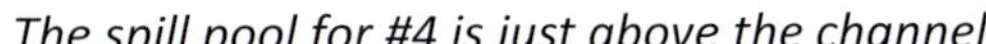

The spill pool for #4 is just above the channel

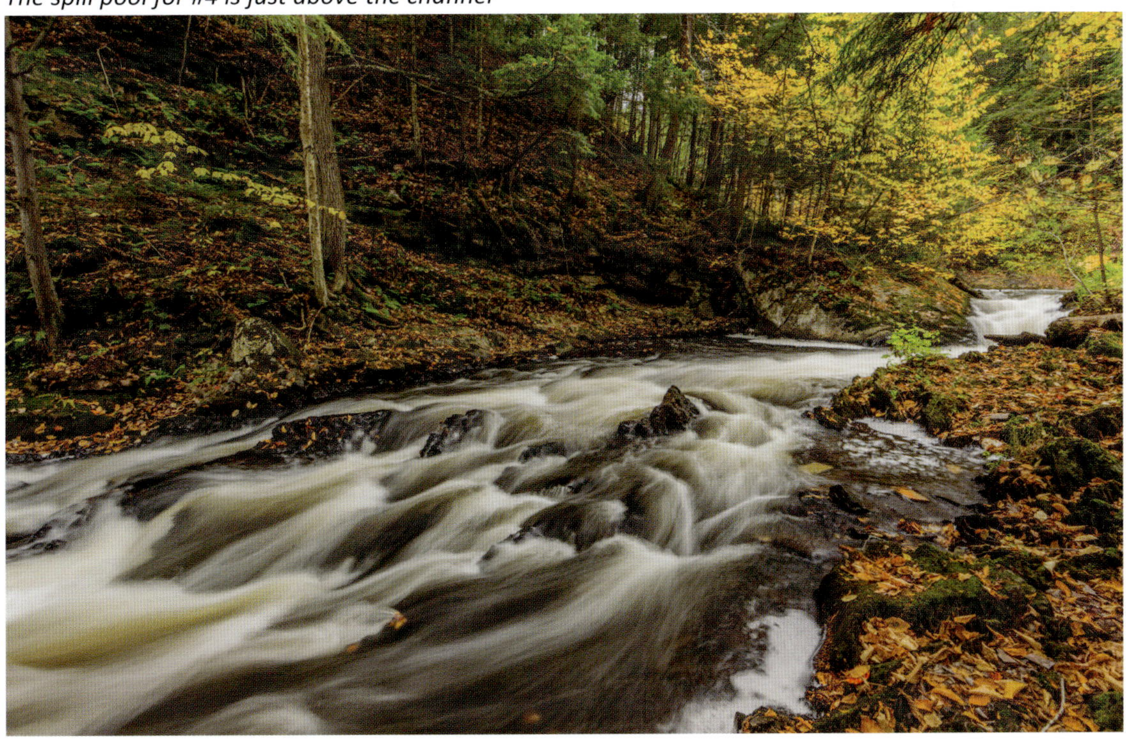

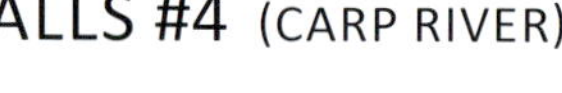

CARP RIVER FALLS #4 (CARP RIVER)

Private

Must See:	9	GPS:	N46 30.228 W87 26.803
Height:	40 feet		
Time:	60-90 minutes	**Hiking Information**	
		Path:	Unimproved footpath
Driving Information		Length:	.50 miles
Signs:	None	Elev. Change:	Moderate
Road:	Dirt road	GPS:	Recommended
Access:	Somewhat difficult	Danger:	Elevated
4WD:	Helpful	WP Boots:	Helpful

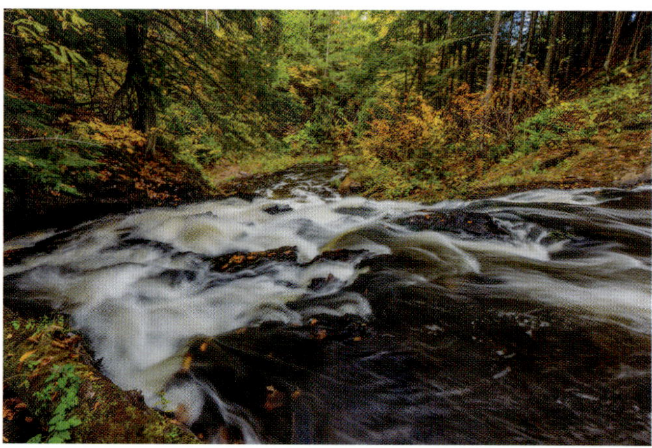

This spectacular waterfall widens out to 40 feet, falling in a triple drop cascade. Frothing white water dominates the river, from side to side. Two final drops arc toward each other at the base of the falls, combining their collective water in a final burst of large white bubbles that are carried downstream. The same footpath at the river's edge from #3 can be hiked the additional 100 feet to view #4 from below the spill pool. The top drop is magnificent in its own right! It's a 15 foot drop that's 10 feet wide. Torrents of water cascade in a very pleasing way to a large spill pool which fans out to slide over the second set of drops, sliding and cascading down another 18 feet. One third of the circumference of the spill pool is involved in this drop as the water follows a cone shaped extension of the pool to its base. The river quickly narrows back down to 10 feet for its final plunge of 7 feet. Clamber up the muddy side next to the falls to view each drop closer.

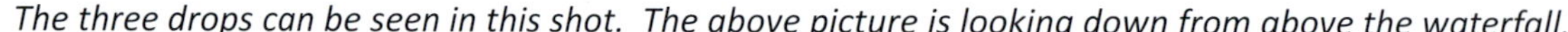

The three drops can be seen in this shot. The above picture is looking down from above the waterfall.

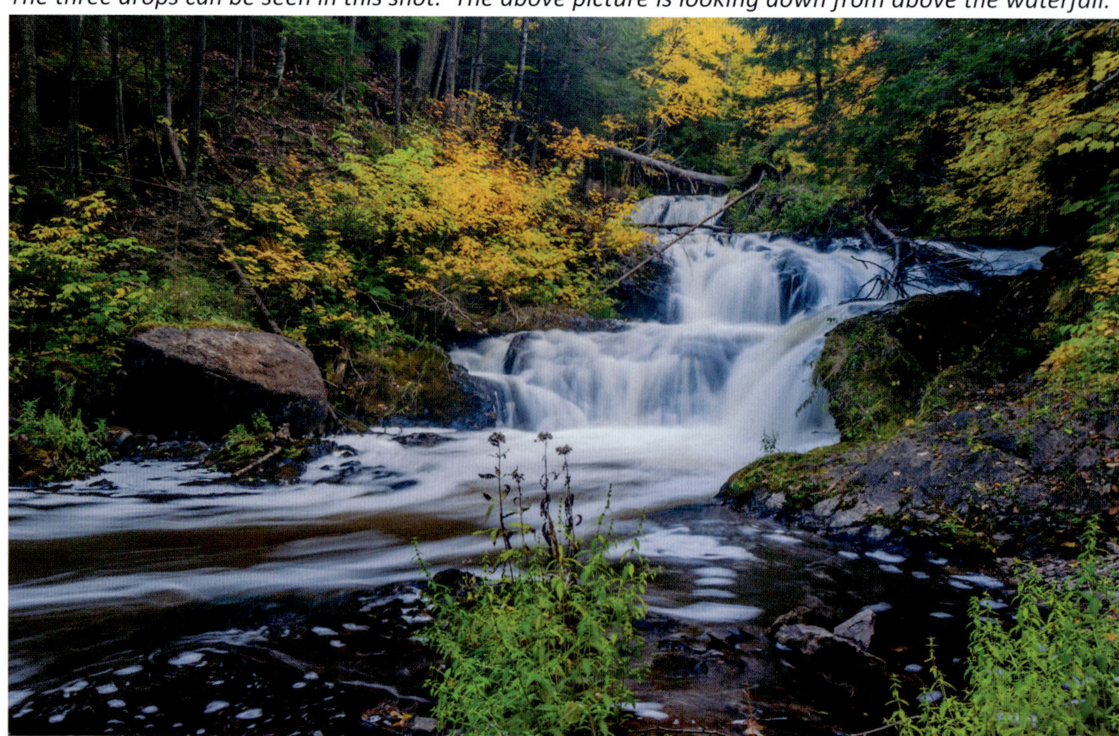

CARP RIVER FALLS #5 (CARP RIVER)

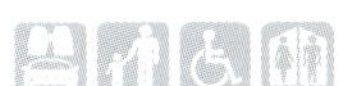

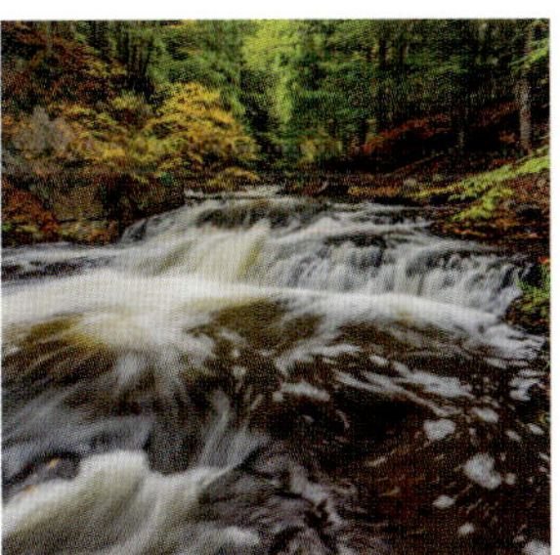

Must See: 5
Height: 10 feet
Time: 60-90 minutes

Driving Information
Signs: None
Road: Dirt road
Access: Somewhat difficult
4WD: Helpful

GPS: N46 30.191 W87 26.820

Hiking Information
Path: Unimproved footpath
Length: .54 miles
Elev. Change: Moderate
GPS: Recommended
Danger: Elevated
WP Boots: Helpful

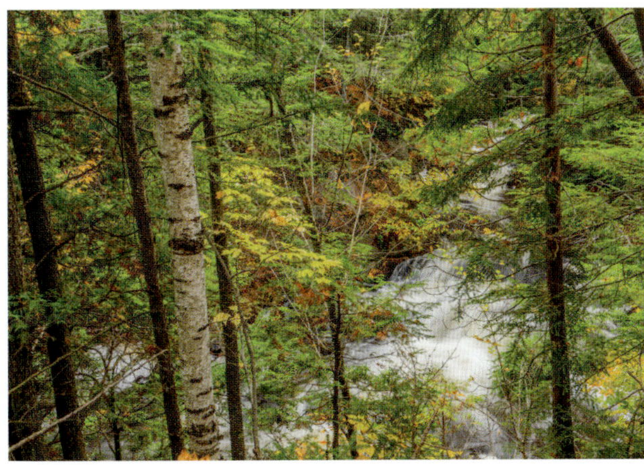

Continue on the footpath next to the river for another 150 feet past the top of #4. The trail narrows to a precarious rocky ledge just inches wide for about 6 feet. A small landing beyond ends at the base of the waterfall. Two irregularly shaped mounds in the center of the river are covered with grasses and flowers. The second drop can just be seen past an imposing crumbling rock edifice. Thimble berries grow along the water and delicate Spotted Touch-me-nots seemingly grow from the rock itself. Back track along the trail and climb to the top of the cliffs to see the rest of the waterfall through pine boughs. The cliff is sheer to the river 40 feet below. The top cascade can be seen 50 feet further upstream from here, but once again, obscured by tree branches. Continue on the trail to the top drop. Climb down the ravine and follow a narrow ledge back to the second drop. There are three drops total in this waterfall, the first two are each 4 feet high and the third is 2 feet for a total of 10 feet.

It's nice to enjoy the waterfall from the river's edge. The view from atop the cliff is seen above.

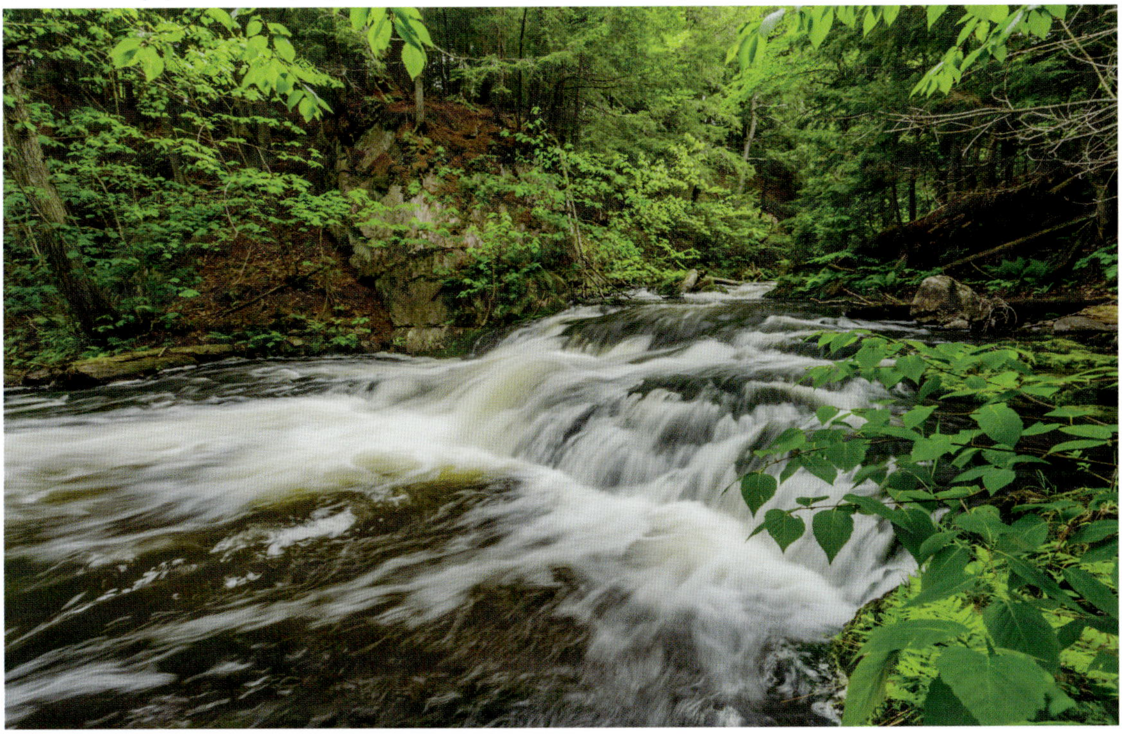

CARP RIVER FALLS #6 (CARP RIVER)

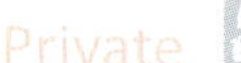

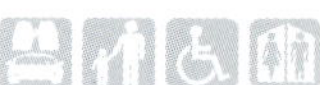

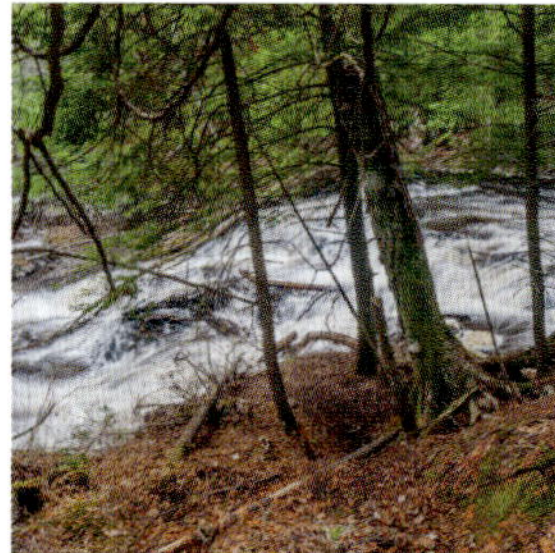

Must See:	7	GPS:	N46 30.156 W87 26.908
Height:	10 feet		
Time:	60-90 minutes	**Hiking Information**	
		Path:	Unimproved footpath
Driving Information		Length:	.65 miles
Signs:	None	Elev. Change:	Moderate
Road:	Dirt road	GPS:	Recommended
Access:	Somewhat difficult	Danger:	Elevated
4WD:	Helpful	WP Boots:	Helpful

Climb down the 15 foot bank to view the waterfall from the river's edge.

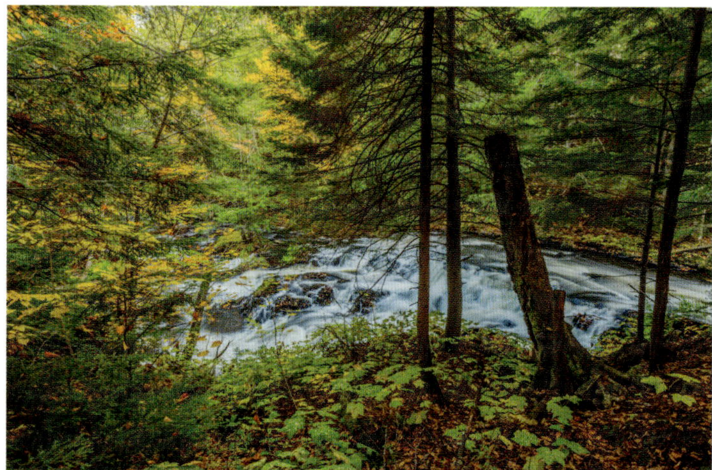

The wide cascading waterfall falls primarily toward the viewing area. A small "overflow" drop is on the far left side, creating an island supporting several trees clustered together. This waterfall collects a large amount of debris (dead branches and tree trunks) for some reason. It would be much nicer if it were cleaned up. At the top of the ravine is a large flat area beneath the trees that has been used as a camping area. A 2-track ends here. Follow it back to get to the water pipe that is used to transport water for the hydroelectric plant.

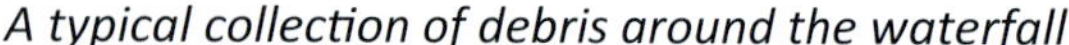

A typical collection of debris around the waterfall

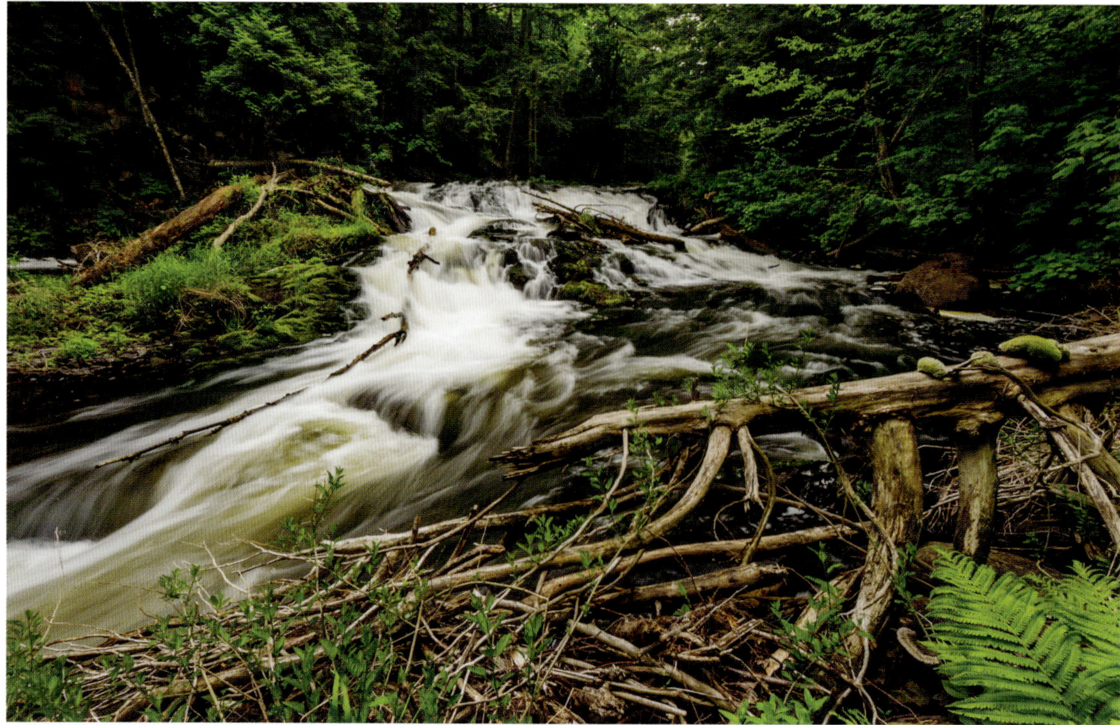

Marquette Mountain Rapids Hike

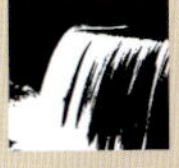

Marquette Mountain Rapids: The river runs near Marquette Branch Prison, an old maximum and minimum-security prison that has been in operation since 1889. The trail to the falls runs next to the grounds. Keep off of the property, which is marked solely by signs scattered through the forest.

Directions: Follow US-41 southeast from Marquette along the Lake Superior shoreline. Just before crossing the Carp River is a road on the south side of the road. Turn right and immediately turn to the left, following the dirt road until it ends at a good sized parking area that has a number of footpaths and bicycle trail heads. Hike south to the Carp River (about 200 yards). A nice footbridge crosses the river. On the south side of the river, a fisherman's trail follows the river to the right (west). It is sometimes close to the river. Other times it ventures further away from the river as it rises up to cross higher bluffs. At these times watch for prison property signs. Stay off the prison property.

MARQUETTE MOUNTAIN RAPIDS (CARP RIVER)

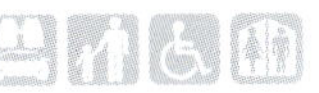

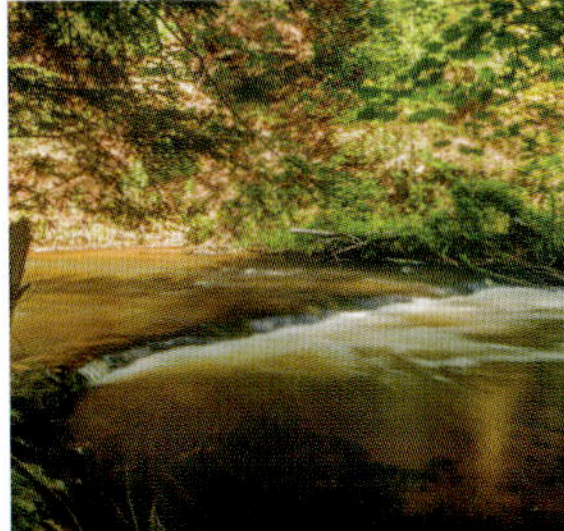

Must See:	2	GPS:	N46 30.498 W87 23.949
Height:	1 foot		
Time:	40-60 minutes	Hiking Information	
		Path:	Footpath
Driving Information		Length:	.54 miles
Signs:	None	Elev. Change:	Moderate
Road:	Dirt road	GPS:	Helpful
Access:	Somewhat difficult	Danger:	Moderate
4WD:	Helpful	WP Boots:	Helpful

Water falls over a plate of rock. There are rapids all along the river, upstream and downstream from here. I believe that there are more small drops further upstream. Continue for the next .25 miles to explore these.

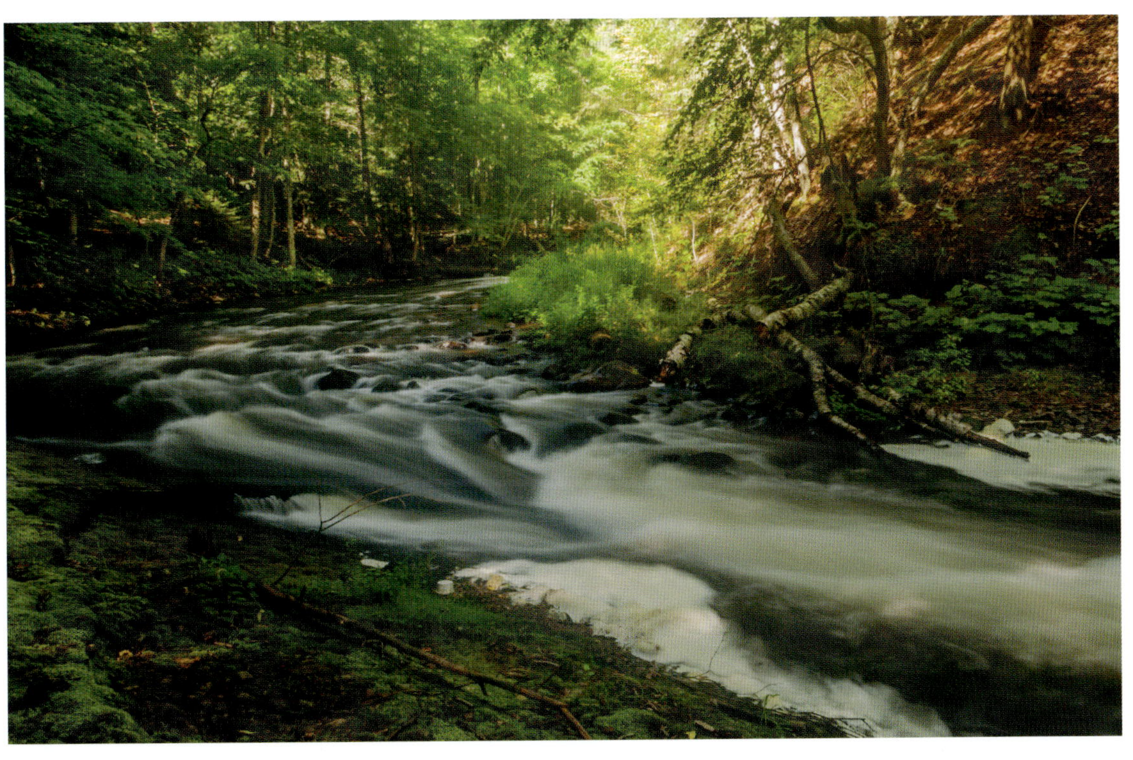

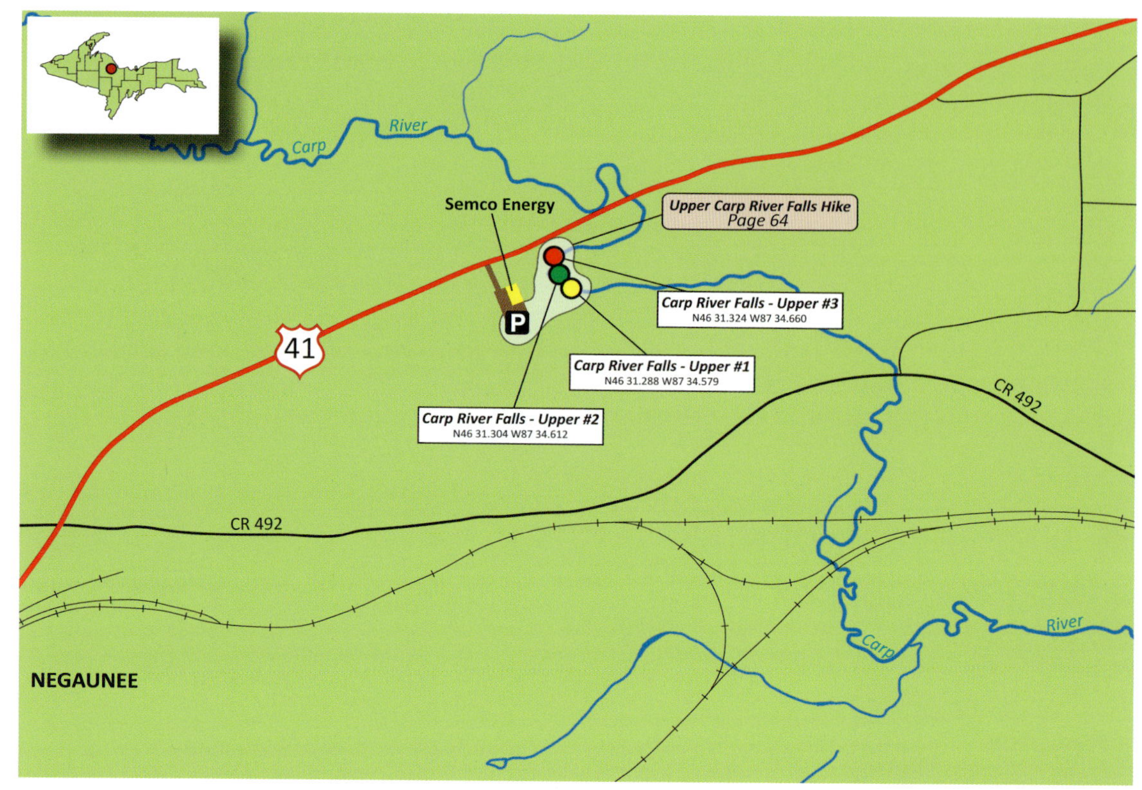

Upper Carp River Falls Hike

The Carp River has its beginning as the drain for Deer Lake, a mere 2 miles north of Ishpeming. Running easterly with a slight southern movement, the Carp River passes beneath US-41, 6 miles further on. The river is now about 1 mile east of Negaunee. In the middle of turning a hard S-curve there are three waterfalls that are scattered over 1/4 mile. The furthest upstream is really a glorified set of rapids. The two further downstream are very nice waterfalls, and equally as nice, they are the closest to the parking area!

Directions: If coming in on US-41 headed west, look for the bridge over the Carp River. Turn left (south) soon afterwards into the parking lot for the Semco Power Company. If driving east on US-41, the road bends left (northwest) right after running next to Teal Lake between Ishpeming and Negaunee. Two miles after that bend, the Semco Power Company will be seen on the right (south). Park in the back of the parking lot. Make sure that you are not interfering with the operations of the power company. Be considerate. Hike to the east behind the fenced-in area of the company. A footpath will be obvious. It runs across a slight ditch and then through a narrow strip of field before entering the woods. Follow the trail to the river. It will lead you directly to the #1 Falls. Follow the trail up river to the #2 Falls. They are not as easily viewed at the #1 Falls. Don't count on a trail to the #3 Falls. It seems that I would find a slight path and then lose it as I hiked between the falls.

CARP RIVER FALLS - UPPER #1 (CARP RIVER)

Private 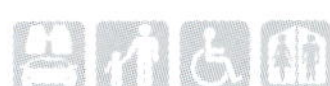

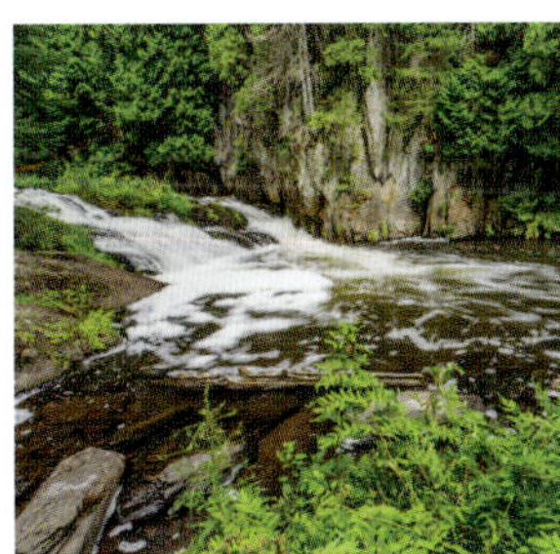

Must See: 6
Height: 5 feet
Time: 20-40 minutes

Driving Information
Signs: None
Road: Main
Access: Easy
4WD: N/A

GPS: N46 31.288 W87 34.579

Hiking Information
Path: Narrow footpath
Length: .15 miles
Elev. Change: Minor
GPS: Helpful
Danger: Slight
WP Boots: Recommended

The river splits around black, moss covered rocks and beside a 25 foot tall massive rock outcropping. The vertical, striated cliff serves as a nice backdrop for the falls. This really has a nice, small, private viewing area. It has the best viewing platform of these three waterfalls.

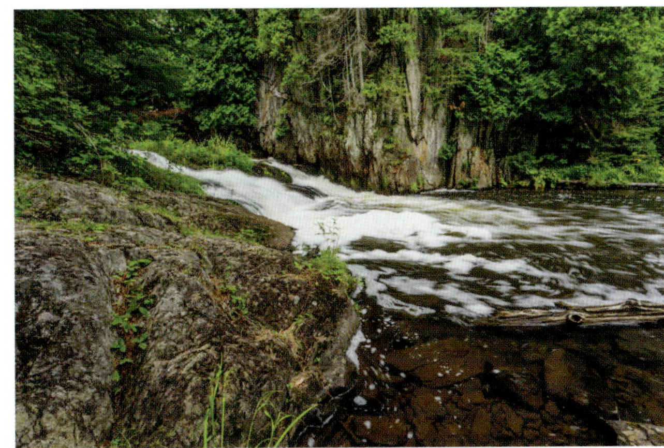

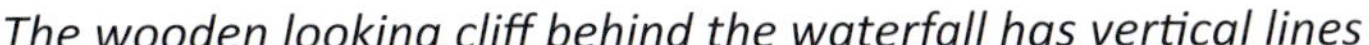

The wooden looking cliff behind the waterfall has vertical lines

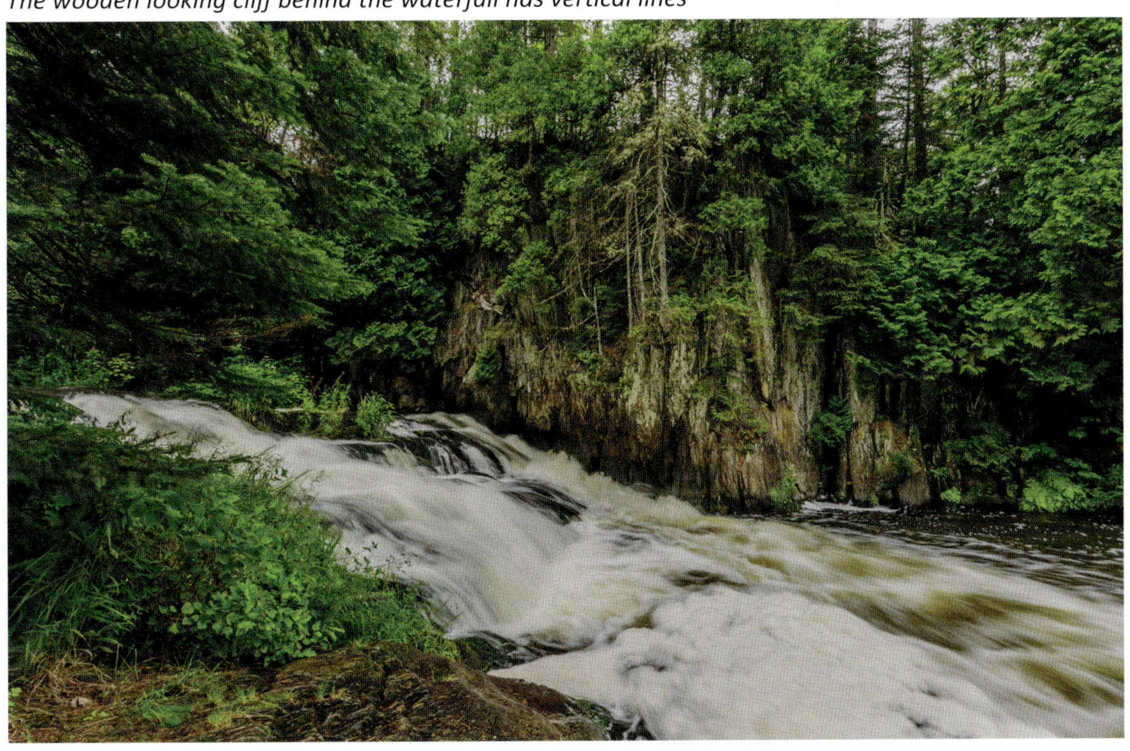

CARP RIVER FALLS - UPPER #2 (CARP RIVER)

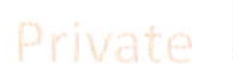

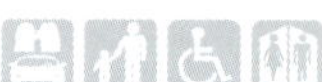

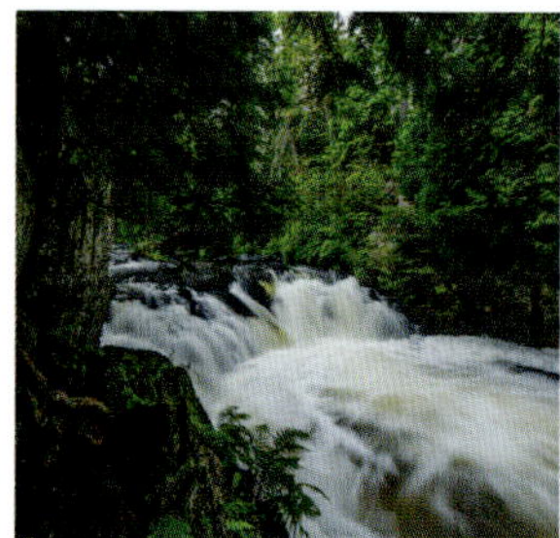

Must See:	7	GPS:	N46 31.304 W87 34.612
Height:	5 feet		
Time:	20-40 minutes		

Driving Information

Signs:	None
Road:	Main
Access:	Easy
4WD:	N/A

Hiking Information

Path:	Narrow footpath
Length:	.20 miles
Elev. Change:	Moderate
GPS:	Helpful
Danger:	Moderate
WP Boots:	Recommended

This is a classic lovely symmetrical cascading waterfall made up of hundreds of little rocky plateaus to catch the water falling. Along the river banks are elegant ferns and thimble berries. Spotted touch-me-nots are interspersed with maple saplings. Cedars overlook the falls, casting green boughs like protective wings over the river.

It requires a bit of a scramble over a rocky ledge to get down to the river's edge. And then there's not much of a ledge on which to stand.

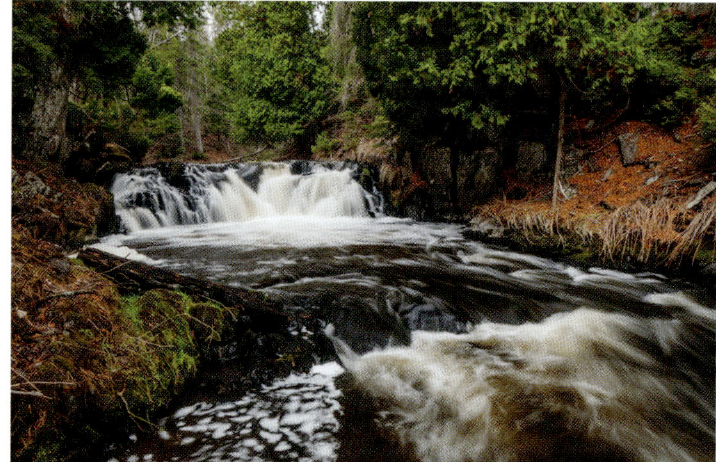

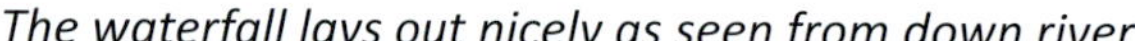
The waterfall lays out nicely as seen from down river

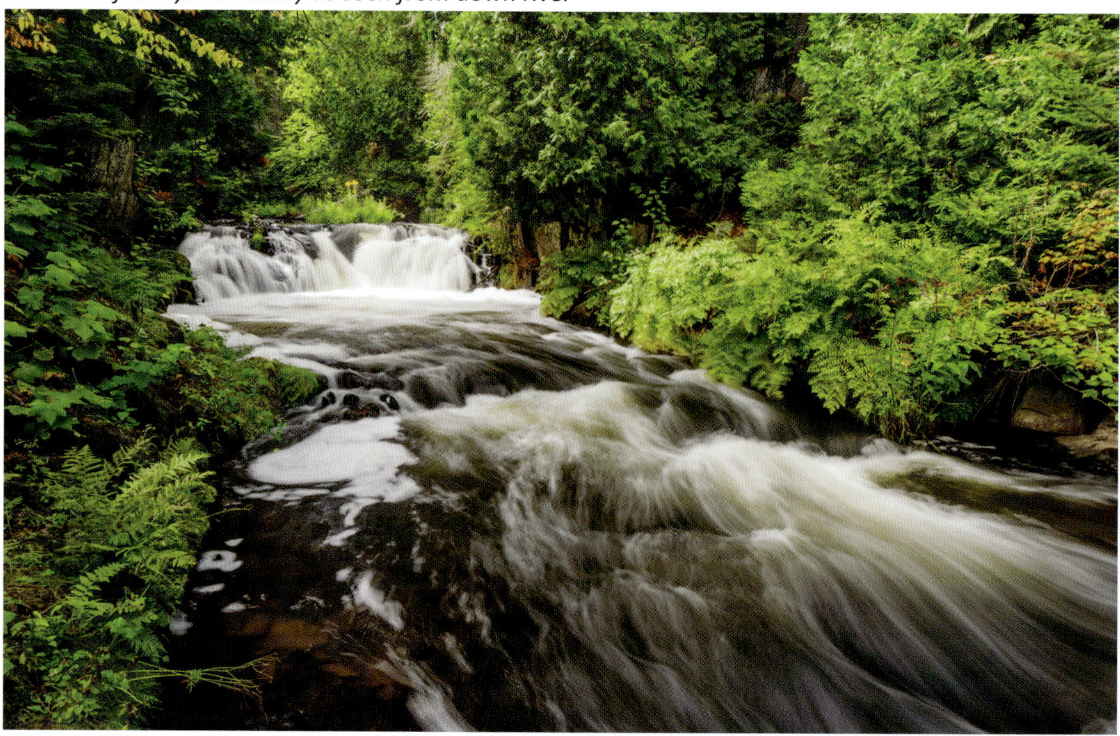

CARP RIVER FALLS - UPPER #3 (CARP RIVER)

Private 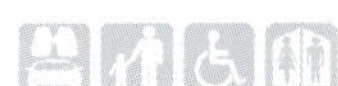

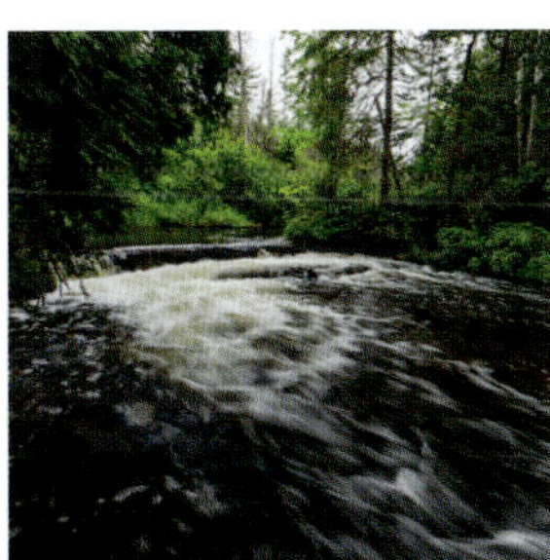

Must See:	2
Height:	2 feet
Time:	20-40 minutes

Driving Information

Signs:	None
Road:	Main
Access:	Easy
4WD:	N/A

GPS:	N46 31.324 W87 34.660

Hiking Information

Path:	Narrow path then none
Length:	.25 miles
Elev. Change:	Moderate
GPS:	Helpful
Danger:	Moderate
WP Boots:	Recommended

There's not much character to this short drop. Glassy water above the falls starts churning after dropping over the edge. The churning water continues all the way down the river past the other waterfalls. This waterfall is not that far from US-41. You'll notice that the road noise is much greater here than back at the first two waterfalls.

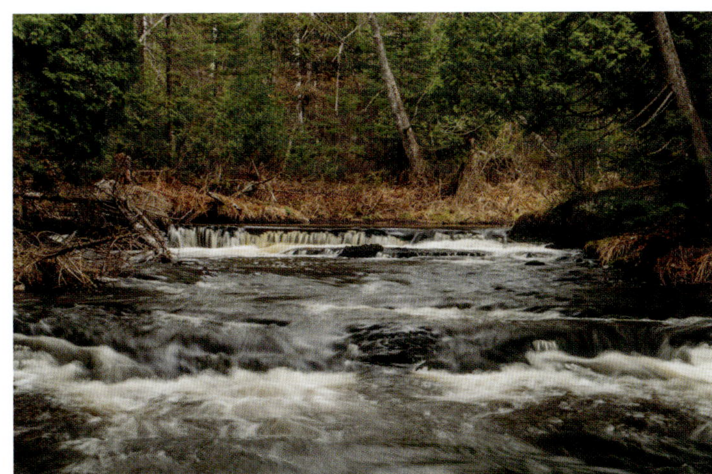

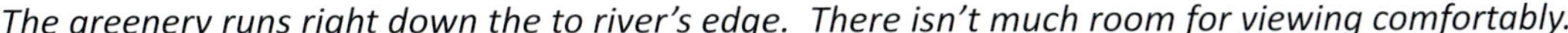

The greenery runs right down the to river's edge. There isn't much room for viewing comfortably.

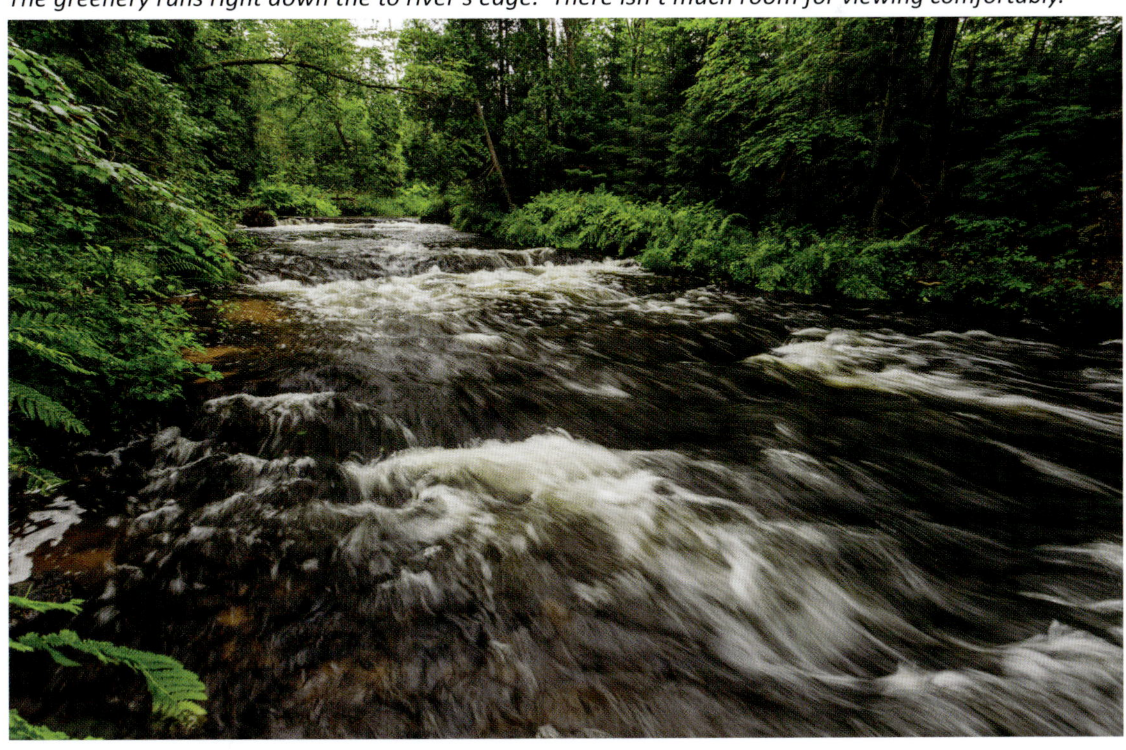

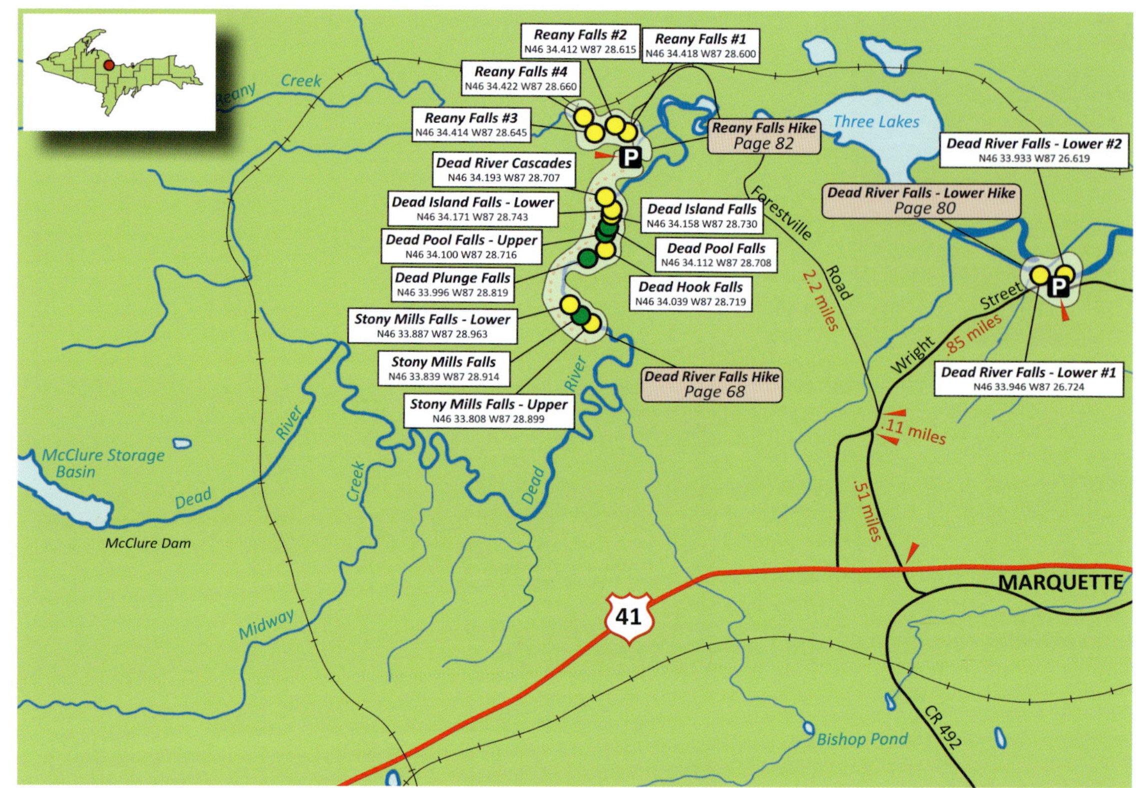

Dead River Falls Hike

The Dead River Falls are best accessed by hiking from the parking lot at the Dead River Power Plant. This is the same place to park for the Reany Falls Hike. The Dead River Falls are often visited and are quite popular. Several of them have wonderful drops in the 15 to 20 foot height range. Be prepared. There is some decent elevation change along the unimproved trail.

College students from Marquette frequent this stretch of river. It is close to town and a couple of the falls have splash pools deep enough to allow diving from rocky perches above the falls.

Directions: Turn north onto Wright Street (CR-492) from US-41. The Westwood Mall Shopping Center is on the northeast corner, Starbucks is on the southwest, with a Culvers to the southeast and a Quiznos on the northwest. In .51 miles turn right to stay on Wright Street. In .11 miles turn left (northwest) onto Forestville Road. After about 1 mile the road makes several sharp bends, crossing the Dead River on an old bridge. From Wright Street to the end of the road is 2.2 miles. The road ends at a parking lot not far from a hydroelectric power plant. Park. (The Reany Falls Hike also begins at this parking lot.) Hike along an obvious dirt road that is to the right of the power plant (DON'T approach the building - it is strictly OFF LIMITS). This road has been under construction for a couple of years, so there may be major changes from the last time I hiked along it. A footpath cuts off to the left after passing by the power house and soon intersects the Dead River. Follow the trail up river, following close to the shoreline. After viewing the seven "Dead River Falls", continue past a large pond that bulges the river to over 300 feet wide. The western shore of the pond is about 350 yards long. The "Stony Mills Falls" are found within the next 800 feet. All told, the hike from the vehicle to the 10th waterfall on the hike, "Stony Mills Falls - Upper" is .85 miles (one way).

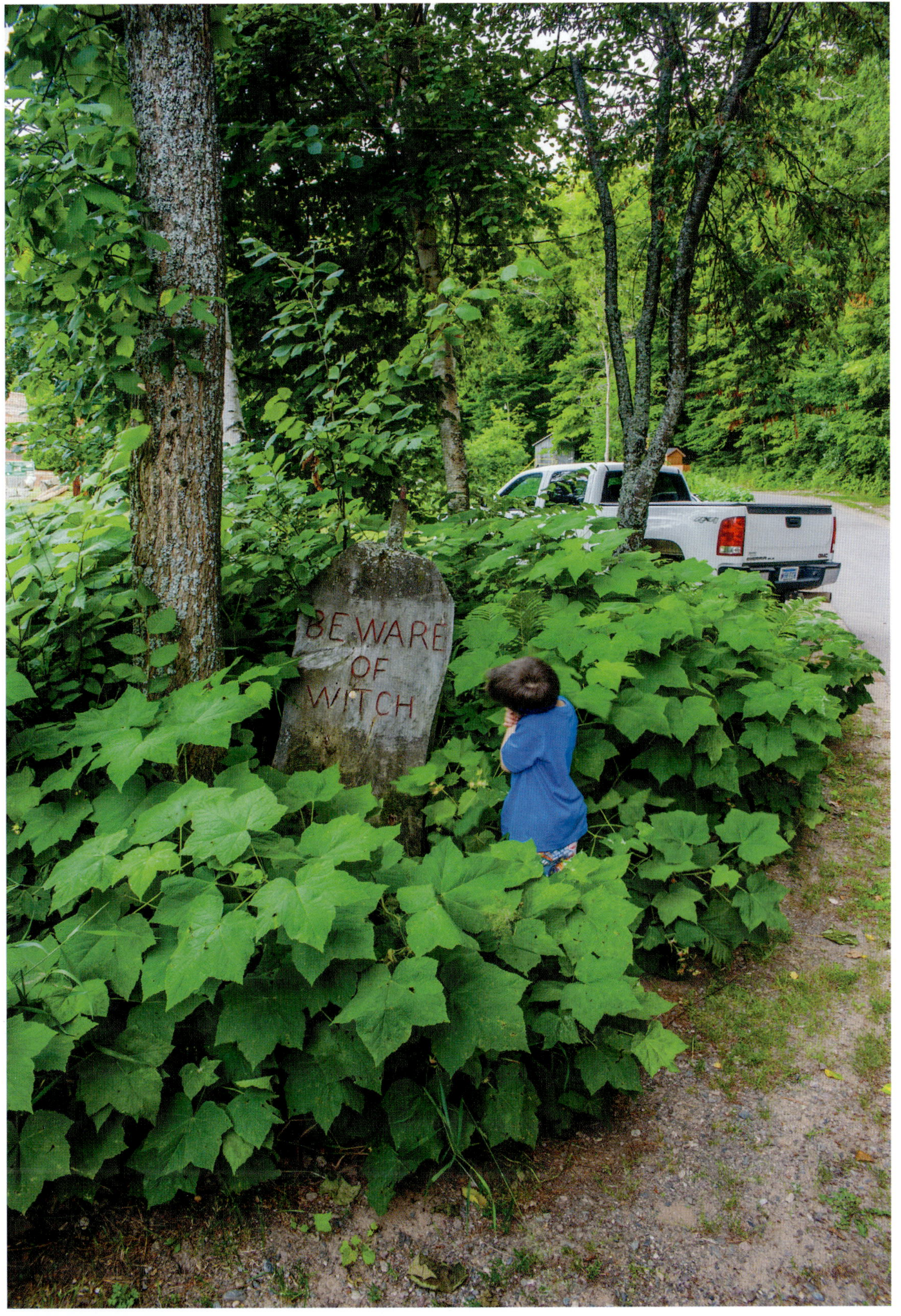

Luke, my youngest son, surrounded by thimbleberry plants, ponders the meaning of a "sign" by the parking lot to the Dead River Falls and Reany Falls.

DEAD RIVER CASCADES (DEAD RIVER)

Private  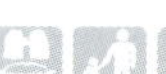  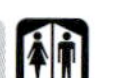

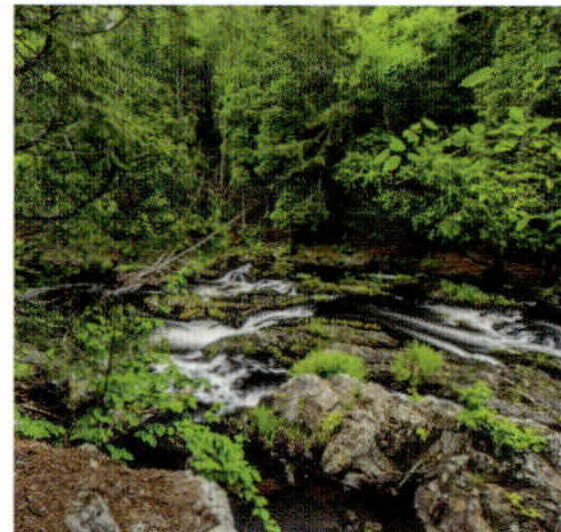

Must See:	5	GPS:	N46 34.193 W87 28.707
Height:	4 feet		
Time:	20-30 minutes	Hiking Information	
		Path:	Footpath
Driving Information		Length:	.23 miles
Signs:	None	Elev. Change:	Moderate
Road:	Secondary road	GPS:	Helpful
Access:	Somewhat difficult	Danger:	Moderate
4WD:	N/A	WP Boots:	N/A

It's good to get to this introductory waterfall. I like to take a break here. After all, it's a bit of a hike from the parking lot up the steep gravel road that parallels the river. Then cut over to the forest at a well marked footpath. Descend back down into the Dead River Gorge and to the top of a good sized bluff that overlooks this first waterfall.

The river drops in a semi-circle over jagged bedrock with ferns topping some of the rocky mounds. This is just a taste of what's to come. It's not spectacular, but the overlook from atop the knobby basalt mass provides a great viewing location. The river splits into several streams as it flows around the matching bedrock some 20 feet below the viewing area. Spindly wildflowers grasp at the sparse soil on the rocky crag, their delicate beauty offering a splash of color to the otherwise gray floor.

The view from the top of the bluff

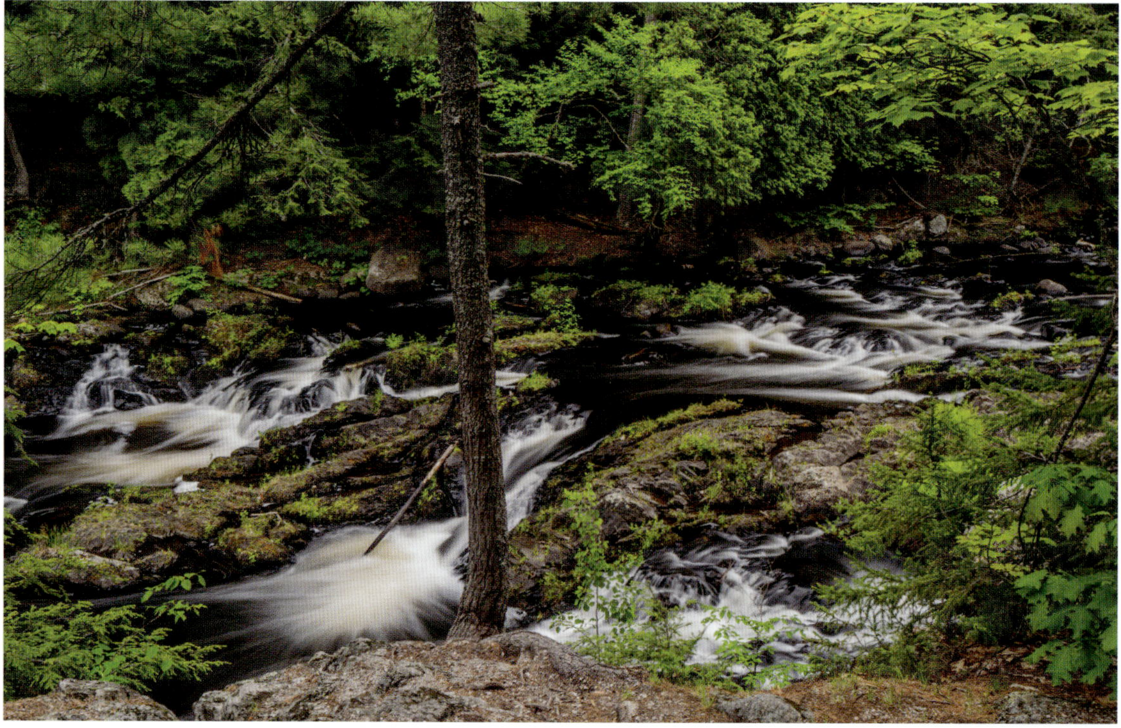

DEAD ISLAND FALLS - LOWER (DEAD RIVER)

Private 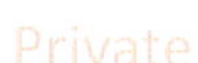  

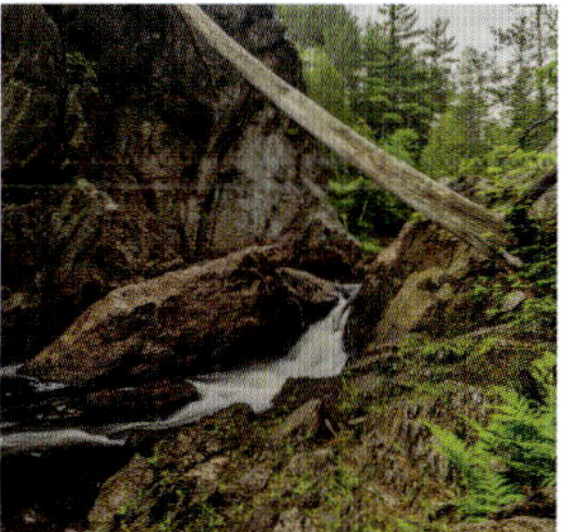

Must See:	5	GPS:	N46 34.171 W87 28.743
Height:	4 feet		
Time:	25-40 minutes	**Hiking Information**	
		Path:	Footpath
Driving Information		Length:	.28 miles
Signs:	None	Elev. Change:	Moderate
Road:	Secondary road	GPS:	Helpful
Access:	Somewhat difficult	Danger:	Moderate
4WD:	N/A	WP Boots:	N/A

Follow the footpath down from the Dead River Cascades to the river's edge along calm waters. A small tributary enters the river and must be crossed. A cluster of logs is typically strategically placed to accommodate this. Follow the base of the ravine (beyond the tributary, another trail climbs the swiftly rising bank) to the bottom of the waterfall. The river here has cut a channel through a 30 foot high mass of bedrock. Several huge chunks have since fallen into the narrow cut. The water pours around the sides of these displaced masses.

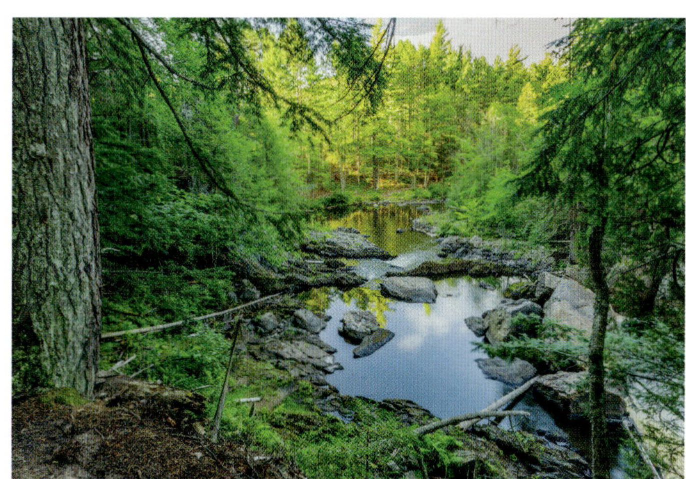

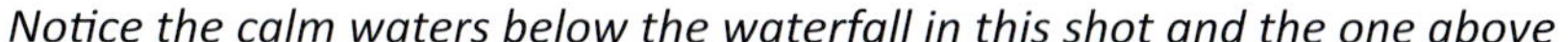

Notice the calm waters below the waterfall in this shot and the one above

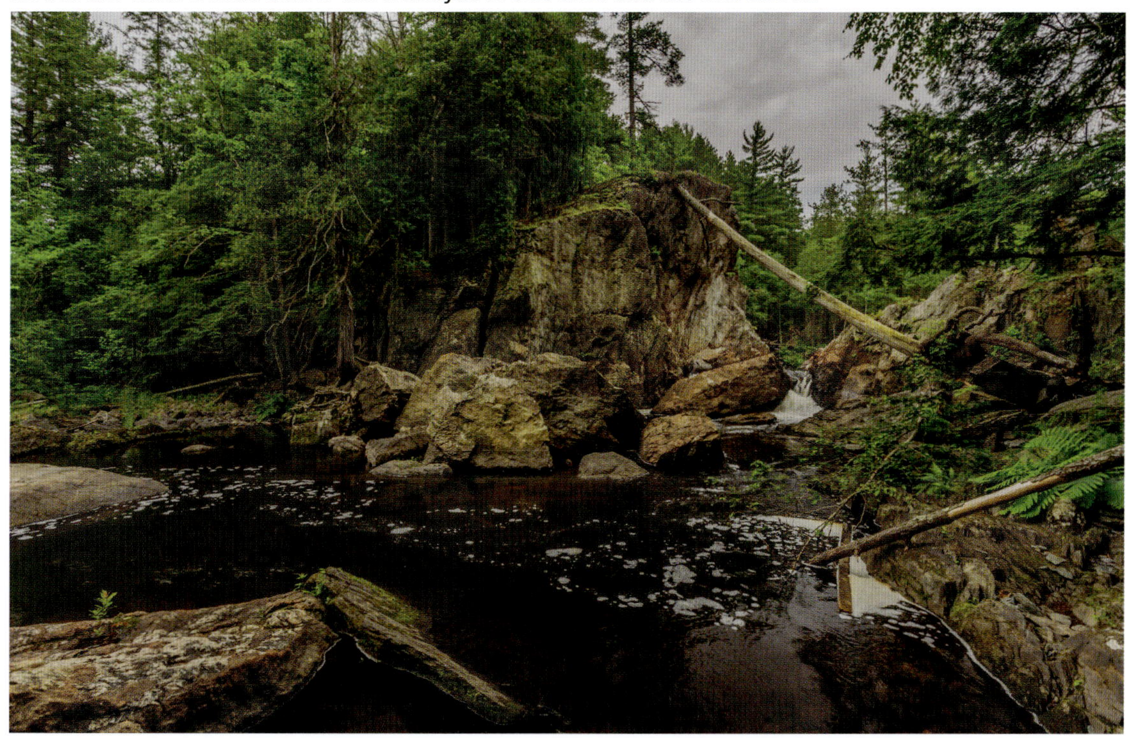

DEAD ISLAND FALLS (DEAD RIVER)

Private

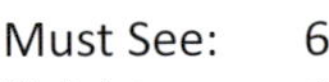

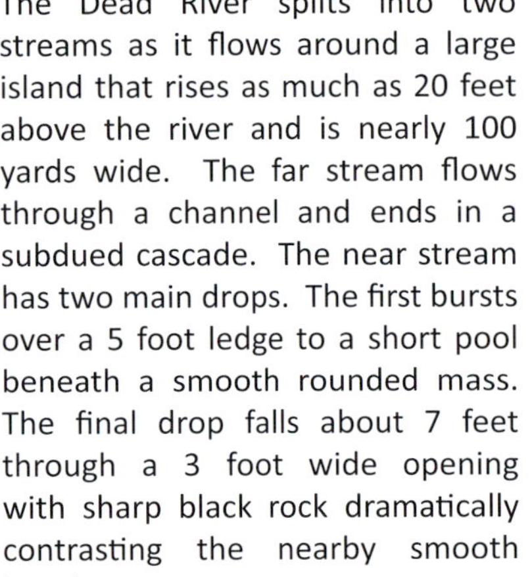

Must See:	6	GPS:	N46 34.158 W87 28.730
Height:	15 feet		
Time:	30-45 minutes	**Hiking Information**	
		Path:	Footpath
Driving Information		Length:	.28 miles
Signs:	None	Elev. Change:	Moderate
Road:	Secondary road	GPS:	Helpful
Access:	Somewhat difficult	Danger:	Moderate
4WD:	N/A	WP Boots:	N/A

The Dead River splits into two streams as it flows around a large island that rises as much as 20 feet above the river and is nearly 100 yards wide. The far stream flows through a channel and ends in a subdued cascade. The near stream has two main drops. The first bursts over a 5 foot ledge to a short pool beneath a smooth rounded mass. The final drop falls about 7 feet through a 3 foot wide opening with sharp black rock dramatically contrasting the nearby smooth basalt.

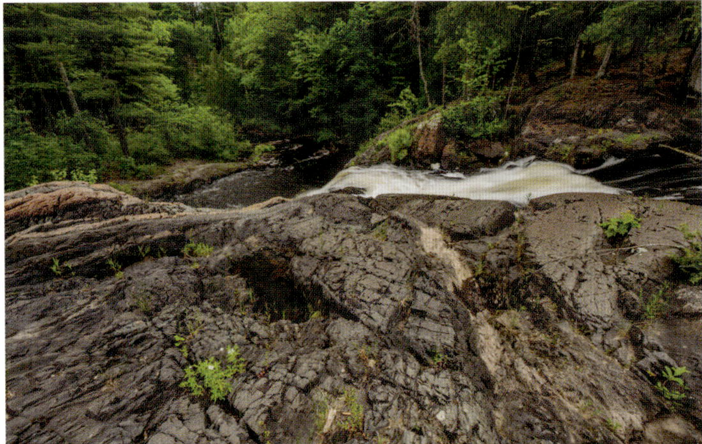

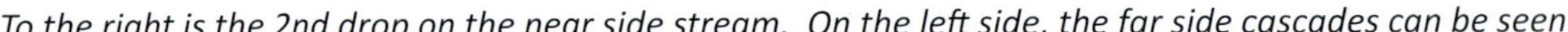

To the right is the 2nd drop on the near side stream. On the left side, the far side cascades can be seen.

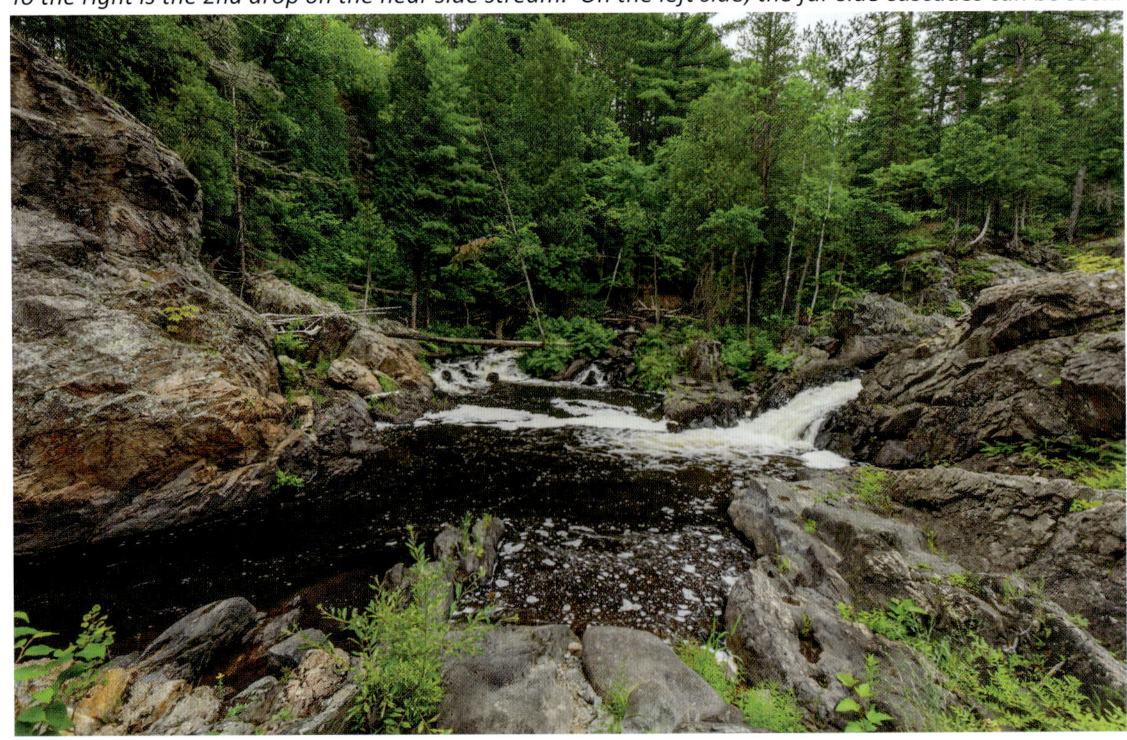

DEAD POOL FALLS (DEAD RIVER)

Private 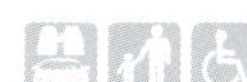 

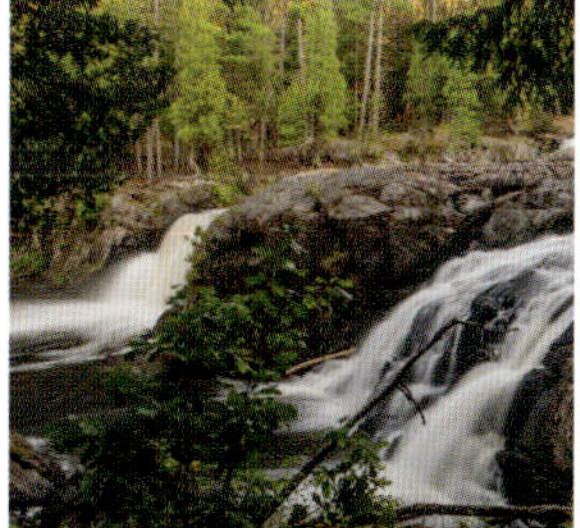

Must See:	7	GPS:	N46 34.112 W87 28.708
Height:	15 feet		
Time:	35-50 minutes	Hiking Information	
		Path:	Footpath
Driving Information		Length:	.33 miles
Signs:	None	Elev. Change:	Moderate
Road:	Secondary road	GPS:	Helpful
Access:	Somewhat difficult	Danger:	Moderate
4WD:	N/A	WP Boots:	N/A

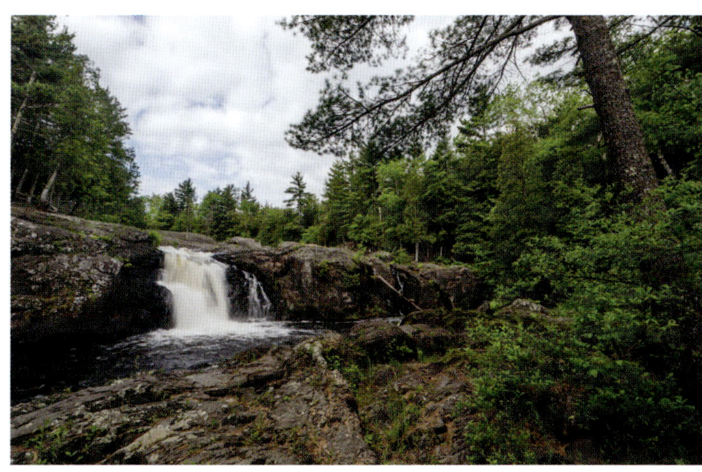

A favorite of college kids, the pool below the main waterfall is often dived into. I'm not recommending this as a safe practice, but I have witnessed it several times on my trips here. When the river is high, it divides and flows heavily over two distinct waterfalls some yards apart. The "black when wet" rock nicely offsets the white frothing river as it cascades down the nearly vertical face. The waterfall tumbles over a long cliff face. At the base of the cliff is a trough. It starts at just a couple feet wide and expands to about 30 feet across at the "main" waterfall. The river then continues around the side of the perfect viewing area to the Dead Island Falls further downstream.

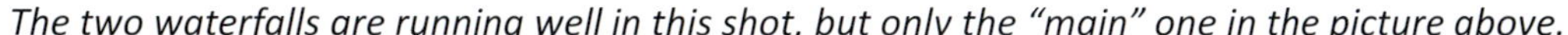

The two waterfalls are running well in this shot, but only the "main" one in the picture above.

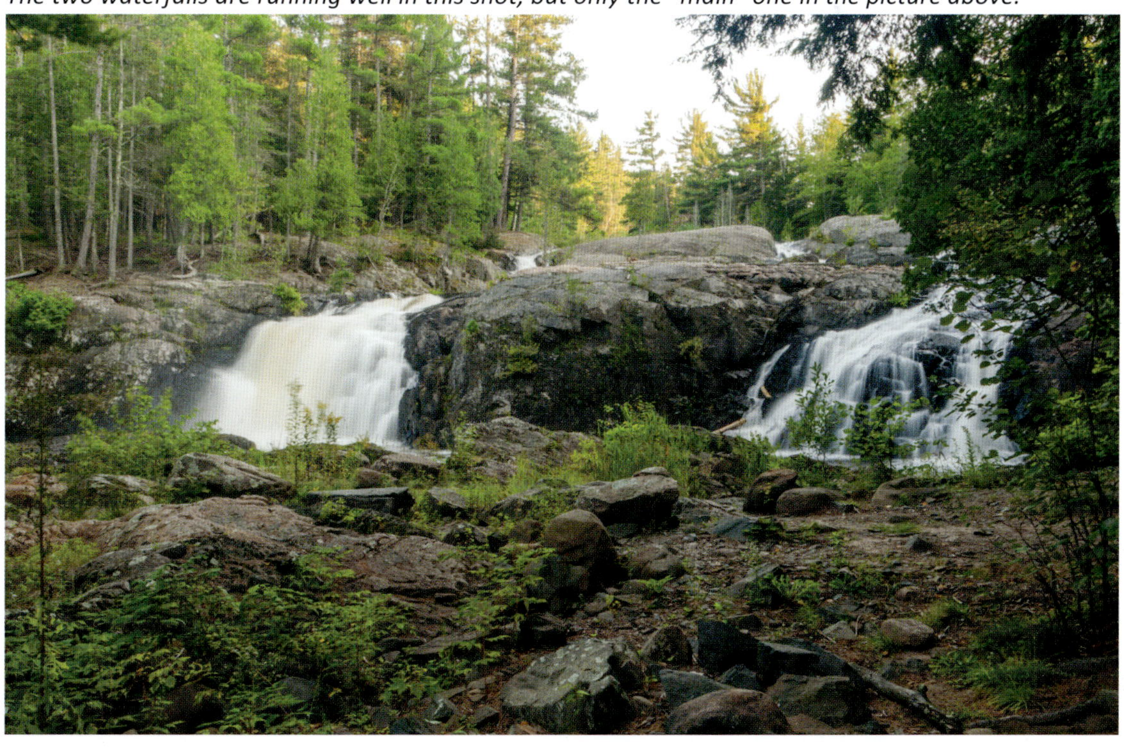

DEAD POOL FALLS - UPPER (DEAD RIVER)

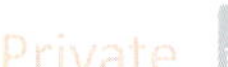

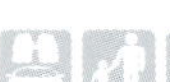

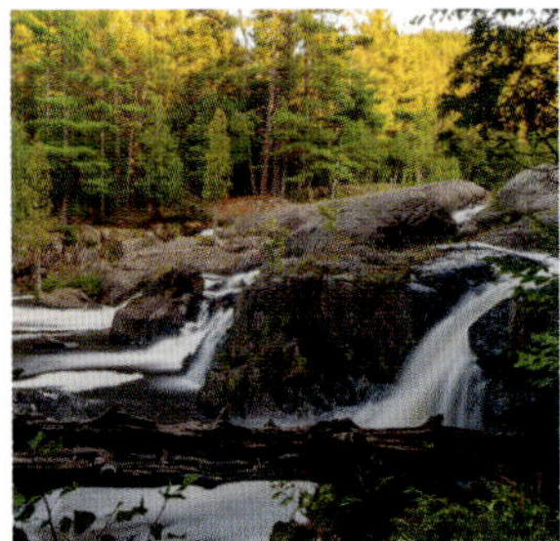

Must See:	7	GPS:	N46 34.100 W87 28.716
Height:	15 feet		
Time:	40-60 minutes	**Hiking Information**	
		Path:	Footpath
Driving Information		Length:	.35 miles
Signs:	None	Elev. Change:	Moderate
Road:	Secondary road	GPS:	Helpful
Access:	Somewhat difficult	Danger:	Moderate
4WD:	N/A	WP Boots:	N/A

Lovely smooth mounds of bedrock lay out before you. Three larger waterfalls and a very tiny one on the left have eroded their way through the basalt and present themselves beautifully. This waterfall is just above Dead Pool Falls. Picnic perfect rock is at the ideal viewing area below the waterfall and at the top of Dead Pool Falls.

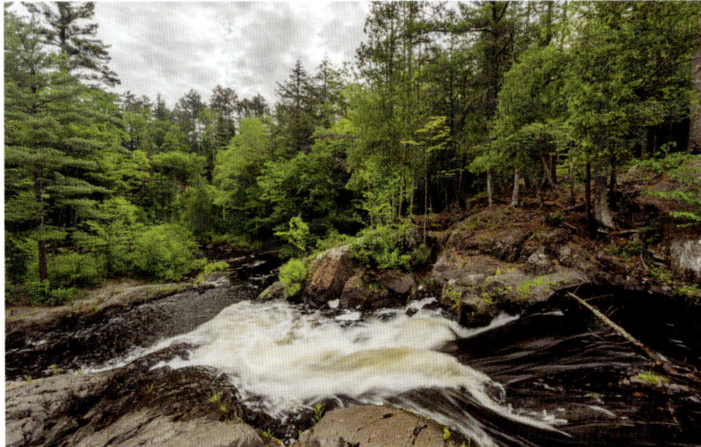

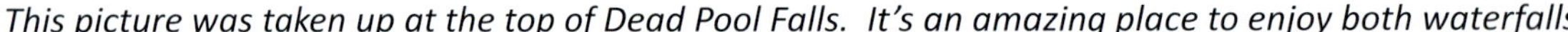
This picture was taken up at the top of Dead Pool Falls. It's an amazing place to enjoy both waterfalls.

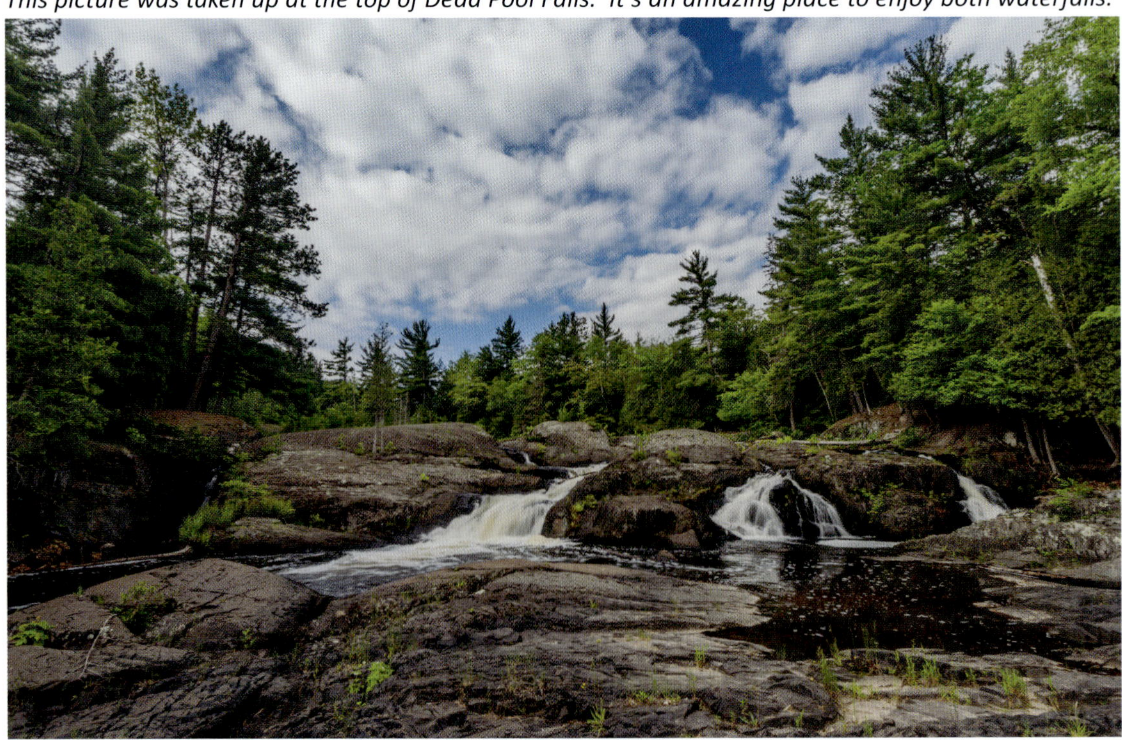

DEAD HOOK FALLS (DEAD RIVER)

Private 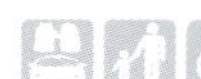 

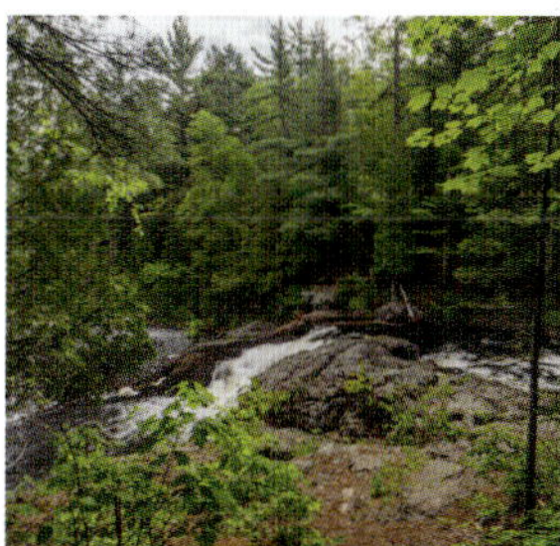

Must See:	6	GPS:	N46 34.039 W87 28.719
Height:	10 feet		
Time:	50-75 minutes	Hiking Information	
		Path:	Footpath
Driving Information		Length:	.44 miles
Signs:	None	Elev. Change:	Moderate
Road:	Secondary road	GPS:	Helpful
Access:	Somewhat difficult	Danger:	Moderate
4WD:	N/A	WP Boots:	N/A

Hike up along the river about .1 miles. Up above the waterfall the river runs along to the edge of a plateau. It angles to the right and then back hard to the left, avoiding a surprisingly hard section of black shiny bedrock. As it “hooks” around the bedrock it cascades, building to a final frothy climax as it enters a large squarish pool.

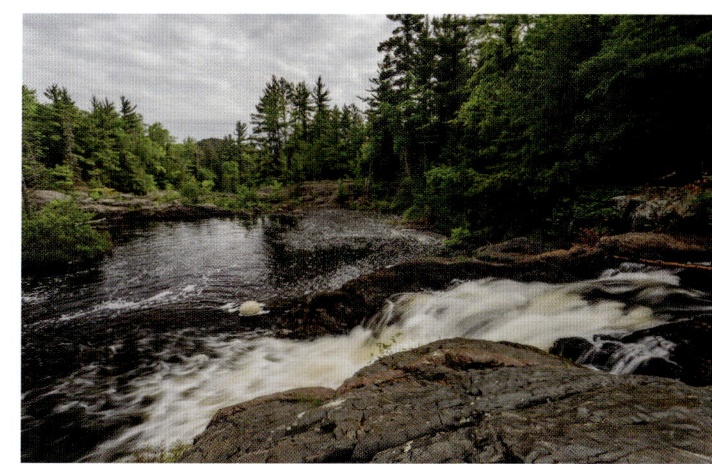

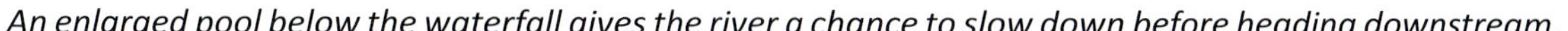

An enlarged pool below the waterfall gives the river a chance to slow down before heading downstream.

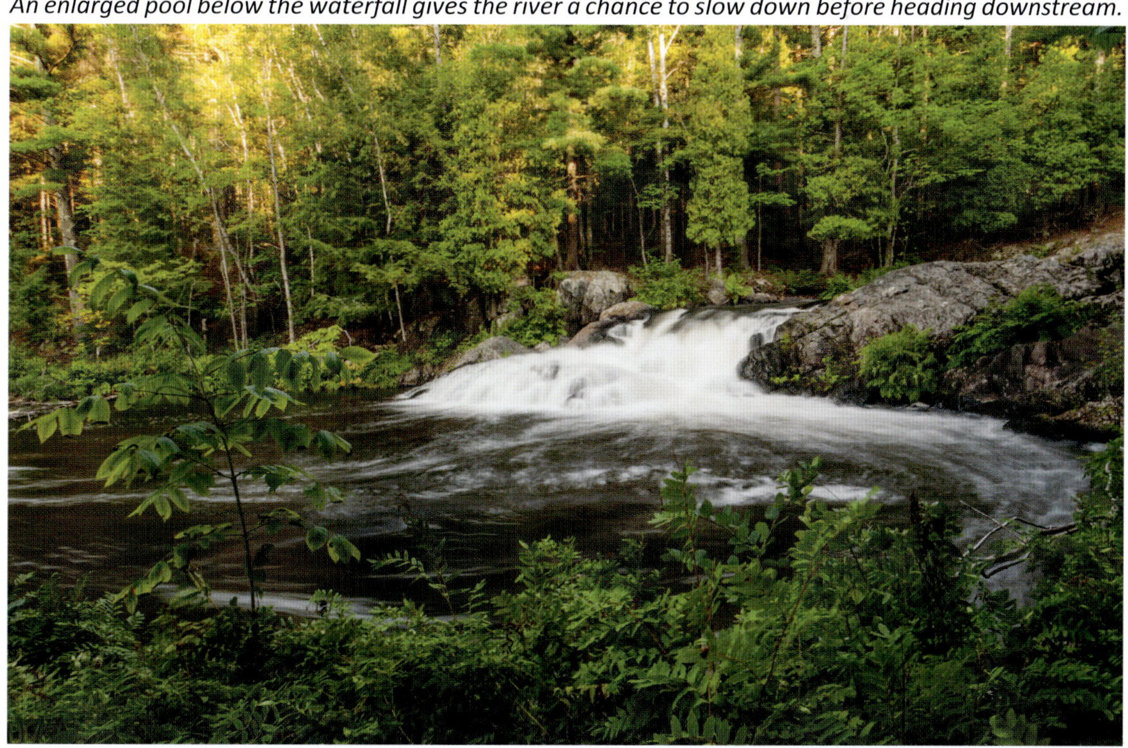

DEAD PLUNGE FALLS (DEAD RIVER)

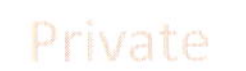 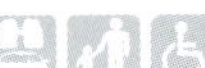  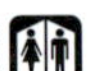

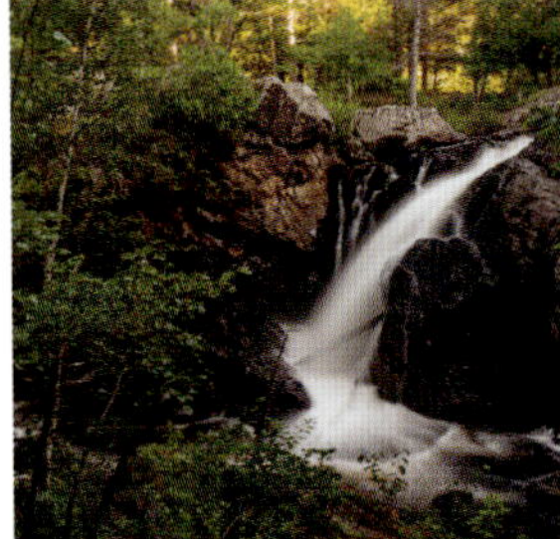

Must See:	8
Height:	20 feet
Time:	60-90 minutes

Driving Information

Signs:	None
Road:	Secondary road
Access:	Somewhat difficult
4WD:	N/A

GPS: N46 33.996 W87 28.819

Hiking Information

Path:	Footpath
Length:	.55 miles
Elev. Change:	Moderate
GPS:	Helpful
Danger:	Moderate
WP Boots:	N/A

Continue hiking .11 miles upstream. Approaching this waterfall, it looks like a beautiful waterfall that is plunging down in a very open space. What a difference there is when actually getting up close! The river courses through a narrow 3 foot wide channel, launching the water in a descending arc into a fairly narrow chasm. The perpetual spray mists the black wall and waters delicate fern and small trees that are growing along the river. It is an intimate setting with a multitude of fractured rocks scattered along the bank, perfect for sitting and contemplating.

It's amazing the difference between the front and side view of this waterfall!

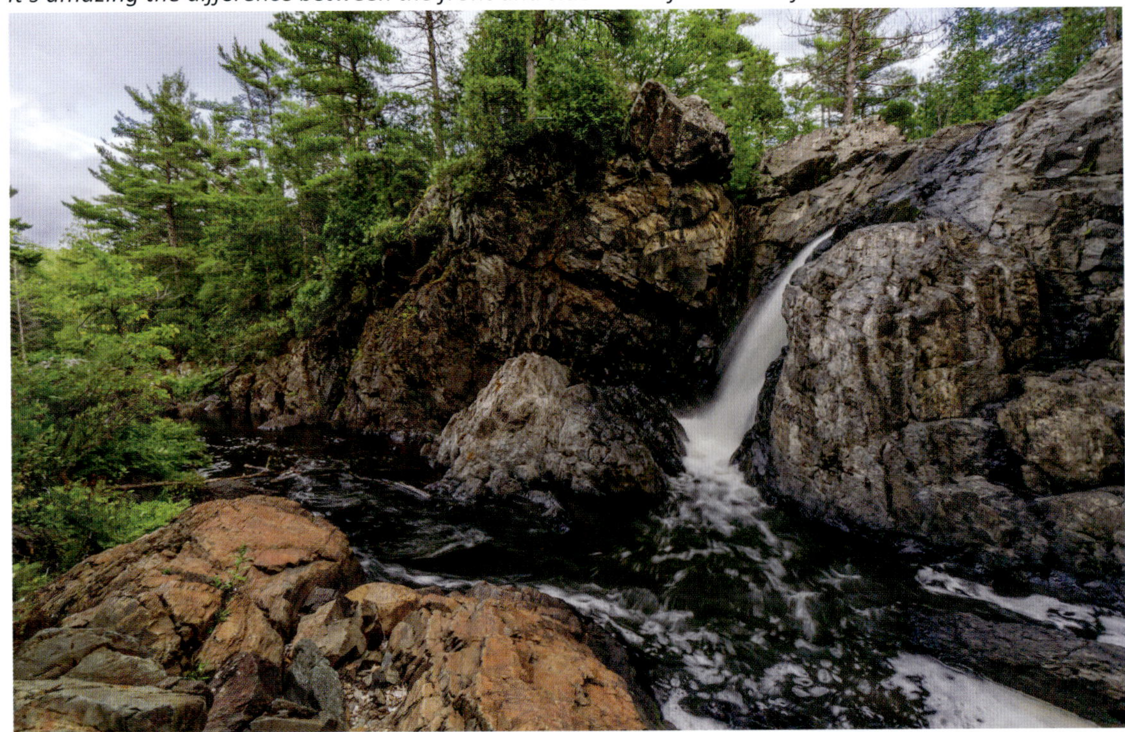

STONY MILLS FALLS - LOWER (DEAD RIVER)

Private 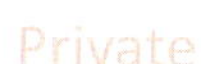 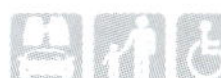 

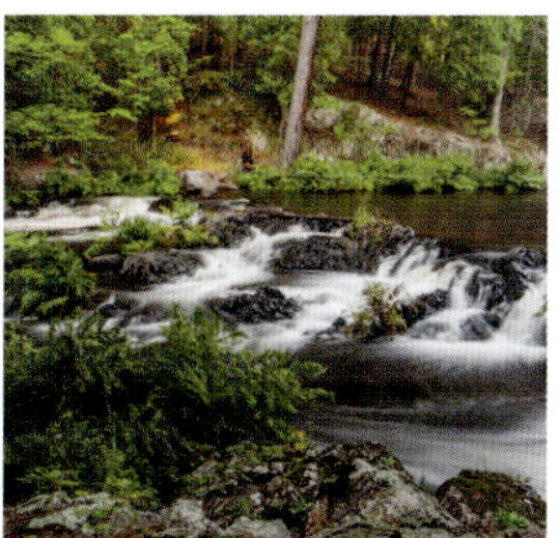

Must See:	4	GPS:	N46 33.887 W87 28.963
Height:	3 feet		
Time:	75-120 minutes	**Hiking Information**	
		Path:	Footpath
Driving Information		Length:	.80 miles
Signs:	None	Elev. Change:	Moderate
Road:	Secondary road	GPS:	Helpful
Access:	Somewhat difficult	Danger:	Moderate
4WD:	N/A	WP Boots:	N/A

Continue to hike .25 miles from Dead Plunge Falls, passing around a good sized pond until once again finding waterfall conducive terrain.

When the river is flowing well, fingers of rock send ribbons of white pouring downstream and over a patch of rapids.

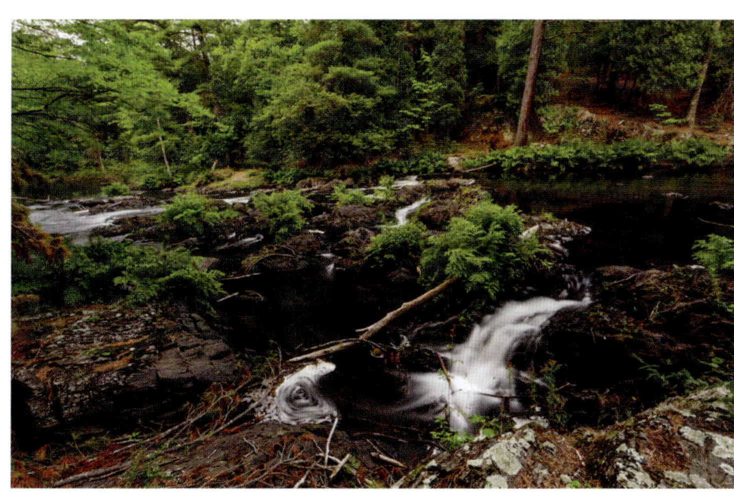

This is a nice spot to stop for a minute after a longer hike from the last waterfall

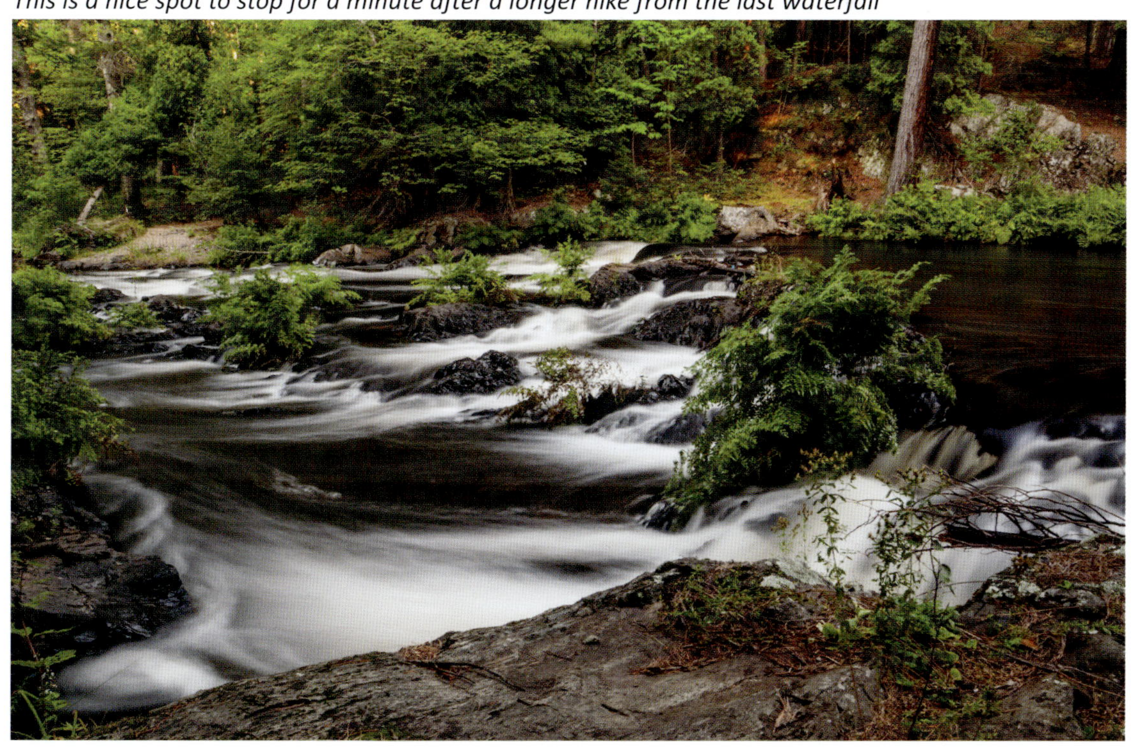

STONY MILLS FALLS (DEAD RIVER)

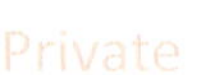

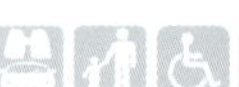

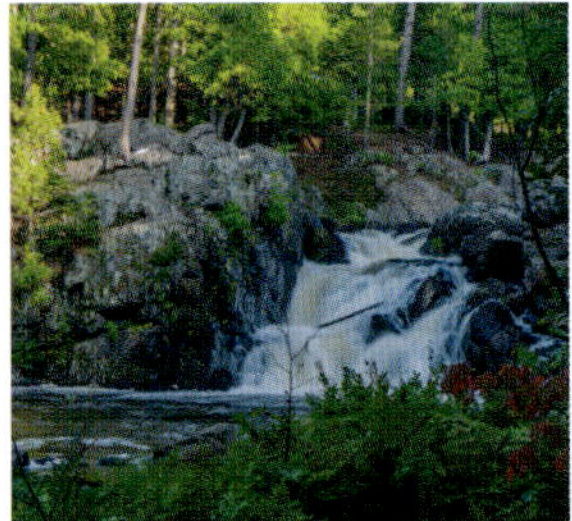

Must See:	8	GPS:	N46 33.839 W87 28.914
Height:	15 feet		
Time:	80-120 minutes	**Hiking Information**	
		Path:	Footpath
Driving Information		Length:	.84 miles
Signs:	None	Elev. Change:	Moderate
Road:	Secondary road	GPS:	Helpful
Access:	Somewhat difficult	Danger:	Moderate
4WD:	N/A	WP Boots:	N/A

Hike another .1 miles upstream. Here you'll find another locally favorite waterfall! It is a great cascading waterfall with a wall of rock on the left and piles of boulders on the right. Local youth dive into the spill pool from the bluff on the left of the falls. There is a way to get to this end of the Dead River without walking so far, but it involves riding an ORV or ATV along power lines and 2-tracks. There is also a way to drive to the far side of the river, coming out at Stony Mills Falls, but I have not been there yet.

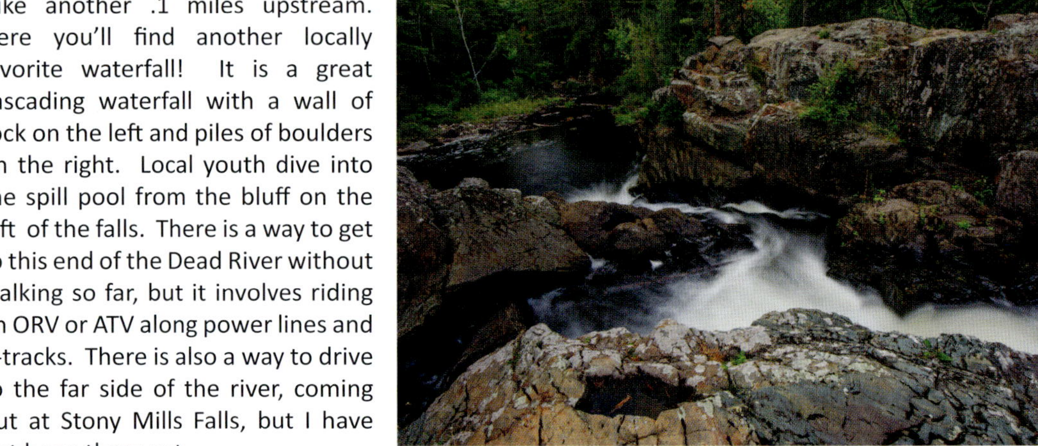

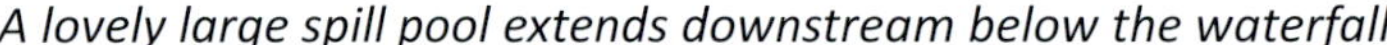
A lovely large spill pool extends downstream below the waterfall

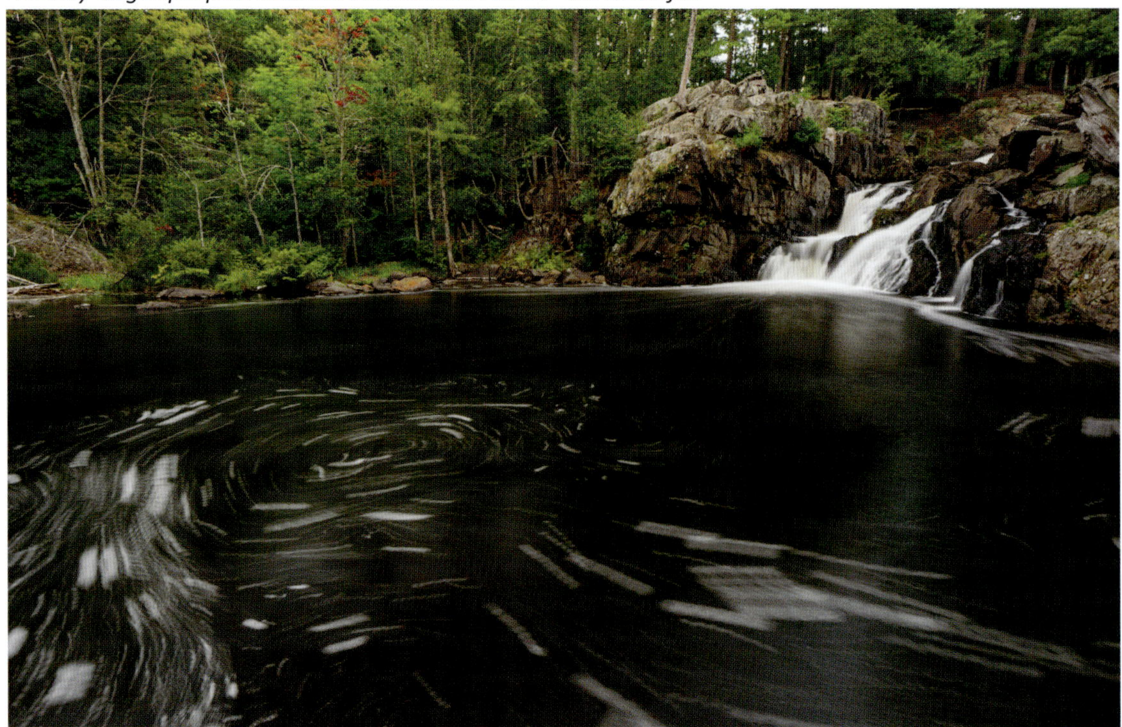

STONY MILLS FALLS - UPPER (DEAD RIVER)

Private 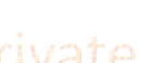 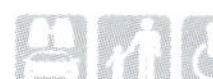 

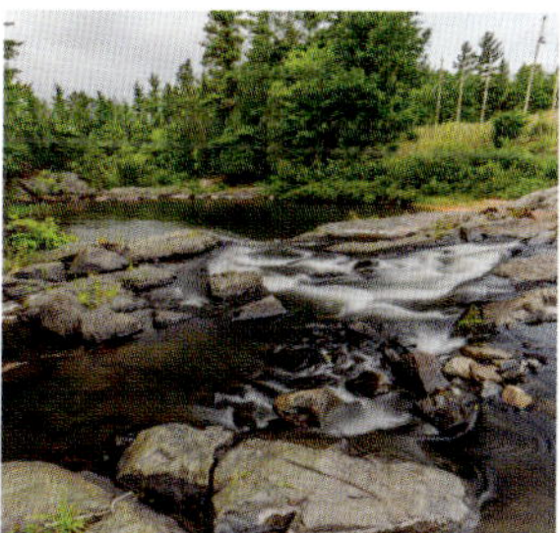

Must See:	5	GPS:	N46 33.808 W87 28.899
Height:	4 feet		
Time:	85-120 minutes	Hiking Information	
		Path:	Footpath
Driving Information		Length:	.89 miles
Signs:	None	Elev. Change:	Moderate
Road:	Secondary road	GPS:	Helpful
Access:	Somewhat difficult	Danger:	Moderate
4WD:	N/A	WP Boots:	N/A

The upper falls are about 200 feet up river from Stony Mills Falls. Here, water pours around rocky masses sticking up out of the river.

I was fortunate to meet a very helpful family on one of my trips to Marquette while looking for another waterfall in the area. Shane Miller, a young lad at the time, guided me via a back way to the Dead River and showed me the Stony Mills Falls. Thanks, Shane!

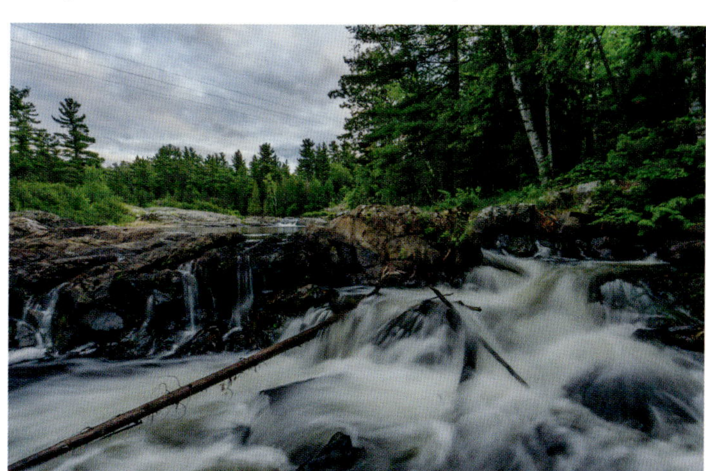

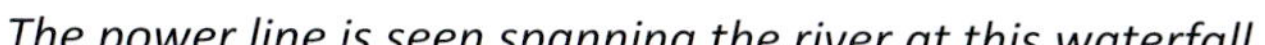

The power line is seen spanning the river at this waterfall

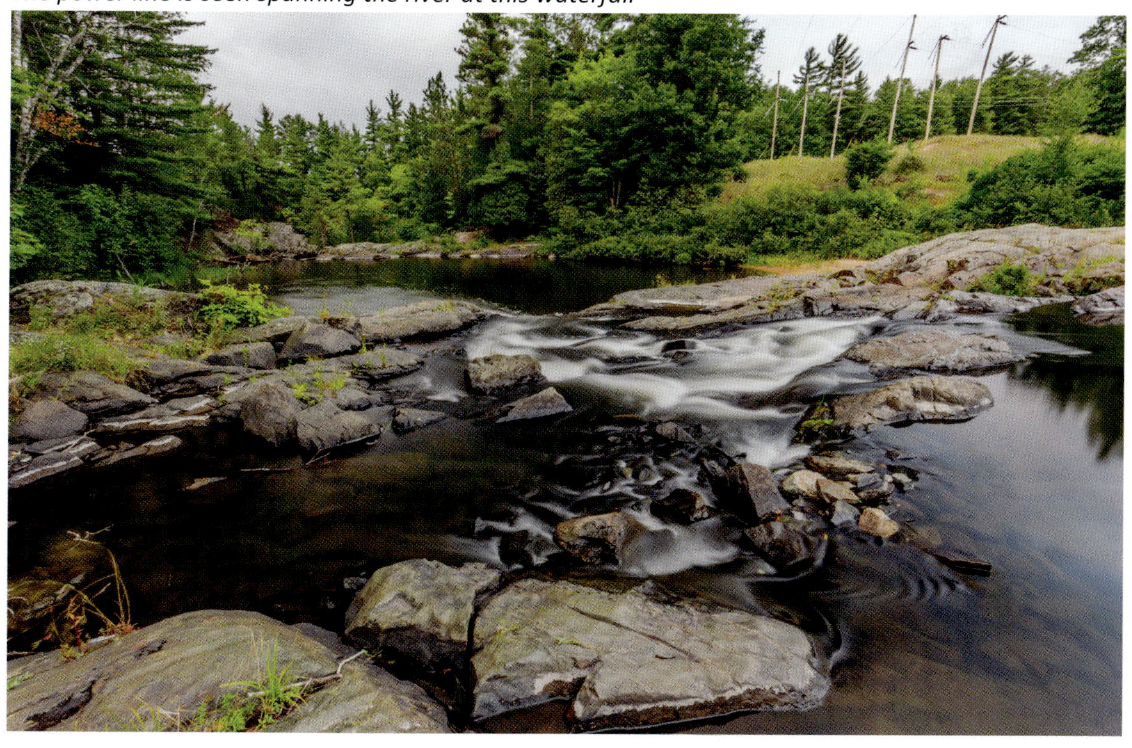

Lower Dead River Falls Hike

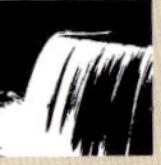

The Lower Dead River Falls are on the outskirts of Marquette. Wright Street runs around the west and north border of the city. The Dead River runs further south at one point on its journey from west to east. It is at this southern bend that it comes quite close to Wright Street. The two lower falls are located within easy walking distance of the street.

Directions: Turn north onto Wright Street (CR-492) from US-41. The Westwood Mall Shopping Center is on the northeast corner, Starbucks is on the southwest, with a Culvers to the southeast and a Quiznos on the northwest. In .51 miles turn right to stay on Wright Street. In .85 miles there is a dirt road to the left (north). Turn and park before the gate that blocks the road. This is an access road for the Upper Peninsula Power Company to work on their water lines. If the gate happens to be open, DO NOT DRIVE BEYOND as it may be closed and locked at any time. Hike past the gate and across the bridge to the falls. The #2 falls are to the right (east) of the bridge and the #1 falls are to the left (west) by a bridge that spans the river right at the base of the falls.

DEAD RIVER FALLS - LOWER #1 (DEAD RIVER)

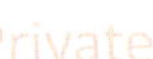

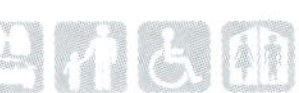

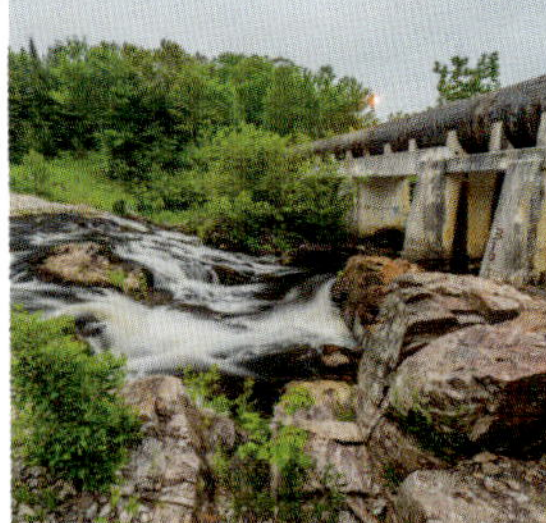

Must See: 6
Height: 18 feet
Time: 10-15 minutes

Driving Information
Signs: None
Road: Secondary road
Access: Easy
4WD: N/A

GPS: N46 33.946 W87 26.724

Hiking Information
Path: N/A
Length: 150 yards
Elev. Change: Moderate
GPS: N/A
Danger: Slight
WP Boots: Helpful

The #1 falls are comprised of three main drops spread over 75 yards. At the top of the waterfall, the river widens out and cascades down 5 feet. It then gathers itself together, passes below the concrete bridge, cascades down another 4 feet, flows alongside the base of a rocky cliff and then drops another 4 feet before turning and heading downstream to the #2 falls.

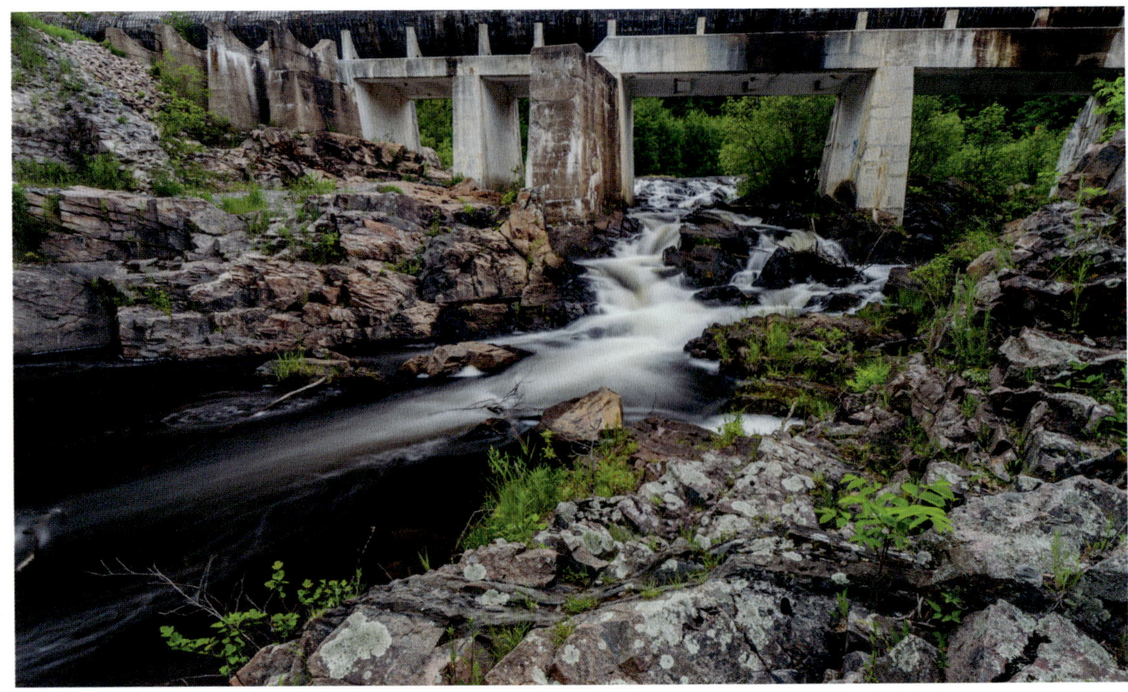

DEAD RIVER FALLS - LOWER #2 (DEAD RIVER)

Private 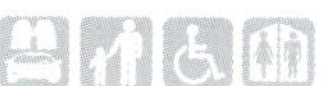

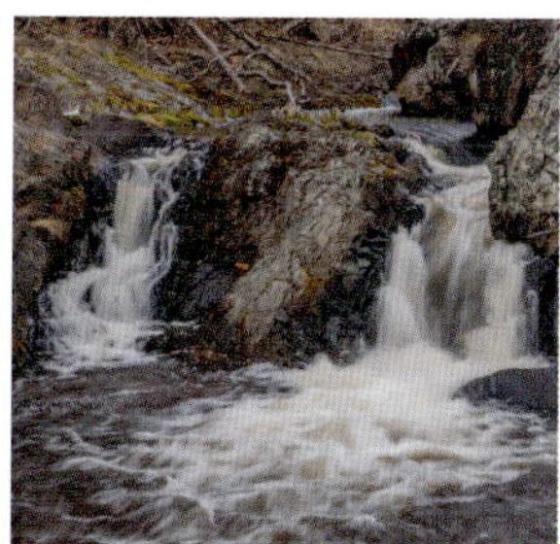

Must See:	5	GPS:	N46 33.933 W87 26.619
Height:	6 feet		
Time:	10-15 minutes	**Hiking Information**	
		Path:	N/A
Driving Information		Length:	100 yards
Signs:	None	Elev. Change:	Moderate
Road:	Secondary road	GPS:	N/A
Access:	Easy	Danger:	Slight
4WD:	N/A	WP Boots:	Helpful

Follow the far side of the river downstream. Climb down the rocky, craggy bank to the river's edge. The 6 foot drop splits around a 30 foot wide island in the middle of the river with several trees growing on it. The bridge over the river can be seen in the distance behind the falls. Be sure to walk down the 2-track (it parallels the river) far enough to get past the most inhospitable area of undergrowth and downed trees before cutting cross country down to the river.

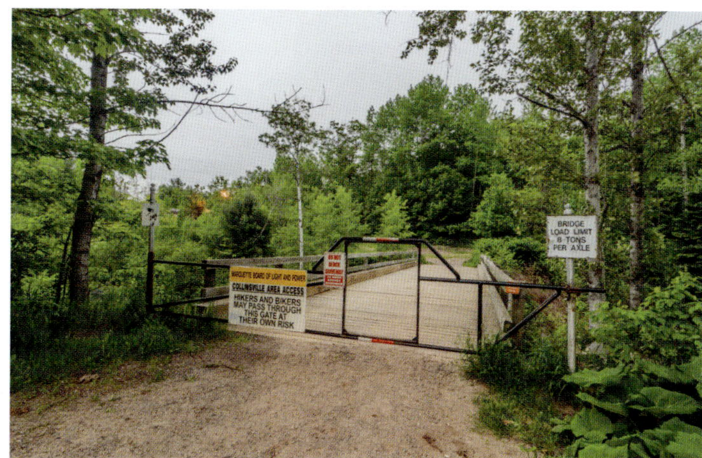

Park by the bridge seen in these shots

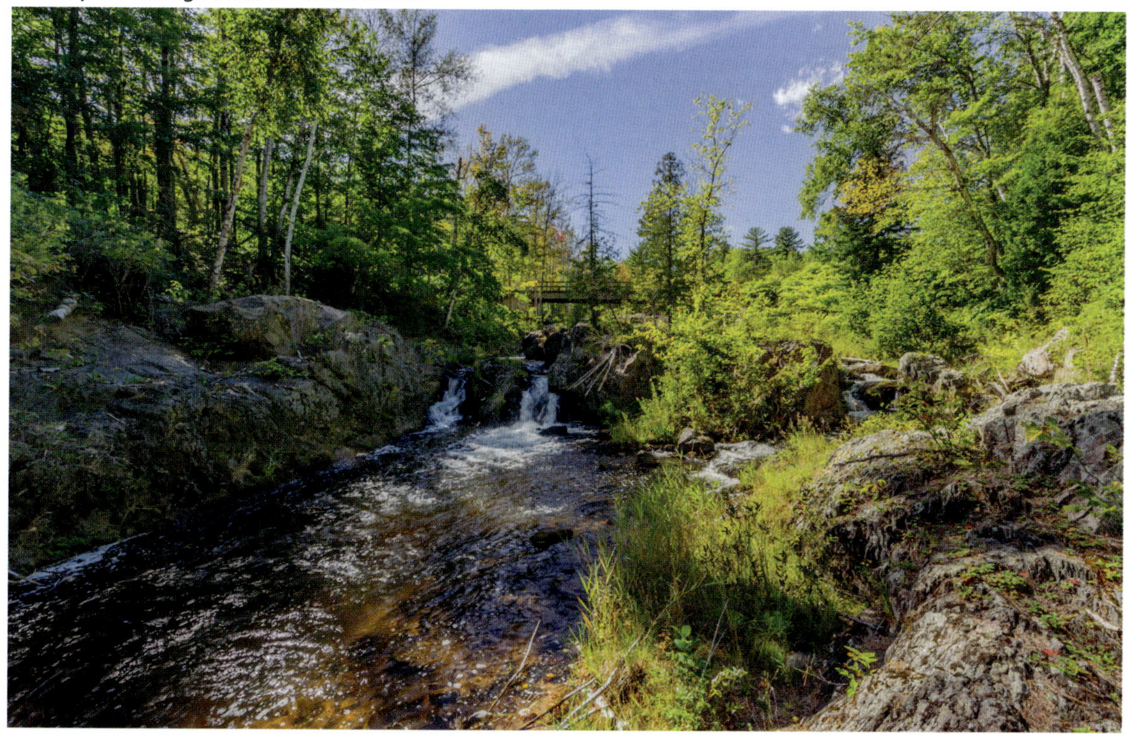

Reany Falls Hike

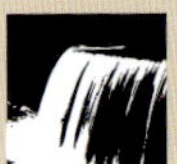

Reany Falls are located on Reany Creek just north of the parking lot for the Dead River Falls. They are very easily accessed and the typically viewed drop (Reany Falls #2) is a small, but nicely presented waterfall.

Directions: Turn north onto Wright Street (CR-492) from US-41. The Westwood Mall Shopping Center is on the northeast corner, Starbucks is on the southwest, with a Culvers to the southeast and a Quiznos on the northwest. In .51 miles turn right to stay on Wright Street. In .11 miles turn left (northwest) onto Forestville Road. After about 1 mile the road makes several sharp bends, crossing the Dead River on an old bridge. From Wright Street to the end of the road is 2.2 miles. The road ends at a parking lot not far from a hydroelectric power plant. Park. Hike 100 yards back up the road until reaching the creek that flows beneath the road. The "main" Reany Falls (#2) is 50 feet to the left (west) of the road. Continue another 100 yards up river to #3 and the #4 falls are another 50 yards upstream at the base of a steep bank. The #1 waterfall is best seen by crossing the road to the east, climbing down the hill and viewing the falls from below the road.

REANY FALLS #1 (REANY CREEK)

Private 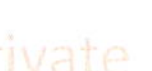 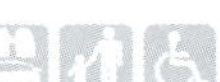 

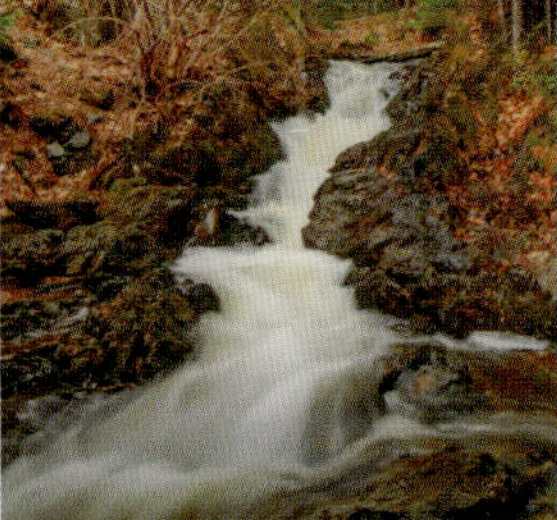

Must See:	6	GPS:	N46 34.418 W87 28.600
Height:	18 feet		
Time:	10-15 minutes	Hiking Information	
		Path:	N/A
Driving Information		Length:	50 yards
Signs:	None	Elev. Change:	Moderate
Road:	Secondary road	GPS:	N/A
Access:	Somewhat difficult	Danger:	Slight
4WD:	N/A	WP Boots:	Helpful

The best way to view this is to climb down to the creek level from the road on the downstream side of the bridge. Wade back up the creek and under the bridge to see the falls. A narrow trough funnels the creek down to the bridge. The creek flattens out below the bridge and then drops another 3 feet as the creek leaves the far side of the bridge.

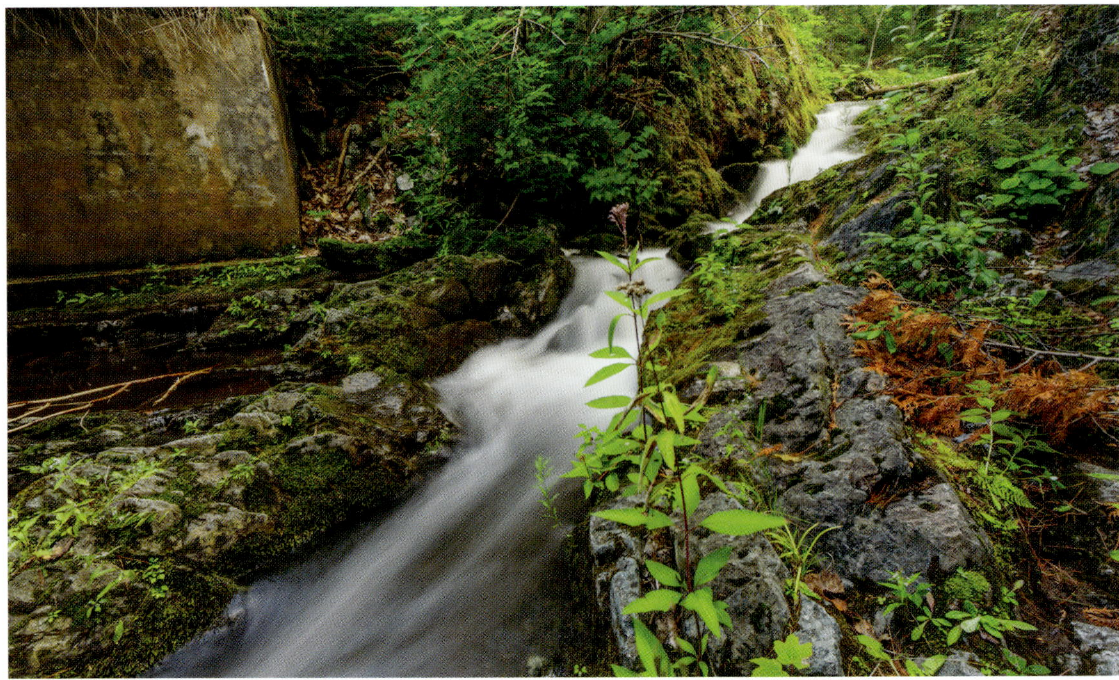

REANY FALLS #2 (REANY CREEK)

Private 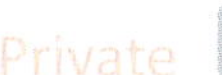  

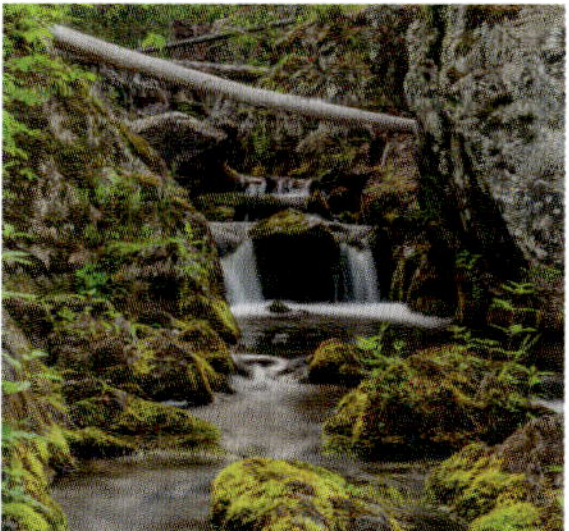

Must See:	6	GPS:	N46 34.412 W87 28.615
Height:	9 feet		
Time:	10-15 minutes	Hiking Information	
		Path:	N/A
Driving Information		Length:	50 yards
Signs:	None	Elev. Change:	Moderate
Road:	Secondary road	GPS:	N/A
Access:	Somewhat difficult	Danger:	Slight
4WD:	N/A	WP Boots:	Helpful

This is the easiest and the most obvious-to-view of the Reany Falls. Moss and lichen covered bedrock is thrust up in a vertical wall 10 feet high on the far side of the creek. A nice three split drop over a nearly hidden mass in the center of the creek is the culmination of three drops in a 100 foot stretch in the creek. Each drop is about 3 feet high for a total of 9 feet.

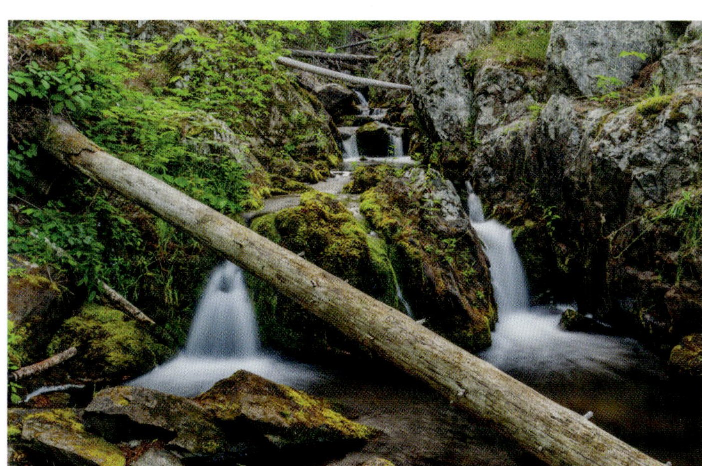

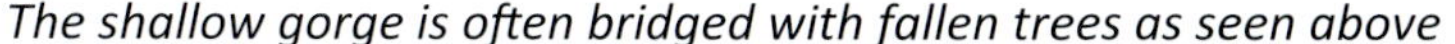

The shallow gorge is often bridged with fallen trees as seen above

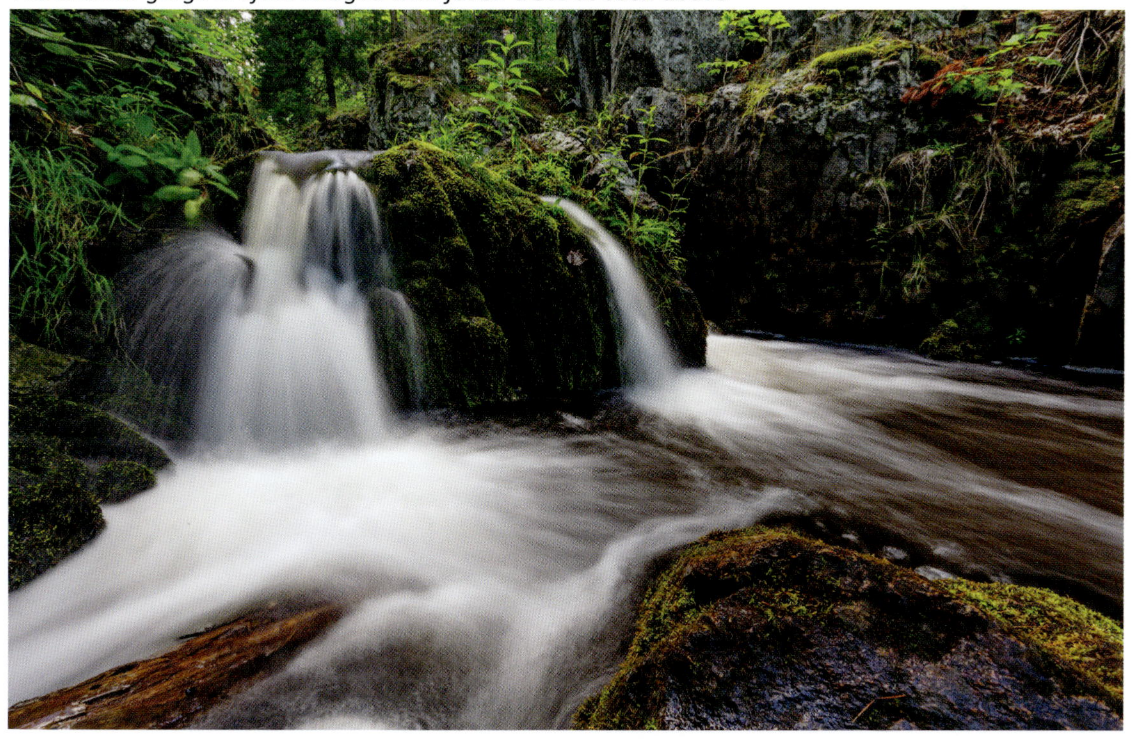

REANY FALLS #3 (REANY CREEK)

Private 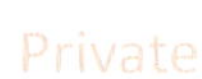  

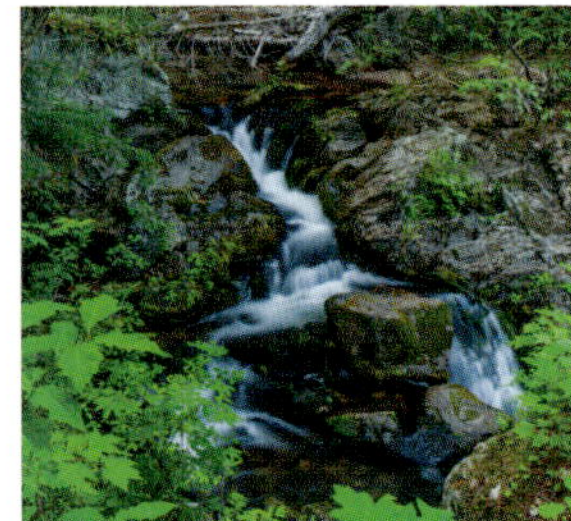

Must See:	6	GPS:	N46 34.414 W87 28.645
Height:	6 feet		
Time:	10-30 minutes	**Hiking Information**	
		Path:	N/A
Driving Information		Length:	100 yards
Signs:	None	Elev. Change:	Moderate
Road:	Secondary road	GPS:	N/A
Access:	Somewhat difficult	Danger:	Slight
4WD:	N/A	WP Boots:	Helpful

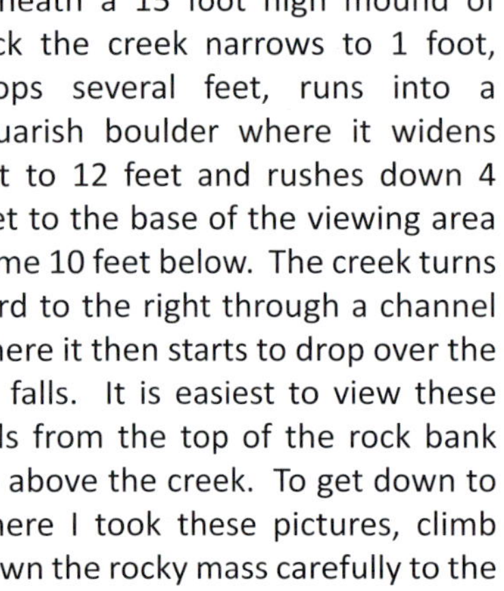

Beneath a 15 foot high mound of rock the creek narrows to 1 foot, drops several feet, runs into a squarish boulder where it widens out to 12 feet and rushes down 4 feet to the base of the viewing area some 10 feet below. The creek turns hard to the right through a channel where it then starts to drop over the #2 falls. It is easiest to view these falls from the top of the rock bank up above the creek. To get down to where I took these pictures, climb down the rocky mass carefully to the narrow ledge just above the creek.

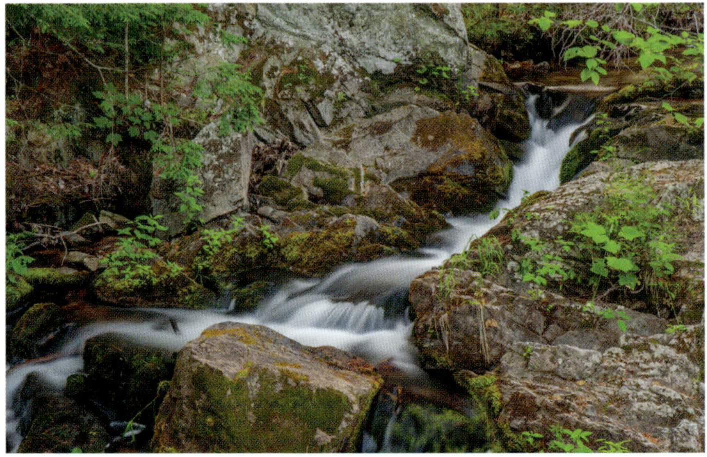

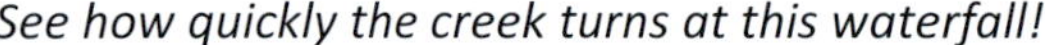

See how quickly the creek turns at this waterfall!

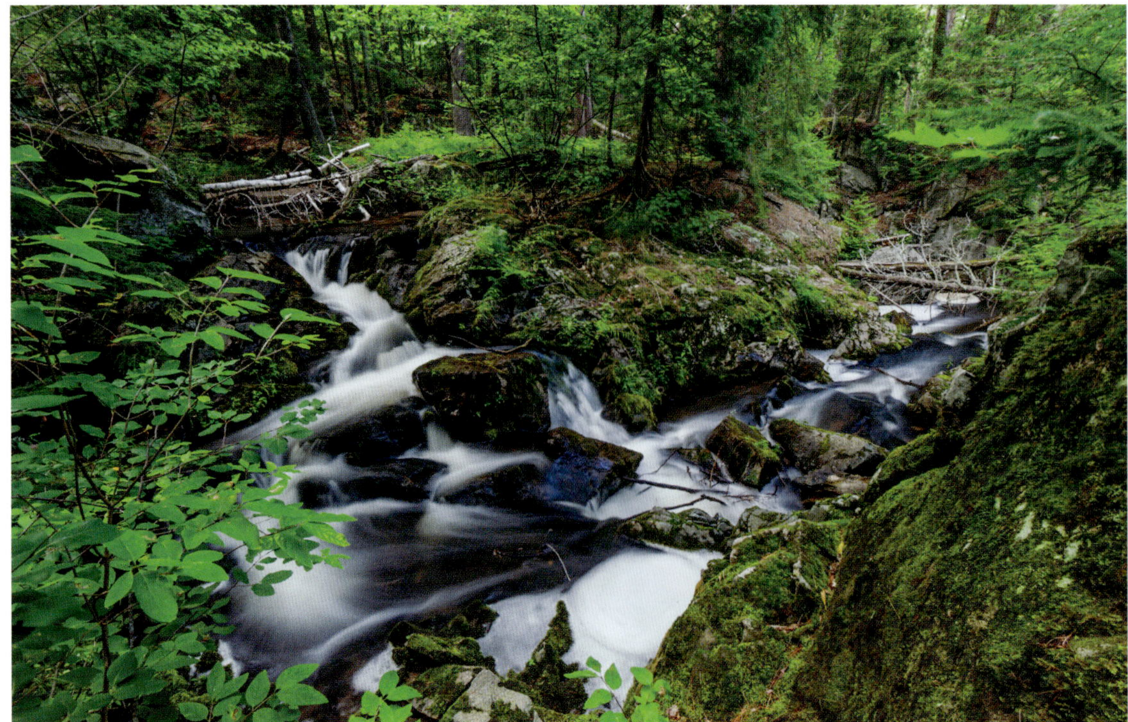

REANY FALLS #4 (REANY CREEK)

Private 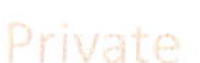 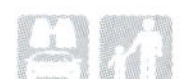 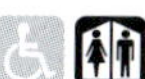 

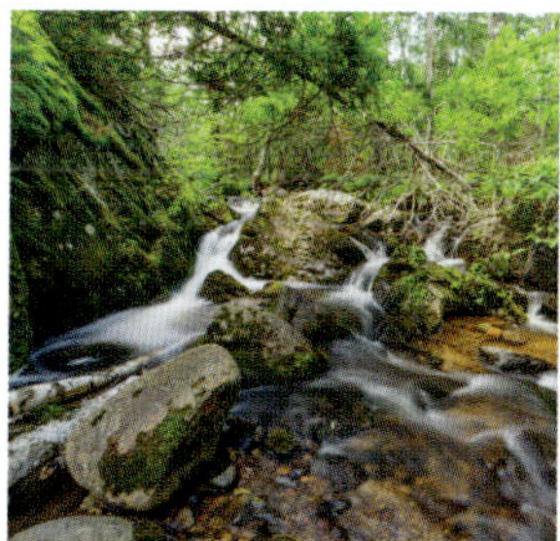

Must See:	5	GPS:	N46 34.422 W87 28.660
Height:	4 feet		
Time:	20-40 minutes	Hiking Information	
		Path:	N/A
Driving Information		Length:	150 yards
Signs:	None	Elev. Change:	Moderate
Road:	Secondary road	GPS:	N/A
Access:	Somewhat difficult	Danger:	Slight
4WD:	N/A	WP Boots:	Helpful

Just above the #3 falls, a gravel filled area in the creek affords a great place to view the last of the Reany Falls. Steep 10 foot high walls on either side of the creek add character to the 4 foot drop that falls around a mass of rock that's centered in the creek. A smaller cedar tree has fallen directly over the cascading falls. Although it is still alive, there are many dead branches hanging down close to the creek.

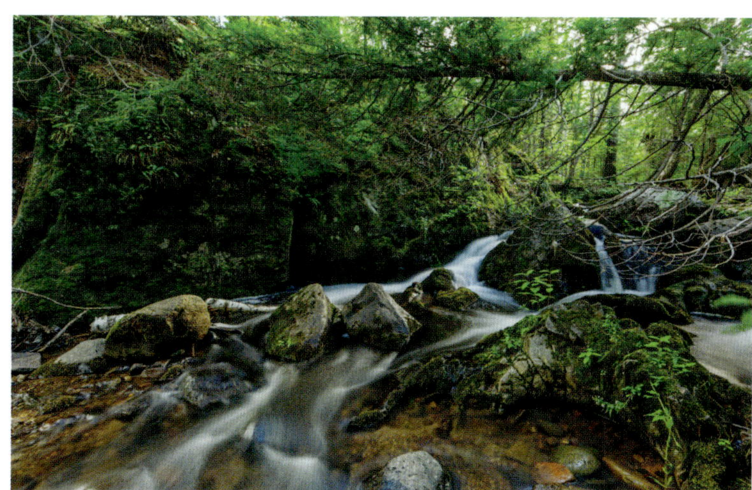

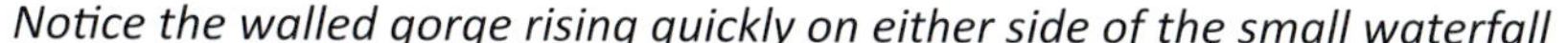

Notice the walled gorge rising quickly on either side of the small waterfall

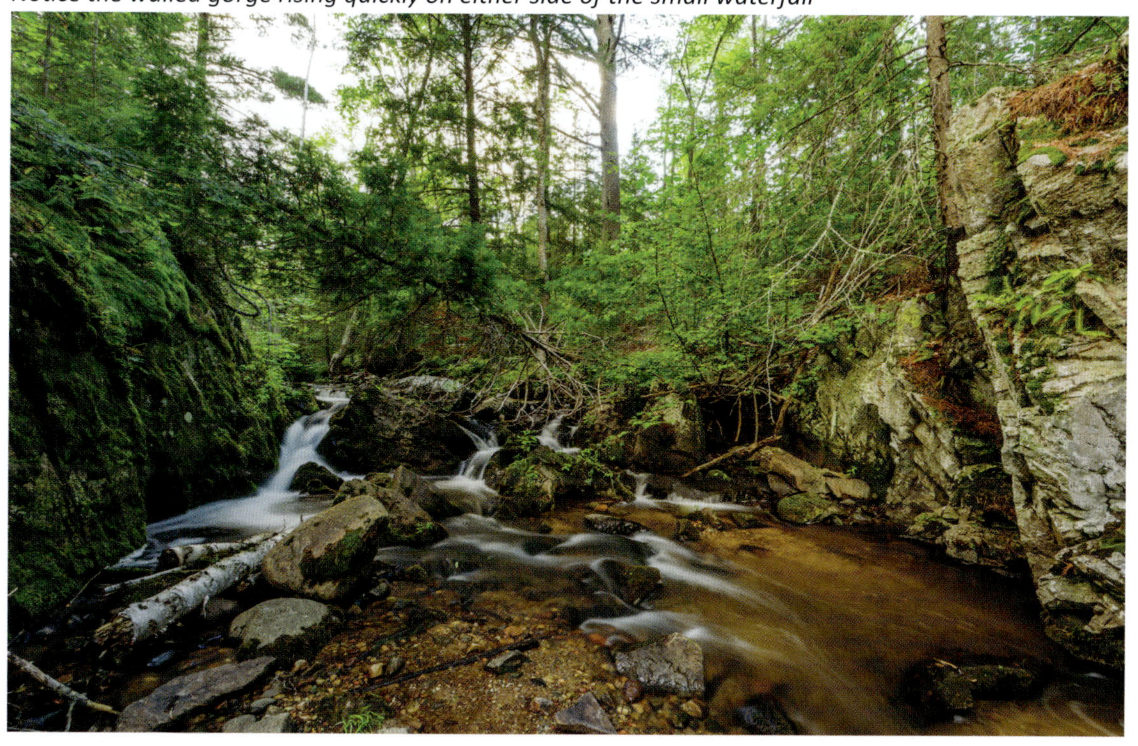

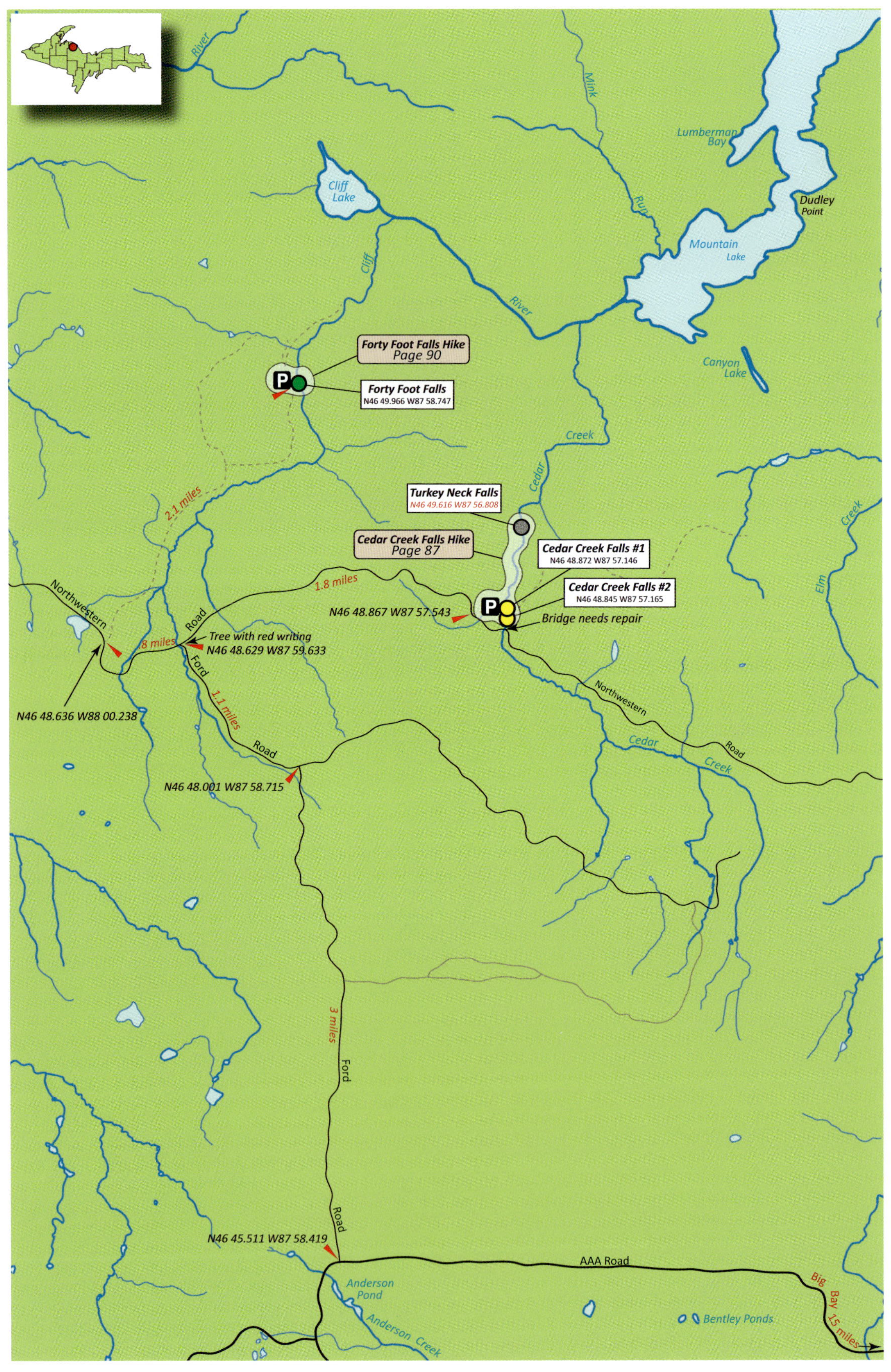

River
Mink
Run
Lumberman Bay
Dudley Point
Cliff Lake
Cliff
River
Mountain Lake
Canyon Lake
Forty Foot Falls Hike
Page 90
Forty Foot Falls
N46 49.966 W87 58.747
Creek
Cedar
Turkey Neck Falls
N46 49.616 W87 56.808
Cedar Creek Falls Hike
Page 87
Cedar Creek Falls #1
N46 48.872 W87 57.146
Cedar Creek Falls #2
N46 48.845 W87 57.165
Bridge needs repair
2.1 miles
1.8 miles
N46 48.867 W87 57.543
Northwestern
Road
.8 miles
Tree with red writing
N46 48.629 W87 59.633
N46 48.636 W88 00.238
Ford
1.1 miles
Road
N46 48.001 W87 58.715
Northwestern
Road
Cedar
Creek
Creek
Elm
3 miles
Ford
Road
N46 45.511 W87 58.419
AAA Road
Anderson Pond
Anderson Creek
Bentley Ponds
Big Bay 15 miles

Cedar Creek Falls Hike

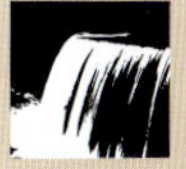

I have had many interesting adventures while looking for waterfalls. Looking for Turkey Neck Falls in the Huron Mountains was one of them. The bridge over Cedar Creek on Northwestern Road in 2010 was missing many of its planks, so it required lining up the tires of the Ranger on existing boards to keep from plunging into the creek below. Just past the creek is a 2-track to the north. I turned on the 2-track, excited to see that it seemed to be heading directly toward the GPS location that I hoped was accurate for the falls. After just a short distance, however, the 2-track came to an end and all-too-familiar wire and postings marked the land beyond as Huron Mountain Club property. Interestingly, from that boundary line the creek was visible down below and there was a small waterfall. I couldn't get a good shot of the falls without trespassing, so I drove back to the road and re-crossed the sparsely planked bridge. In about .4 miles I found a 2-track that cut back toward the creek until it died out just before the creek. I was able to get down to the base of the falls without encountering any "No Trespassing" signs on this side of the creek, but viewing the falls would obviously be MUCH better from the other side. I took some shots of the falls. Since that trip I have become fairly well convinced that it probably is a different waterfall than Turkey Neck Falls, so I named it after Cedar Creek. I need to get back to this area and see if hiking further down the creek is possible on this side and if the elusive Turkey Neck Falls can be found!

Directions: After driving west on CR-AAA for 4.7 miles past the main portion of the Eagle Mine, turn north (right) just before CR-AAA turns to the south. Follow Ford Road (not marked) north for 3 miles. Turn left to continue on Ford Road. After 1.1 miles turn right (east) onto Northwestern Road. In 1.8 miles there is a 2-track on the left (east). Follow the 2-track a couple tenths of a mile to a small clearing. Park. Climb through the undergrowth down to the creek and the falls.

TURKEY NECK FALLS (CEDAR CREEK)

Private   

Must See:	?	GPS:	N46 49.616 W87 56.808
Height:	? feet		*(Not verified)*
Time:	? minutes	Hiking Information	
		Path:	None
Driving Information		Length:	? yards
Signs:	None	Elev. Change:	?
Road:	2-track	GPS:	Recommended
Access:	Difficult	Danger:	?
4WD:	Recommended	WP Boots:	?

There are waterfalls beyond "Cedar Creek Falls" but they may be on Huron Mountain Club property. Their property is marked on the east side of the creek. Obey all "Do Not Trespass" signs.

CEDAR CREEK FALLS #1 (CEDAR CREEK)

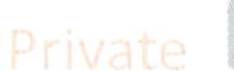

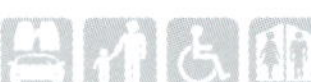

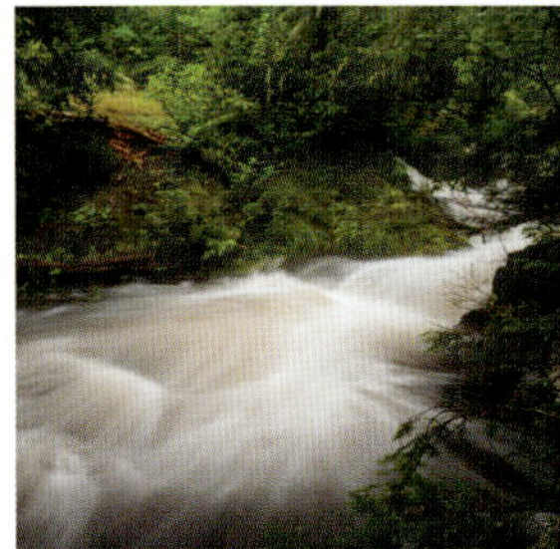

Must See:	6	GPS:	N46 48.872 W87 57.146
Height:	10 feet		
Time:	15-30 minutes	Hiking Information	
		Path:	None
Driving Information		Length:	100 yards
Signs:	None	Elev. Change:	Moderate
Road:	2-track	GPS:	Recommended
Access:	Difficult	Danger:	Moderate
4WD:	Recommended	WP Boots:	Helpful

The creek narrows and zigzags back and forth through the falls that can't be viewed from the Huron Mountain Club side. Climb down through the undergrowth and pine branches to the creek. There is very little footing along the creek for good viewing of the falls. It really does present itself better on the other side.

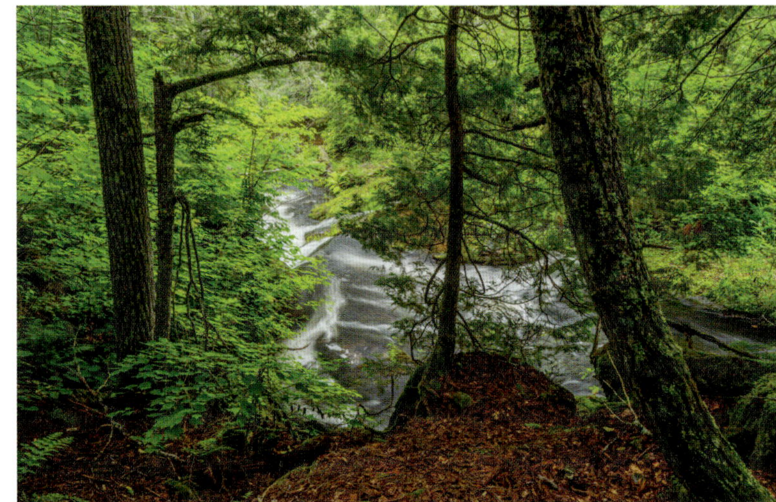

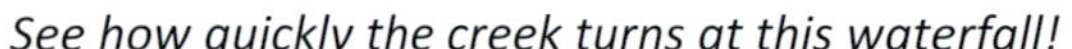

See how quickly the creek turns at this waterfall!

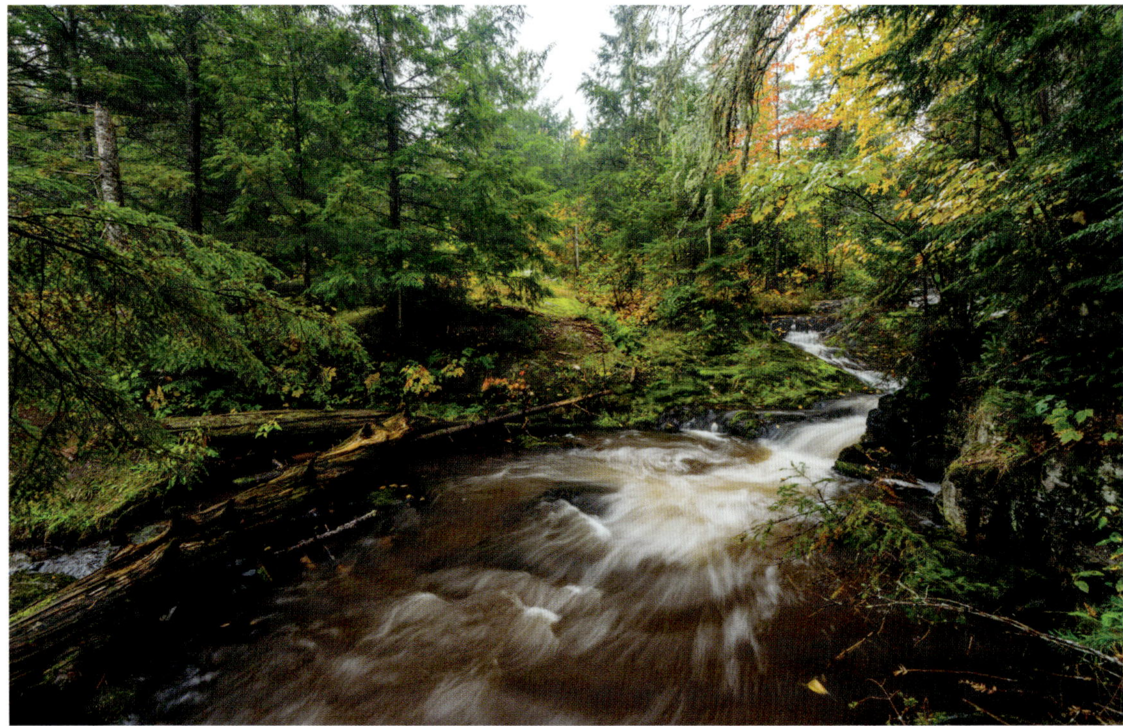

CEDAR CREEK FALLS #2 (CEDAR CREEK)

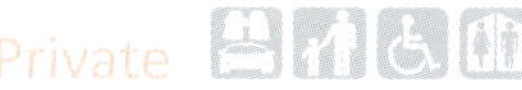

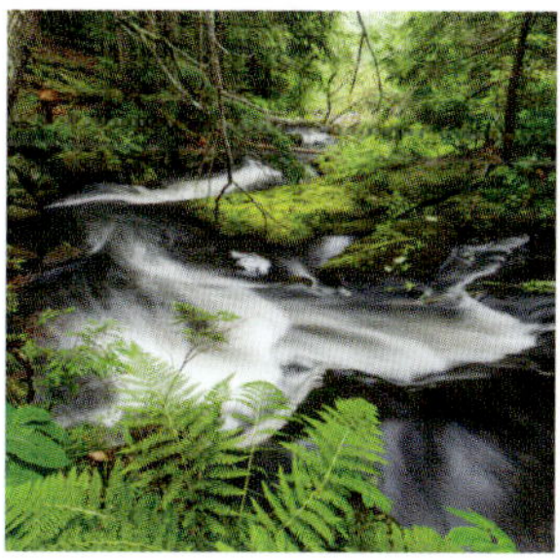

Must See:	4	GPS:	N46 48.845 W87 57.165
Height:	5 feet		
Time:	20-40 minutes	**Hiking Information**	
		Path:	None
Driving Information		Length:	165 yards
Signs:	None	Elev. Change:	Moderate
Road:	2-track	GPS:	Recommended
Access:	Difficult	Danger:	Moderate
4WD:	Recommended	WP Boots:	Helpful

Hike upstream 65 yards to this small waterfall. Above the waterfall, the creek runs placidly. It then abruptly drops in a horseshoe arc about a foot as it turns quickly about a moss encrusted rock mass. While flowing by the far side, the creek narrows, sliding down into a trough. The force of the water being turned back upon itself shoots up a rooster tail of white water.

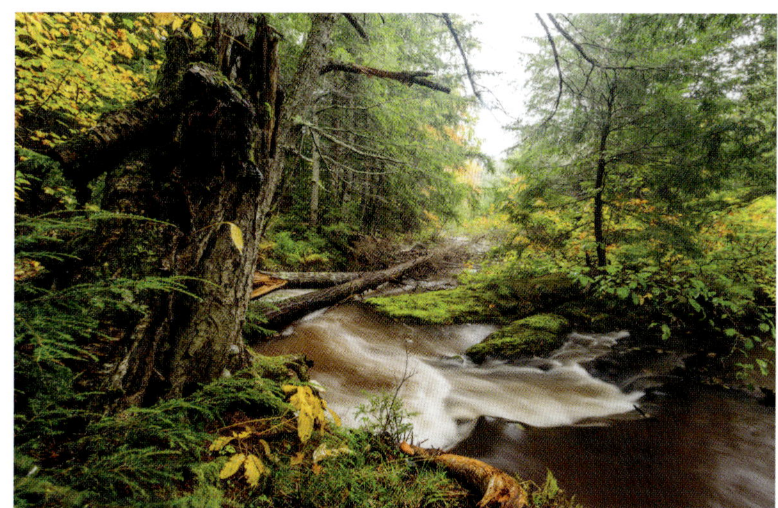

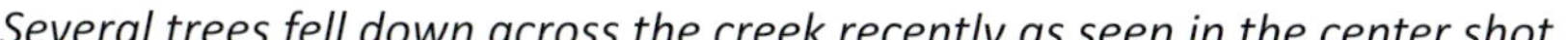

Several trees fell down across the creek recently as seen in the center shot

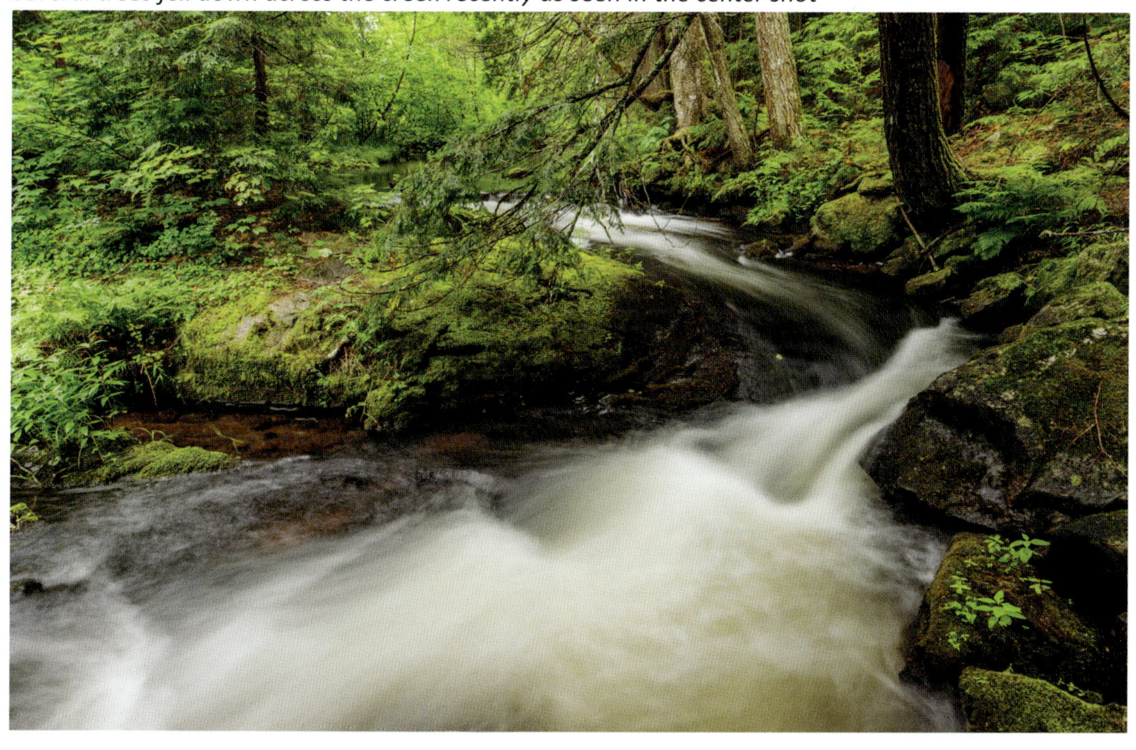

MARQUETTE COUNTY

Forty Foot Falls Hike

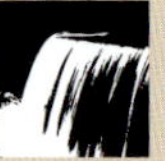

Forty Foot Falls is in the Huron Mountains. When you haven't seen a road sign for 20 miles, and the best indication of where to turn is by memorizing the number of beer cans piled at a corner or by looking for painted trees, you know that you have left civilization in the dust some time ago. The winding roads keep degenerating until you arrive near the top of the waterfall some 2 miles down a pot-holed 2-track. Don't be discouraged, however. On most days any vehicle with decent clearance should be able to get to the falls. I would recommend having a GPS unit with you in case you lose track of exactly where you are on the route. There really are NO road signs out here!

Directions: After driving west on CR-AAA for 4.7 miles past the main portion of the Eagle Mine, turn north (right) just before CR-AAA turns to the south. Follow Ford Road (not marked) north for 3 miles. Turn left to continue on Ford Road. After 1.1 miles turn left (west) onto Northwestern Road. In .8 miles there is a 2-track on the right (northeast). Follow the 2-track for 2.1 miles. Park at the small parking area near the top of the falls. The waterfall is less than 100 yards from the parking area.

FORTY FOOT FALLS (CLIFF RIVER)

Private 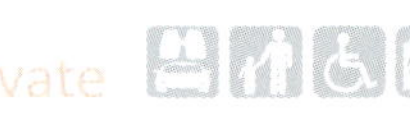

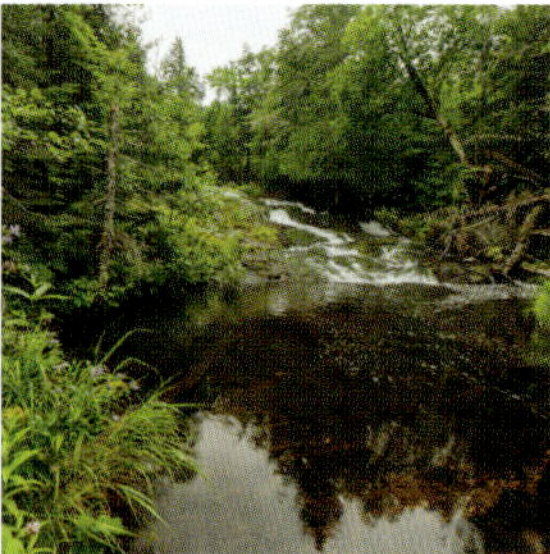

Must See: 8
Height: 40 feet
Time: 5-20 minutes

Driving Information
Signs: None
Road: 2-track
Access: Difficult
4WD: Recommended

GPS: N46 49.966 W87 58.747

Hiking Information
Path: Unimproved footpath
Length: 50 yards
Elev. Change: Slight
GPS: Recommended
Danger: Slight
WP Boots: N/A

Forty Foot Falls, or Cliff Falls, has to rank as one of my more interesting discoveries. Finding the falls right next to the 2-track was a special treat. But unexpectedly, there were assorted pots and pans hanging from the trunk of a tree near the top of the falls. A grill was also there. These were not "accidently" left there, but looked quite at home in this remote setting. My guess is that an old hunting club located not too far from the falls keeps cooking utensils for some on-the-spot eating of fish caught below the falls. Be considerate and do not touch them.

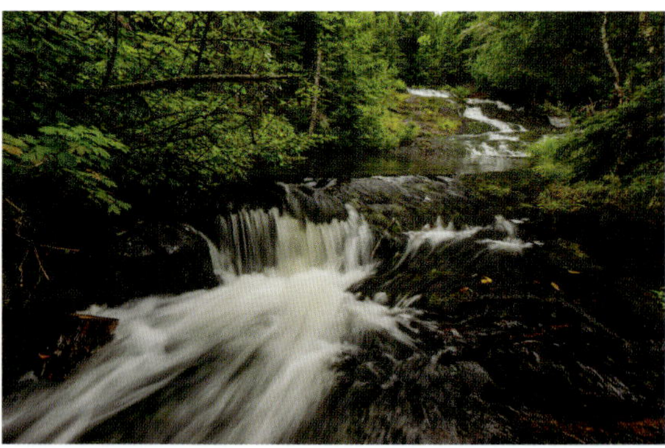

Looking down the fast running waterfall

At the base of the main cascade

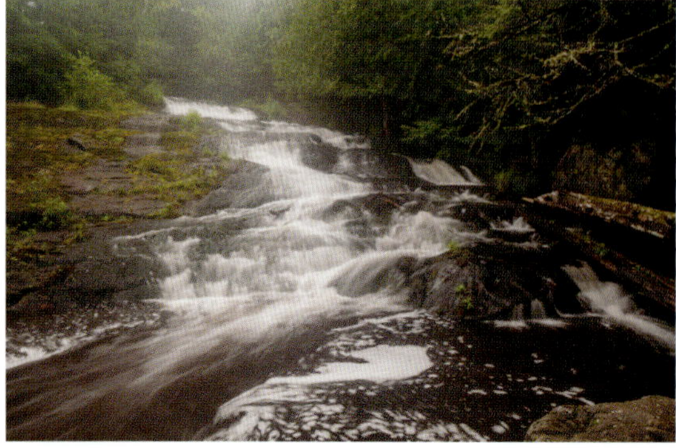

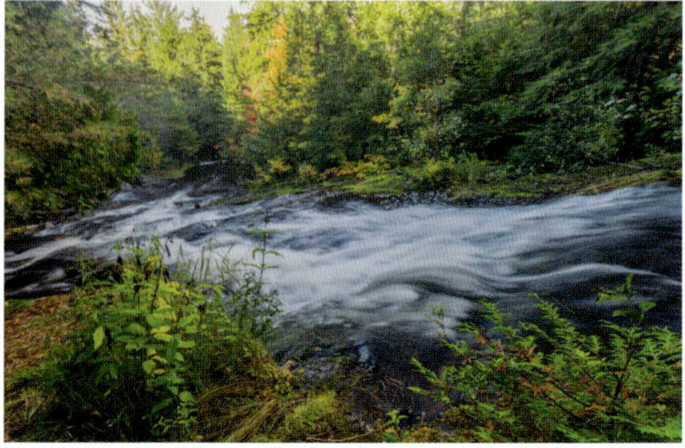

Forty Foot Falls

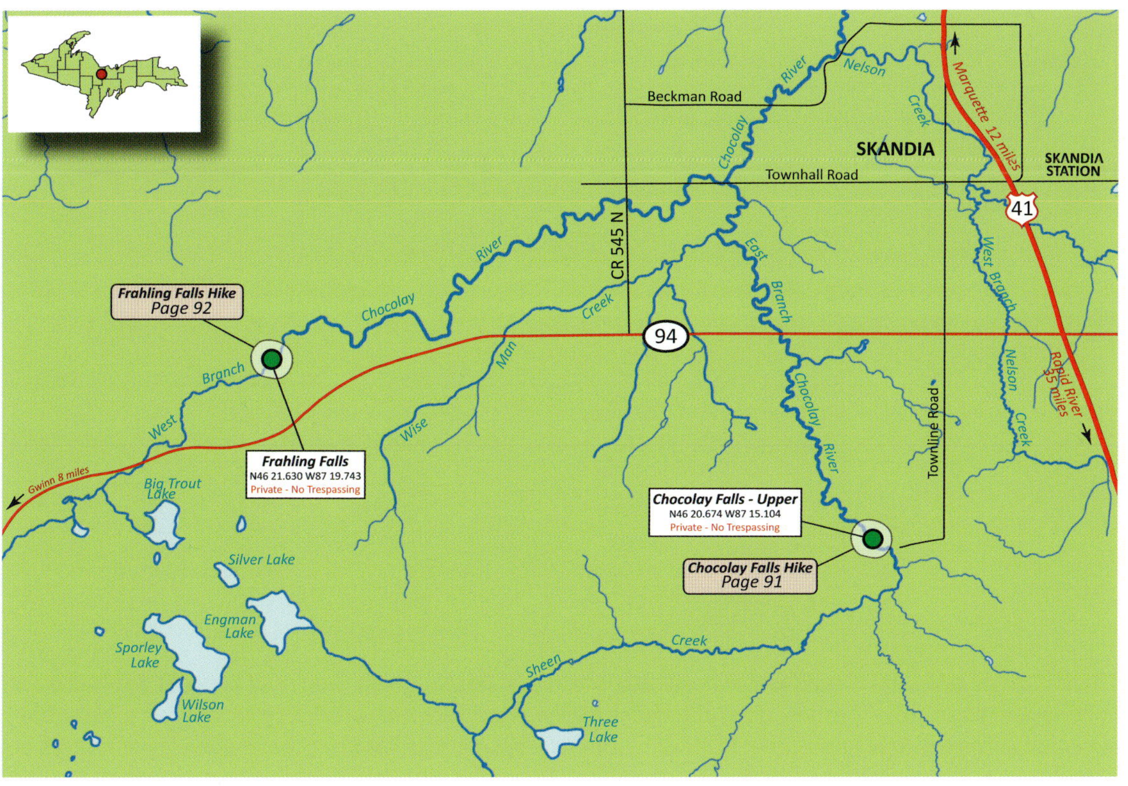

Chocolay Falls Hike

Chocolay Falls - Upper is on private property and the owner doesn't allow visitors to hike down to the falls. A bad experience with some of his cows being let loose years ago has understandably soured him toward waterfall explorers. This is a good place to remind ourselves again to be considerate and thoughtful with all the land owners that we may come in contact with.

Directions: The waterfall is on private property and not accessible.

CHOCOLAY FALLS - UPPER (EAST BRANCH CHOCOLAY RIVER) Private

Must See:	7	GPS:	N46 20.674 W87 15.104
Height:	7 feet		
Time:	N/A	**Hiking Information**	
		Path:	None
Driving Information		Length:	N/A
Signs:	None	Elev. Change:	Moderate
Road:	Secondary	GPS:	Recommended
Access:	Somewhat easy	Danger:	Moderate
4WD:	N/A	WP Boots:	Helpful

Do not attempt to get to these falls without permission. It is land locked by private property on both sides of the river.

Frahling Falls Hike

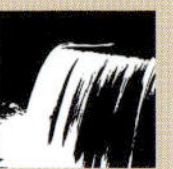

This waterfall seems to have several spellings. I have seen it listed as Frohling Falls, Frahling Falls and Froeling Falls. In 2012, I was met with signs that stated that the waterfall was on private property and no trespassing was allowed. This waterfall is now off limits.

Directions: The waterfall is on private property and not accessible.

FRAHLING FALLS (WEST BRANCH CHOCOLAY RIVER)

Private

Must See:	8	GPS:	N46 21.630 W87 19.743
Height:	35 feet		
Time:	N/A	Hiking Information	
		Path:	N/A
Driving Information		Length:	N/A
Signs:	None	Elev. Change:	Slight
Road:	2-track	GPS:	Recommended
Access:	Difficult	Danger:	Slight
4WD:	ATV needed	WP Boots:	Helpful

There is a nice spill pool to wade in. A bowl shaped area under the main drop may serve as an interesting "whirlpool" to sit in. The falls are split, most of the water flowing on the right side. It's in a quiet, secluded setting with a small "beach" area by the falls base and a flat area that can be used to park an ATV. There are remnants of a small campfire here. This is on posted private property. Do not attempt to access without permission

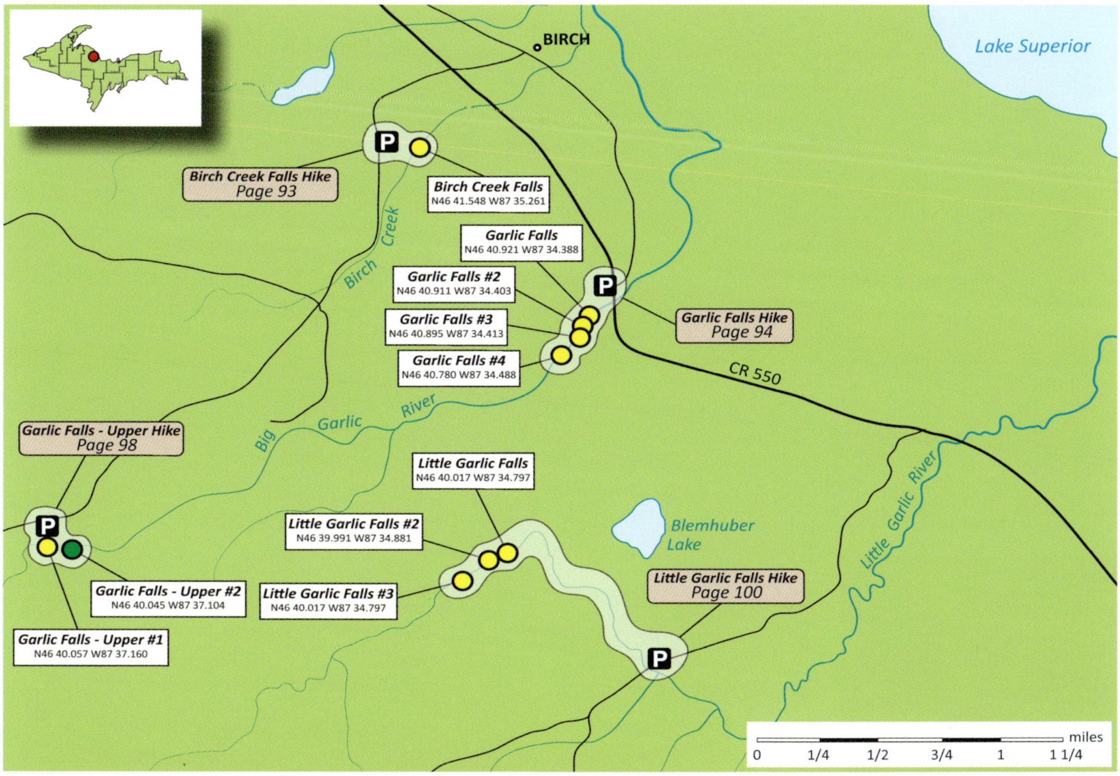

BIRCH
Lake Superior
Birch Creek Falls Hike
Page 93
Birch Creek Falls
N46 41.548 W87 35.261
Birch Creek
Garlic Falls
N46 40.921 W87 34.388
Garlic Falls #2
N46 40.911 W87 34.403
Garlic Falls #3
N46 40.895 W87 34.413
Garlic Falls #4
N46 40.780 W87 34.488
Garlic Falls Hike
Page 94
CR 550
Big Garlic River
Garlic Falls - Upper Hike
Page 98
Little Garlic Falls
N46 40.017 W87 34.797
Little Garlic Falls #2
N46 39.991 W87 34.881
Little Garlic Falls #3
N46 40.017 W87 34.797
Blemhuber Lake
Little Garlic River
Little Garlic Falls Hike
Page 100
Garlic Falls - Upper #2
N46 40.045 W87 37.104
Garlic Falls - Upper #1
N46 40.057 W87 37.160
miles
0 1/4 1/2 3/4 1 1 1/4

Birch Creek Falls Hike

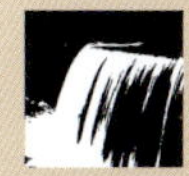

Birch Creek is a narrow, low volume creek. It does, however, have a cascading drop as the creek descends quickly through a shallow but steep canyon. The terrain is a bit rugged and the hike is best suited for those familiar with hiking cross country without the assistance of a trail. A logging operation went through here recently (the first 2/3 of the hike). Branches and stumps left behind create hiking hazards, and new undergrowth fighting for sunlight can also add difficulty to the hike.

Directions: Drive about 13 miles north of Marquette on CR-550. Turn left (west) off of CR-550 on the dirt road just past Birch Creek (N46 41.854 W87 35.077). Drive .5 miles to N46 41.618 W87 35.458. Park here. An old logging road heads to the east. It is not drivable, but a faint footpath runs down it. About halfway to the falls the footpath veers off to the right. Follow the VERY FAINT footpath. USE A GPS to get to the falls. The footpath is too faint to be a reliable guide. It is .16 miles from the parking spot to the falls.

BIRCH CREEK FALLS (BIRCH CREEK)

Private 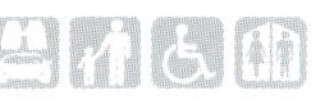

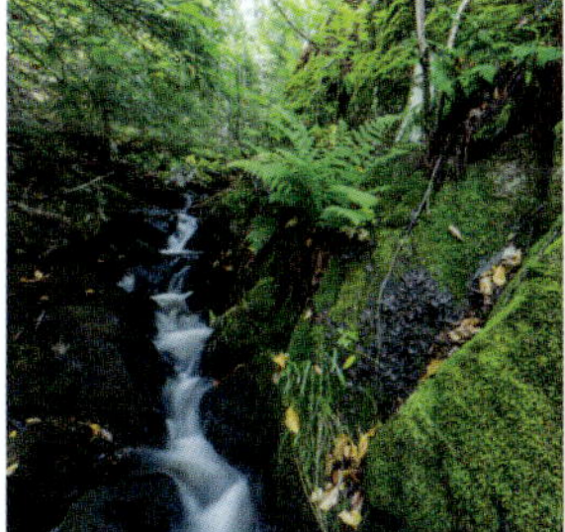

Must See:	5	GPS:	N46 41.548 W87 35.261
Height:	15 feet		
Time:	20-40 minutes	Hiking Information	
		Path:	Faint to none
Driving Information		Length:	.16 miles
Signs:	None	Elev. Change:	Moderate
Road:	Dirt	GPS:	Required
Access:	Somewhat difficult	Danger:	Moderate
4WD:	Helpful	WP Boots:	Helpful

A long, slow cascade cuts a small canyon down to a lower plateau. Lichen, moss and ferns cling to the sides of the canyon. The boulders that line the creek bed are angular and slippery. Take care if trying to walk up them!

Garlic Falls Hike

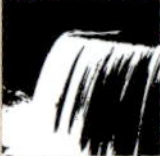

Big Garlic River runs through a swampy area between CR-550 and Lake Superior. But higher, dry ground lies just up river from the bridge. It is through this land that four waterfalls carry the Big Garlic over some interesting rock formations with my favorite being a sweeping, sliding waterfall over a sheet of bedrock.

Directions: Drive 11.5 miles on CR-550 north from Marquette to the Big Garlic River. Park safely along the roadside. Hike through waist to shoulder high grasses, goldenrod, ferns, and thimbleberries as you parallel the river on the north side, heading upstream. In about 100 yards you'll be in the forest proper, and the thick undergrowth will dwindle. The river splits into several branches and you many need to ford one or more to find the easiest route to the falls. All but the last of the falls are not easily viewed. Branches, uneven ground, and steep gorge walls make it difficult to view the falls and hike between them. The first waterfall is found in about 350 yards and the furthest is .36 miles from the bridge.

GARLIC FALLS (BIG GARLIC RIVER)

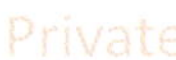

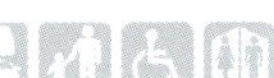

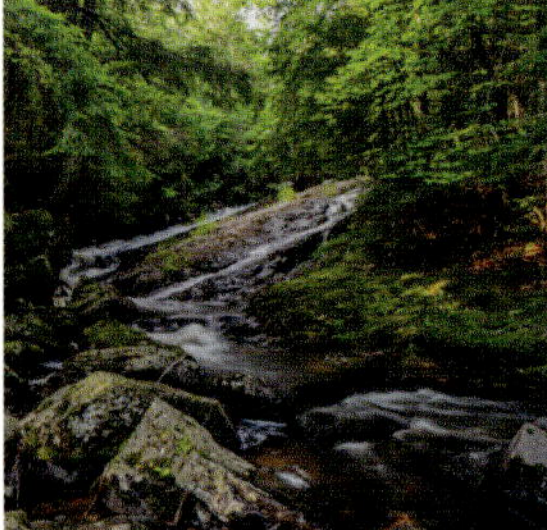

Must See: 6
Height: 15 feet
Time: 30-45 minutes

Driving Information
Signs: None
Road: Secondary
Access: Somewhat easy
4WD: N/A

GPS: N46 40.921 W87 34.388

Hiking Information
Path: Intermittent
Length: 300 yards
Elev. Change: Moderate
GPS: Recommended
Danger: Moderate
WP Boots: Recommended

This is one of Michigan's more unique waterfalls. A rounded mass of bedrock set at a fairly steep decline ushers the river down the far side of the hump (both sides when the river is high) until it abruptly runs into a bulwark of layered rock standing up to 15 feet high. This forces the river to turn sharply to pass by the descending bluff. The river then drops another 3 feet over a small tiered ledge. After this, the river runs quietly on its short journey to Lake Superior.

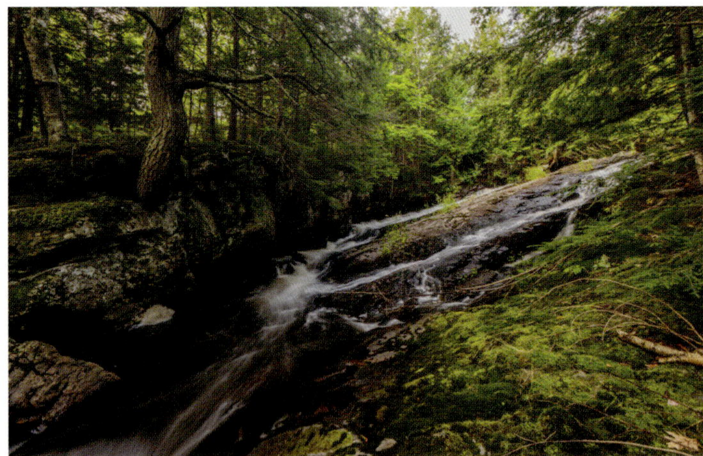

Along the main slide

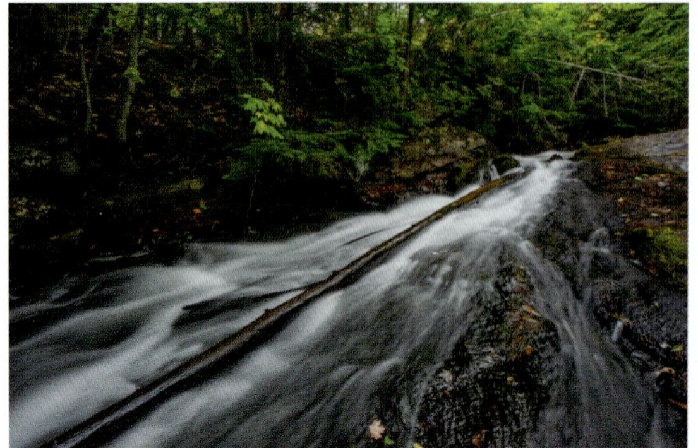

Standing at the top of the waterfall, looking down

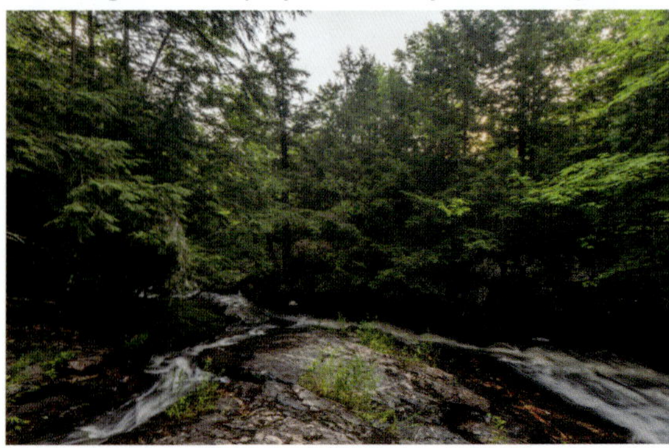

GARLIC FALLS #2 (BIG GARLIC RIVER)

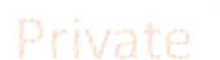

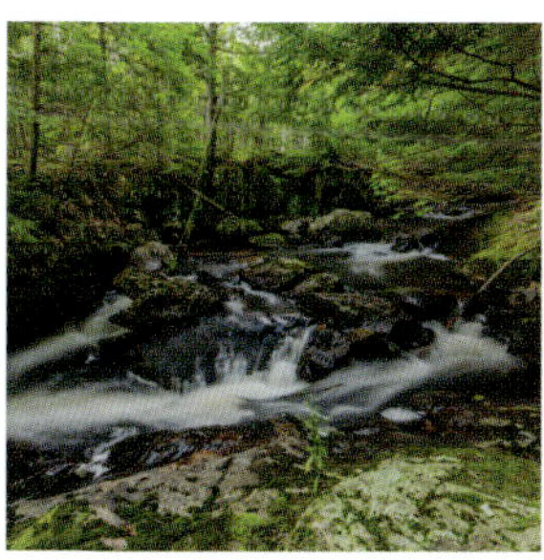

Must See:	4
Height:	5 feet
Time:	35-50 minutes

Driving Information

Signs:	None
Road:	Secondary
Access:	Somewhat easy
4WD:	N/A

GPS:	N46 40.911 W87 34.403

Hiking Information

Path:	Intermittent
Length:	350 yards
Elev. Change:	Moderate
GPS:	Recommended
Danger:	Moderate
WP Boots:	Recommended

Just above Garlic Falls, this little waterfall is tucked around a boulder ensconced corner. The river widens out to 20 feet, drops in three split cascades before coming together again for a final 1 foot drop into the pool that is just above Garlic Falls. Evergreens stretch out their boughs, greeting each other over the waterfall.

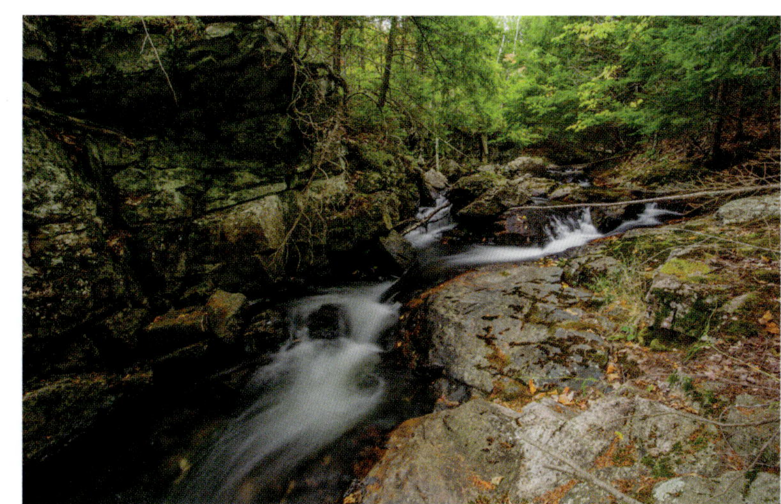

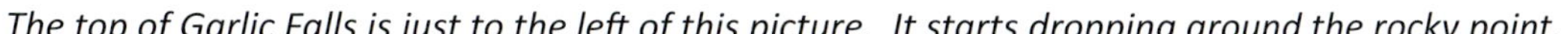

The top of Garlic Falls is just to the left of this picture. It starts dropping around the rocky point.

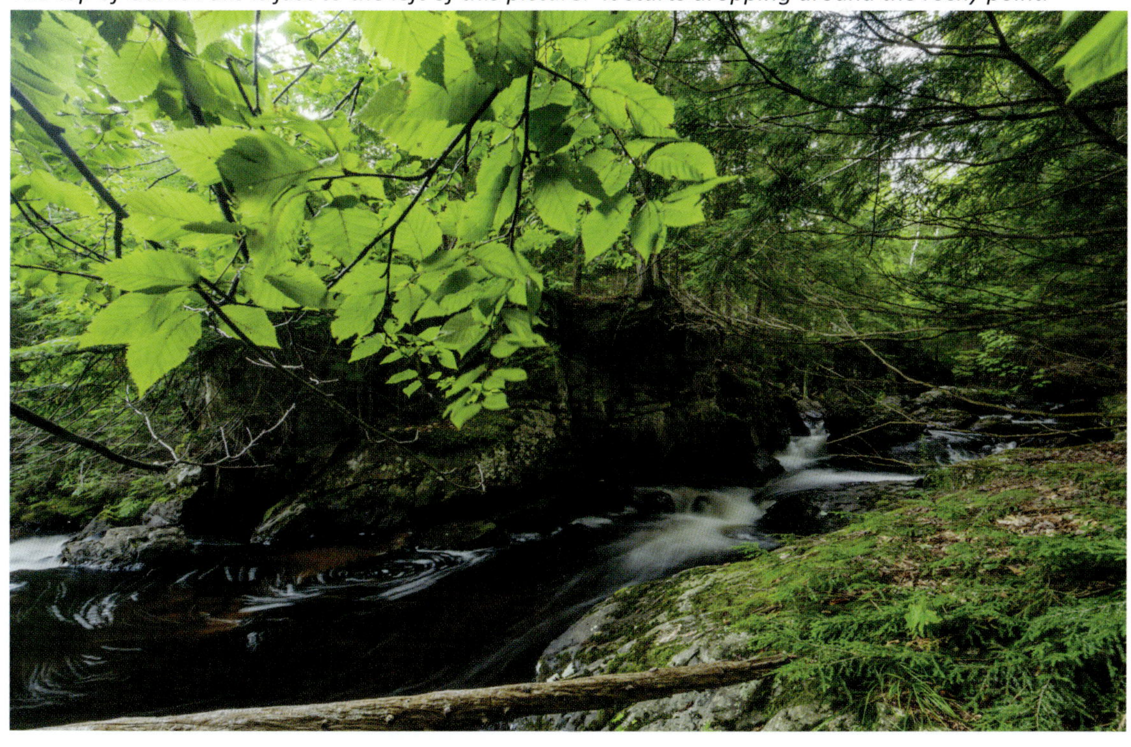

GARLIC FALLS #3 (BIG GARLIC RIVER)

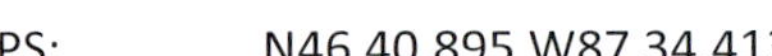

Private

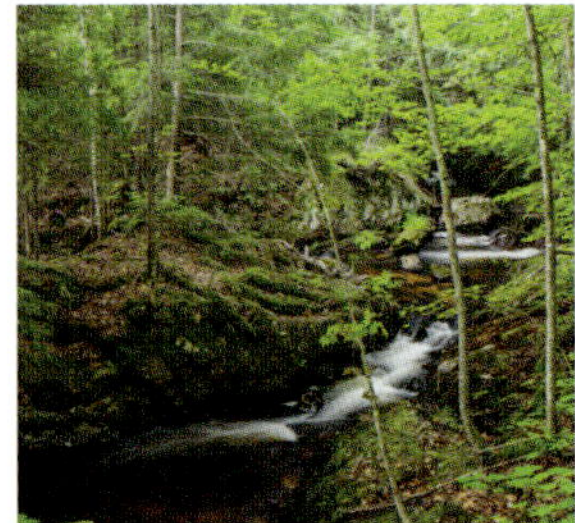

Must See:	6
Height:	8 feet
Time:	40-60 minutes

Driving Information

Signs:	None
Road:	Secondary
Access:	Somewhat easy
4WD:	N/A

GPS:	N46 40.895 W87 34.413

Hiking Information

Path:	Intermittent
Length:	.20 miles
Elev. Change:	Moderate
GPS:	Recommended
Danger:	Moderate
WP Boots:	Recommended

The 75 yard long waterfall is mostly channelled, although it does break into a double stream to surround a rocky island. It runs quickly, with several cascades (2 feet high at the most) along its length. There's a tangle of downed trees caught near the end of the island. The bottom of the waterfall is about 50 yards upstream from #2. Down here, at the end of the channel, it churns into a good sized spill pool. The current is on the far side of the river, shoved up against a nearly vertical wall.

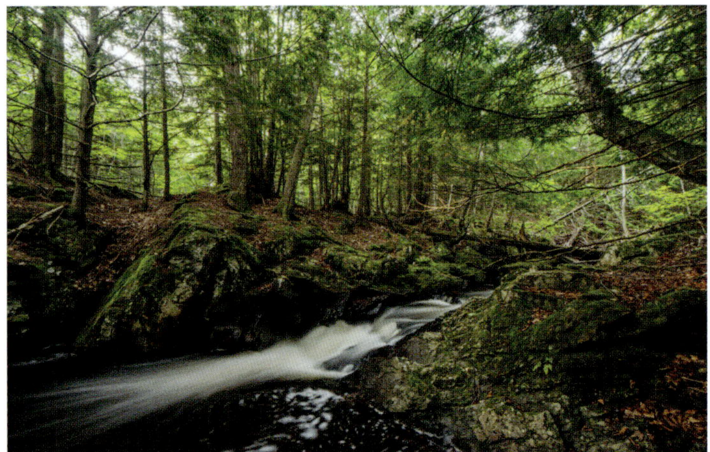

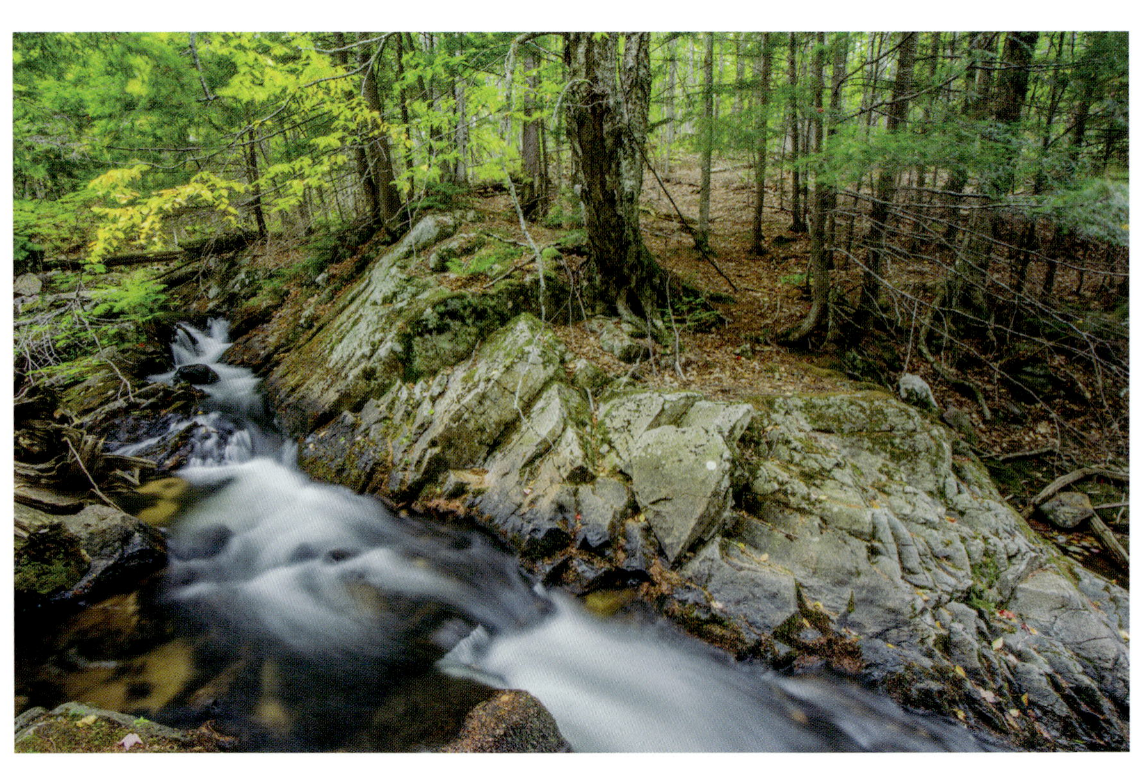

GARLIC FALLS #4 (BIG GARLIC RIVER)

Private

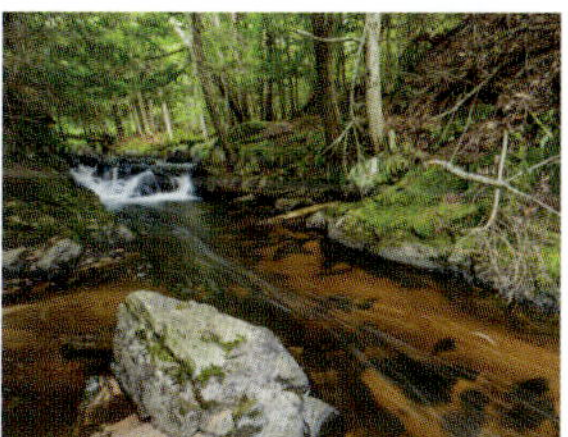

Must See:	4	GPS:	N46 40.780 W87 34.488
Height:	5 feet		
Time:	50-70 minutes	Hiking Information	
		Path:	Intermittent
Driving Information		Length:	.36 miles
Signs:	None	Elev. Change:	Moderate
Road:	Secondary	GPS:	Recommended
Access:	Somewhat easy	Danger:	Moderate
4WD:	N/A	WP Boots:	Recommended

This is the most easily viewed of the waterfalls along this hike. However, you must ford the river, or climb over a 15 foot rise to get to the waterfall from #3. I prefer to cross the river to the far side for viewing, as there is a flat grassy spot at the river's edge just downstream from the waterfall. It's a perfect place to enjoy the soothing sight.

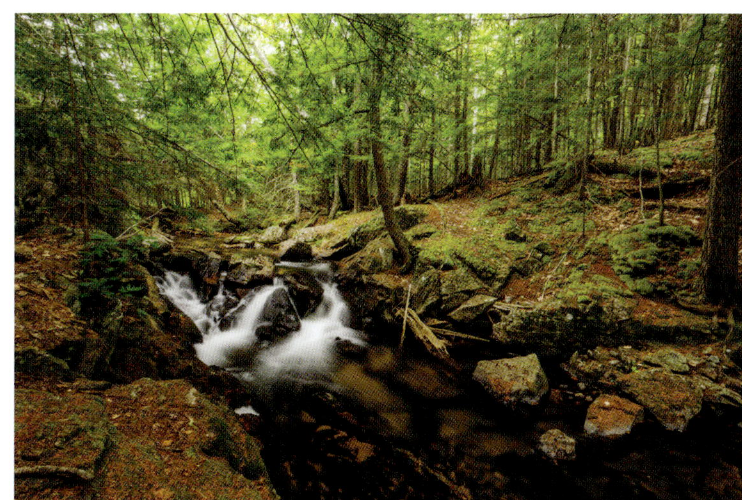

The waterfall cascades through blackened rock fingers, dividing the river into pleasing sections. Enjoy the rapids and small cascades between #3 and #4.

It's beautiful to view the waterfall from the sandbar seen on the left side of the river

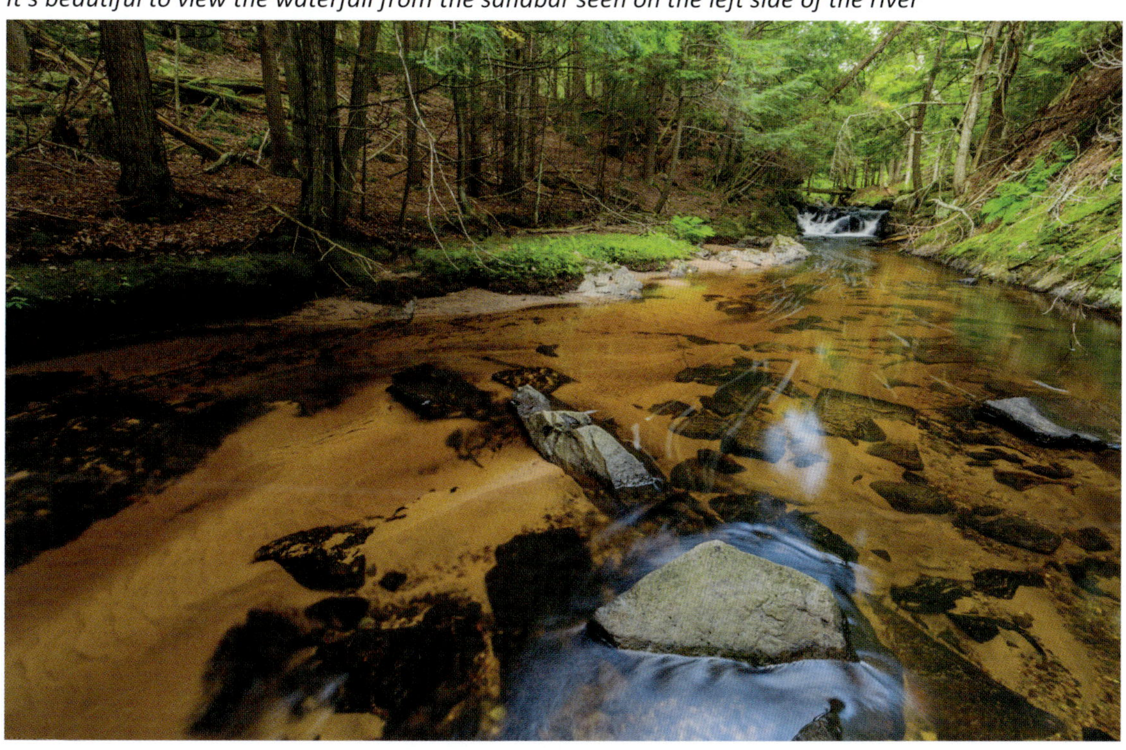

Garlic Falls - Upper Hike

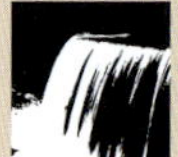

A walk through thick pines abruptly ends at the river with the Upper #1 Falls. The forest in this area is quite thick, with the lower dead branches of evergreens seemingly everywhere!

Directions: Follow CR-550 north from Marquette about 13 miles. Turn left (west) off of CR-550 onto the dirt road that is just past Birch Creek (N46 41.854 W87 35.077). (This is the same road as the route to Birch Creek Falls.) Follow the dirt road for 2.8 miles. Turn left (south) at N46 40.150 W87 37.104. Drive 100 yards to the end of the 2-track. Hike the well-worn trail to the river. Upper #1 is there. Upper #2 is downstream 85 yards in a small ravine.

GARLIC FALLS - UPPER #1 (BIG GARLIC RIVER)

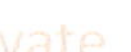

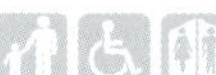

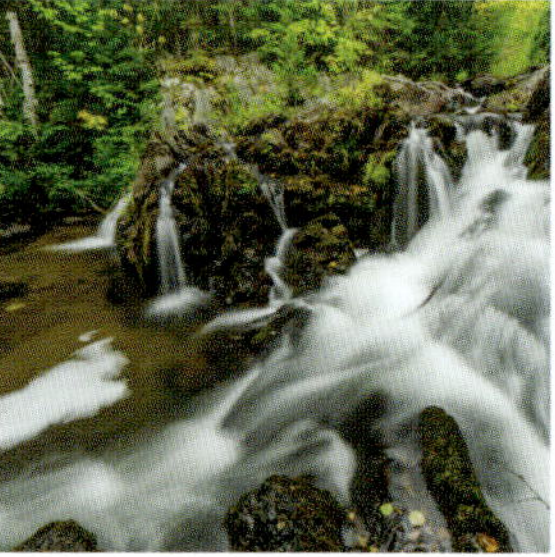

Must See:	6	GPS:	N46 40.057 W87 37.160
Height:	15 feet		
Time:	15-30 minutes	Hiking Information	
		Path:	Well-worn footpath
Driving Information		Length:	150 yards
Signs:	None	Elev. Change:	Moderate
Road:	2-track	GPS:	Recommended
Access:	Somewhat difficult	Danger:	Minor
4WD:	Helpful	WP Boots:	Recommended

Although this set of waterfalls is in a somewhat remote area, there is a relatively nice path to the falls. These falls are much easier to get to than the "regular" Garlic Falls!

This waterfall is a multi-tiered cascade pouring around a rounded mass of rock in the center of the river. Water-warn boulders look like they were strategically placed in the river just below the falls. The rock walls and boulders are covered with moss. Sit on the bare rocks and absorb the feeling of antiquity and timelessness as the waterfall babbles and the unchanging river rushes on.

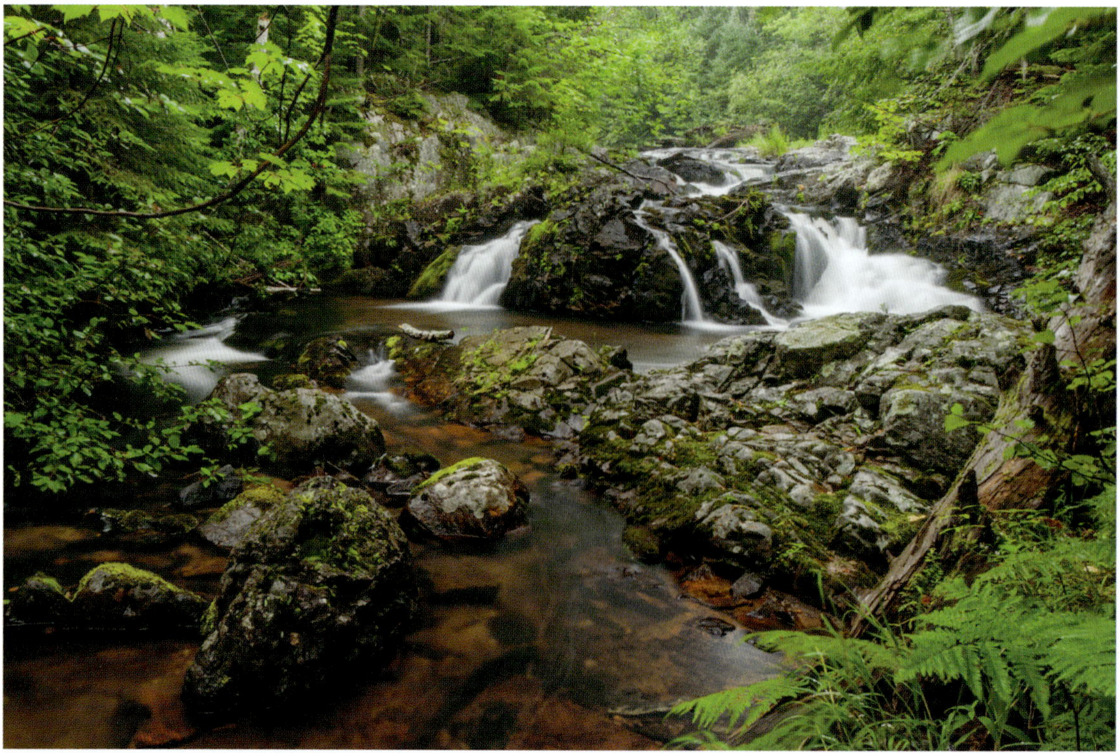

GARLIC FALLS - UPPER #2 (BIG GARLIC RIVER)

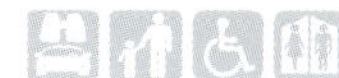

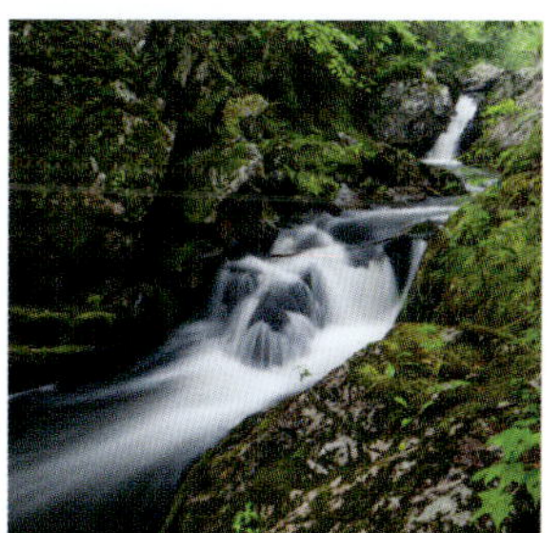

Must See:	7	GPS:	N46 40.045 W87 37.104
Height:	18 feet		
Time:	30-45 minutes	**Hiking Information**	
		Path:	Well-worn footpath
Driving Information		Length:	250 yards
Signs:	None	Elev. Change:	Moderate
Road:	2-track	GPS:	Recommended
Access:	Somewhat difficult	Danger:	Moderate
4WD:	Helpful	WP Boots:	Recommended

The Garlic River runs down a narrow chute to a 20 foot long pool and then plunges another 2 feet over moss covered rocks for a nice end to this waterfall. It is much more challenging to get to this waterfall than the Upper #1 Falls. But the view makes it worth the extra work!

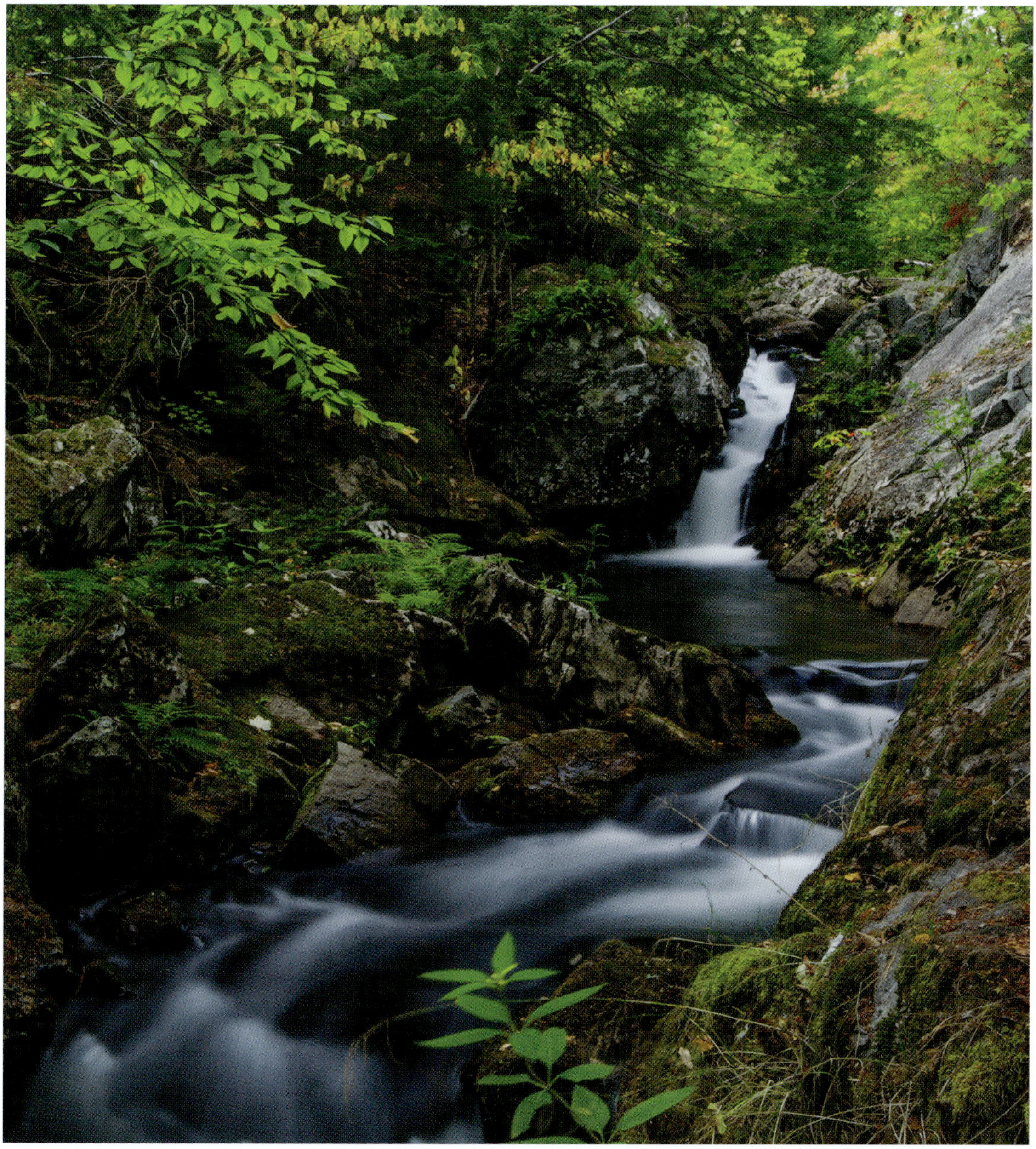

Little Garlic Falls Hike

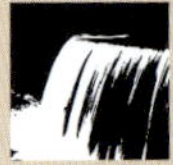

The Little Garlic River empties into Lake Superior between Garlic Island and Little Presque Isle. Upstream 4.5 miles are a trio of small waterfalls. The popular North Country Trail passes by Little Garlic Falls, so there is a well maintained trail that leads to this back country location.

Directions: Follow CR-550 north from Marquette about 10 miles. Turn left (west) off of CR-550 onto the dirt road just past the Little Garlic River (N46 40.478 W87 32.706). In 1.7 miles there is a small area to park on the left (south) side of the dirt road. This is just before a bridge that crosses over Little Garlic River. Park. The North Country Trail with its tell-tale blue triangles fastened to tree trunks (perhaps they have been upgraded to the blue rectangles by now) should be obvious on the northern side of the road. Follow it for 1 mile to the falls. The next 2 falls are found upstream in the next .3 miles.

LITTLE GARLIC FALLS (LITTLE GARLIC RIVER)

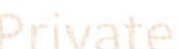

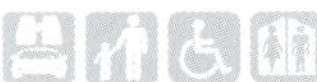

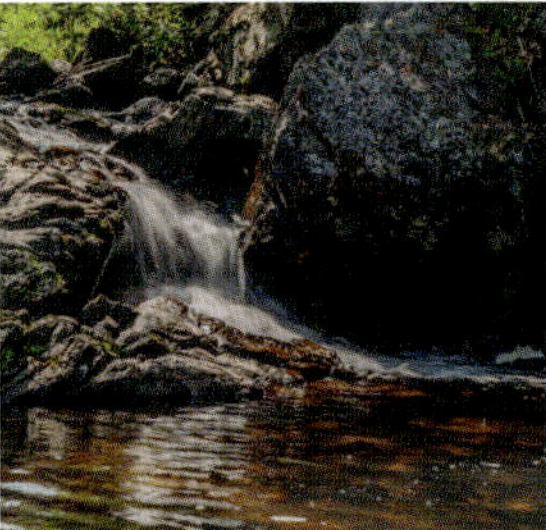

Must See:	5	GPS:	N46 40.017 W87 34.797
Height:	6 feet		
Time:	60-90 minutes	Hiking Information	
		Path:	Well-worn footpath
Driving Information		Length:	1.0 miles
Signs:	None	Elev. Change:	Elevated
Road:	Dirt road	GPS:	Recommended
Access:	Difficult	Danger:	Moderate
4WD:	Helpful	WP Boots:	Required (to cross river)

There is a 30 foot rock face on the right above the deep spill pool. These kind of cliffs can make you feel small or at least lend a sense of awe to the location! From the south side of the river there is a fisherman's path that leads along the river upstream to the next two falls. It was a pleasant surprise to run across a fellow photographer at this waterfall in August of 2010. It is rare to meet anyone at remote waterfalls.

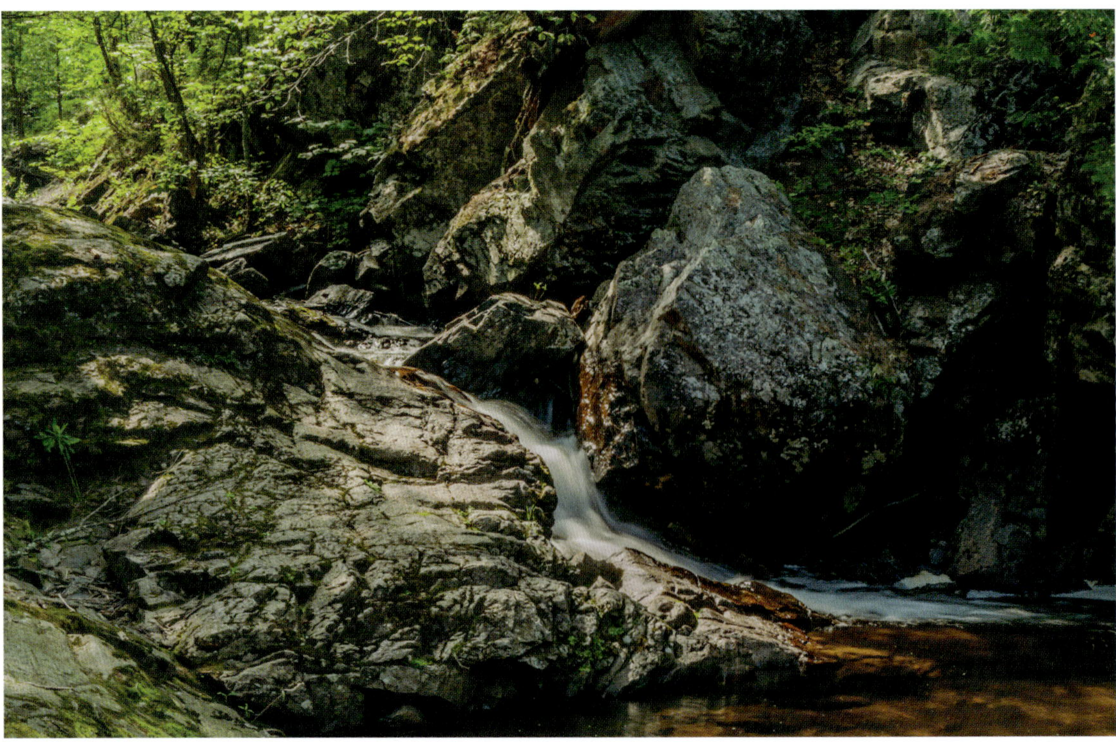

LITTLE GARLIC FALLS #2 (LITTLE GARLIC RIVER)

Private 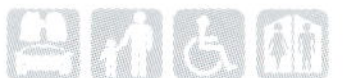

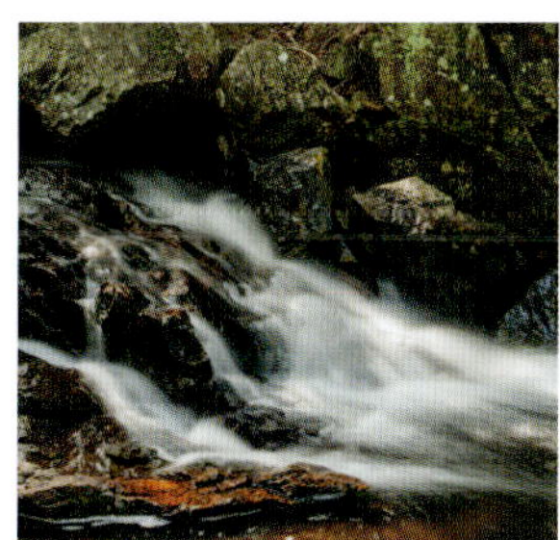

Must See:	4	GPS:	N46 39.991 W87 34.881
Height:	4 feet		
Time:	65-95 minutes	**Hiking Information**	
		Path:	Well-worn footpath
Driving Information		Length:	1.1 miles
Signs:	None	Elev. Change:	Elevated
Road:	Dirt road	GPS:	Recommended
Access:	Difficult	Danger:	Moderate
4WD:	Helpful	WP Boots:	Required (to cross river)

The river tumbles over rough stone fingers into a clear, calm pool. There is a flat moss-covered area that is perfect for a picnic next to the wading pool. It can be seen in the foreground of the picture below.

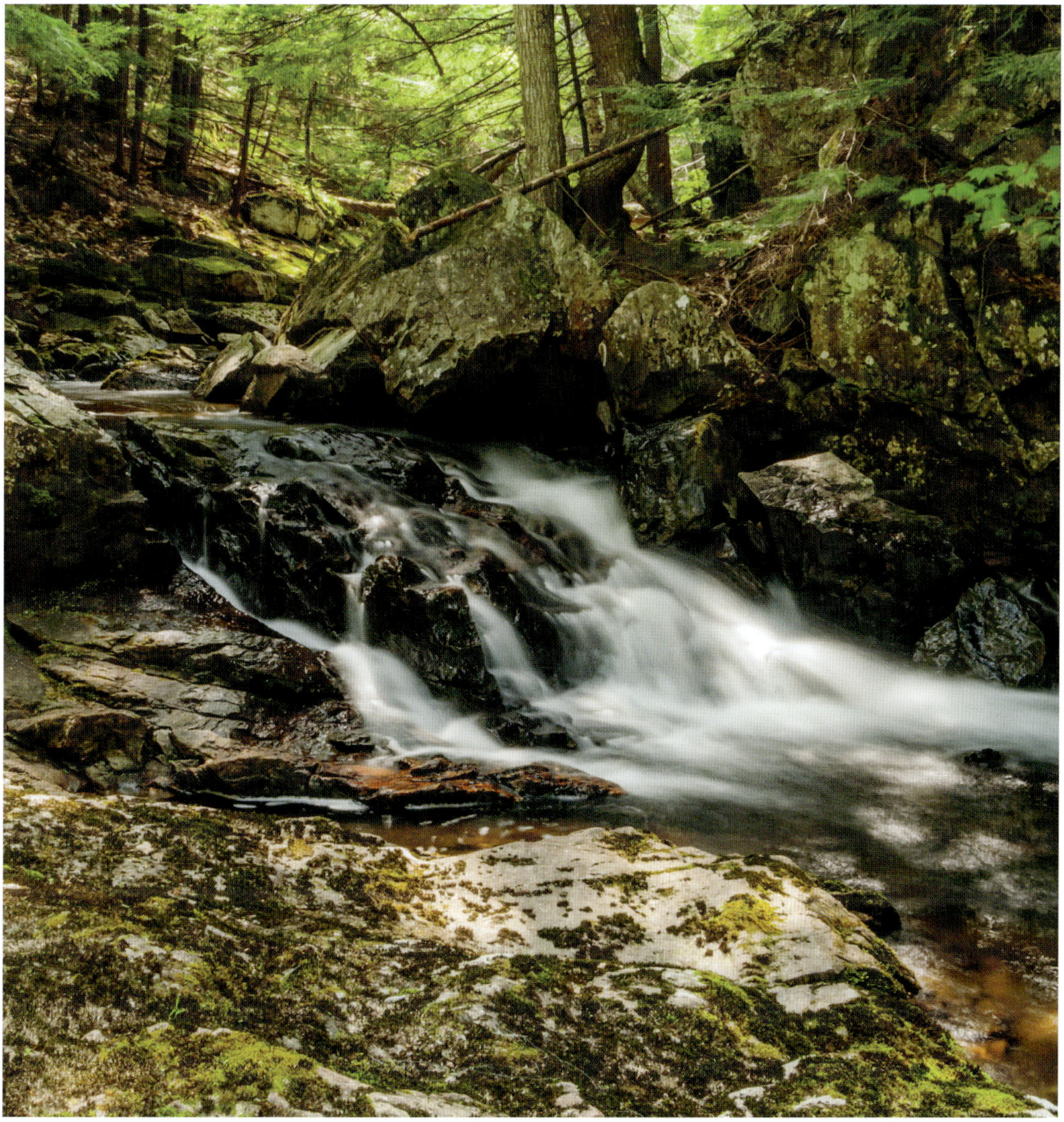

LITTLE GARLIC FALLS #3 (LITTLE GARLIC RIVER)

Private 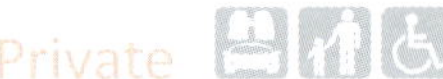

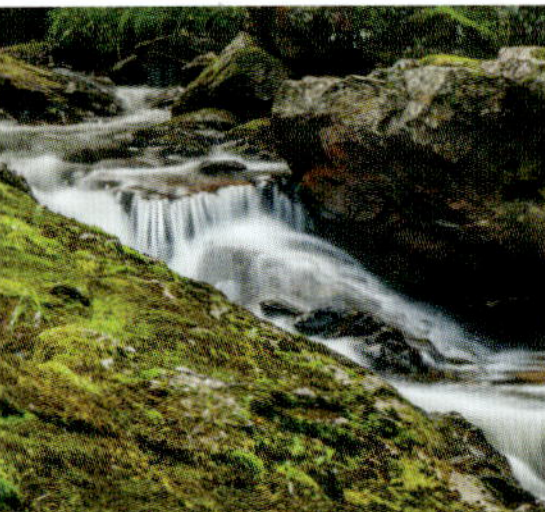

Must See:	4
Height:	7 feet
Time:	75-110 minutes

Driving Information

Signs:	None
Road:	Dirt road
Access:	Difficult
4WD:	Helpful

GPS:	N46 40.017 W87 34.797

Hiking Information

Path:	Well-worn footpath
Length:	1.3 miles
Elev. Change:	Elevated
GPS:	Recommended
Danger:	Moderate
WP Boots:	Required (to cross river)

Hike .17 miles upstream along the narrow river from #2. The southern side of the river is lower ground. The river runs along the base of a rocky bluff than extends for nearly a mile on the northern side of the river.

The #3 falls sport several cascades, with the largest about 2 feet tall. Below the falls is a nice, mossy rock bank with large rocks littering the river. A hunter's camp is not far from here. As always, be considerate.

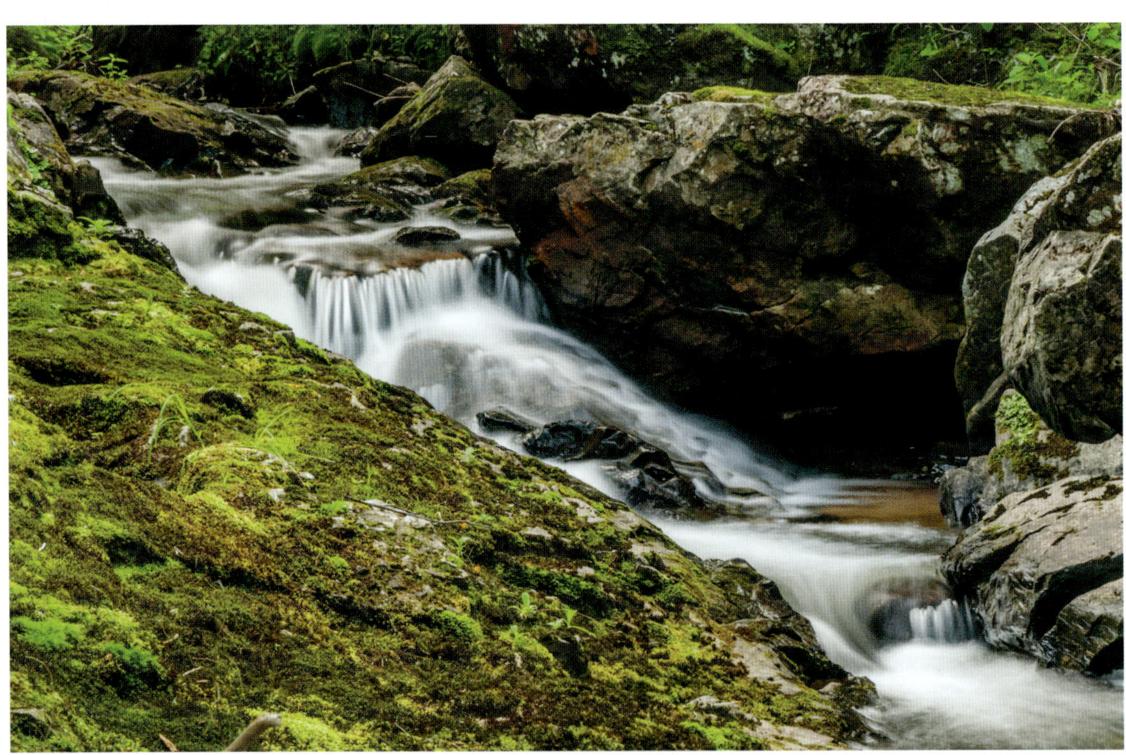

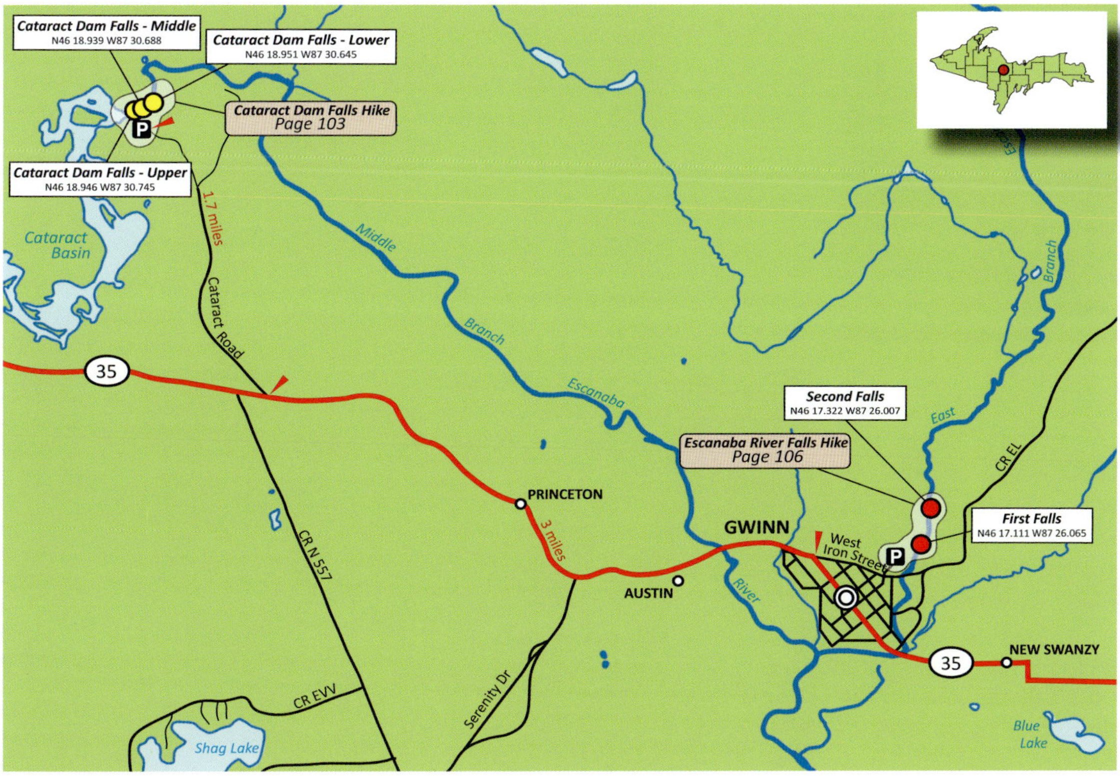

Cataract Dam Falls - Middle
N46 18.939 W87 30.688

Cataract Dam Falls - Lower
N46 18.951 W87 30.645

Cataract Dam Falls Hike
Page 103

Cataract Dam Falls - Upper
N46 18.946 W87 30.745

1.7 miles

Cataract Basin

Middle Branch Escanaba River

Cataract Road

35

Second Falls
N46 17.322 W87 26.007

Escanaba River Falls Hike
Page 106

East Branch

CR EL

PRINCETON

3 miles

GWINN

West Iron Street

First Falls
N46 17.111 W87 26.065

CR N 557

AUSTIN

NEW SWANZY

CR EVV

Serenity Dr

Shag Lake

Blue Lake

Cataract Dam Falls Hike

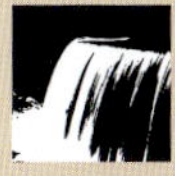

Cataract Dam is now owned by U.P. Hydro, LLC. The FRCC Operating License was transferred to them from UPPCO in early 2011. At the base of the hydroelectric plant's dam is the base of a waterfall, now known as Cataract Dam Falls. The river then runs through a shallow box canyon. Partway through the canyon is the Middle Falls, with the Lower Falls at the end of the canyon. I have encountered fishermen often at the base of the Lower Falls. The trail runs above the canyon. There are no guard rails to protect from dropping over the sheer walls. Be careful with young children.

Directions: Drive on M-35 west from Gwinn for 3 miles. Turn right (northwest) onto Cataract Road. Follow it to the end. There is a parking lot at the dam with a boat launch and pit toilet. Several rough footpaths head over to the river below the falls. Follow the paths along the edge of the canyon to see the falls along the way.

CATARACT DAM FALLS - UPPER (MIDDLE BRANCH ESCANABA RIVER)

Private 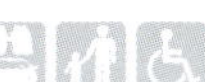 

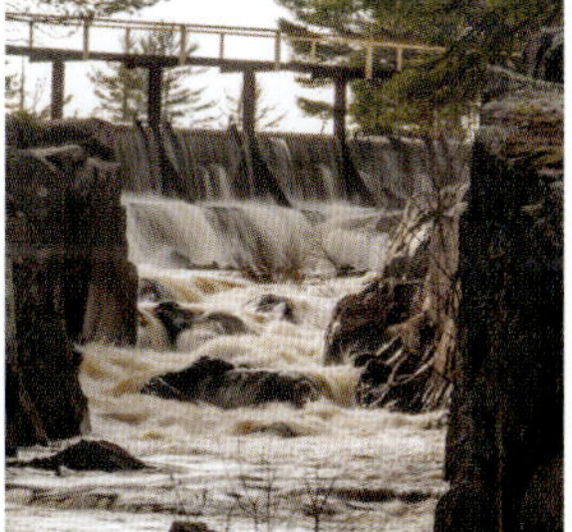

Must See:	6	GPS:	N46 18.946 W87 30.745
Height:	12 feet		
Time:	10-20 minutes	Hiking Information	
		Path:	Footpath
Driving Information		Length:	50 yards
Signs:	None	Elev. Change:	Slight
Road:	Dirt road	GPS:	N/A
Access:	Somewhat easy	Danger:	Moderate
4WD:	N/A	WP Boots:	N/A

The lower portion of the original falls is incorporated into the base of the dam. There are only several dams in Michigan that have integrated any of the natural waterfall structure.

CATARACT DAM FALLS - MIDDLE (MIDDLE BRANCH ESCANABA RIVER) Private

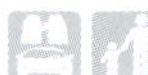

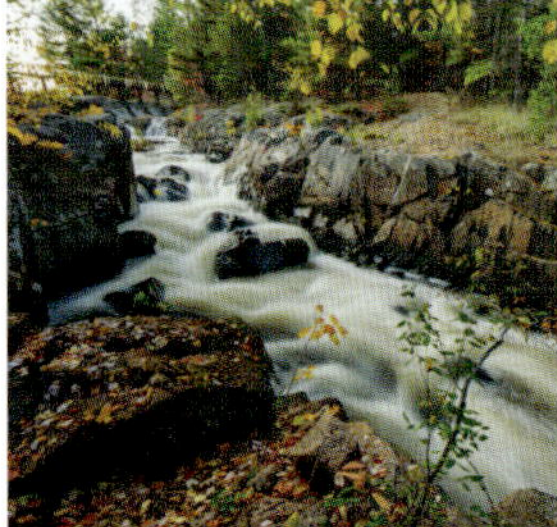

Must See:	4	GPS:	N46 18.939 W87 30.688
Height:	4 feet		
Time:	15-25 minutes	Hiking Information	
		Path:	Footpath
Driving Information		Length:	100 yards
Signs:	None	Elev. Change:	Slight
Road:	Dirt road	GPS:	N/A
Access:	Somewhat easy	Danger:	Moderate
4WD:	N/A	WP Boots:	N/A

It's not a long walk between the Upper and Lower Falls, but in that short walk along the top of the canyon the Middle Falls can be seen as a shallow set of cascades that surround a knob of bedrock that rises up in the river. The Upper Falls can be seen in the distance.

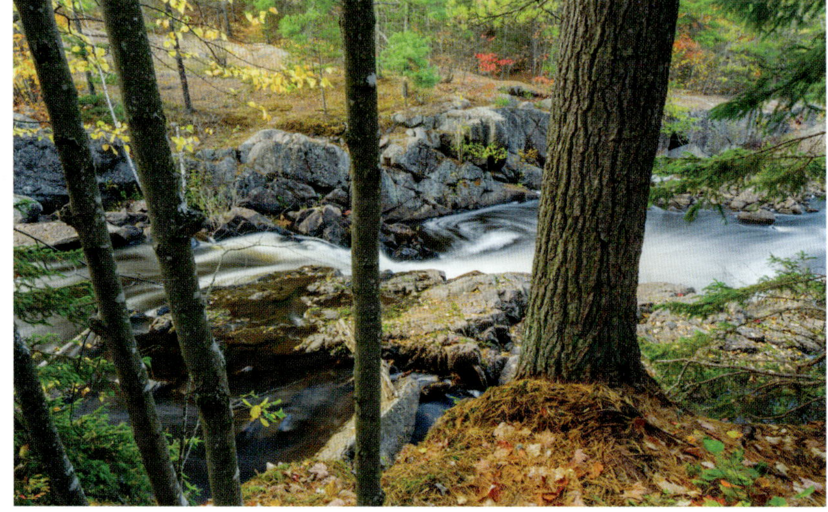

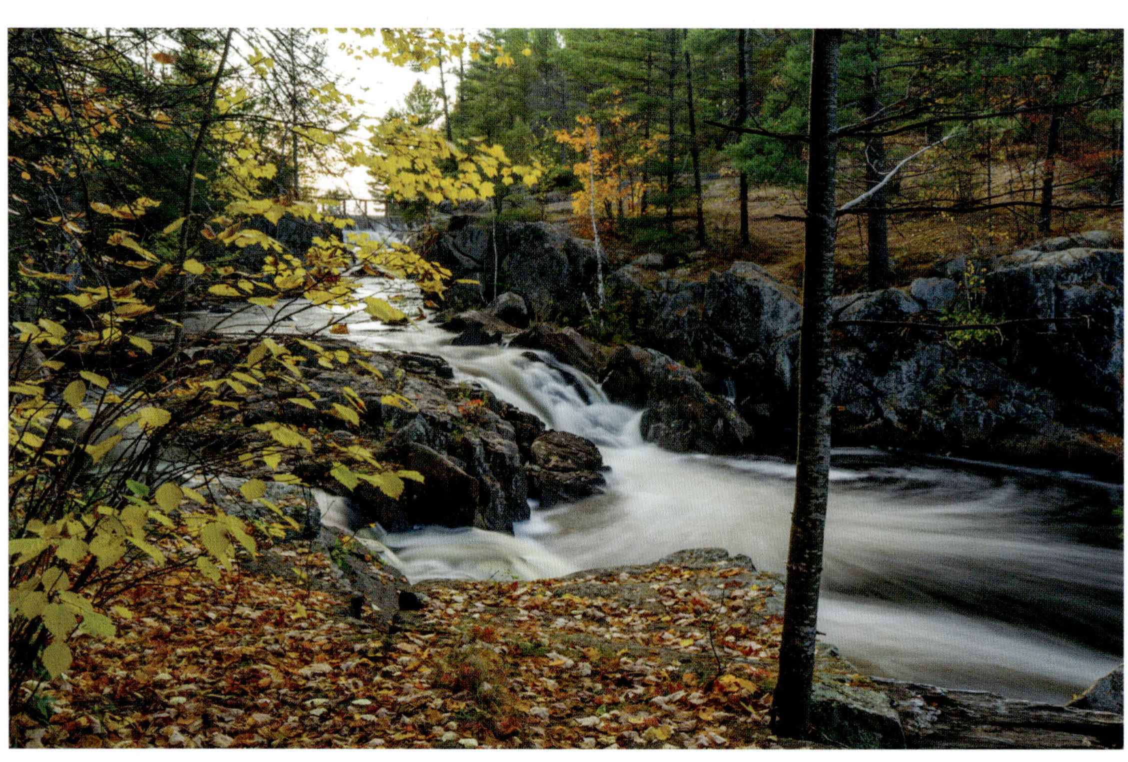

CATARACT DAM FALLS - LOWER (MIDDLE BRANCH ESCANABA RIVER) Private

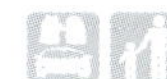 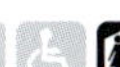 

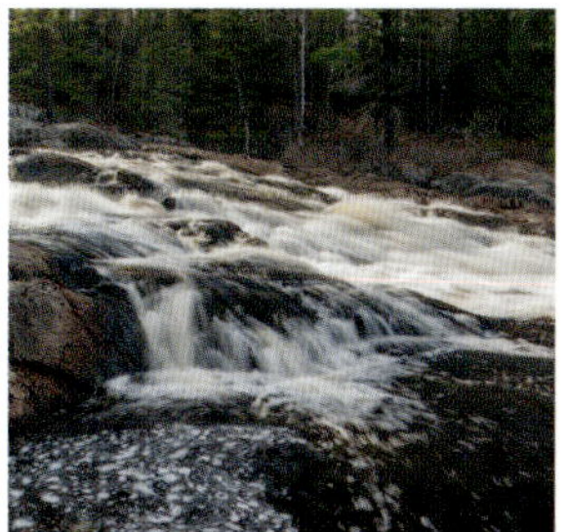

Must See:	6	GPS:	N46 18.951 W87 30.645
Height:	15 feet		
Time:	15-25 minutes	Hiking Information	
		Path:	Footpath
Driving Information		Length:	150 yards
Signs:	None	Elev. Change:	Moderate
Road:	Dirt road	GPS:	N/A
Access:	Somewhat easy	Danger:	Moderate
4WD:	N/A	WP Boots:	N/A

The river makes a hard bend to the left just below the falls. This is also where the rocky banks that line the sides of the river from here to the dam fade down to nothing. The river widens out and spills down into a good fishing hole. Come in April to watch Brook Trout jump up the falls!

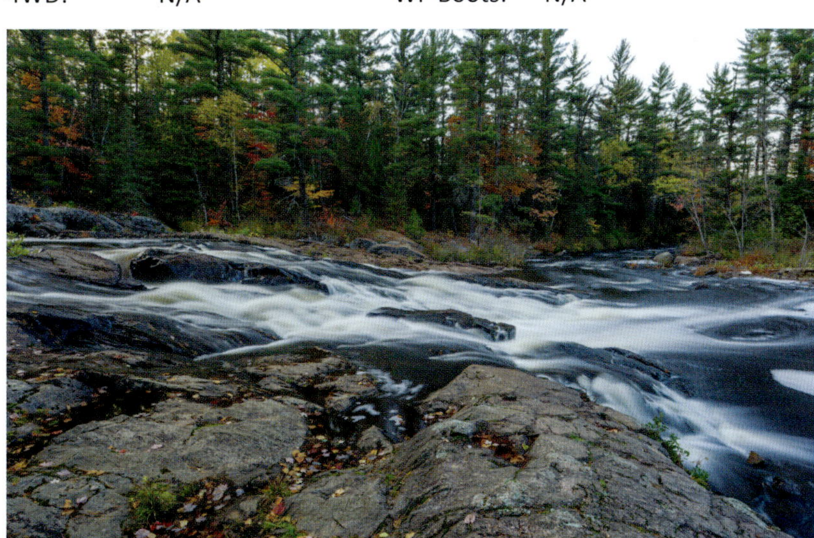

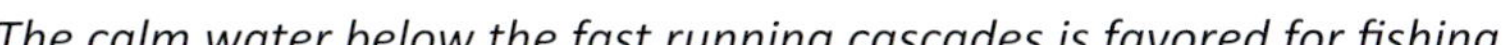

The calm water below the fast running cascades is favored for fishing

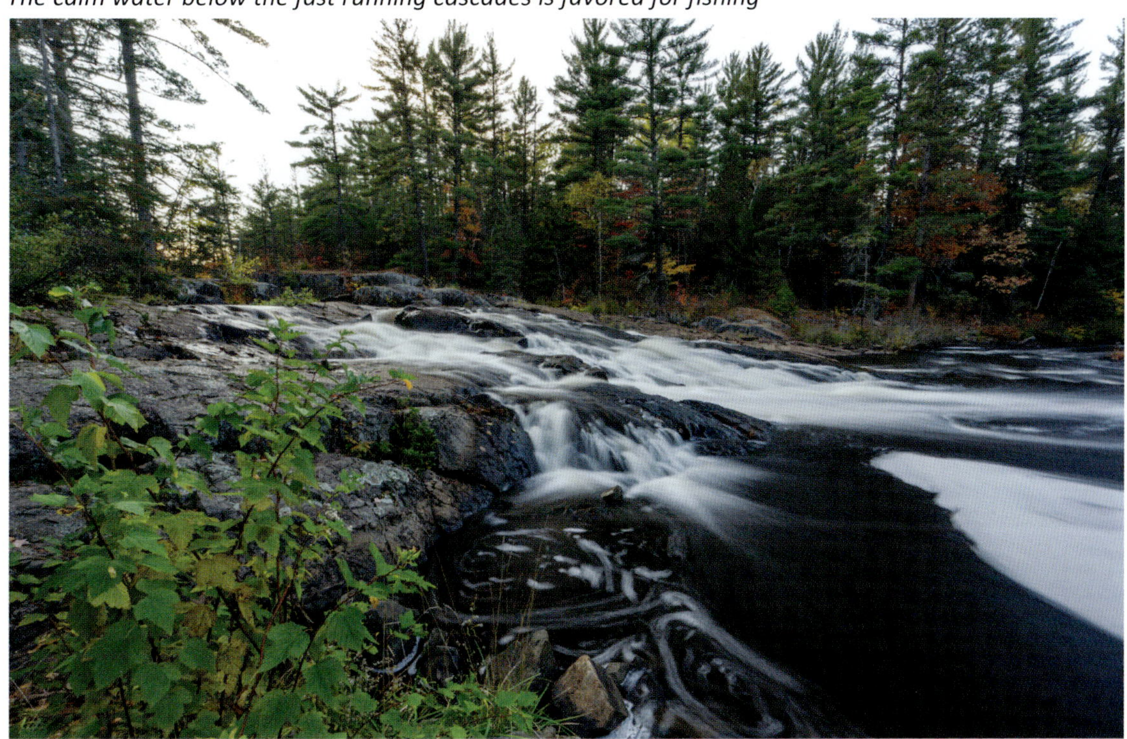

Escanaba River Falls Hike

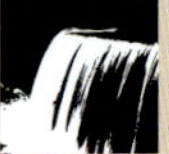

Farquar-Metsa Tourist Park is several blocks north of Gwinn on the west side of the East Branch of the Escanaba River. It underwent a large renovation in 2012. A large unsupervised swimming area on the river is just down river from First Falls. Both of the falls in the park are really just a couple of rapids, but since they are found on some atlases, I am including them for documentation purposes.

Directions: From the northwestern end of Gwinn, take West Iron Street sharply to the east for nearly .5 miles. The park is on the left (north). Drive past the camping area to behind the building on the left (I think it's a bathhouse). Park in the parking lot back there. Head down to the river (east) which is only about 100 yards. First Falls are at the mouth of the swimming area. It should be easy to find. Follow the narrow footpath north along the river to Second Falls. The trail heads through a forest of mostly evergreens.

FIRST FALLS (EAST BRANCH ESCANABA RIVER)

Private 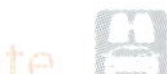 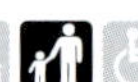 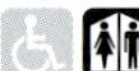

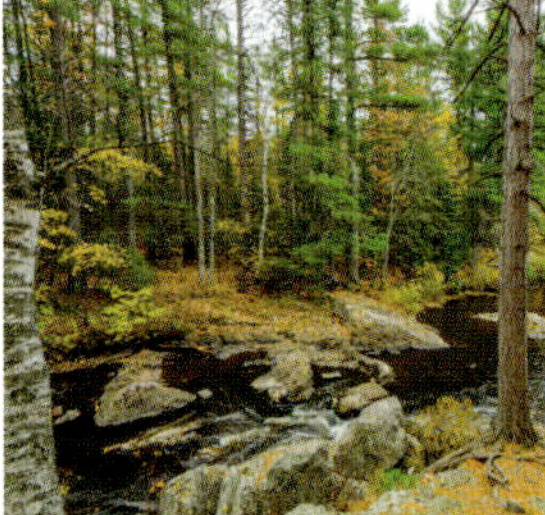

Must See:	1	GPS:	N46 17.111 W87 26.065
Height:	2 feet		
Time:	10-20 minutes	Hiking Information	
		Path:	Mowed fields
Driving Information		Length:	100 yards
Signs:	None	Elev. Change:	Slight
Road:	Secondary	GPS:	N/A
Access:	Mostly Easy	Danger:	Slight
4WD:	N/A	WP Boots:	N/A

With mowed grass along the river and several structures visible from the falls, this feels like a tamed waterfall compared to the vast majority in Michigan! It does make it more kid friendly, however. Enjoy frisbee in the open field next to the river or maybe a picnic on the bedrock next to the falls.

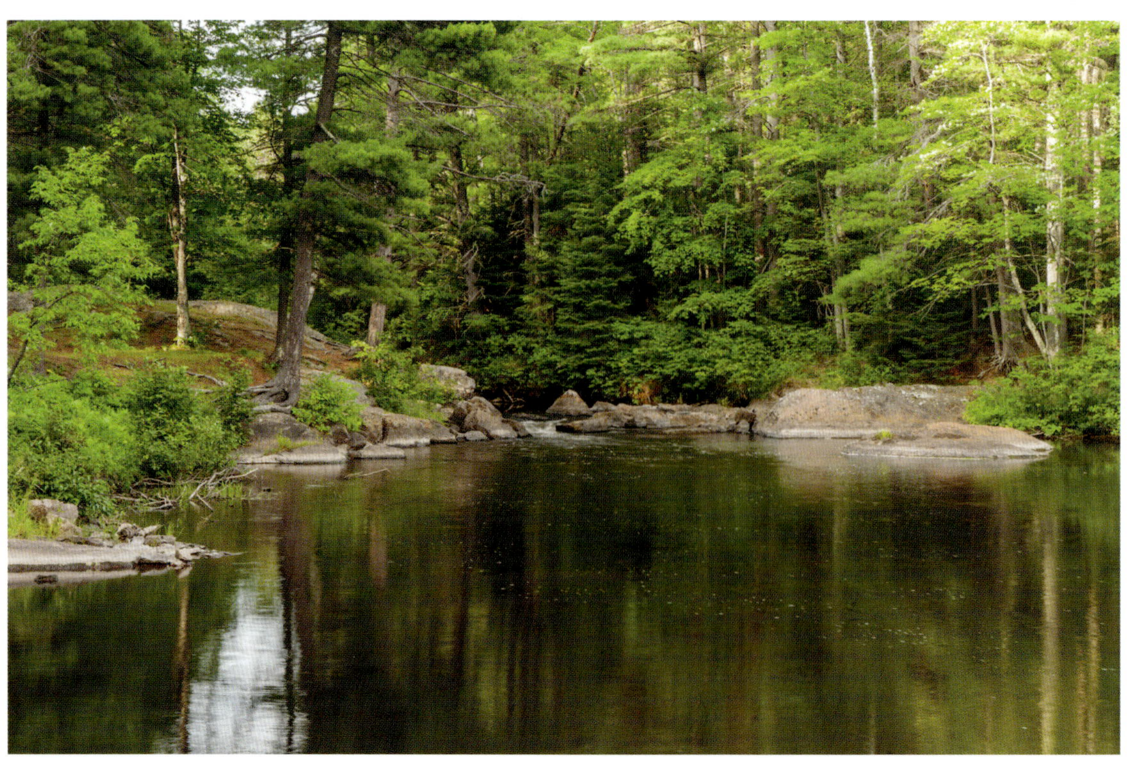

SECOND FALLS (EAST BRANCH ESCANABA RIVER)

Private 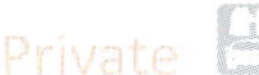 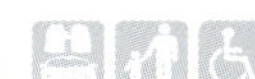 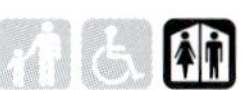

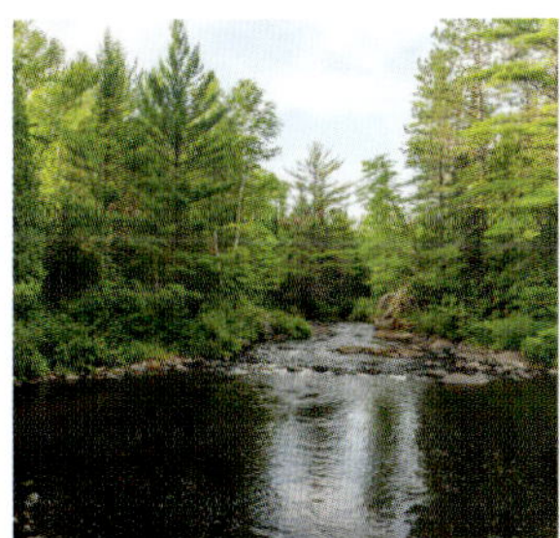

Must See:	1	GPS:	N46 17.322 W87 26.007
Height:	2 feet		
Time:	30-45 minutes		

Driving Information

Signs:	None
Road:	Secondary
Access:	Mostly Easy
4WD:	N/A

Hiking Information

Path:	Mowed fields
Length:	.3 miles
Elev. Change:	Slight
GPS:	N/A
Danger:	Slight
WP Boots:	N/A

These falls are almost a third of a mile back from "civilization", so imagine my amazement when, after taking several pictures here in October, I turned around, startled to hear someone speaking to me. A hunter wanted to know if I'd seen any black bears. I hadn't, which was just fine with me. But it did make me keep a closer eye and ear to my surroundings for the rest of the day! It was a good reminder that bear season was open, and I really should keep that in mind.

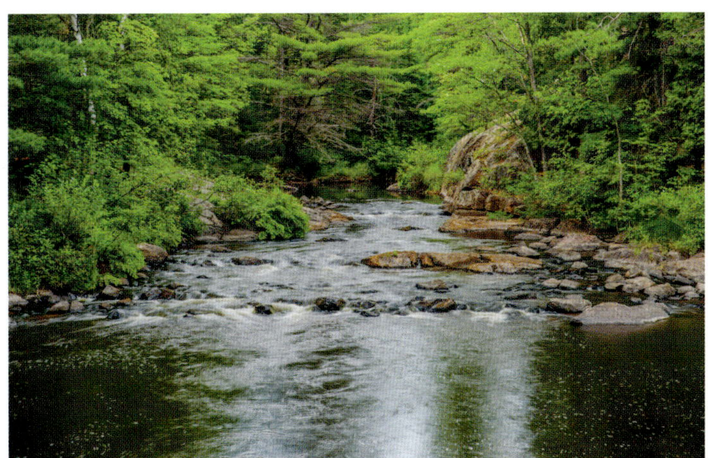

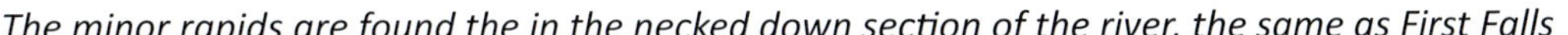

The minor rapids are found the in the necked down section of the river, the same as First Falls

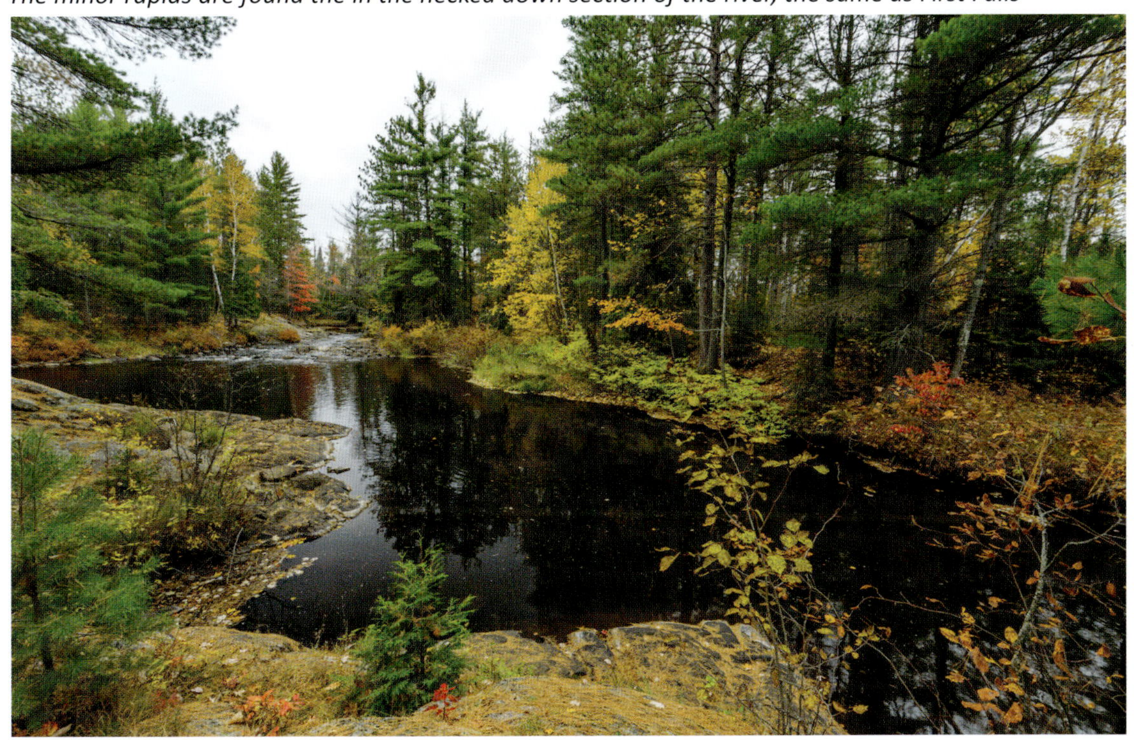

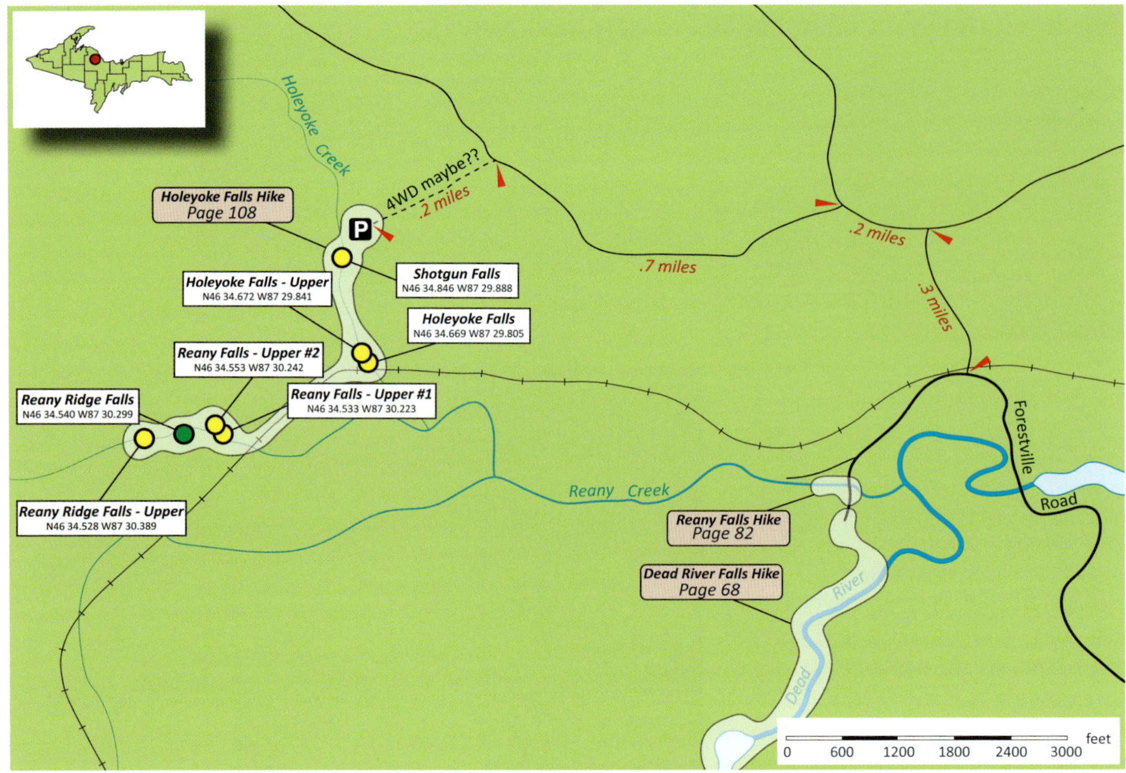

Holeyoke Falls Hike

This hike is not for the beginner! There is no trail. Plan on climbing in and out of several deep ravines. Oh, and it's nearly a 2 mile round trip. There are railroad tracks that cut between the two creeks and it may be tempting to walk down the tracks. (Keep in mind, however, that they are privately owned and it is trespassing to hike along them. Also, trains can appear with no warning. They can be quite silent. The steep banks alongside the tracks could make it nearly impossible to get to safety.) And then there are the rocky creek banks that must be climbed over in order to get to the upper reaches of the creeks.

I don't want to create the impression that this hike is impossible, but I also don't want anyone to attempt it without being aware of the difficulties.

Directions: (The basic directions for getting to the Dead River Falls will get you into this vicinity) Take Wright Street (the road that runs around the outskirts of Marquette from US-41 on the west up to the north of Marquette and then cuts east, intersecting with CR-550 and then basically ending at Presque Isle Avenue, which runs north and south through Marquette) north from US-41. Turn left (northwest) onto Forestville Road in .6 miles. In 1.7 miles turn right onto a dirt road. In .3 miles turn left. In .2 miles turn left again and drive for .7 miles on a good dirt road. Turn left at the power lines and drive .2 miles to an obvious parking area at the top of a very deep ravine. (You may need a 4WD vehicle to make the last leg of this drive) Thousands of shotgun shells litter the ground along with broken bottles and remnants of campfires. Hike over into the trees to the south, working your way down to the bottom of the ravine. Shotgun Falls, named after the profusion of spent shotgun casings found not far away, is found on the other side of the ravine. Follow Holeyoke Creek down river until meeting up with more waterfalls just before the railroad tracks. Hike over to Reany Creek. Just 100 yards west of the railroad here is the beginning of a series of waterfalls. Follow the creek upstream to see them all.

SHOTGUN FALLS (HOLEYOKE CREEK)

Private 

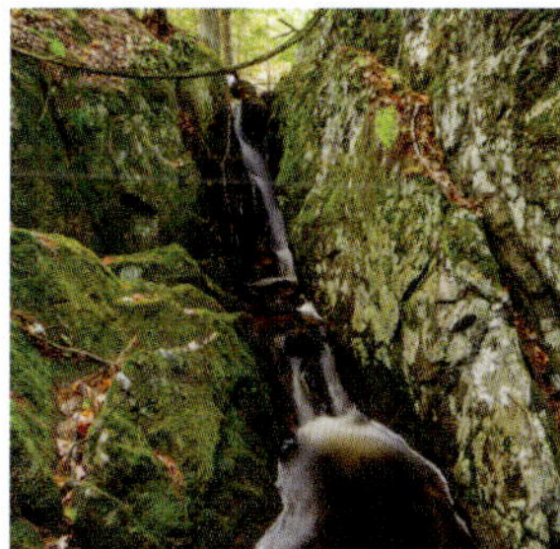

Must See:	5	GPS:	N46 34.846 W87 29.888
Height:	9 feet		
Time:	20-30 minutes	**Hiking Information**	
		Path:	None
Driving Information		Length:	150 yards
Signs:	None	Elev. Change:	Elevated
Road:	2-track	GPS:	Recommended
Access:	Difficult	Danger:	Moderate
4WD:	Recommended	WP Boots:	N/A

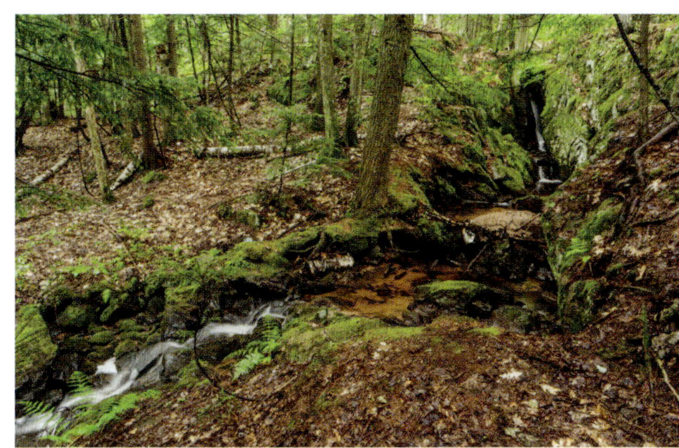

The creek runs down through the bottom of a heavily wooded, 60 foot deep ravine. Toward the bottom of the ravine, as the creek flows down into it, a mass of rock blocks its journey. Over time, the creek has worn a slit 2 feet wide through a weak portion of the bedrock. Shotgun Falls is the result. After the initial "hidden" 5 foot drop, a couple narrow cascades follow until the creek emerges from the narrow rift into a slightly wider spill pool. Several more cascades take the creek down to the base of the ravine where the creek turns and easily follows the ravine.

The ancient cleft in the rock practically hides the thin ribbon of a waterfall. The entire area exudes "green"! Large evergreen overhead, thick green moss and lichen cling to the rugged bedrock, and scattered ferns and grasses downstream from the waterfall all show off their various shades of green.

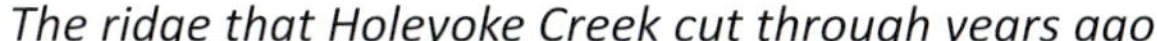

The ridge that Holeyoke Creek cut through years ago

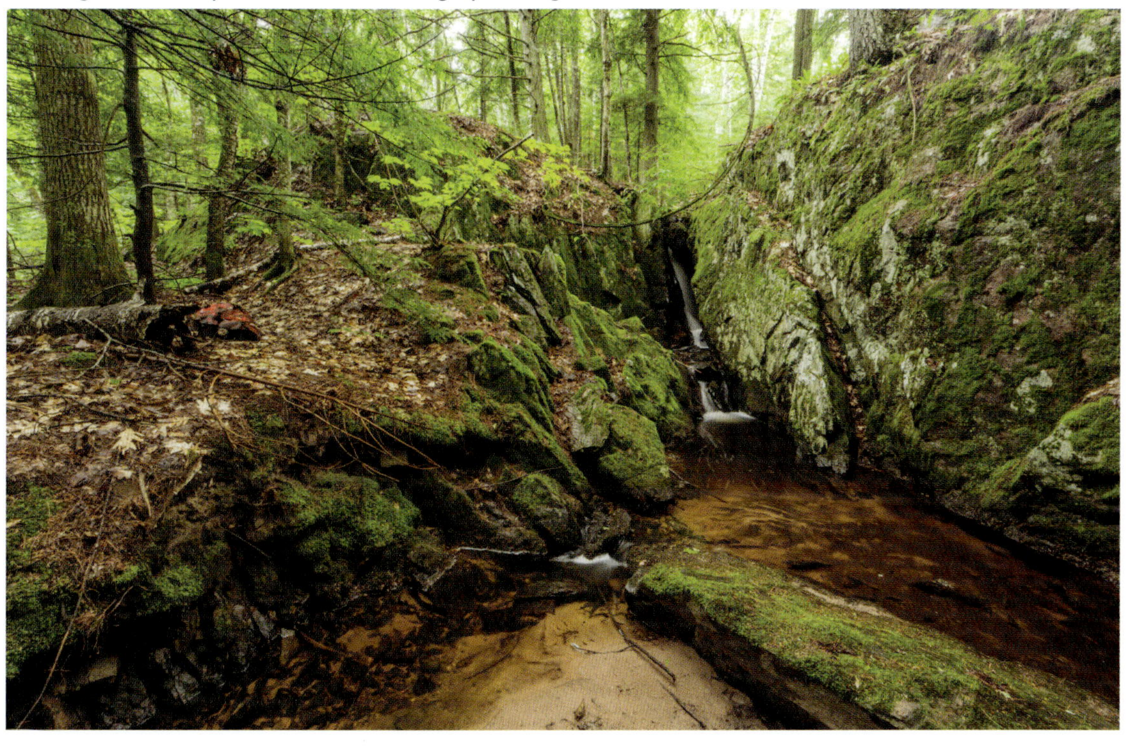

HOLEYOKE FALLS - UPPER (HOLEYOKE CREEK)

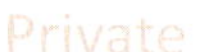

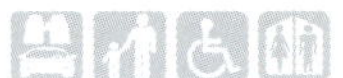

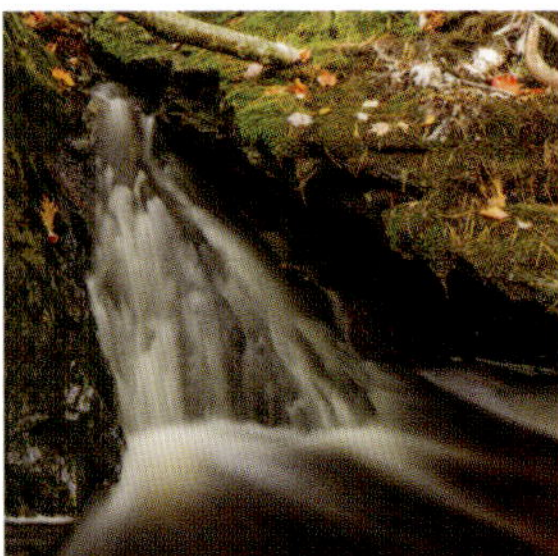

Must See:	5	GPS:	N46 34.672 W87 29.841
Height:	3 feet		
Time:	40-60 minutes	Hiking Information	
		Path:	None
Driving Information		Length:	.29 miles
Signs:	None	Elev. Change:	Elevated
Road:	2-track	GPS:	Recommended
Access:	Difficult	Danger:	Elevated
4WD:	Recommended	WP Boots:	N/A

This drop is .22 miles downstream from Shotgun Falls. After a relatively smooth journey through the forest, the terrain becomes more rocky and restless. The creek starts a more rapid journey down. This tiny waterfall has neat character as the water fans out, running down a rippled slide to a widened out pool below that is full of interesting eddies.

The waterfall splays out over a "V" shaped rock secreted into a 4 x 10 foot hollowed out "cave". A small, but relatively deep spill pool necks down before the creek runs another 10 feet.

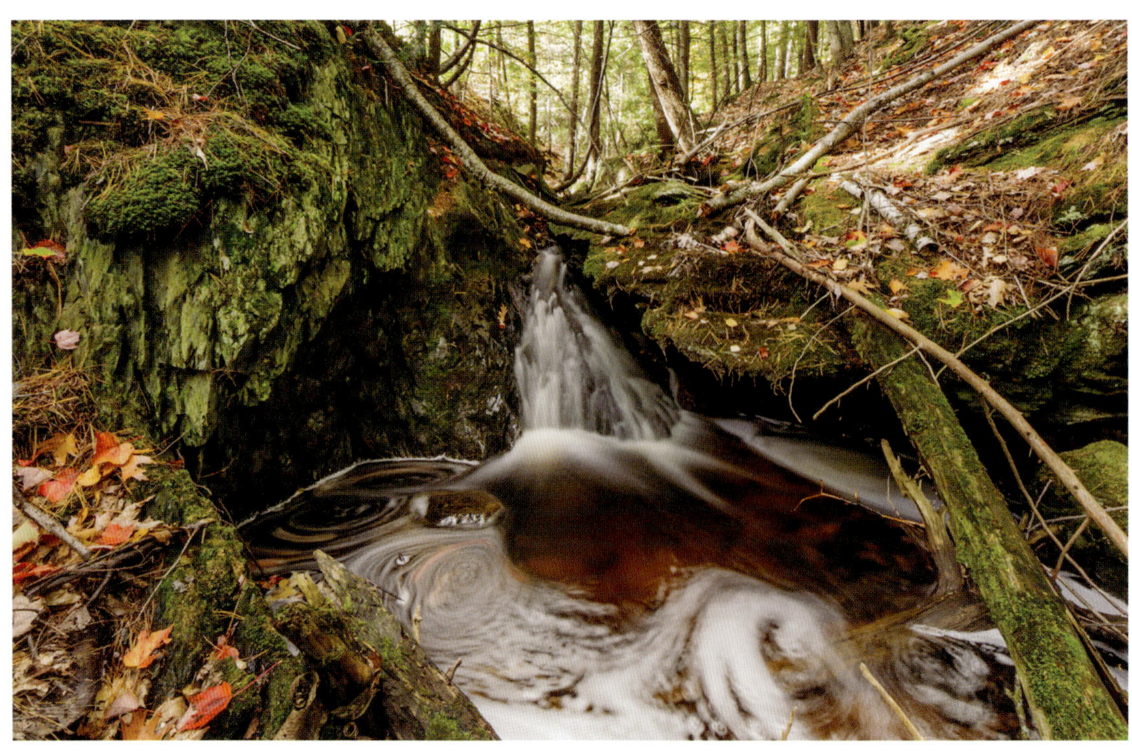

HOLEYOKE FALLS (HOLEYOKE CREEK)

Private 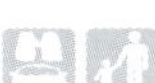 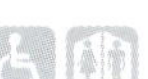

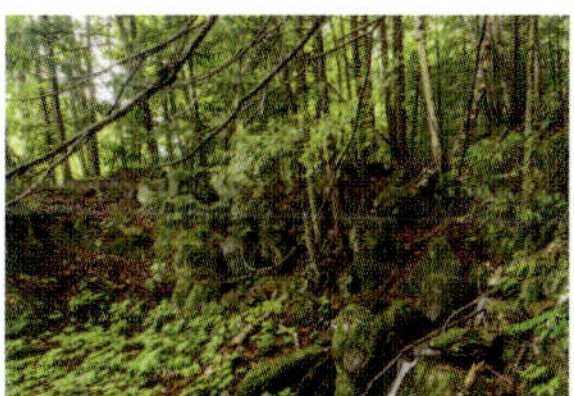

Must See:	6	GPS:	N46 34.669 W87 29.805
Height:	30 feet		
Time:	45-70 minutes	Hiking Information	
		Path:	None
Driving Information		Length:	.33 miles
Signs:	None	Elev. Change:	Elevated
Road:	2-track	GPS:	Recommended
Access:	Difficult	Danger:	Elevated
4WD:	Recommended	WP Boots:	N/A

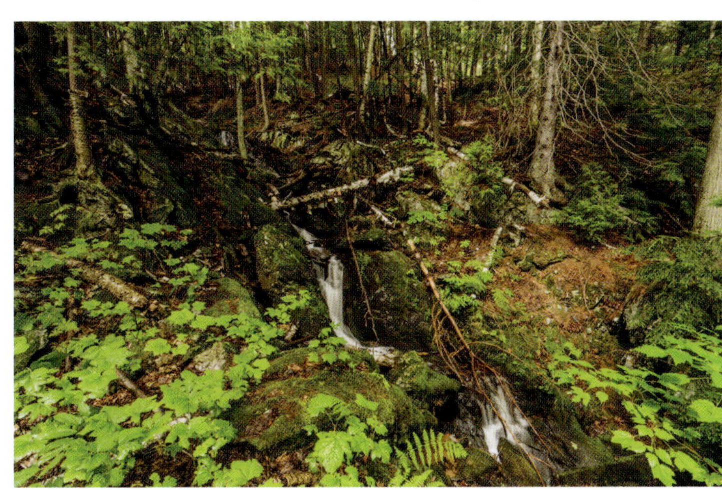

The 1/4 mile hike from Shotgun Falls to Holeyoke Falls requires some effort. There is no trail, and a quickly descending creek at the end make it an exhausting hike. Sometimes it's better to travel right down the creek bed. Other times there are level spots in the forest that are more easily traveled. When approaching the waterfall, several small drops give warning (like the Upper Falls). It's a steep climb down to the bottom, so pick your way carefully. The waterfall is a series of fast dropping cascades that culminate at an old moss-covered concrete entrance to a culvert that passes beneath a set of railroad tracks. The creek eventually meets up with Reany Creek.

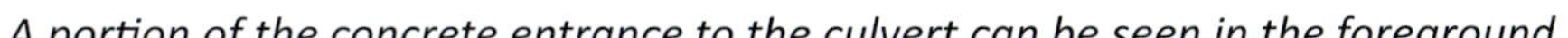

A portion of the concrete entrance to the culvert can be seen in the foreground

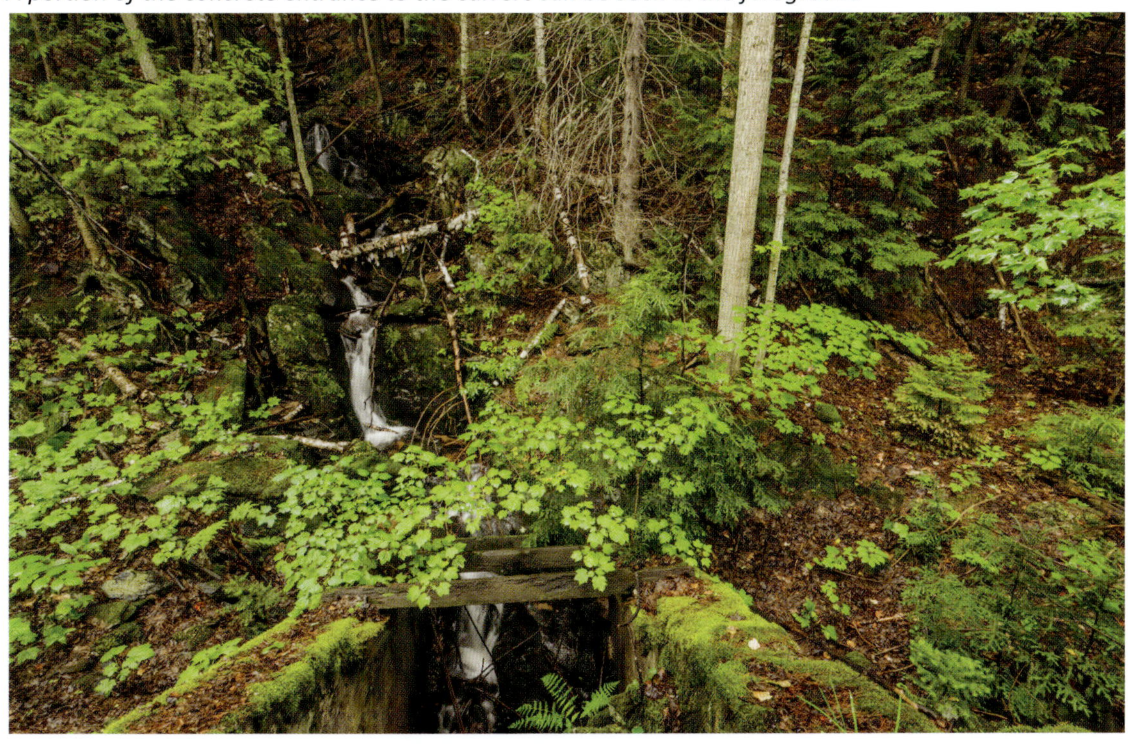

REANY FALLS - UPPER #1 (REANY CREEK)

Private 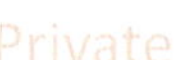  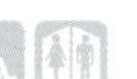

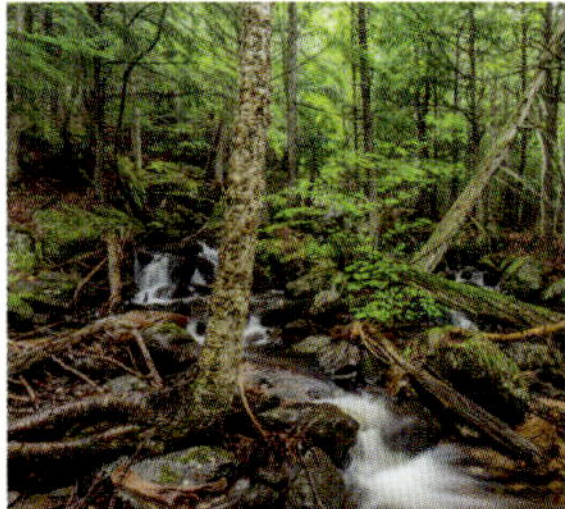

Must See:	5	GPS:	N46 34.533 W87 30.223
Height:	20 feet		
Time:	60-90 minutes	**Hiking Information**	
		Path:	None
Driving Information		Length:	.73 miles
Signs:	None	Elev. Change:	Elevated
Road:	2-track	GPS:	Recommended
Access:	Difficult	Danger:	Elevated
4WD:	Recommended	WP Boots:	N/A

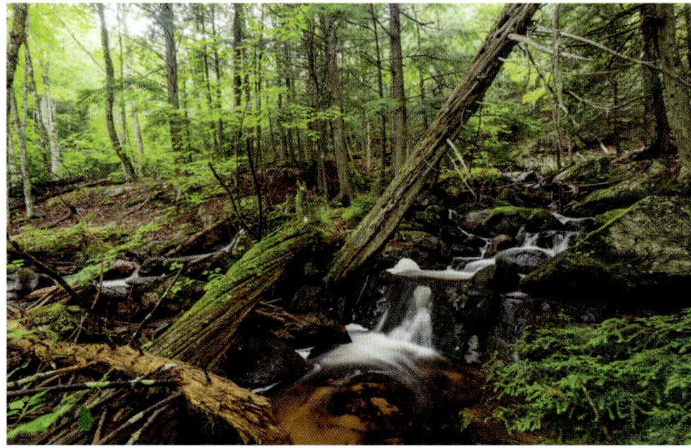

Hike parallel to the railroad tracks between Holeyoke Falls and Reany Creek. The waterfall should be heard at this point. Follow the creek upstream a short distance to the base of the widened waterfall.

The river comes tumbling down a rocky hillside, dividing around a fairly wide island populated with large boulders and cedar trees. Numerous cascades fall amongst boulders and downed trees. The creek comes back together at the base of the falls only to split again almost immediately. The waterfall looks something like an oversized Holeyoke Falls. This creek contains a lot more water, and the hillside waterfall is substantially wider. But much of the water coming down the hill is hidden beneath the large boulders that fill the divided waterway. Unfortunately, because so much of the creek is hidden, there is no easy way to appreciate the amount of drop that is laid out before you.

Mossy rocks are everywhere!

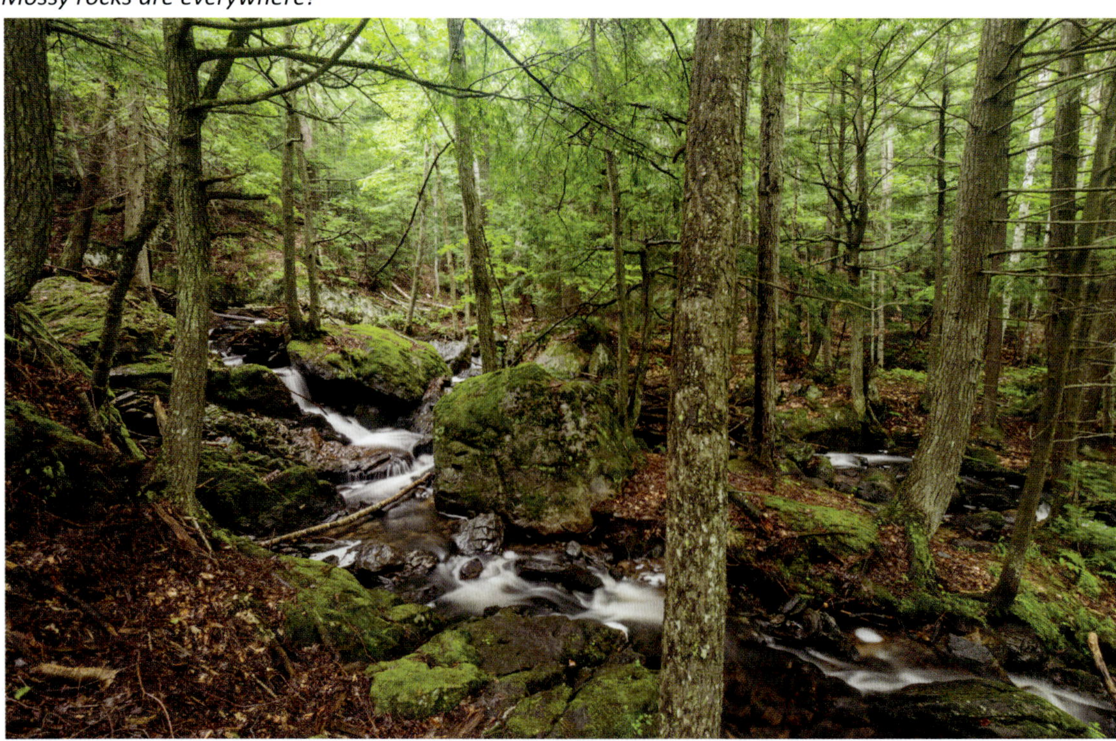

REANY FALLS - UPPER #2 (REANY CREEK)

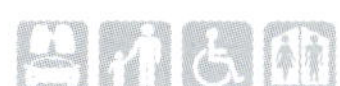

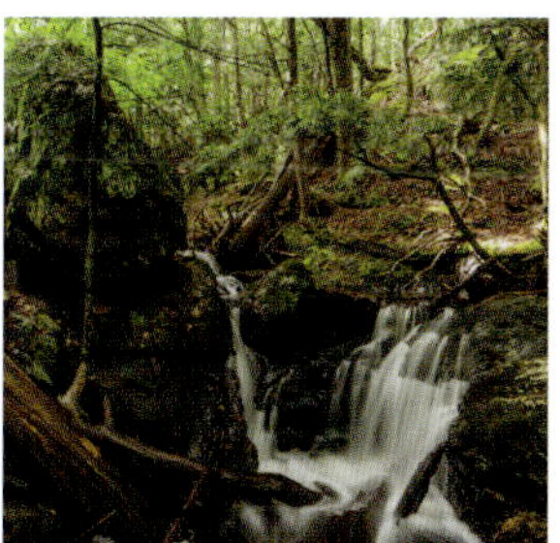

Must See:	6
Height:	10 feet
Time:	70-100 minutes

Driving Information

Signs:	None
Road:	2-track
Access:	Difficult
4WD:	Recommended

GPS:	N46 34.553 W87 30.242

Hiking Information

Path:	None
Length:	.76 miles
Elev. Change:	Elevated
GPS:	Recommended
Danger:	Elevated
WP Boots:	N/A

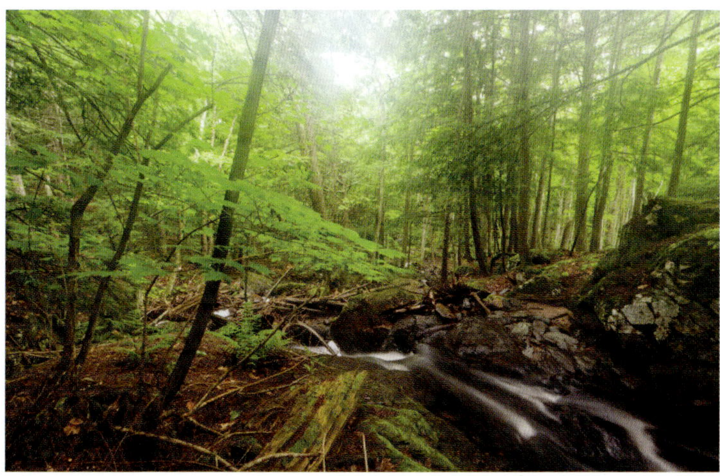

A triple-split drop falls around a cluster of large rock masses that have tumbled into the creek with most of them somehow landing vertically. Steep ravine walls rise on either side. Climb up around the lower viewing area of the waterfall to see the top portion. Up here, the creek turns quickly, falling over a seemingly flattened rock plateau, with a large boulder standing guard on the near side, and a pile of rocks laying the foundation for the waterfall. Tapered bedrock points the way downstream. And with the masses of rock on the near side, the upstream and downstream views are hidden from view.

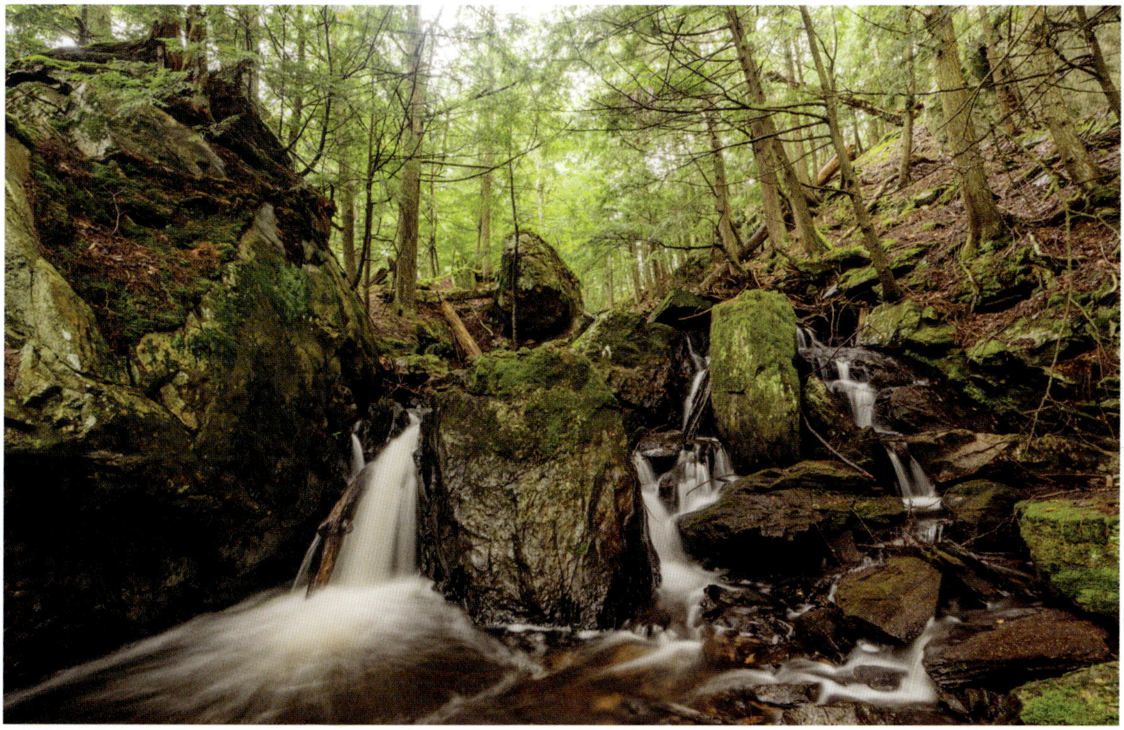

REANY RIDGE FALLS (REANY CREEK)

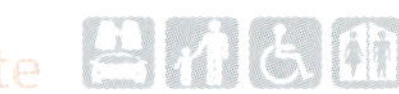

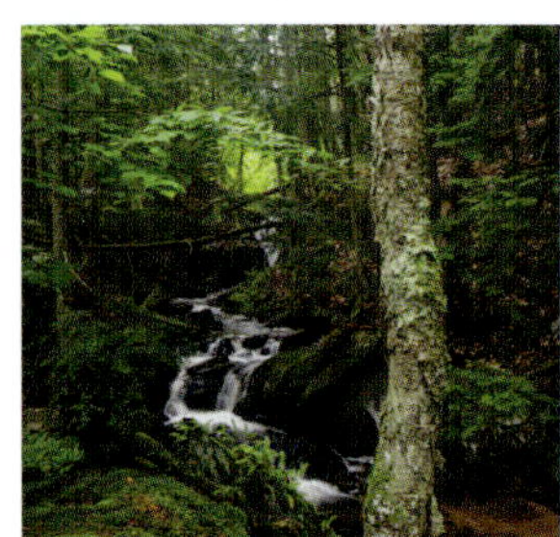

Must See:	7
Height:	8 feet
Time:	90-120 minutes

Driving Information

Signs:	None
Road:	2-track
Access:	Difficult
4WD:	Recommended

GPS:	N46 34.540 W87 30.299

Hiking Information

Path:	None
Length:	.82 miles
Elev. Change:	Elevated
GPS:	Recommended
Danger:	Elevated
WP Boots:	N/A

Hike along the top of the southern side of the gorge wall for about 85 yards. From here, you'll see this lovely waterfall and a couple smaller drops laid out in front of you! Pick your way down to the creek when possible, carefully hiking along the wet rocks. Long, narrow rocks standing on edge divide the creek into narrow strands of water, like fingers held under a faucet. The waterfall is nicely presented with a flat viewing area. This is my favorite waterfall in this section of the creek.

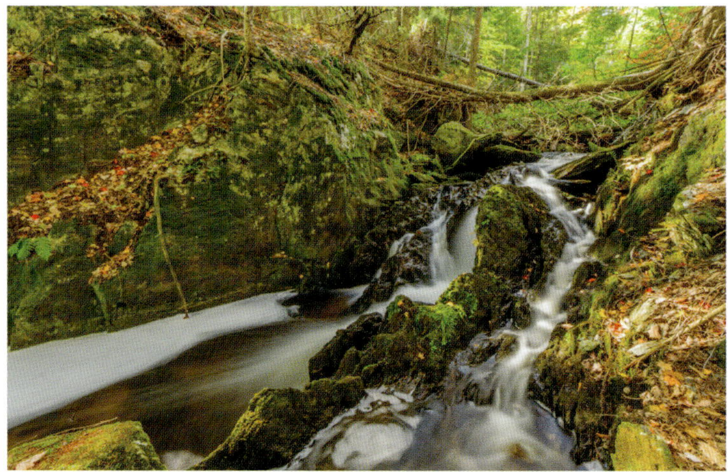

This is a rugged section of Michigan! No trail - and very uneven footing everywhere!

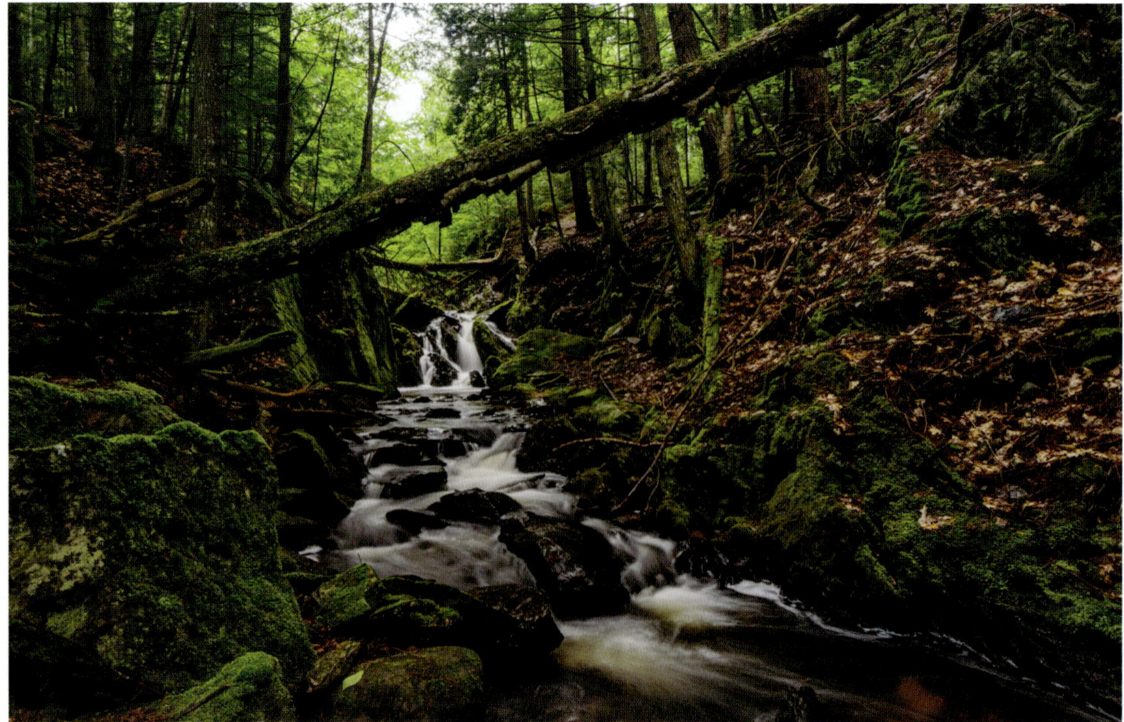

REANY RIDGE FALLS - UPPER (REANY CREEK)

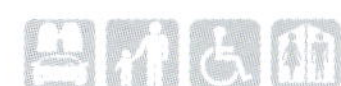

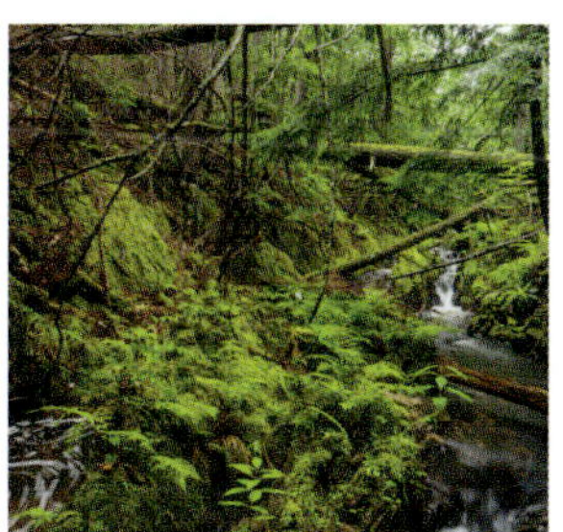

Must See:	5	GPS:	N46 34.528 W87 30.389
Height:	6 feet		
Time:	100-130 minutes	**Hiking Information**	
		Path:	None
Driving Information		Length:	.90 miles
Signs:	None	Elev. Change:	Elevated
Road:	2-track	GPS:	Recommended
Access:	Difficult	Danger:	Elevated
4WD:	Recommended	WP Boots:	N/A

Hike .10 miles further upstream. This passes through rough terrain.

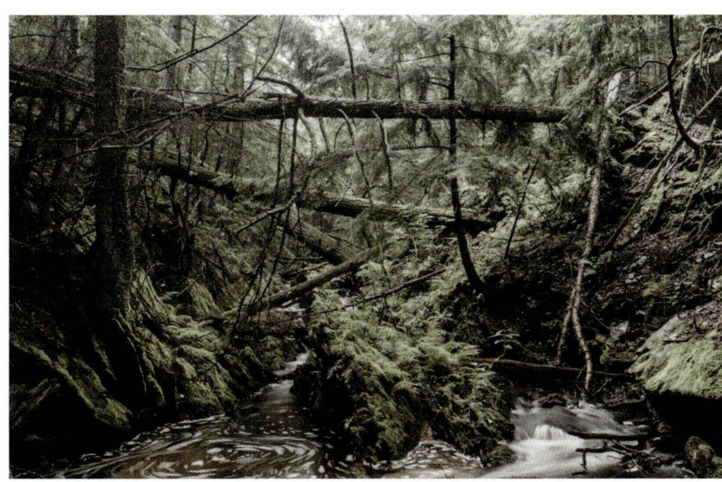

The ridges seen downstream at Reany Ridge Falls are present here in even more dramatic fashion! In fact, the creek is actually split in half for a ways with a large moss-covered spine running right down the middle of the bed. Several small cascades add up to about 6 feet of drop over 150 feet in this back country creek. Lush, soft moss stands in contrast to the rugged terrain all around.

For a shorter way back to the vehicle, hike cross country for .21 miles to the power line. Head to N46 34.694 W87 30.444. From there hike along the ATV trail to the vehicle (.56 miles).

The unique waterfall looks like a deeply rutted 2-track!

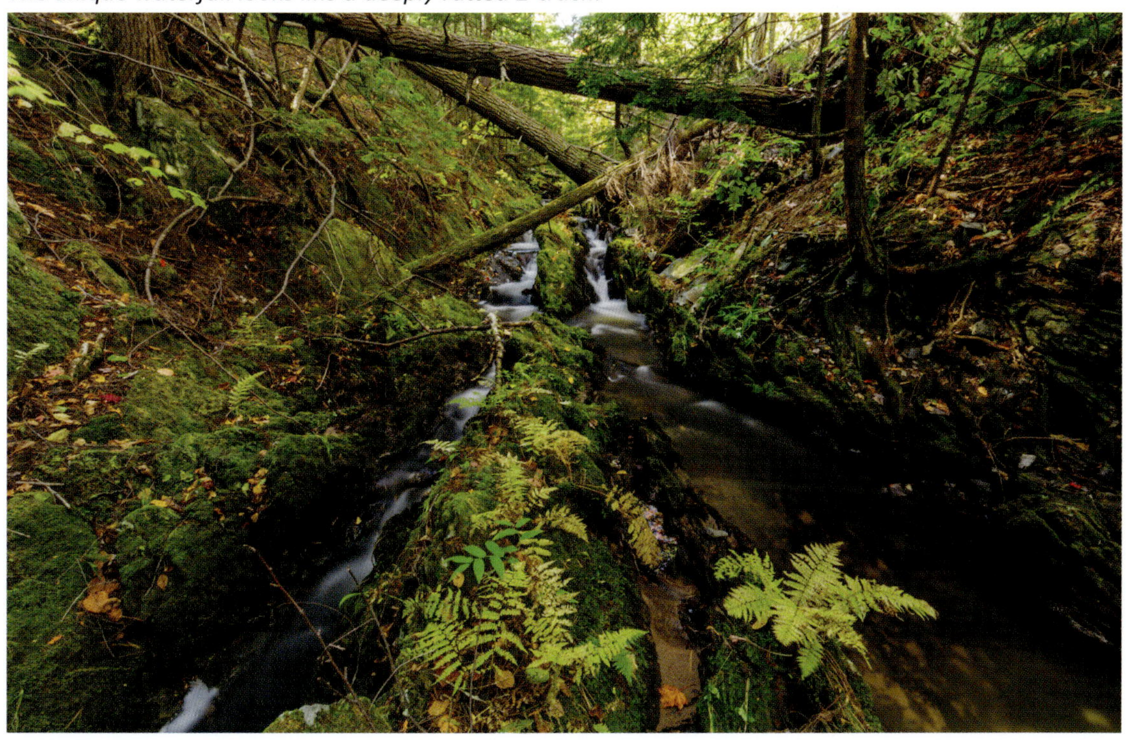

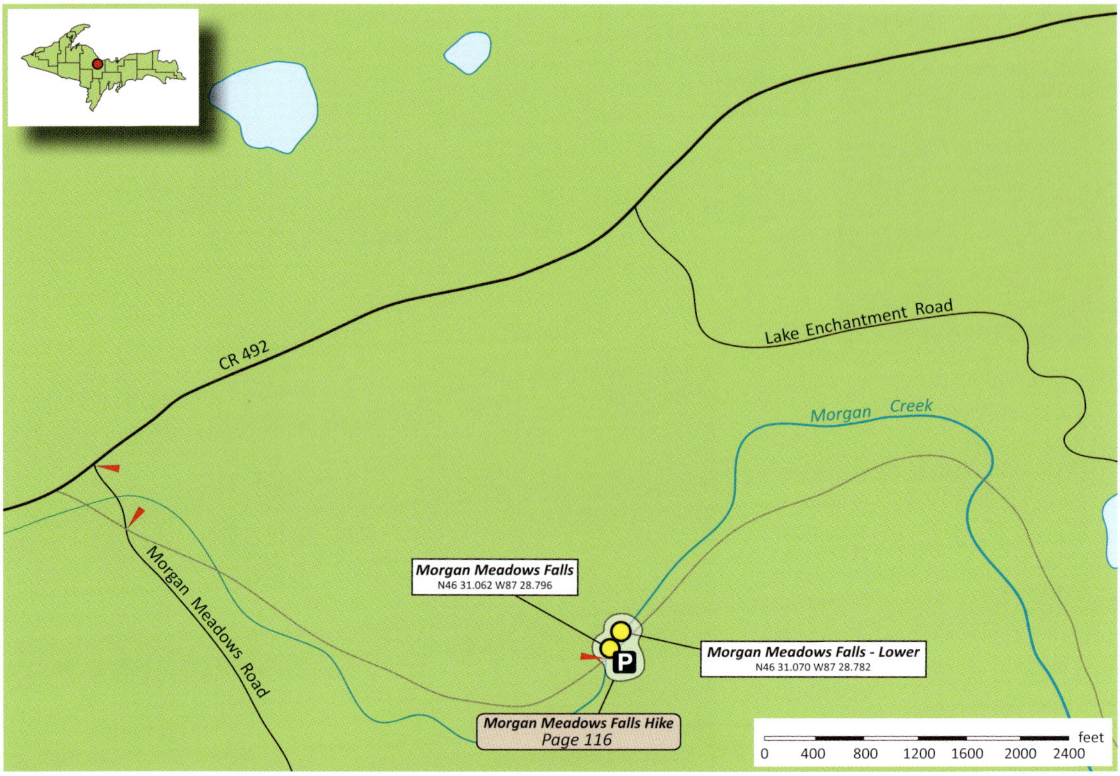

CR 492
Lake Enchantment Road
Morgan Creek
Morgan Meadows Road
Morgan Meadows Falls
N46 31.062 W87 28.796
Morgan Meadows Falls - Lower
N46 31.070 W87 28.782
Morgan Meadows Falls Hike
Page 116
feet
0 400 800 1200 1600 2000 2400

Morgan Meadows Falls Hike

Bad data is a bummer! I had information to look for these falls about a mile downstream from here. So... after hiking to the creek from Lake Enchantment Road, I followed it down river all the way to Morgan Falls. Of course, there were no waterfalls. It was on my third attempt that I finally had it right... somewhat. When I arrived at the correct parking spot, the information I had sent me the wrong way. I hiked over 1/4 mile up the creek before coming back to the vehicle only to discover a waterfall just on the other side of the road! What an easy set of waterfalls to find, if you only know where to look!

The dirt road that runs past the waterfall

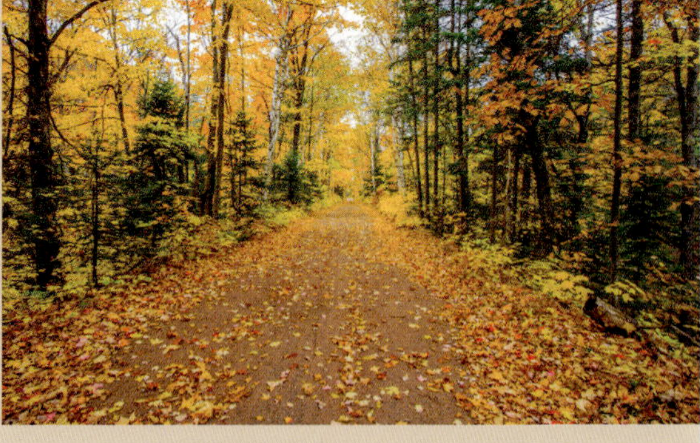

The drive down the 2-track can be a little bumpy, but most vehicles should be able to make it. The creek makes a hard turn to the right, drops over a set of cascades, meanders through a small flat area and then, as it starts to parallel the road, tumbles down through a wild and steep tangle of undergrowth in the lower falls.

Directions: Off of US-41 in Marquette, turn south onto CR-492 (next to Starbucks) and drive for 3.5 miles. Turn left (south) onto Morgan Meadow Drive. The road crosses a creek almost immediately. Turn left (southeast) at the first dirt road following the creek. Follow it for .7 miles. Park on the right. The falls are on the left.

MORGAN MEADOWS FALLS (MORGAN CREEK)

Private 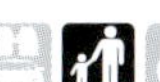 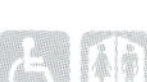

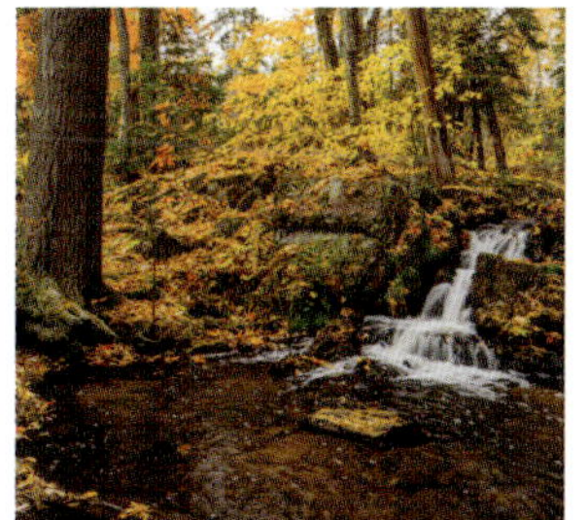

Must See:	5	GPS:	N46 31.062 W87 28.796
Height:	5 feet		
Time:	5-10 minutes	Hiking Information	
		Path:	None needed
Driving Information		Length:	100 feet
Signs:	None	Elev. Change:	Slight
Road:	Dirt road	GPS:	N/A
Access:	Somewhat easy	Danger:	Slight
4WD:	N/A	WP Boots:	N/A

Block shaped rocks push the creek to the right over falls through a three-step cascade to a sandy and pebble filled spill pool. This is only 100' from the parking spot! There is a good sized flat area that works for picnicking near the falls and playing with kids!

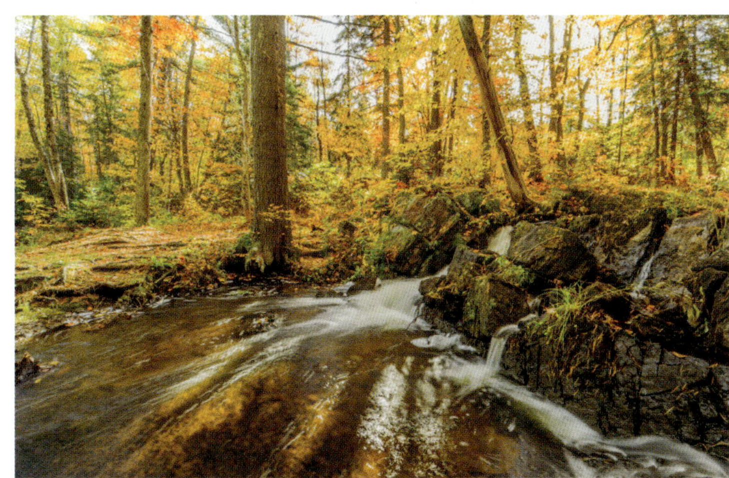

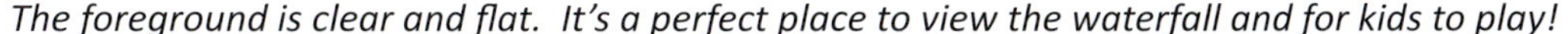

The foreground is clear and flat. It's a perfect place to view the waterfall and for kids to play!

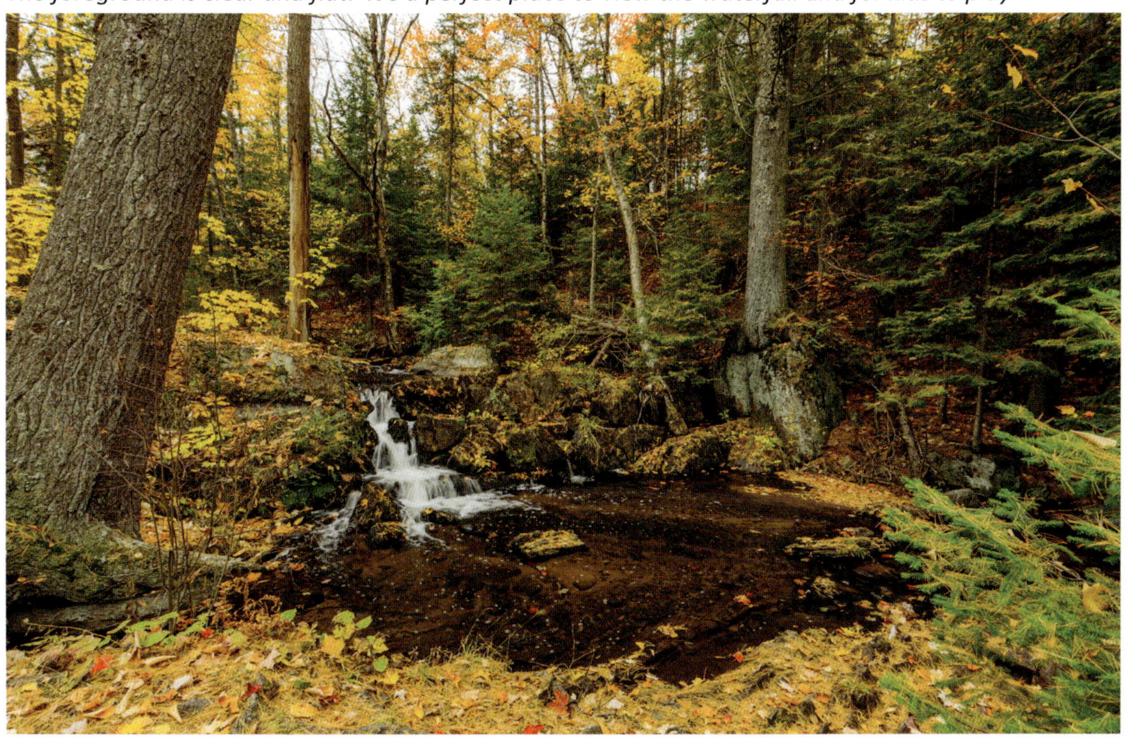

MORGAN MEADOWS FALLS - LOWER (MORGAN CREEK)

Private 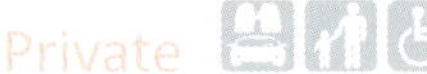

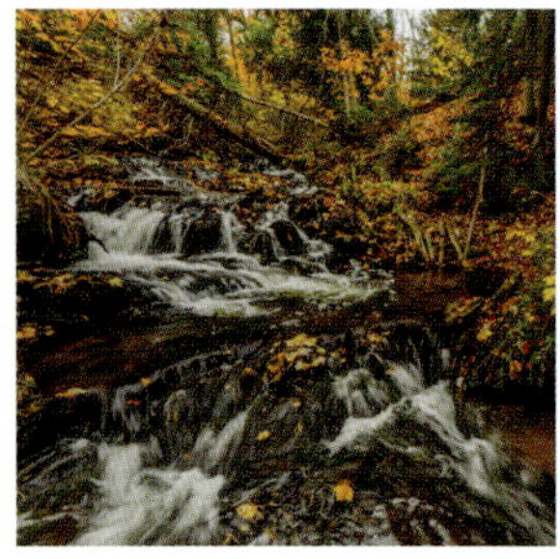

Must See:	6	GPS:	N46 31.070 W87 28.782
Height:	8 feet		
Time:	10-20 minutes	Hiking Information	
		Path:	None needed
Driving Information		Length:	200 feet
Signs:	None	Elev. Change:	Moderate
Road:	Dirt road	GPS:	N/A
Access:	Somewhat easy	Danger:	Moderate
4WD:	N/A	WP Boots:	Helpful

Climb down the 15 foot ravine to the base of the lower falls just 75 feet downstream from Morgan Meadows Falls. There is no trail. Follow the dirt road until the undergrowth thins out perpendicular to the base of the falls. The creek drops in many little cascades over a 30 foot stretch of creek.

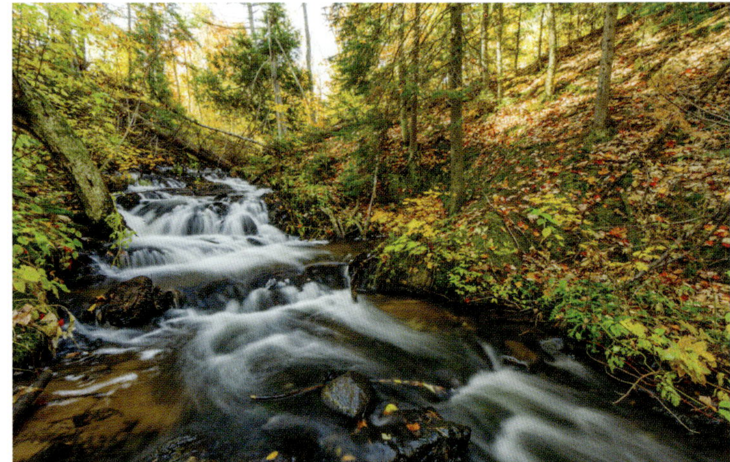

This view is along a steep hillside and not nearly as viewer friendly as the waterfall up above

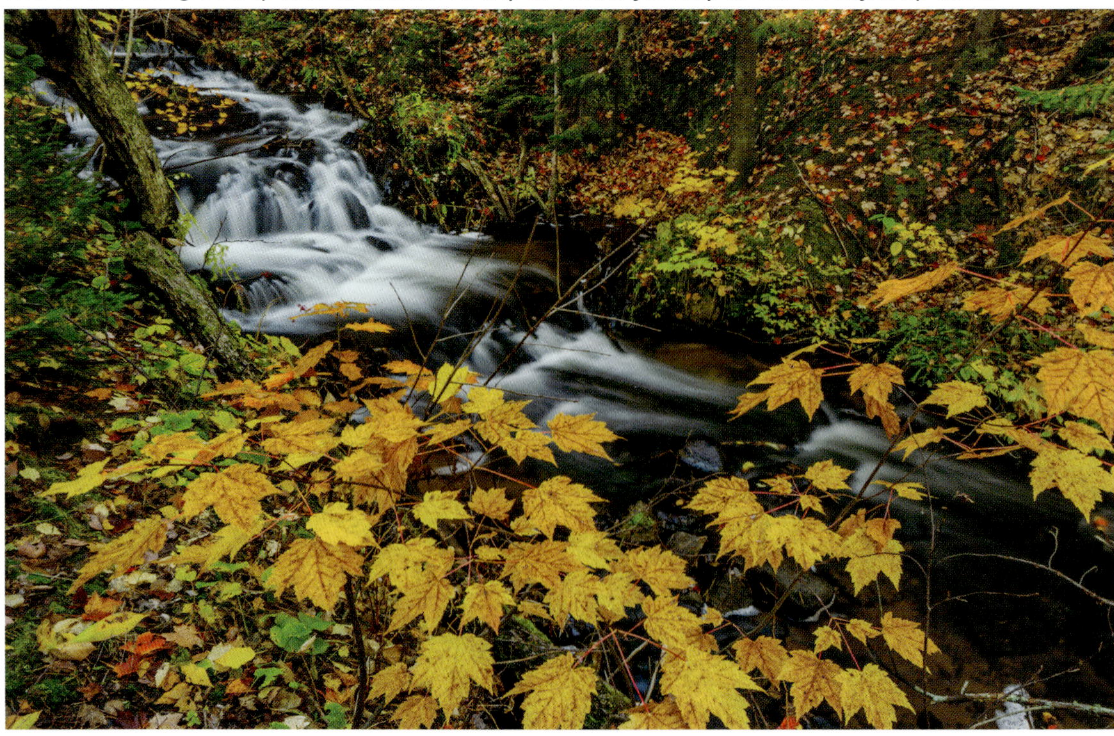

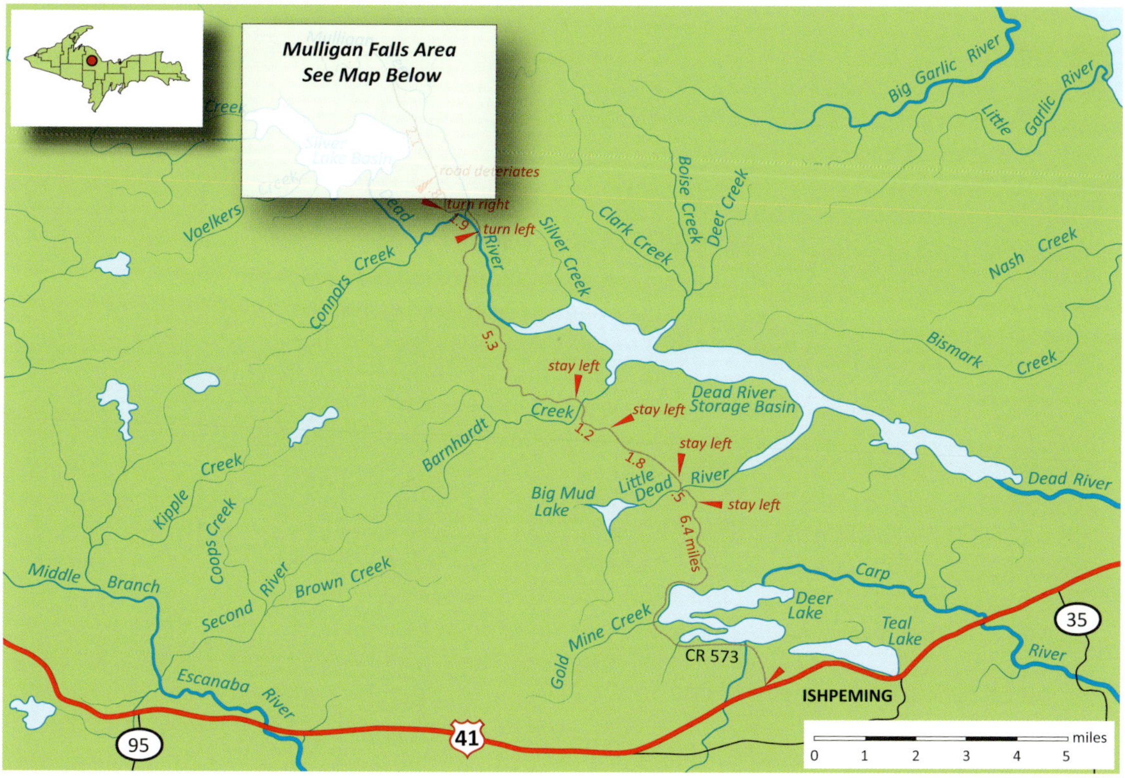

Mulligan Falls Area
See Map Below

turn right
turn left
stay left
stay left
stay left
stay left

Big Garlic River
Little Garlic River
Voelkers Creek
Connors Creek
Dead River
Silver Creek
Clark Creek
Boise Creek
Deer Creek
Nash Creek
Bismark Creek
Dead River Storage Basin
Barnhardt Creek
Little Dead River
Big Mud Lake
Kipple Creek
Coops Creek
Middle Branch
Second River
Brown Creek
Escanaba River
Gold Mine Creek
Deer Lake
Teal Lake
Carp River
CR 573
ISHPEMING

0 1 2 3 4 5 miles

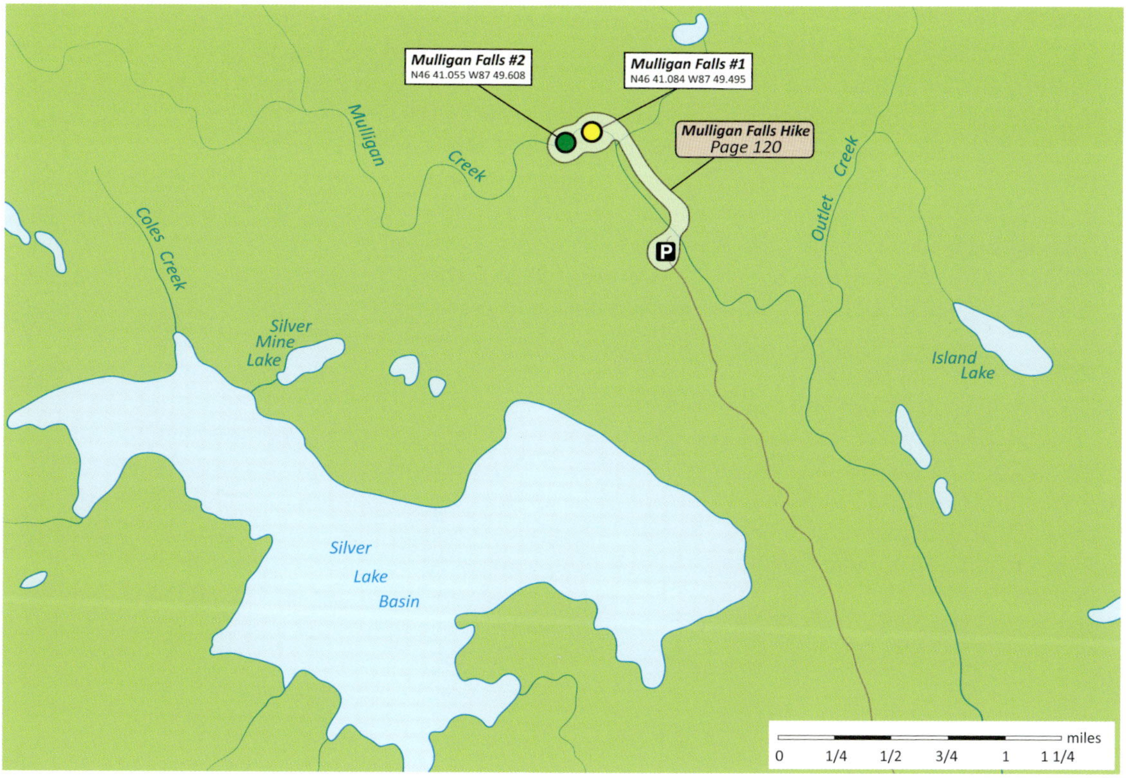

Mulligan Falls #2
N46 41.055 W87 49.608

Mulligan Falls #1
N46 41.084 W87 49.495

Mulligan Falls Hike
Page 120

Mulligan Creek
Outlet Creek
Coles Creek
Silver Mine Lake
Island Lake
Silver Lake Basin

0 1/4 1/2 3/4 1 1 1/4 miles

Mulligan Falls Hike

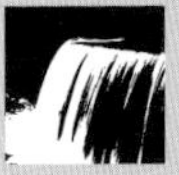

This is a more difficult hike. For some reason, these are the hikes that I look back on with more fondness! Perhaps it's the "I survived it!" mentality, or the raw emotion at the time, or maybe just the amount of time spent looking for a particular waterfall that embeds the mind with more hooks on which to place memories.

I have to admit that I was not looking forward to finding the Mulligan Falls. I had practically no data about what I was looking for; just a couple of GPS coordinates. From past experience, I had learned that those were often terribly unreliable. The lack of roads in the area made me wonder how close I could drive. I was pulling a Polaris Ranger behind my GMC Sierra. This had its pluses and minuses. I was able to go down 2-tracks and really rough dirt roads with the ORV, but the amount of time that it took to unload and load it back up kept me from using it as merely a "scout vehicle". Too often I had exercised poor judgment and had to turn around in nearly impossible quarters. Once I was forced to back up over 1/4 mile down a narrow 2-track with the trailered Polaris making it a most difficult drive! As it turned out, although the dirt road kept winding and twisting, I kept getting closer to Mulligan Creek. When the road finally became too much of a concern to drive the truck any further, I unloaded the Ranger and was able to go the next couple of miles with no difficulties. And then I reached the creek. There was a bridge, but too narrow for my vehicle. There was no other way across, so I parked and started hiking. Just then several ATV's came from the other side and crossed the bridge. I talked briefly with the drivers and mentioned Mulligan Falls. They said it was flowing well. That gave me considerable relief. There really WAS at least one waterfall and it must be fairly easy to get to! I followed the 2-track until the GPS coordinates that I had forced me to cross through a thick stand of pines and head down to the creek. There was nothing there but swampy lowland. Discouraged, but undeterred, I kept working my way upstream, figuring the falls had to be that direction. Finally, a third of a mile later, I stumbled upon the lower falls, pouring out of the only high ground I had seen along the creek. The falls were not easily viewed, as a large spill pool dominated the foreground. Still, it was a very welcome sight, and the late evening sun was allowing for nice photos. But that late sun also meant that dark would be upon me soon, and I still had a return trip to make. I took several shots and recorded some data. Then quickly hiking up the creek, I was rewarded by finding the upper falls in only about 100 yards. I have since been told that there is another waterfall about 1/2 mile further upstream. (But that is for another day!) I decided to call it a day and get back, before dark if possible! Getting out of the river gorge proved to be more difficult that I thought. Rock outcroppings, fallen trees, and steep hillsides wouldn't let me cut straight up and out to the mostly flat plateau. I did finally get out and discovered a hunting cabin with a faint trail heading down to the falls. It was at the end of a 2-track. Following it wasn't a direct route back to the bridge, but it was easier than cutting through the trees. Once again, an adventure came to a close with that satisfied feeling of accomplishment!

Directions: In Ishpeming turn north off of US-41 onto North 2nd Street. (This is across from the National Ski and Snowboard Hall of Fame.) Drive for 6.4 miles. (The road becomes CR-573 after just a couple of blocks.) Stay left and drive another .5 miles. Again, stay left and continue for 1.8 miles. Once again, stay left. Drive for 1.2 miles. (The road turns to gravel toward the end of this section.) Stay left. In 5.3 miles turn left and drive another 1.9 miles. Turn right and continue for .8 miles. The road deteriorates here. A 4WD with good clearance is needed for the next 2.1 miles. This is where most people will need to park. A narrow wooden bridge just wide enough for ATV and foot traffic crosses Mulligan Creek. Follow the 2-track (staying to the left) to a hunting cabin @ N46 41.114 W87 49.391. There is a faint trail from here to the falls.

MULLIGAN FALLS #1 (MULLIGAN CREEK)

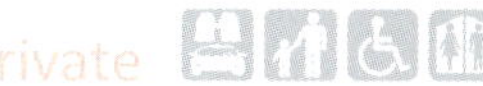

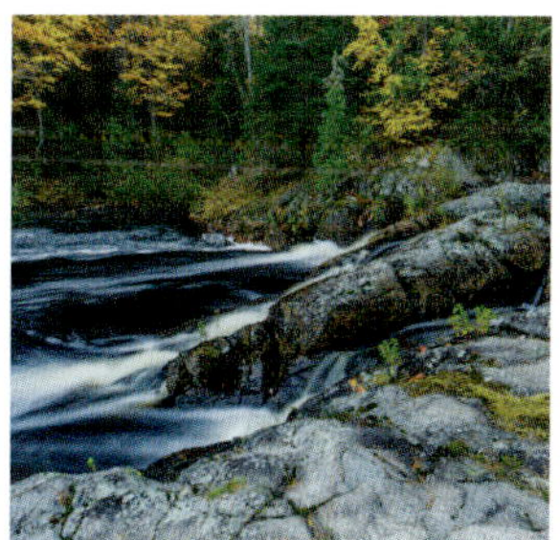

Must See:	6	GPS:	N46 41.084 W87 49.495
Height:	7 feet		
Time:	1-2 hours	Hiking Information	
		Path:	Slight
Driving Information		Length:	1.2 miles from the bridge
Signs:	None	Elev. Change:	Moderate
Road:	2-track	GPS:	Required
Access:	Very difficult	Danger:	Moderate
4WD:	Required	WP Boots:	Recommended

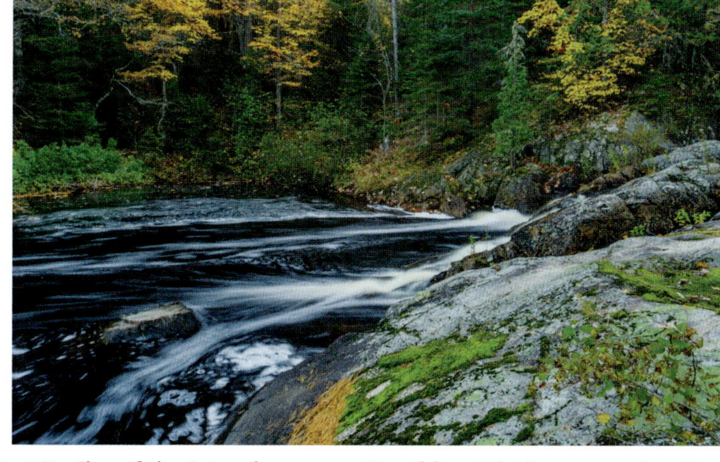

The creek runs through a narrow, short walled canyon. At the end of the canyon it narrows to 4 feet, drops 2 feet around a chunk of basalt, widens back out to 20 feet, and then divides into thirds as it drops 5 feet around rounded basalt mounds. The large spill pool below the falls marks the beginnings of the long, slow journey the creek takes through marshy lands.

Without a narrow 4WD with good clearance there is a good chance the hike will need to be longer. The last 2 miles of the 2-track are questionable, with the very end getting nearly impossible for a conventional vehicle.

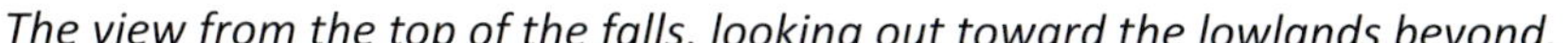

The view from the top of the falls, looking out toward the lowlands beyond.

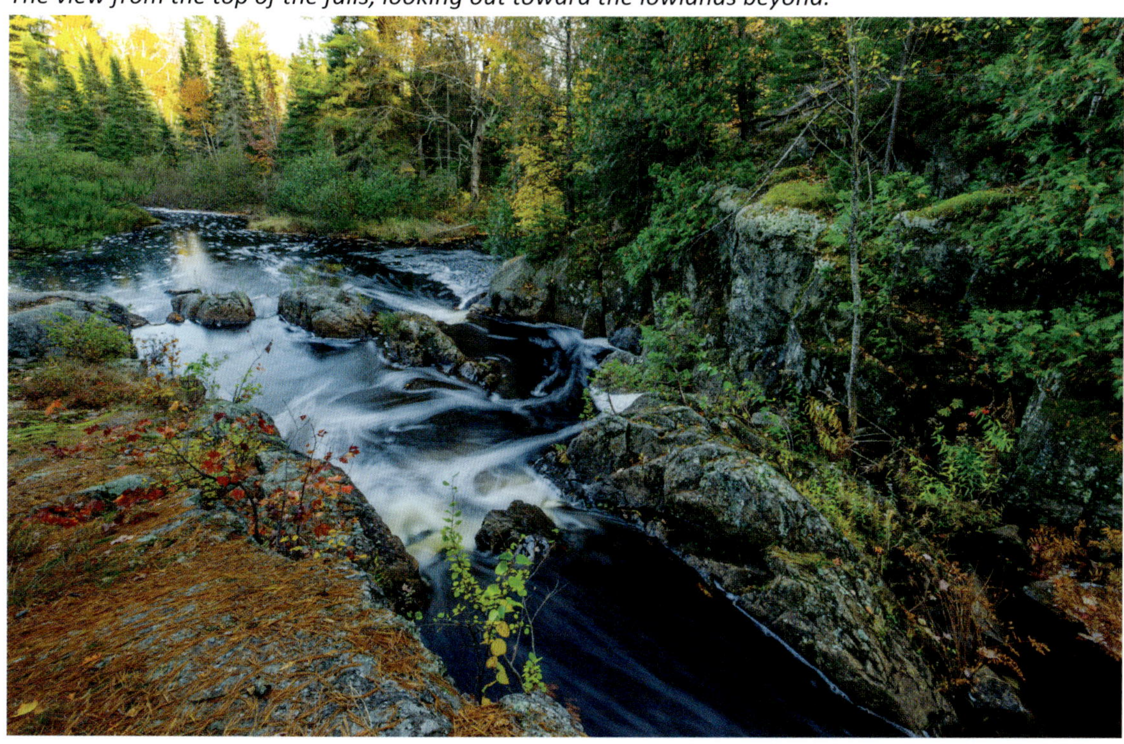

MULLIGAN FALLS #2 (MULLIGAN CREEK)

Private 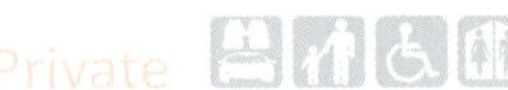

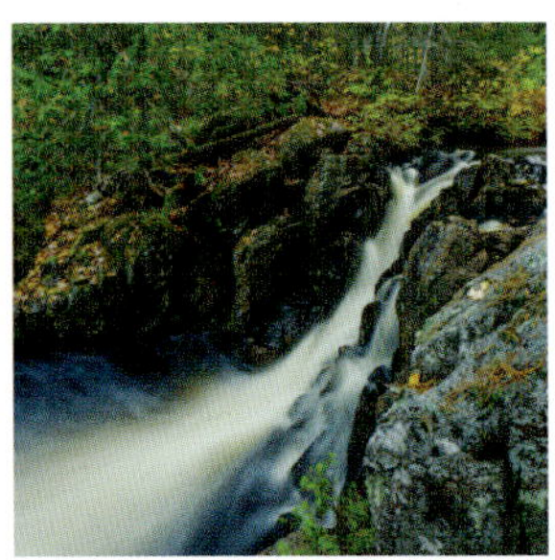

Must See: 8
Height: 10 feet
Time: 1-2 hours

Driving Information
Signs: None
Road: 2-track
Access: Very difficult
4WD: Required

GPS: N46 41.055 W87 49.608

Hiking Information
Path: Slight
Length: 1.3 miles from the bridge
Elev. Change: Moderate
GPS: Required
Danger: Moderate
WP Boots: Recommended

This waterfalls occurs as the creek enters the canyon. Craggy rocks break up the drop, with rushing water shooting down through narrow crevasses in the rock. The creek widens out to fill the 20 foot wide canyon. A small, cute drop is found about halfway between the upper and lower falls. I got one picture of it.

Without a narrow 4WD with good clearance there is a good chance the hike will need to be longer. The last 2 miles of the 2-track are questionable, with the very end getting nearly impossible for a conventional vehicle.

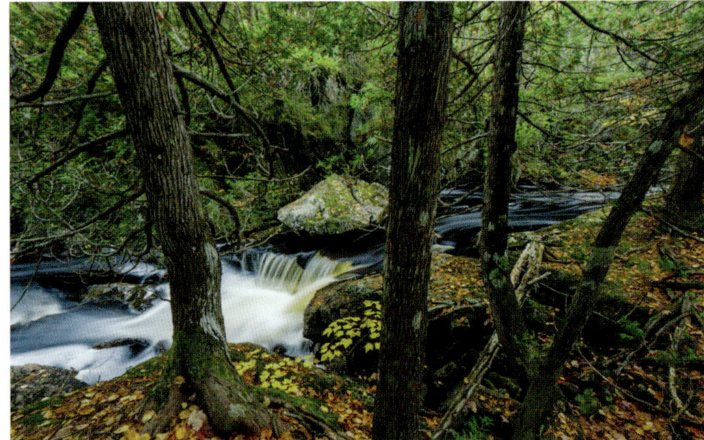

A small drop between #1 and #2

The good sized spill pool below the narrow waterfall

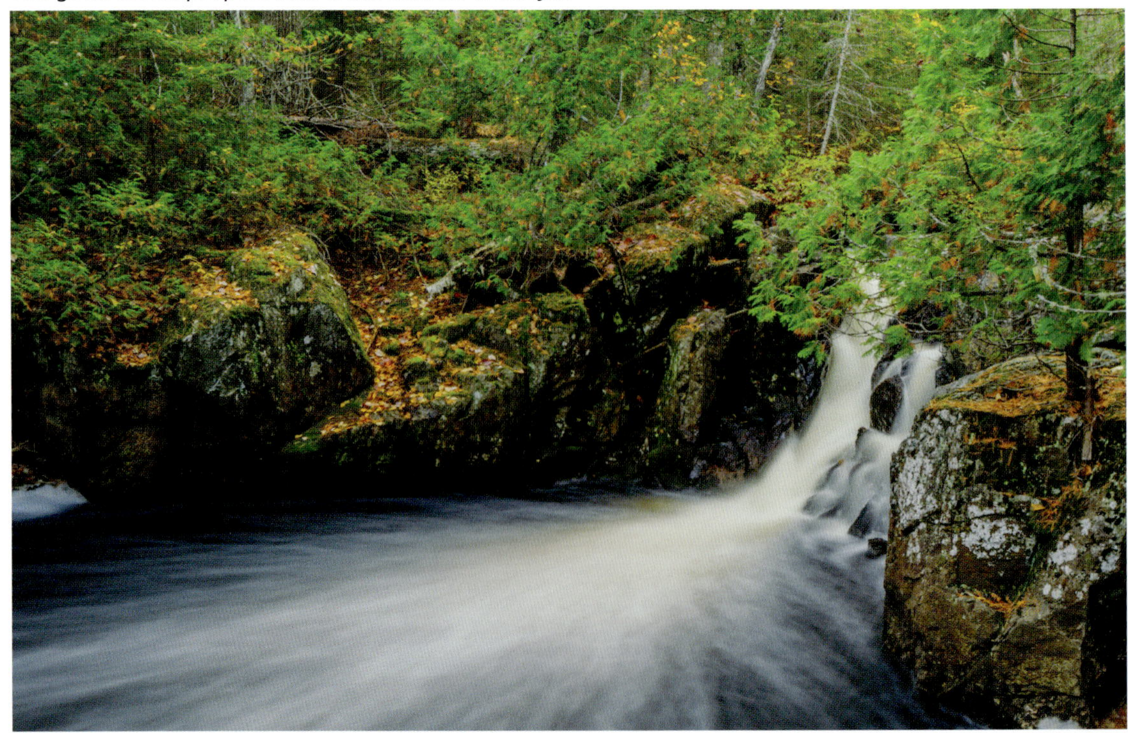

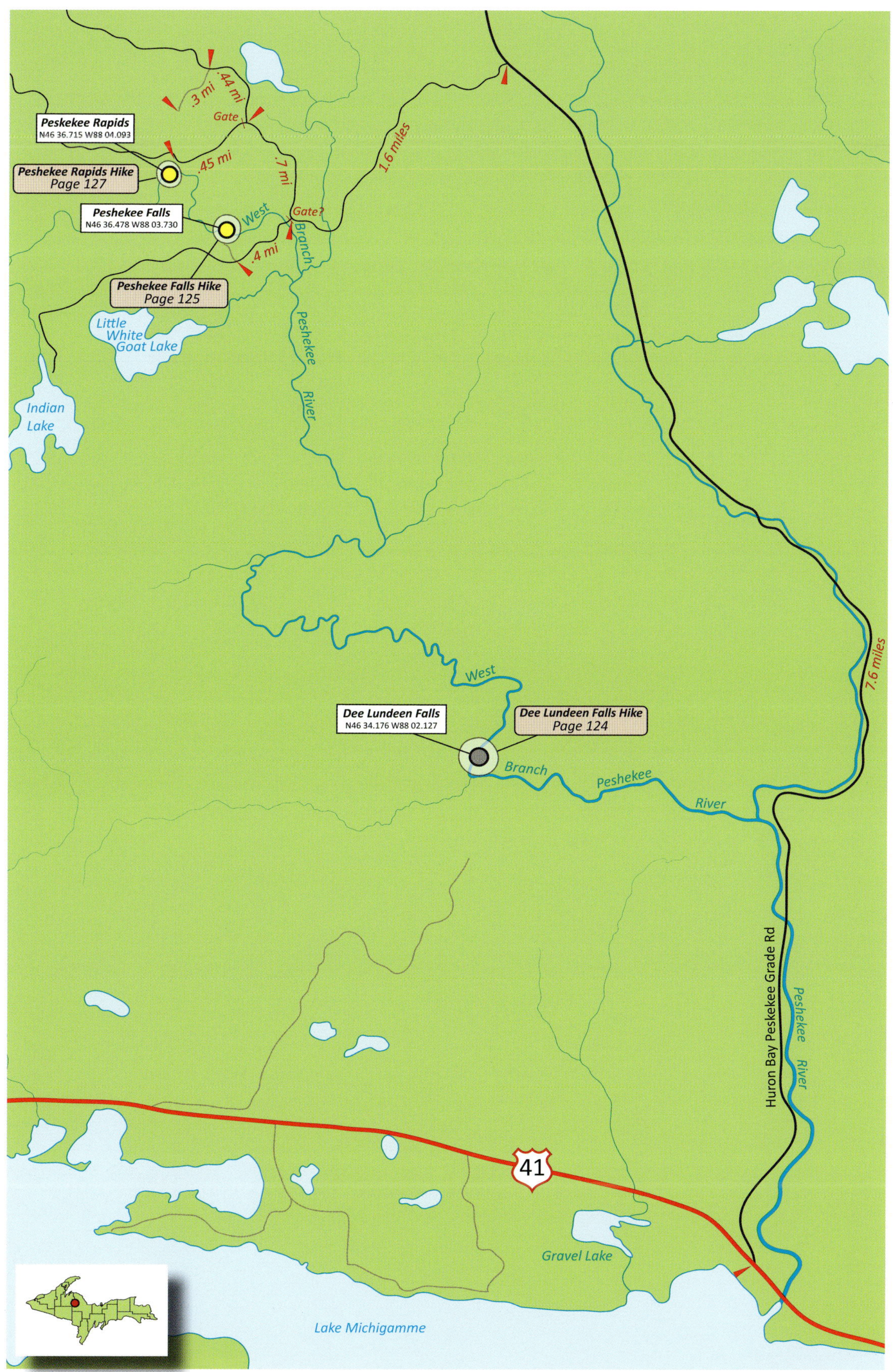

Peshekee Rapids
N46 36.715 W88 04.093
Peshekee Rapids Hike
Page 127
Peshekee Falls
N46 36.478 W88 03.730
Peshekee Falls Hike
Page 125
.3 mi
.44 mi
Gate
.45 mi
.7 mi
Gate?
.4 mi
1.6 miles
West
Branch
Peshekee
River
Little
White
Goat Lake
Indian
Lake
Dee Lundeen Falls
N46 34.176 W88 02.127
Dee Lundeen Falls Hike
Page 124
West
Branch
Peshekee
River
7.6 miles
Huron Bay Peskekee Grade Rd
Peshekee
River
41
Gravel Lake
Lake Michigamme

Dee Lundeen Falls Hike

Dee Lundeen Falls is on private property and beyond a gated driveway.

Directions: A dirt road to the north of Lake Michigamme winds around and branches a couple of times. One of these branches is eventually blocked by a gate on the way to a cabin and the waterfall. Do not attempt to pass without permission from the owner.

DEE LUNDEEN FALLS (WEST BRANCH PESHEKEE RIVER)

Private

Must See:	N/A	GPS:	*N46 34.176 W88 02.127 (not verified)*
Height:	N/A		
Time:	N/A	**Hiking Information**	
		Path:	N/A
Driving Information		Length:	N/A
Signs:	None	Elev. Change:	N/A
Road:	Dirt road	GPS:	Helpful
Access:	Somewhat difficult	Danger:	N/A
4WD:	Helpful	WP Boots:	N/A

This waterfall is on private property. Do not enter without permission!

Peshekee Falls Hike

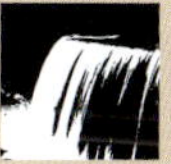

The West Branch of the Peshekee River has its beginning in the southwest corner of the Huron Mountains in Baraga County, just south of Mount Curwood. It runs southeasterly, crossing into Marquette County. Just a short distance north of Lake Michigamme it joins forces with the Peshekee River. Back closer to the Marquette/Baraga County border is where Peshekee Falls occurs.

Directions: Turn north on Huron Bay/Peshekee Grade Road off of US-41. The rough road is found just west of the bridge over the Peshekee River. This is just 5.5 miles east of the Baraga County line. Head north on the "old railroad grade" road for 7.6 miles. Turn left on a gravel road (west). Follow the winding road 1.6 miles. There is a road to southwest. (On my excursion to this waterfall, I came in from the north. Access from the south would be easier, if it is not trespassing. The directions I'm now giving need to be proved out.) I think it is gated. If so, see if walking down the road is permitted. If it is, hike for .4 miles to a 2-track to the right (north). Once again, make sure it is not posted, private property. Follow the 2-track to its end (.15 miles). Hike north to the waterfall. There may or may not be a trail for the short 75 yards to the waterfall.

If this route is not permitted, continue driving north past the "gated" road. Get past the lower ground along the river. Park. Hike the .4 miles to the waterfall through the forest (no trail). As always, be respectful of property owners and obey all property signs.

PESHEKEE FALLS (PESHEKEE RIVER - WEST BRANCH)

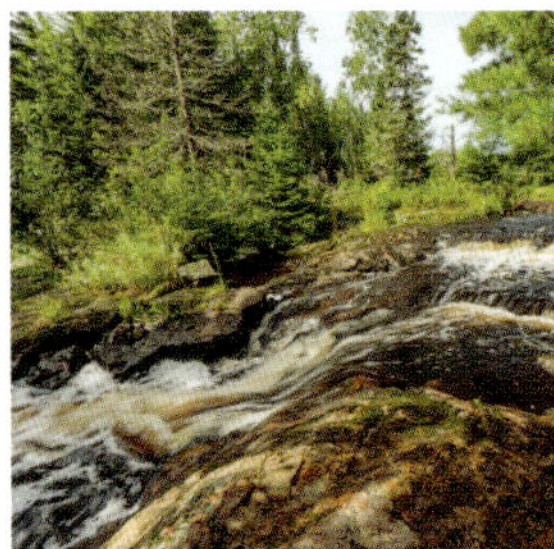

Must See:	6	GPS:	N46 36.478 W88 03.730
Height:	10 feet		
Time:	.5-1.5 hours	Hiking Information	
Driving Information		Path:	Unknown/none
Signs:	None	Length:	75 yards/.4 miles
Road:	2-track/gravel	Elev. Change:	Moderate
Access:	Difficult	GPS:	Helpful/required
4WD:	Helpful	Danger:	Moderate
		WP Boots:	May be helpful

Beavers have dammed the river above the waterfall. They have made a 1.5 foot drop up above the waterfall proper. The river then "S" curves down over flat plates, dropping 1 to 3 feet each time. Squarish blocks of rock line the river's walls, which makes good viewing areas along the northern side of the river quite sparse.

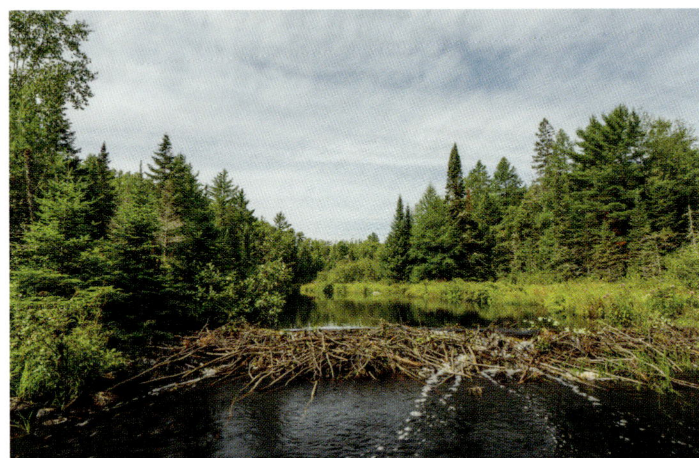

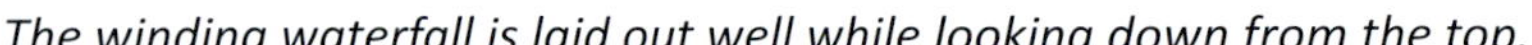

The winding waterfall is laid out well while looking down from the top.

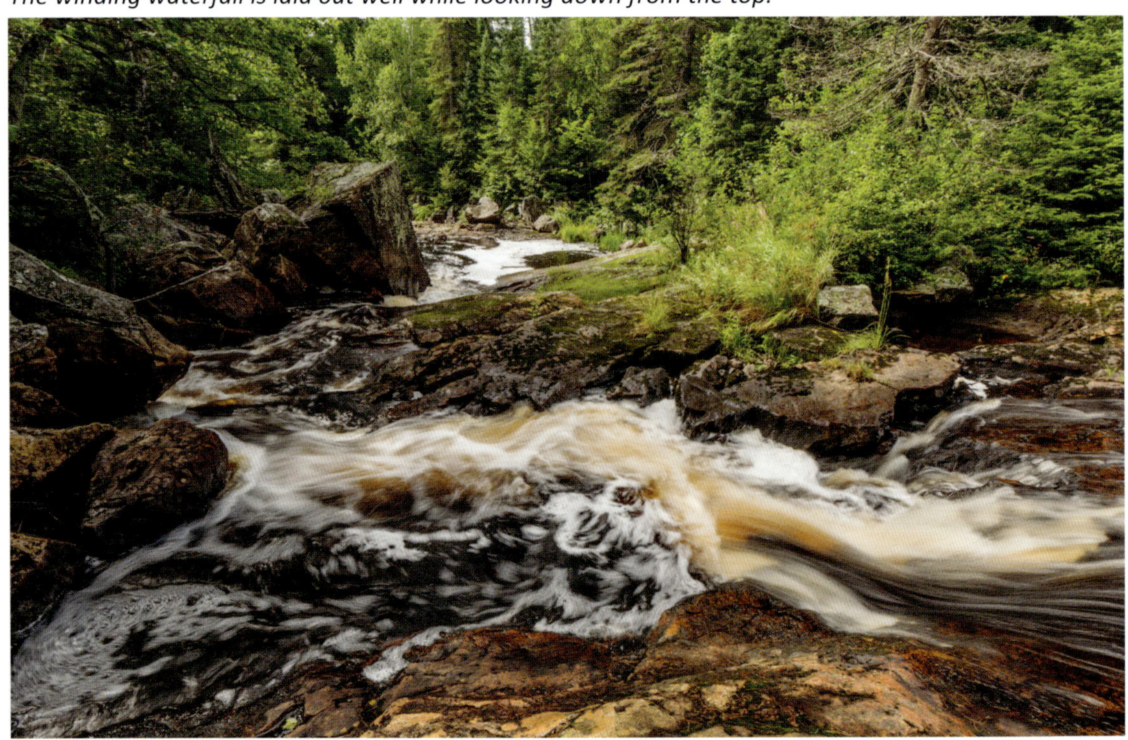

Peshekee Rapids Hike

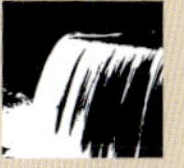

The .6 miles between the Peshekee Rapids and Peshekee Falls, the West Branch of the Peshekee River runs lazily and widens out into wet, marshy areas. At these two points, the river is pinched down into extremely narrow waterways, as the river is naturally dammed up by bedrock ridges. At low points along these ridges, the river leaks down and creates points of interest.

Directions: Turn north on Huron Bay/Peshekee Grade Road off of US-41. The rough road is found just west of the bridge over the Peshekee River. This is just 5.5 miles east of the Baraga County line. Head north on the "old railroad grade" road for 7.6 miles. Turn left on a gravel road (west). Follow the winding road 2.3 miles. As I recall, there is a gated road to the left (west). (Similar to Peshekee Falls, on my excursion to these rapids, I came in from the north. Access from the east would be easier, if it is not trespassing. These directions I'm now giving also need to be verified.) Park. Hike to the southwest if it is permissible to walk down the road. In .45 miles you will have just passed by an enlarged portion of the river and the road will turn to the north. Follow the road 50 yards to the north. Enter the forest, hiking west 75 yards to get past a low point. Then turn south and hike 120 yards down to the rapids.

If it's not permissible to hike down the road beyond the gate, continue driving along the gravel road .44 miles. Turn left (southwest) onto a 2-track (a 4WD may be needed). Follow the 2-track (staying to the left) to the end (.3 miles). Park. Hike through the sometimes dense woods to the GPS coordinates for the rapids (.31 miles).

PESHEKEE RAPIDS (PESHEKEE RIVER - WEST BRANCH)

Private 

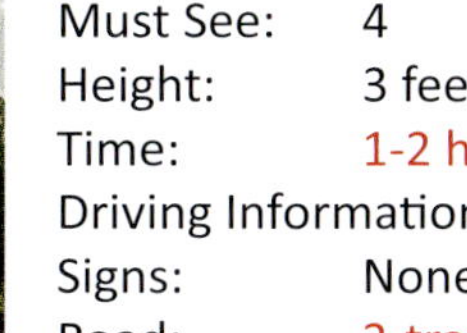

Must See:	4	GPS:	N46 36.715 W88 04.093
Height:	3 feet		
Time:	1-2 hours	Hiking Information	
Driving Information		Path:	2-track then none
Signs:	None	Length:	.3 -.4 miles
Road:	2-track	Elev. Change:	Moderate
Access:	Difficult	GPS:	Required
4WD:	Recommended	Danger:	Moderate/increased
		WP Boots:	May be helpful

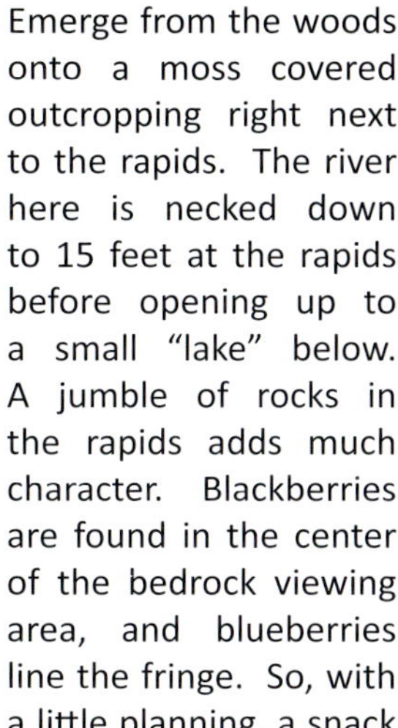

Emerge from the woods onto a moss covered outcropping right next to the rapids. The river here is necked down to 15 feet at the rapids before opening up to a small "lake" below. A jumble of rocks in the rapids adds much character. Blackberries are found in the center of the bedrock viewing area, and blueberries line the fringe. So, with a little planning, a snack at the end of this journey may just be possible!

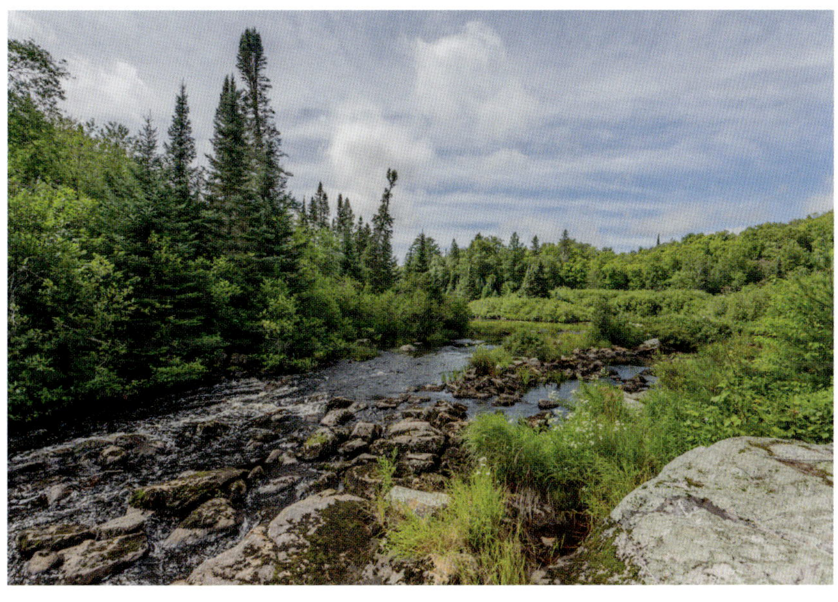

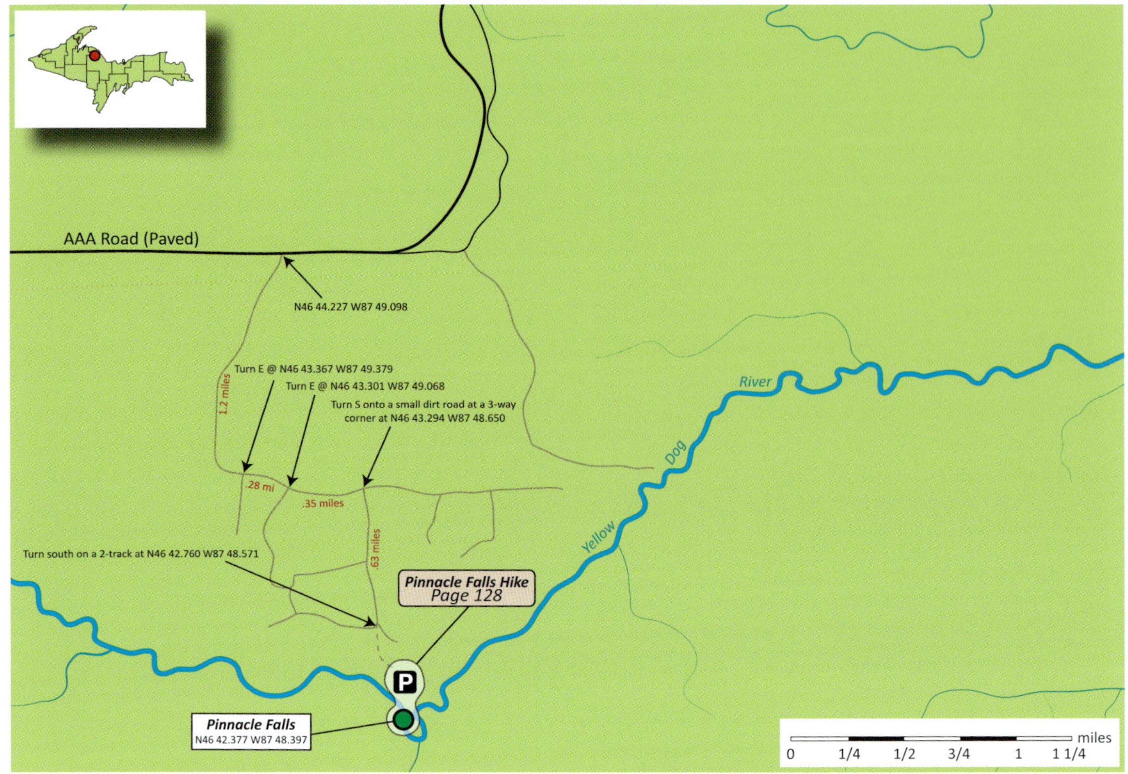

Pinnacle Falls Hike

Pinnacle Falls has a rich history that still impacts us today. In fact, I heard that the Yellow Dog River was named by an event that took place at Pinnacle Falls hundreds of years ago. Several bands of Chippewa Indians were trapped at the bend in the river by a superior force of Iroquois warriors. It was only by an ingenious plan crafted by the chief which relied on the brave actions of five young members of the "Yellow Dog" family that the Chippewas were able to escape under cover of darkness.

Pinnacle Falls is also unique in that it retains relics from the logging days. At the top of the falls are rings of iron that are fastened to the solid granite. They were used to create a sluice gate that kept logs lined up correctly as they tumbled over the falls in the late 1800's. Countless pine trees made their way from the Yellow Dog Plains down the Yellow Dog River and across Lake Independence to the sawmill at Big Bay.

We are fortunate to have Pinnacle Falls now under the ownership of the Yellow Dog Watershed Preserve, a land trust that is designed to keep the falls open to the general public for generations to come. To learn more about the Yellow Dog Watershed Preserve please visit their website at http://www.yellowdogwatershed.org

Directions: Turn off of CR-AAA Road to the southwest @ N46 44.227 W87 49.098. There are a couple of excavation areas after turning off of CR-AAA. Continue past this area. Turn east 1.2 miles after leaving CR-AAA Road. In .28 miles turn east again. After .35 miles turn south at a 3-way corner. The road here is a smaller dirt road. In another .63 miles turn south onto a 2-track that will dead end at a small parking area for the falls. Hike down the obvious footpath. It descends about 200 feet into the Yellow Dog Gorge on the hike. The path loops along the side of the river back to the north until opening up beneath hardwoods and a beautiful place for a picnic below the falls.

PINNACLE FALLS (YELLOW DOG RIVER)

Private 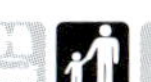  

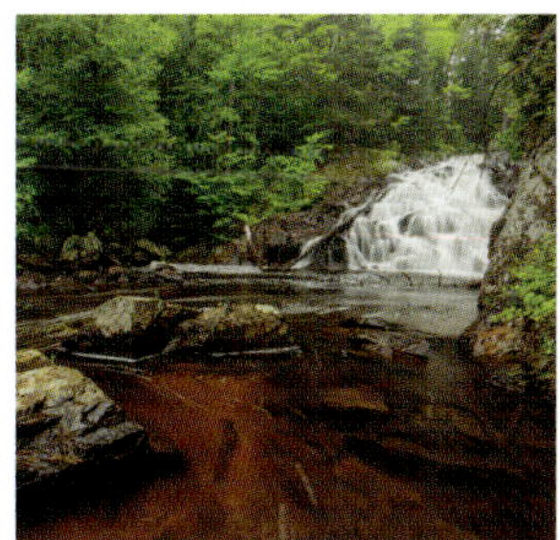

Must See:	9	GPS:	N46 42.377 W87 48.397
Height:	25 feet		
Time:	45-75 minutes	Hiking Information	
		Path:	Semi-improved footpath
Driving Information		Length:	1/4 mile
Signs:	None	Elev. Change:	Major
Road:	2-track	GPS:	Helpful
Access:	Difficult	Danger:	Moderate
4WD:	Helpful	WP Boots:	N/A

This is a classic cascading waterfall! The Pinnacle rises to the right of the falls about 50 feet above the viewing area. The river below the falls is boulder strewn. There is about a 100 foot elevation change from the parking area. This makes for a strenuous hike back from the falls.

I rate this a "Kid Friendly" waterfall. Take this with a grain of salt! The hike down and especially back up the trail may be too much for little ones. But for those that can handle a steep hike, the river below the falls is shallow and the terrain flat and pleasing.

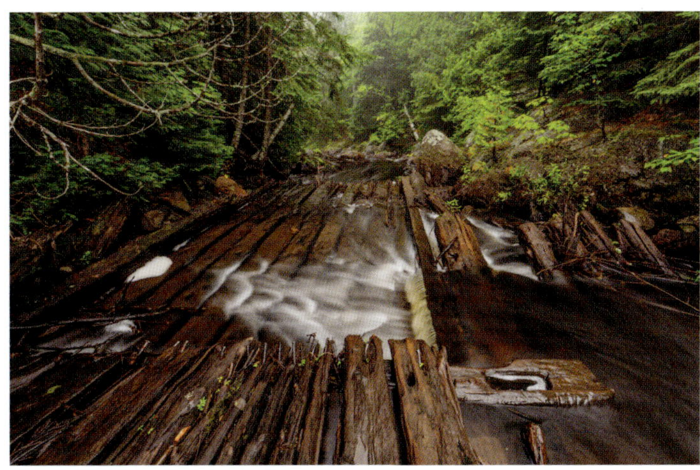

Remnants from the logging days are still up above the waterfall

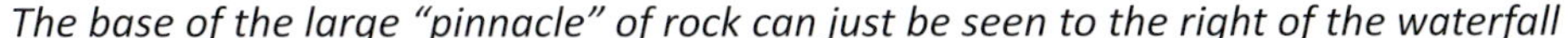

The base of the large "pinnacle" of rock can just be seen to the right of the waterfall

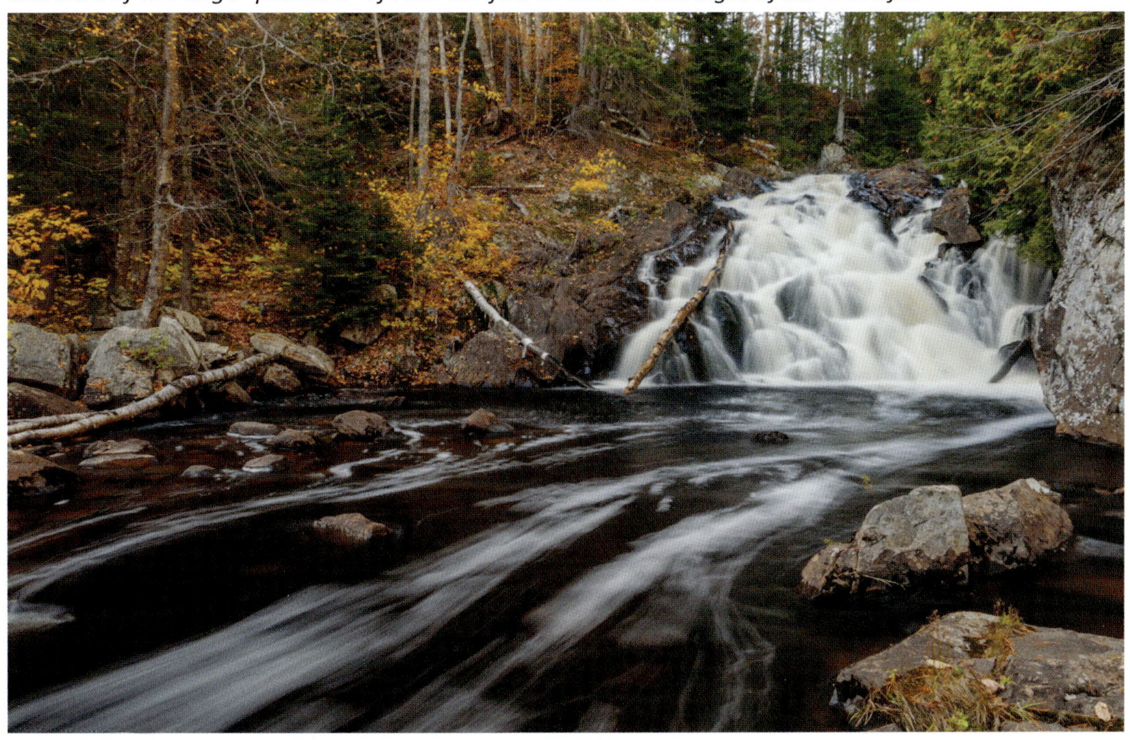

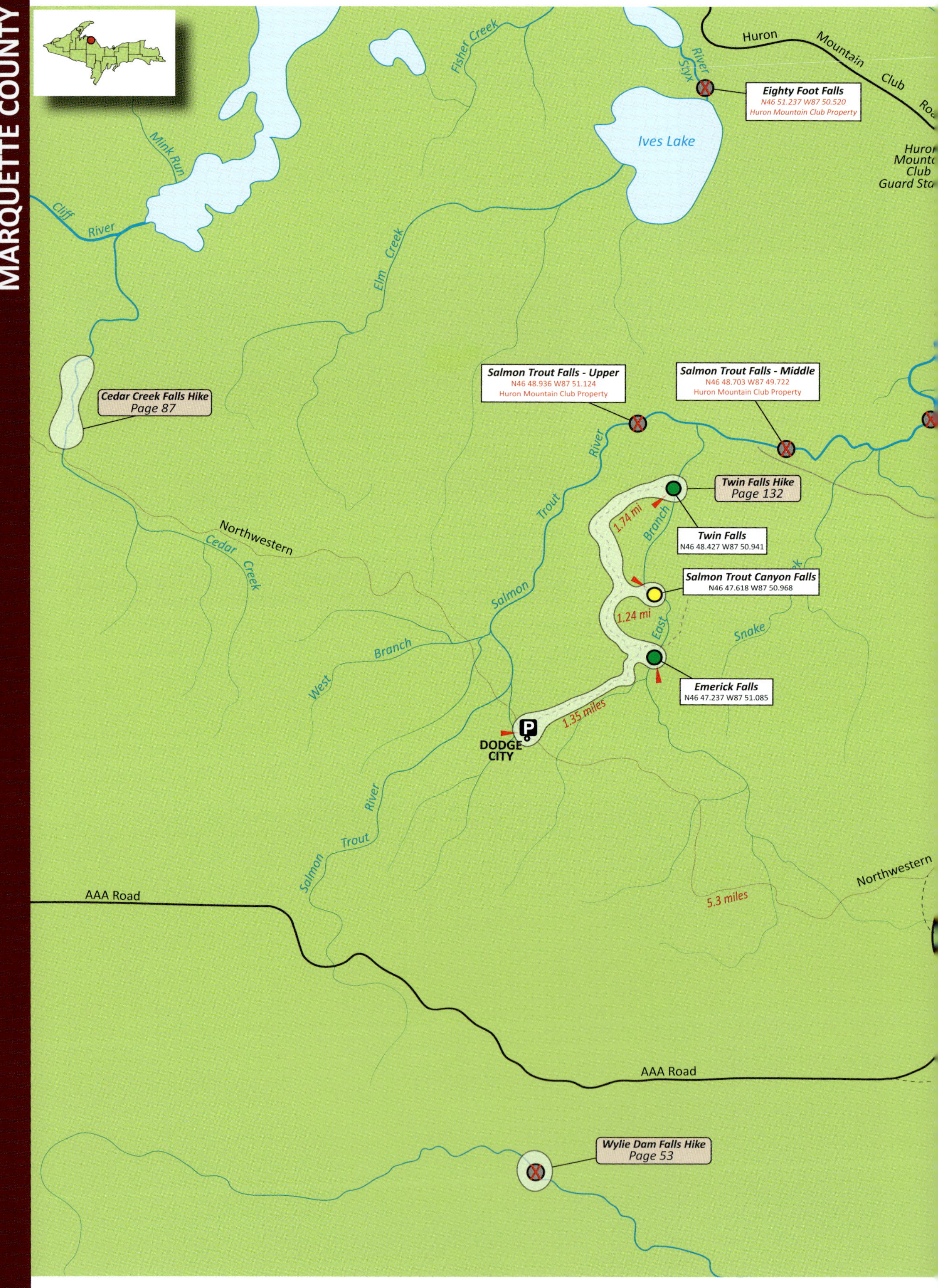

Eighty Foot Falls
N46 51.237 W87 50.520
Huron Mountain Club Property
Huron Mountain Club Road
Ives Lake
Styx River
Fisher Creek
Mink Run
Cliff River
Elm Creek
Cedar Creek Falls Hike
Page 87
Salmon Trout Falls - Upper
N46 48.936 W87 51.124
Huron Mountain Club Property
Salmon Trout Falls - Middle
N46 48.703 W87 49.722
Huron Mountain Club Property
Twin Falls Hike
Page 132
Twin Falls
N46 48.427 W87 50.941
Salmon Trout Canyon Falls
N46 47.618 W87 50.968
Emerick Falls
N46 47.237 W87 51.085
1.74 mi
1.24 mi
1.35 miles
5.3 miles
East Branch
Snake
Salmon Trout River
West Branch
Northwestern
Cedar Creek
DODGE CITY
AAA Road
Wylie Dam Falls Hike
Page 53

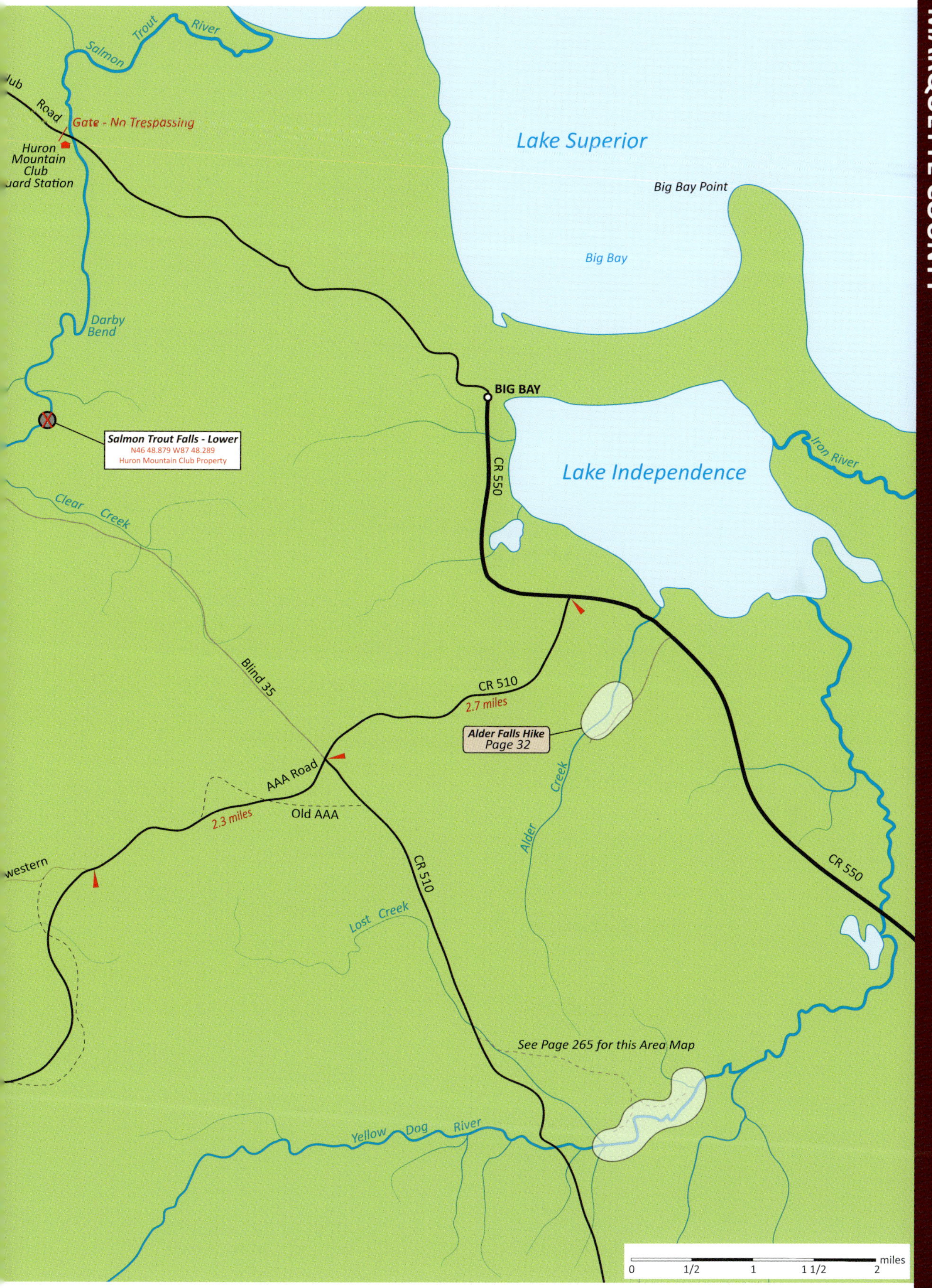
Salmon Trout River
Gate - No Trespassing
Huron Mountain Club
Road
Lake Superior
Big Bay Point
Big Bay
Darby Bend
BIG BAY
Salmon Trout Falls - Lower
N46 48.879 W87 48.289
Huron Mountain Club Property
CR 550
Lake Independence
Iron River
Clear Creek
Blind 35
CR 510
2.7 miles
Alder Falls Hike
Page 32
AAA Road
Old AAA
2.3 miles
Alder Creek
CR 510
CR 550
western
Lost Creek
See Page 265 for this Area Map
Yellow Dog River
0
1/2
1
1 1/2
2
miles

Huron Mountain Club Waterfalls

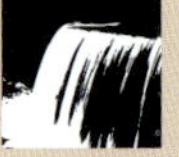

The Huron Mountain Club owns a large amount of property in the northern portion of Marquette County. This includes much of the Salmon Trout River and areas north and west of it. Their borders are clearly marked with wire stretching from tree to tree and signs nailed to the trees. Trespassing is not allowed and the borders are monitored by paid guards. The waterfalls that I am aware of on the Huron Mountain Club property include the Upper, Middle, and Lower falls on the Salmon Trout River as well as Eighty Foot Falls on the River Styx. It is probable that Turkey Neck Falls on Cedar Creek and possibly Hogback Falls (unless this is also called "Twin Falls") on the Eastern Branch of the Salmon Trout River are also on HMC property. I have not found them yet and therefore do not know.

Do not attempt to visit any of the waterfalls in Huron Mountain Club property.

Twins Falls Hike

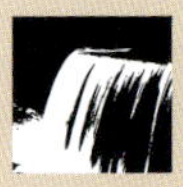

This area is being divided into parcels and sold off. This is the information that was provided to me by a local resident in 2014. At that time it was possible to park by the gated road and hike to the waterfalls. I trust that is still possible

Directions: Continue onto CR-AAA Road off of CR-510. In 2.3 miles turn right (west) onto Northwestern Road at N46 45.741 W87 47.940. Stay on the good dirt road for about 5 miles. Just past Dodge City, park at N46 46.784 W87 52.484. Hike toward the falls, staying on the road as much as possible. There are various 2-tracks that branch off every once in a while. For the most part, stay on the main road. There is a 2-track that gets close to Emerick Falls, but I don't know of one near Salmon Trout Canyon Falls. There is a bridge that crosses over to the east side of the river. I don't recommend viewing the Canyon Falls from that side as there is a high bluff along the river over there. It looked like the western side had more manageable viewing opportunities. From Salmon Trout Canyon Falls, head back to the road and follow the trails to Twin Falls. The road here is a minor 2-track (at least it was the last time I was there). Be prepared for wet conditions along the way. This is a tough, long hike. Be prepared!

EMERICK FALLS (EAST BRANCH - SALMON TROUT RIVER)

Private 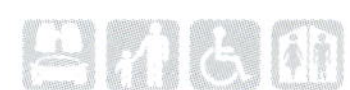

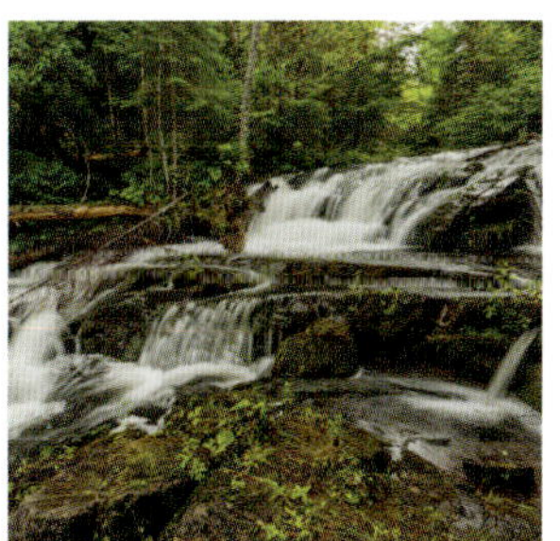

Must See:	8	GPS:	N46 47.237 W87 51.085
Height:	15 feet		
Time:	1.5-2 hours	Hiking Information	
		Path:	2-track then none
Driving Information		Length:	1.35 miles
Signs:	None	Elev. Change:	Moderate
Road:	Gravel Road	GPS:	Required
Access:	Very difficult	Danger:	Elevated
4WD:	Helpful	WP Boots:	Recommended

This waterfall is found in a shallow ravine. A 5 foot cascade spills into a shallow, wide pool, which in turn cascades another 10 feet, favoring the far side of the river. This is a very nice waterfall with no trail to it. Rock walls on the viewing side give way suddenly to the river. This unfortunately limits the viewing options.

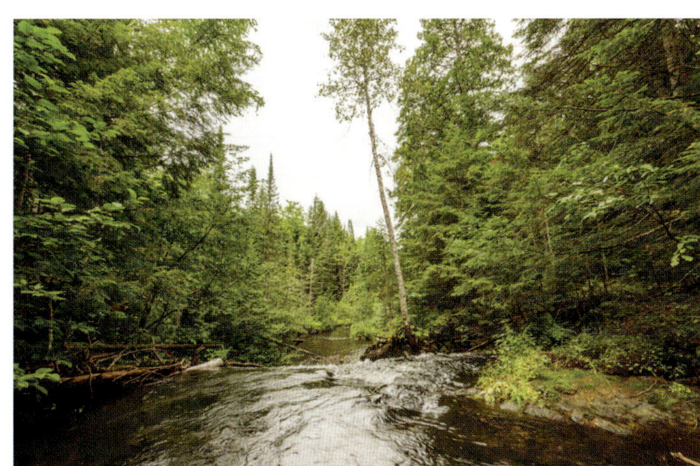

The view from the top of the waterfall

Thanks to Jacob Emerick for letting me know about this waterfall! His work on Michigan's waterfalls (especially in the Keweenaw area) is very informative. See _www.waterfallsofthekeweenaw.com_ to view his information.

From this vantage place downstream a little way the waterfall lays out nicely

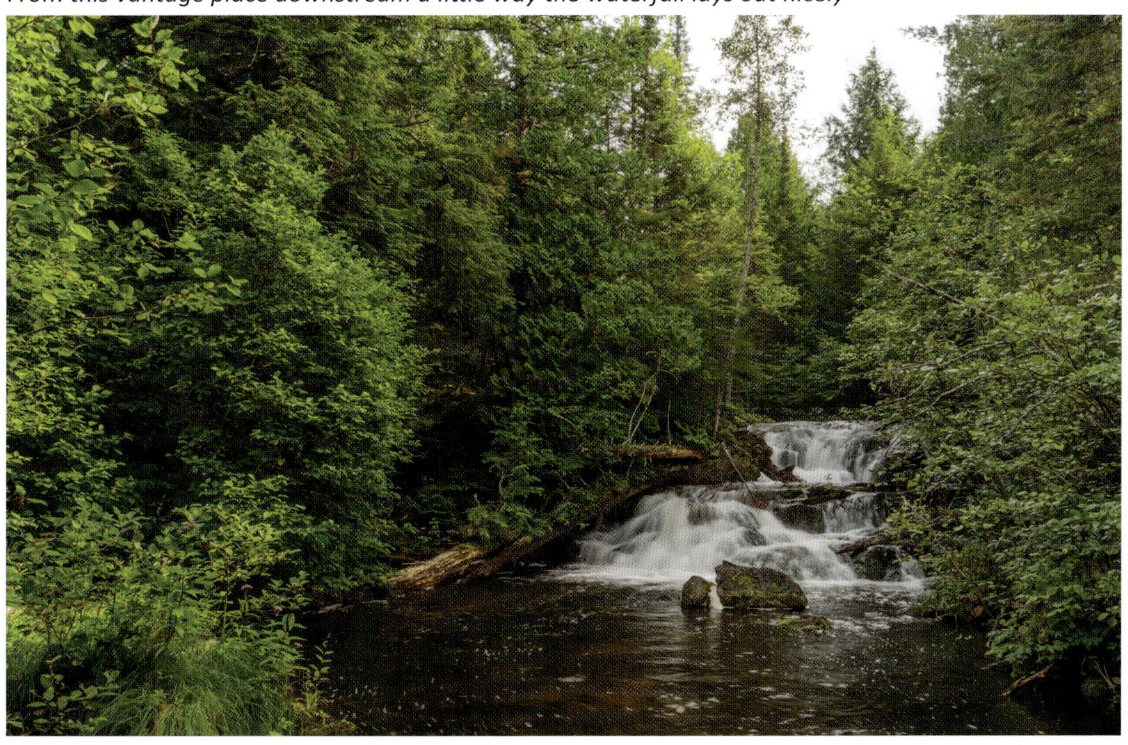

SALMON TROUT CANYON FALLS (EAST BRANCH - SALMON TROUT RIVER)

Private

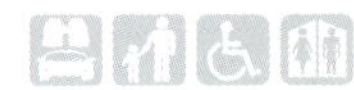

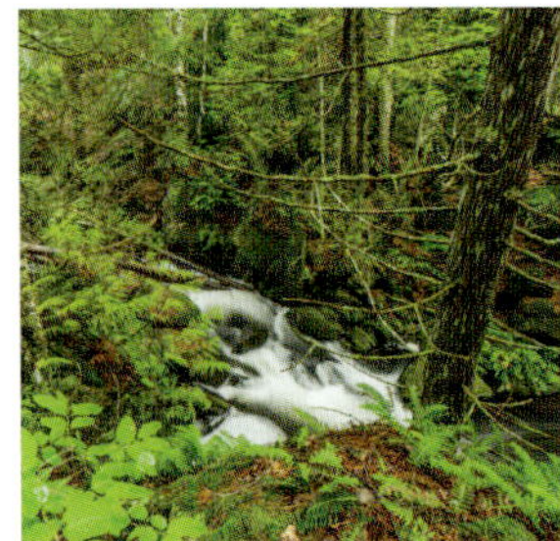

Must See:	4	GPS:	N46 47.618 W87 50.968
Height:	5 feet		
Time:	3-4 hours	Hiking Information	
		Path:	None
Driving Information		Length:	2.38 miles
Signs:	None	Elev. Change:	Elevated
Road:	2-track	GPS:	Required
Access:	Very difficult	Danger:	Elevated
4WD:	ATV required	WP Boots:	Recommended

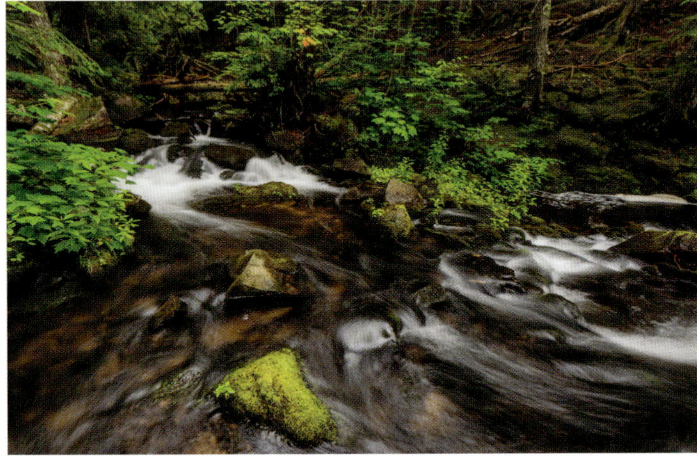

Hike about 1.24 miles from Emerick Falls to Salmon Trout Canyon Falls. This is a round-about hike if sticking to the road as much as possible. It's a much shorter hike if going cross-country directly from waterfall to waterfall.

Falls occur along the rugged canyon with precipitous walls on either side. The falls begin by pouring through a jagged pile of rocks at the start of the canyon. Some of these rocks have been pushed down river. This is where the end of the waterfall can best be seen. The rough, disheveled bedrock walls are most impressive, rising to dizzying heights (according to Michigan standards)!

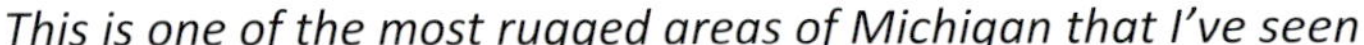

This is one of the most rugged areas of Michigan that I've seen

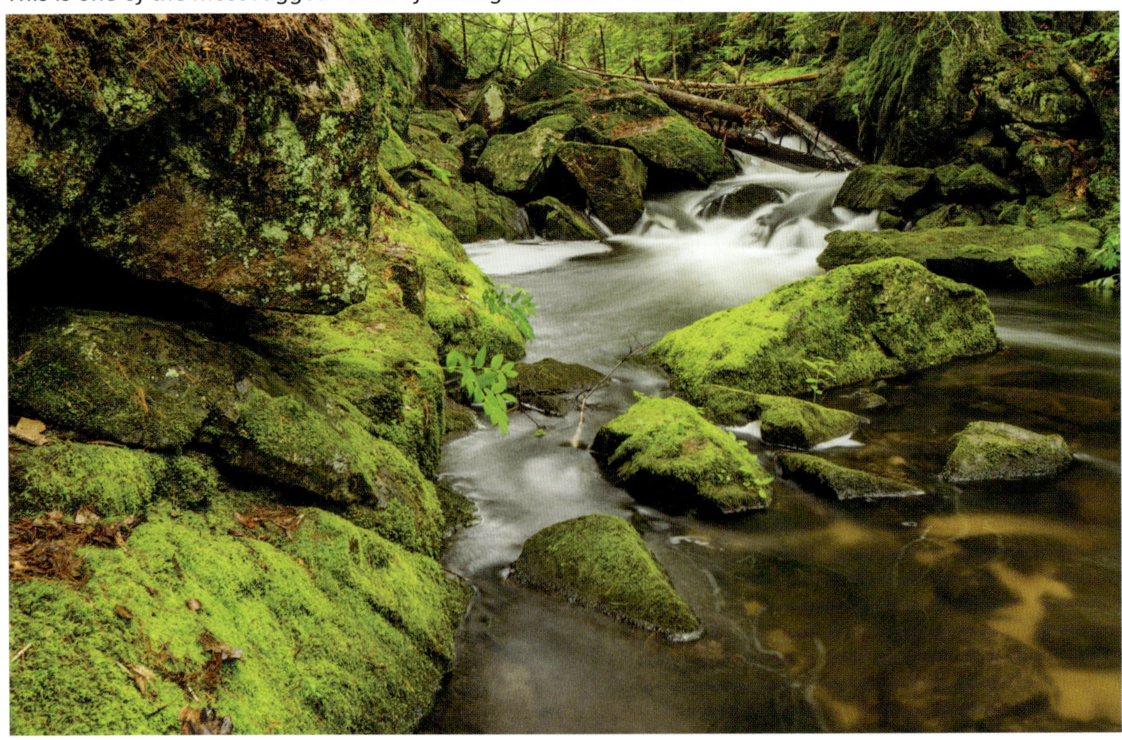

TWIN FALLS (EAST BRANCH - SALMON TROUT RIVER)

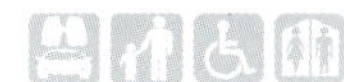

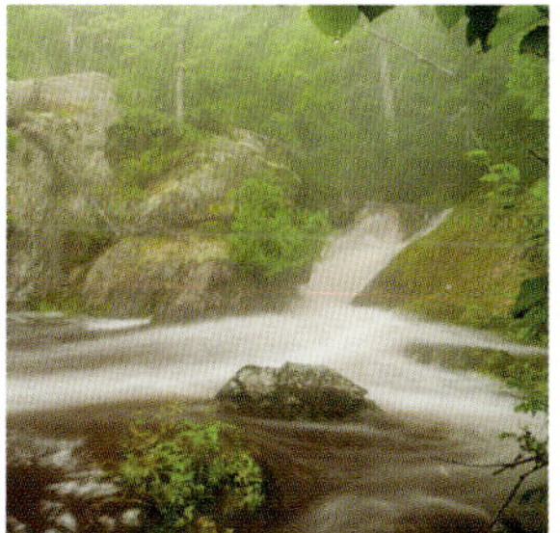

Must See:	7	GPS:	N46 48.427 W87 50.941
Height:	15 feet		
Time:	20-40 minutes	**Hiking Information**	
		Path:	None
Driving Information		Length:	150 yards
Signs:	None	Elev. Change:	Moderate
Road:	2-track	GPS:	Required
Access:	Very difficult	Danger:	Elevated
4WD:	ATV required	WP Boots:	Recommended

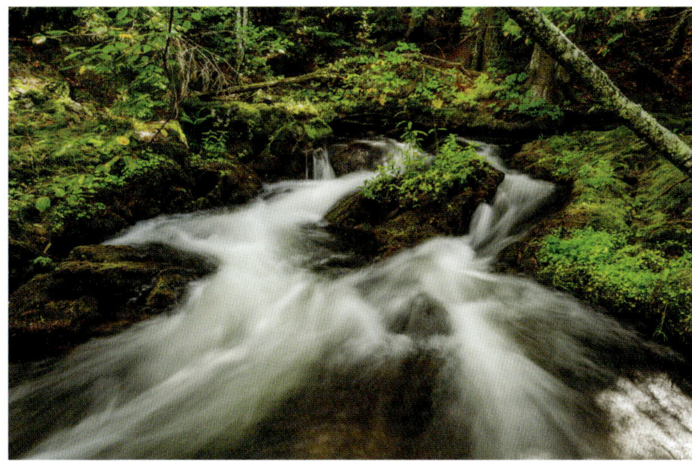

It's about 1.75 miles from Salmon Trout Canyon Falls to Twin Falls. This is the last leg of one of the most difficult hikes in Michigan.

The river comes pouring down from higher ground in a small cascade, then the river turns and drops the last 9 feet in a torrent. A large outcropping blocks its path, turning the river to the left as it drops. And then as suddenly as it swerves to the left, the river cuts back to the right at the base of the falls, expanding into a good sized spill pool. The river slows and widens out as it now enters a swampier area.

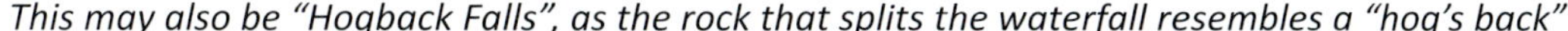

This may also be "Hogback Falls", as the rock that splits the waterfall resembles a "hog's back"

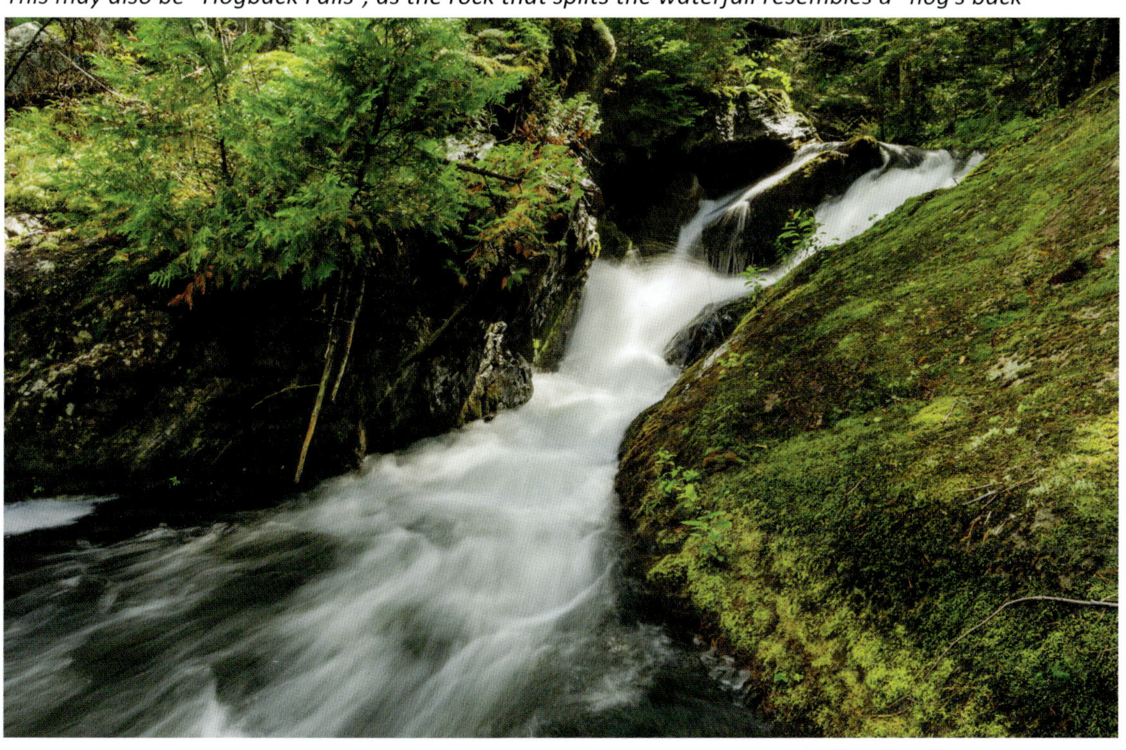

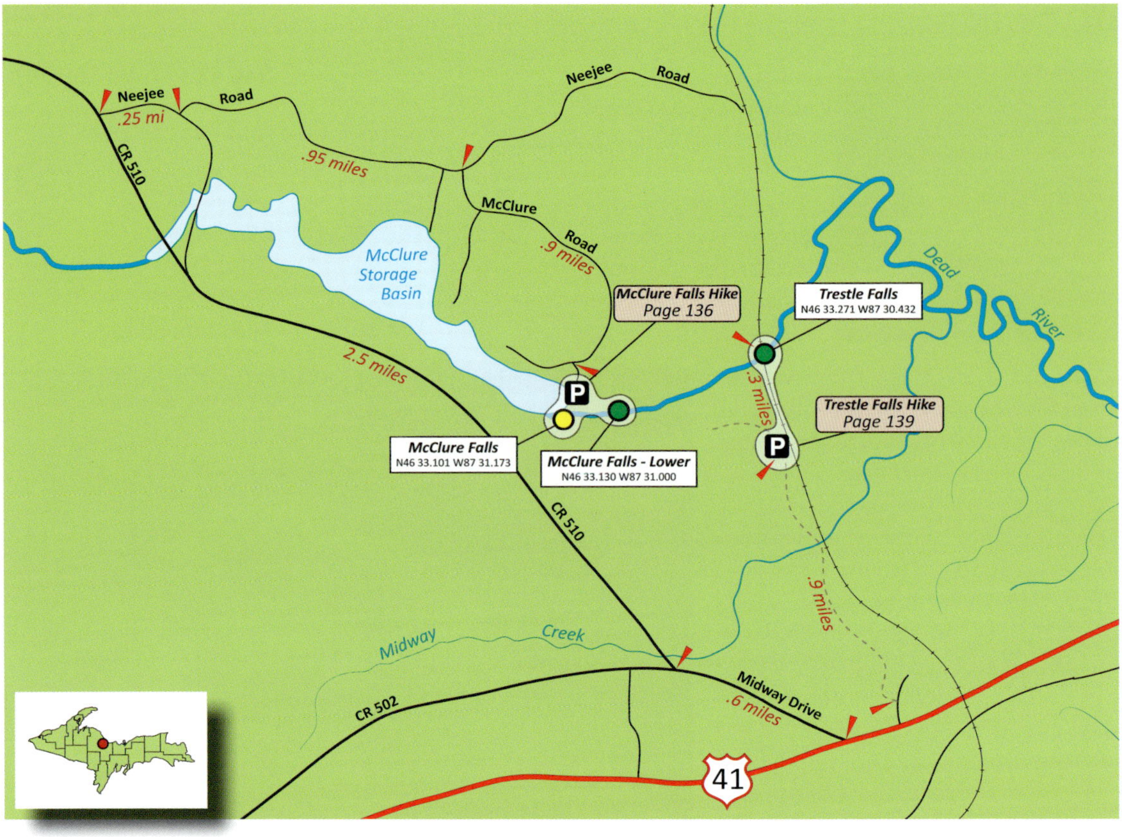

McClure Falls Hike

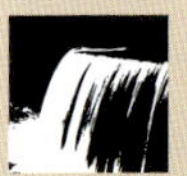

McClure Dam was built up above a waterfall on the Dead River. A section of the falls is still visible, and although a good portion of the river is diverted for power generation purposes, the waterfalls still maintain some of their original charm.

Directions: Turn northwest onto Midway Drive off of US-41. In .6 miles turn right (northwest) onto CR-510 (the "back way" to Big Bay). In 2.5 miles turn right (east) onto Neejee Road. In .25 miles turn left to stay on Neejee Road. In .95 miles turn left (south) onto McClure Road. In .9 miles turn left (south) to the parking area along the dam. Park. Hike down to the base of the dam to McClure Falls. The lower falls are accessed via a faint footpath that winds through the forest back closer to the parking area. When the path gets close to the river, a rope tied to trees gives assistance for hiking down into the Dead River gorge. The easiest way to view the waterfall is from a fairly flat area at the river's edge downstream from the waterfall.

MCCLURE FALLS (DEAD RIVER)

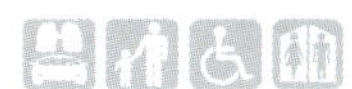

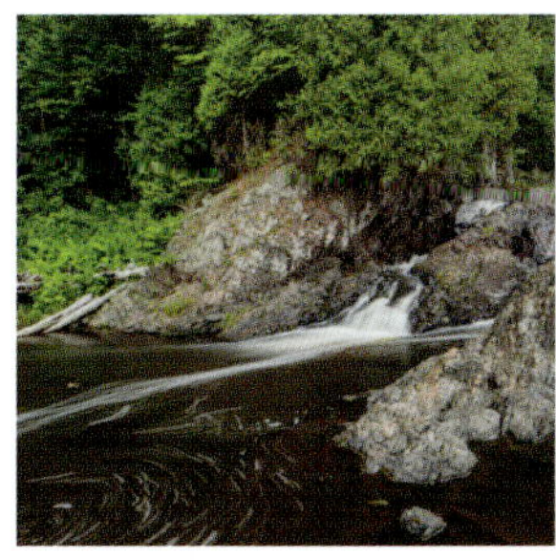

Must See:	6	GPS:	N46 33.101 W87 31.173
Height:	15 feet		
Time:	10-25 minutes	**Hiking Information**	
		Path:	N/A
Driving Information		Length:	100 yards
Signs:	None	Elev. Change:	Minor
Road:	Gravel	GPS:	N/A
Access:	Somewhat difficult	Danger:	Minor
4WD:	N/A	WP Boots:	N/A

Knobby bedrock is exposed all across the river below the dam. The overflow from the dam that is allowed to run down this portion of the river meanders around higher parts of the rocks, dropping the most right at the dam, and then continuing to drop over the next 75 yards.

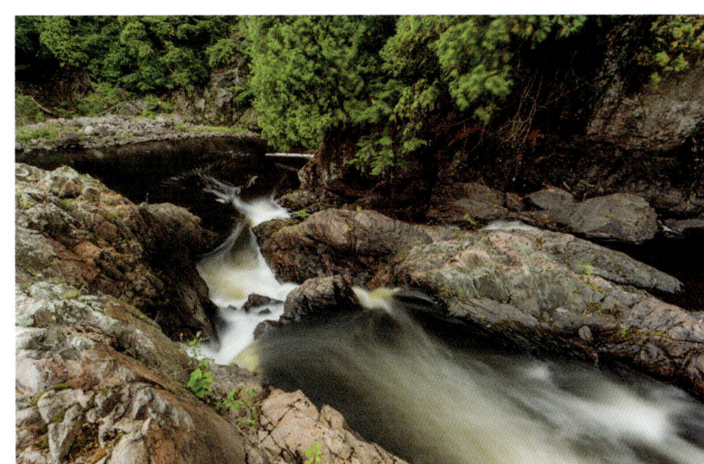

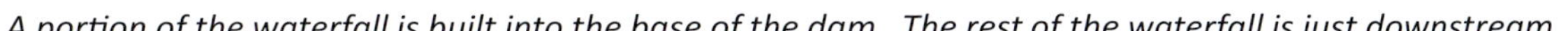

A portion of the waterfall is built into the base of the dam. The rest of the waterfall is just downstream.

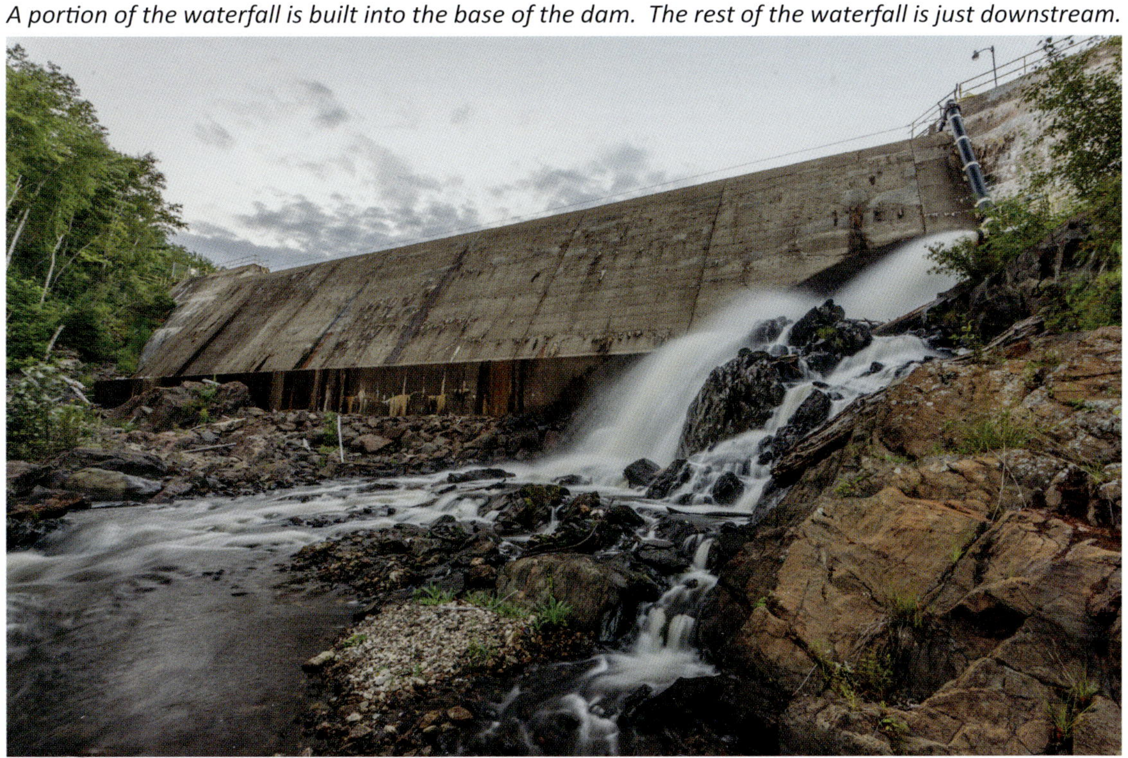

MCCLURE FALLS - LOWER (DEAD RIVER)

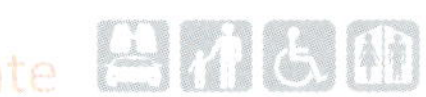

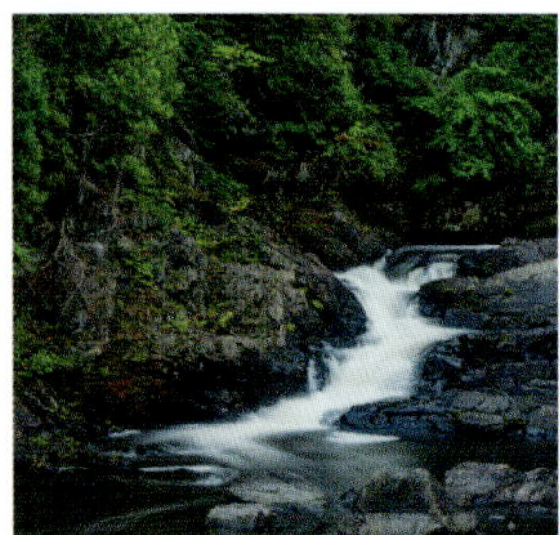

Must See:	7	GPS:	N46 33.130 W87 31.000
Height:	10 feet		
Time:	30-60 minutes	Hiking Information	
		Path:	Slight footpath
Driving Information		Length:	.15 miles
Signs:	None	Elev. Change:	Moderate
Road:	Gravel	GPS:	Helpful
Access:	Somewhat difficult	Danger:	Moderate
4WD:	N/A	WP Boots:	N/A

The walk through the woods and then down into the ravine is interesting and a bit dangerous. The rope tied from tree to tree is certainly helpful in getting down into the gorge. A large amount of crushed bedrock has been dumped into the gorge at the end of the hike. The shifting rocks need to be navigated carefully while climbing the rest of the way down to the river's edge. Various wildflowers grow in this rocky viewing area.

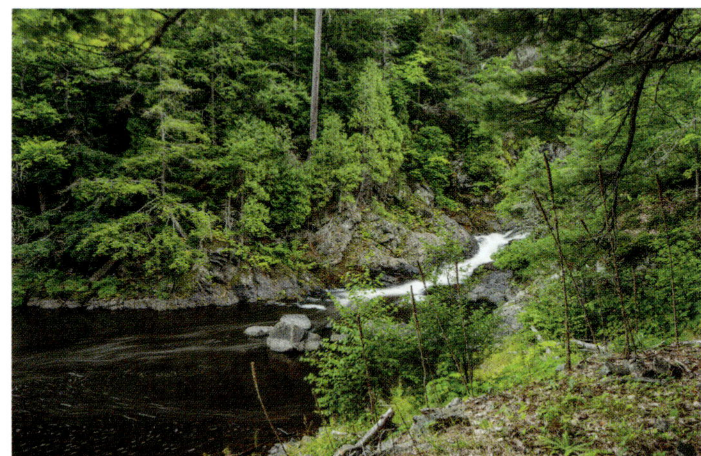

The river widens out below the waterfall into a good sized pool

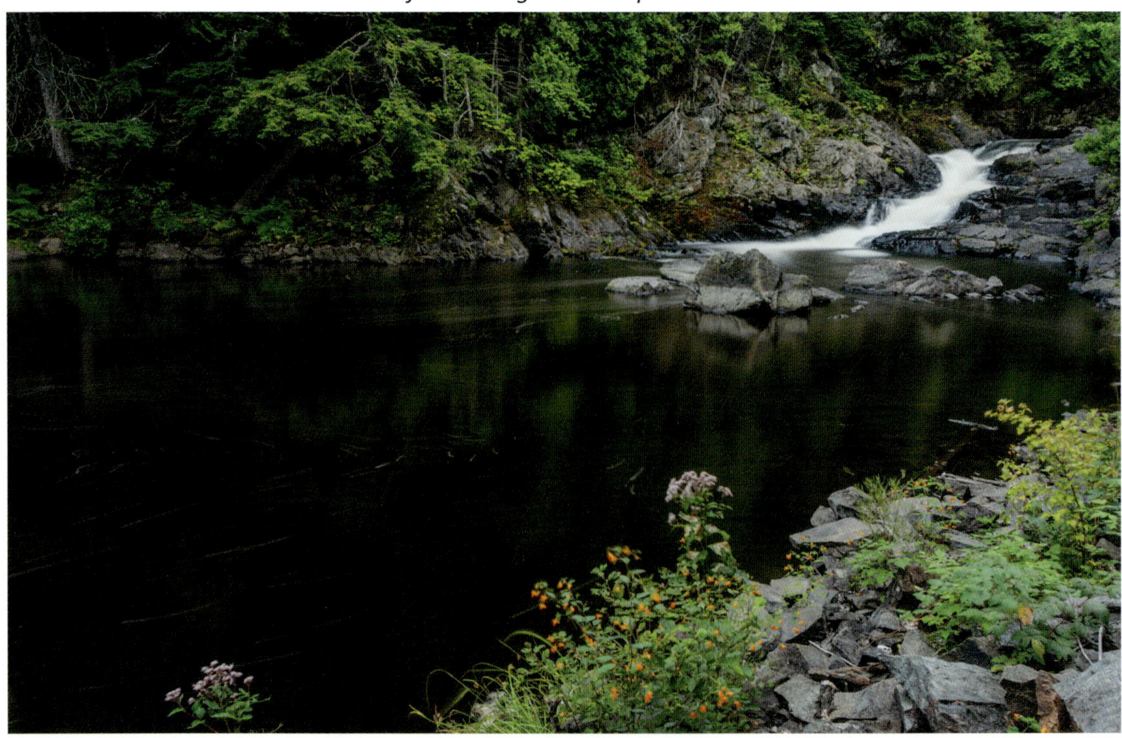

Trestle Falls Hike

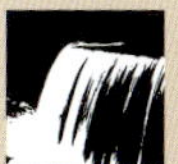

This impressive waterfall is found below a trestle that spans the Dead River. The steel structure, high overhead, is impressive in its own right.

Directions: Off of US-41, turn north into Midway Rentals driveway just west of the overhead railroad tracks. Before the rental company is a large propane tank. About 100 yards later is a building with a sign for "H&L Mesabi" on the left (west). Turn left (west) just before the building. Drive past the building. There is a dirt road that starts on the far side of the parking lot. Drive down it and into the woods (.9 miles). The road diminishes in size to a narrow 2-track by the end of the drive. Park on the side of the 2-track by another small ATV trail that heads to the right (east). Park at N46 33.019 W87 30.362. Hike 30 yards down the ATV trail. The trail will suddenly come upon a set of railroad tracks. Turn left and parallel the tracks for .3 miles. DO NOT hike down the tracks. It is dangerous and illegal. The tracks will continue over the trestle. DO NOT go out onto the trestle. It is extremely dangerous. Head east (downstream) along the top of the gorge. Follow a faint trail. The gorge wall will descend down to the riverbed in a couple hundred yards. Follow the rocks in the river back upstream to get close to the waterfall.

TRESTLE FALLS (DEAD RIVER)

Private 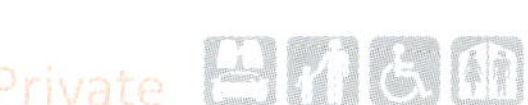

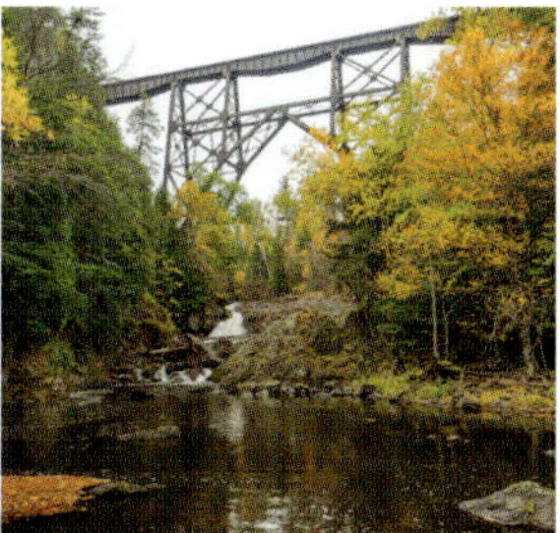

Must See:	7	GPS:	N46 33.271 W87 30.432
Height:	20 feet		
Time:	1-1.5 hours	Hiking Information	
		Path:	Slight Footpath
Driving Information		Length:	.5 miles
Signs:	None	Elev. Change:	Major
Road:	2-track	GPS:	Recommended
Access:	Quite difficult	Danger:	Increased
4WD:	Helpful	WP Boots:	N/A

Trestle Falls reminds me of a miniature Agate Falls. There is much less water and the trestle is lower, but the feel is similar. The waterfall is nested below the trestle, crossing the top of the gorge some 60 feet above. The Dead River runs through the gorge with descending walls overlooking the rock strewn river way below. Unlike Agate Falls, this railroad is still active. In fact, as I sat there writing my field notes, I heard a train whistle. I quickly got back to my camera and tripod which was on a large flat rock in the riverbed. I was able to take some pictures of the train over the waterfall! The numerous cars were filled with iron balls headed to the smelters.

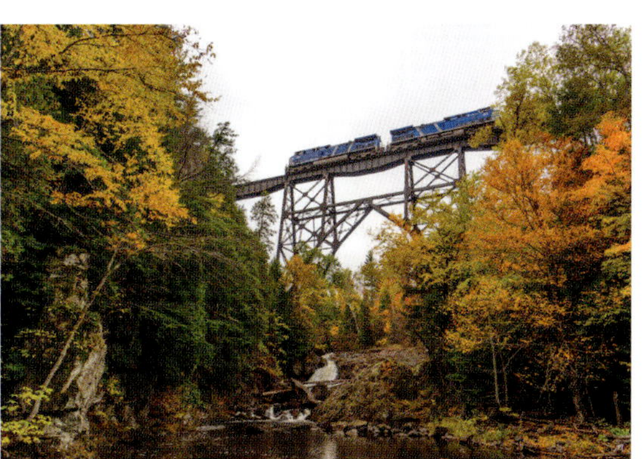

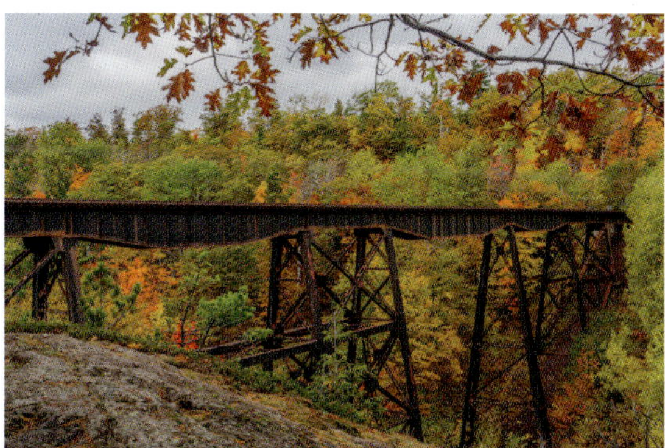

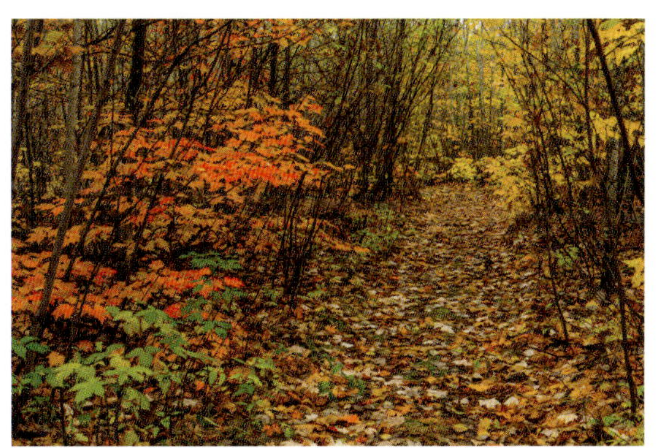

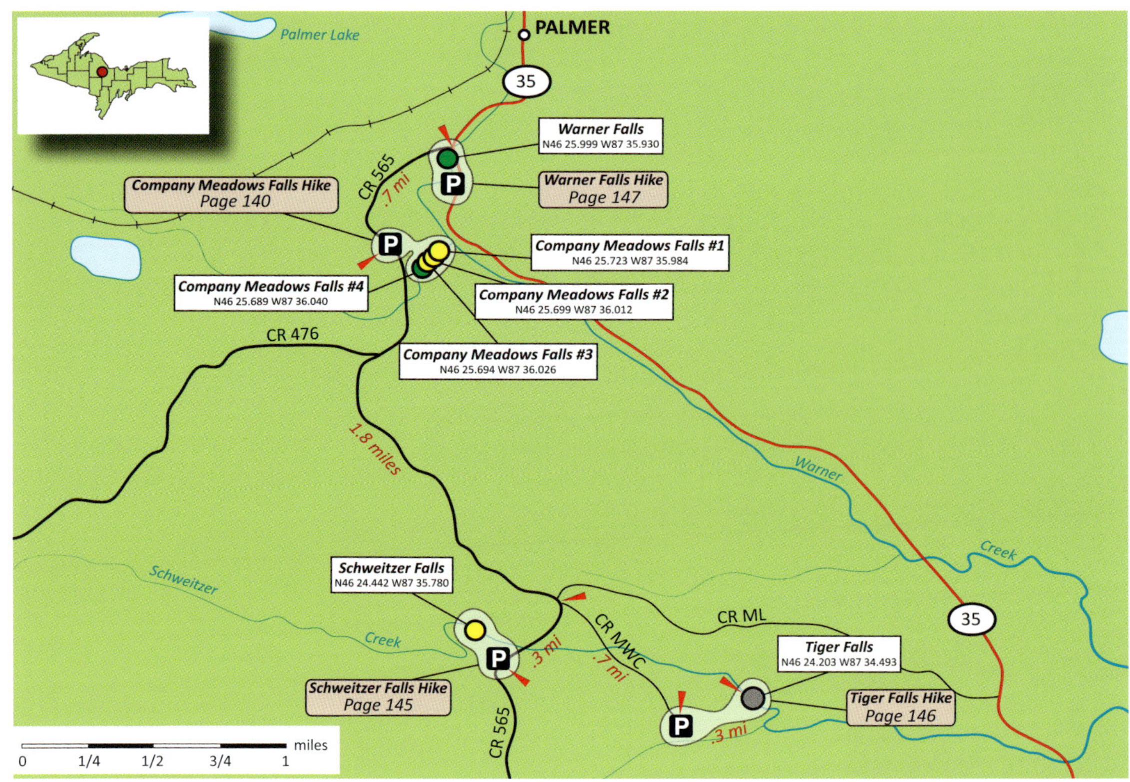

Company Meadows Falls Hike

I was informed of a set of little known waterfalls at a motel that I frequent in Marquette. The owner talked of waterfalls near Palmer and instructed me to talk to the owner of the gas station in Palmer. The elderly proprietor thought for a minute before telling me of a small creek that his grandfather had taken him to on occasion to go fishing when he was young. He remembered that there had been some drops along its course between CR-565 and M-35. He gave me directions and, voila... there were the falls! What a great memory! It had been many years since he had been to the creek, and he nailed it! He said that the creek (or maybe the area) was called "Company Meadows" so I thought it only appropriate to call the falls the "Company Meadows Falls".

Directions: Drive south from Palmer on M-35 to CR-565 (just north of Warner Falls). Turn to the west. Drive .7 miles to N46 25.719 W87 36.197. Park by the "curving road" sign. Stay on the high ground if possible while heading to the GPS coordinates for the waterfalls.

COMPANY MEADOWS FALLS #1 (COMPANY MEADOWS CREEK) Private

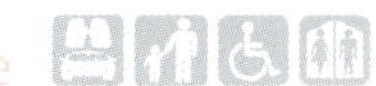

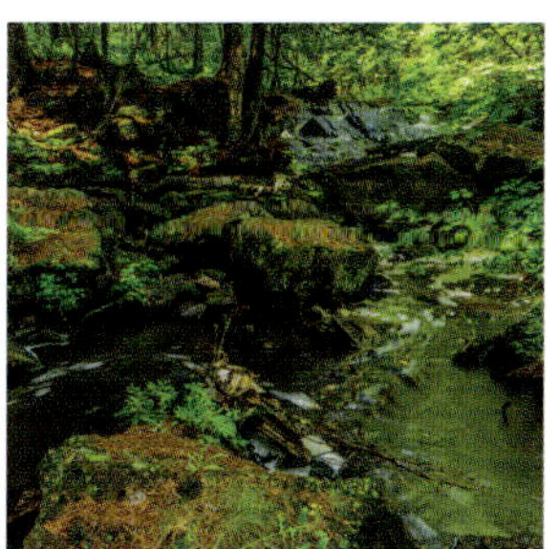

Must See:	4	GPS:	N46 25.723 W87 35.984
Height:	8 feet		
Time:	30-45 minutes	Hiking Information	
		Path:	None
Driving Information		Length:	.17 miles
Signs:	None	Elev. Change:	Moderate
Road:	Main	GPS:	Required
Access:	Somewhat difficult	Danger:	Moderate
4WD:	N/A	WP Boots:	Required (to cross creek)

The waterfall slides underneath two large boulders that are very typical in this area of the creek. I strongly recommend a GPS for this hike since the creek can be elusive to find. The terrain is not the easiest to hike through with a good deal of undergrowth and uneven ground in the area.

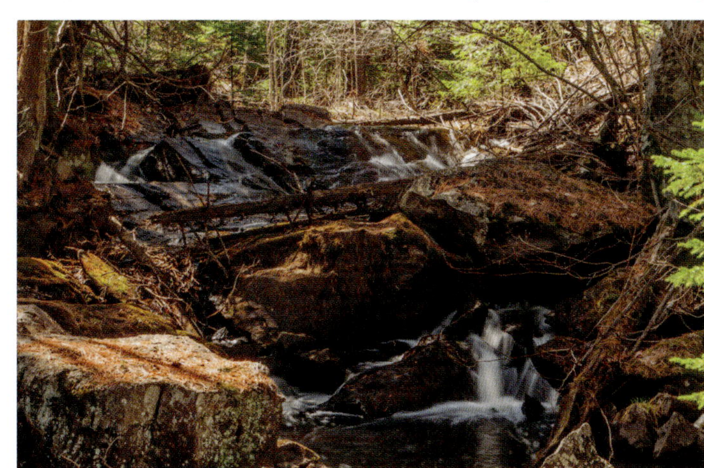

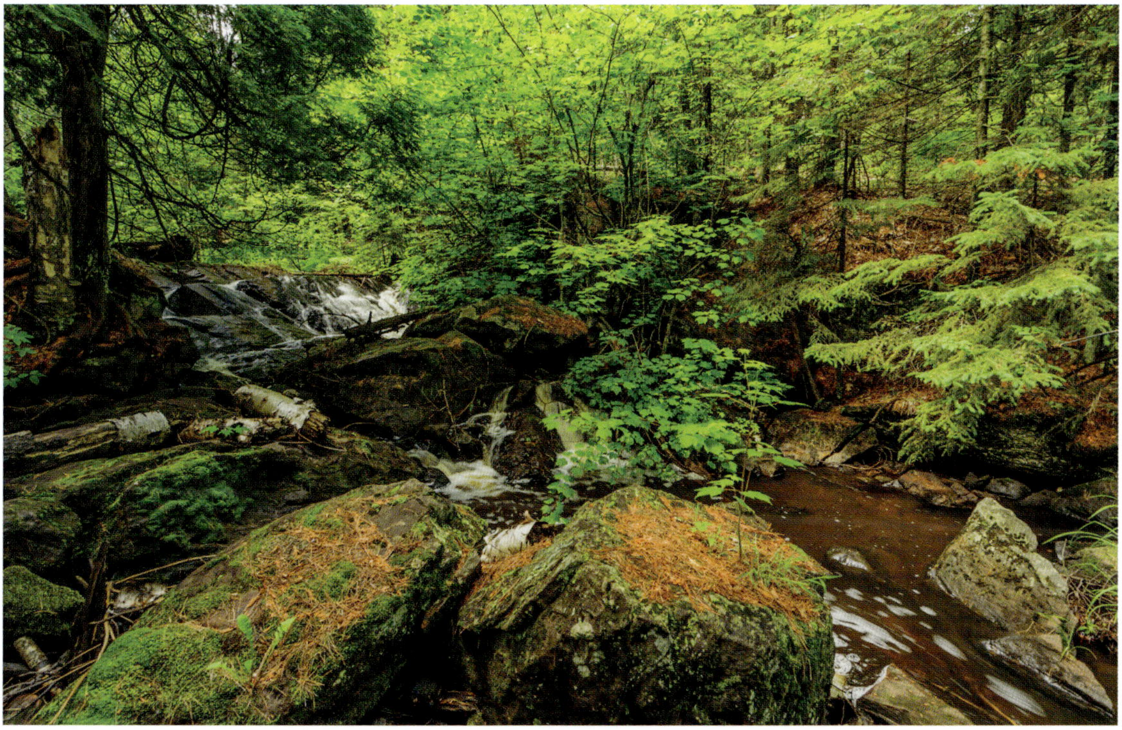

COMPANY MEADOWS FALLS #2 (COMPANY MEADOWS CREEK) Private

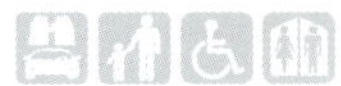

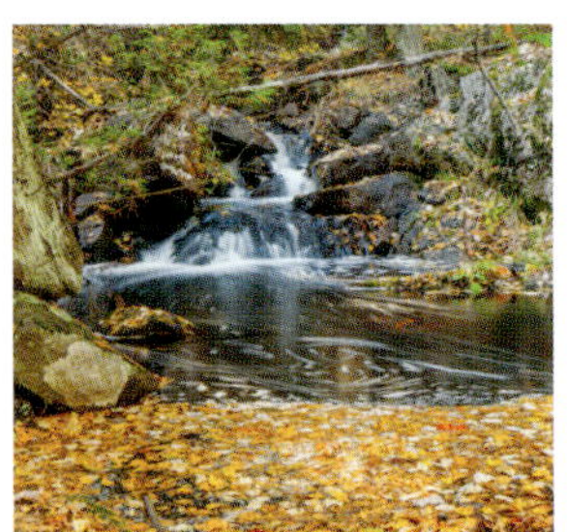

Must See:	5	GPS:	N46 25.699 W87 36.012
Height:	5 feet		
Time:	35-50 minutes	Hiking Information	
		Path:	None
Driving Information		Length:	.21 miles
Signs:	None	Elev. Change:	Moderate
Road:	Main	GPS:	Required
Access:	Somewhat difficult	Danger:	Moderate
4WD:	N/A	WP Boots:	Required (to cross creek)

This small waterfall is about 50 yards upstream from the #1 falls.

The double cascading main drop ends in a nice sized spill pool. Perhaps this is one of the holes that a small boy and his grandpa fished years ago...

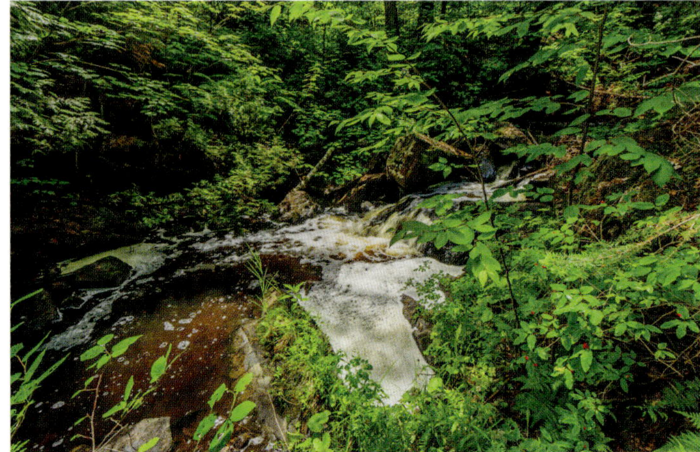

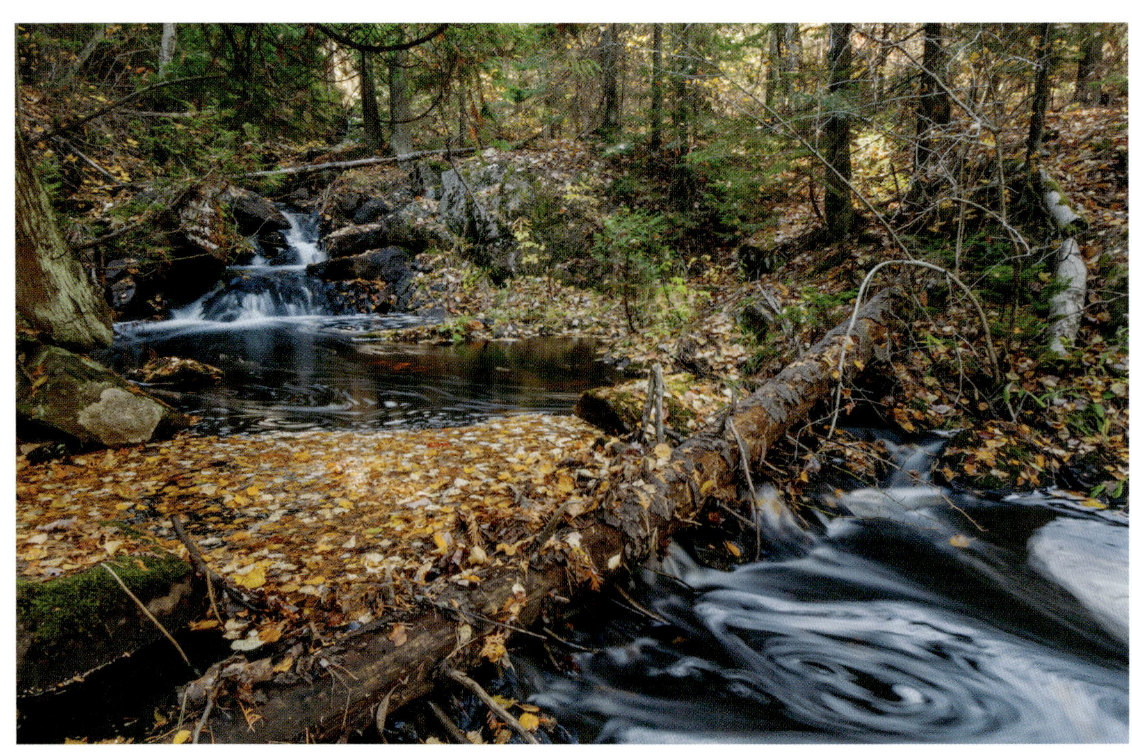

COMPANY MEADOWS FALLS #3 (COMPANY MEADOWS CREEK) Private

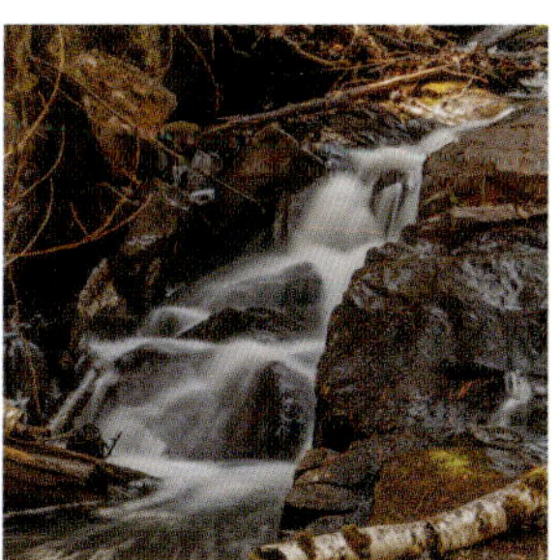

Must See:	4	GPS:	N46 25.694 W87 36.026
Height:	5 feet		
Time:	40-55 minutes	**Hiking Information**	
		Path:	None
Driving Information		Length:	.25 miles
Signs:	None	Elev. Change:	Moderate
Road:	Main	GPS:	Required
Access:	Somewhat difficult	Danger:	Moderate
4WD:	N/A	WP Boots:	Required (to cross creek)

The last three falls here, #2, #3, and #4 are all quite close together. In fact, #3 is only about 50 feet further upstream from #2.

A rocky channel was cut into the bedrock over time by the flowing creek. The resulting cascading waterfall sits at the base of a stone hill covered with a thin layer of soil.

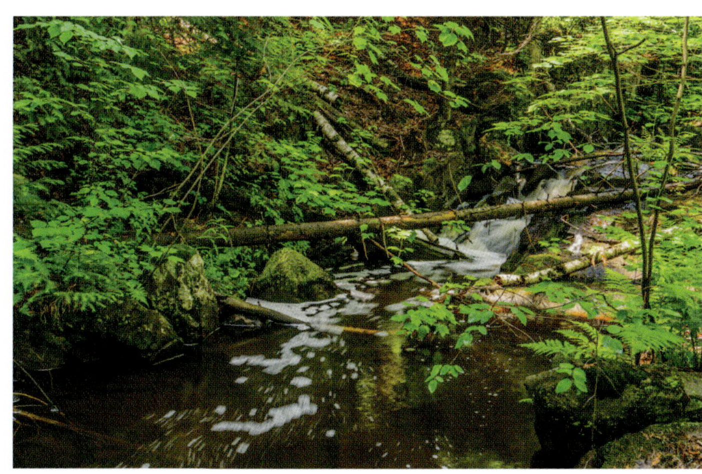

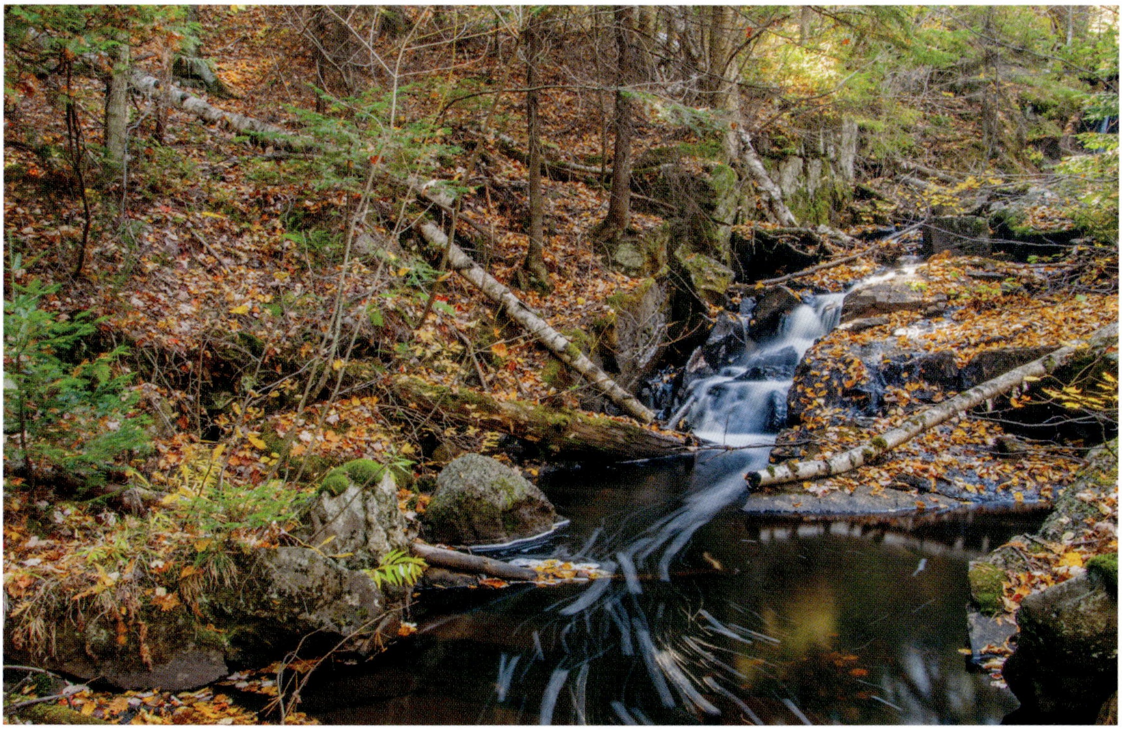

COMPANY MEADOWS FALLS #4 (COMPANY MEADOWS CREEK) Private

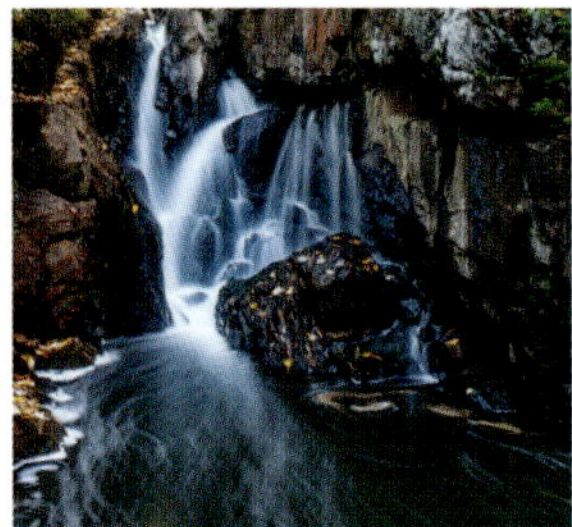

Must See:	7	GPS:	N46 25.689 W87 36.040
Height:	10 feet		
Time:	45-60 minutes	**Hiking Information**	
		Path:	None
Driving Information		Length:	.27 miles
Signs:	None	Elev. Change:	Moderate
Road:	Main	GPS:	Required
Access:	Somewhat difficult	Danger:	Moderate
4WD:	N/A	WP Boots:	Required (to cross creek)

The creek sports a 10 foot drop through a narrow canyon as it starts its rapid descent to Warner Creek. I love the look of the water gushing out of the rock "face". It really is a unique look for Michigan!

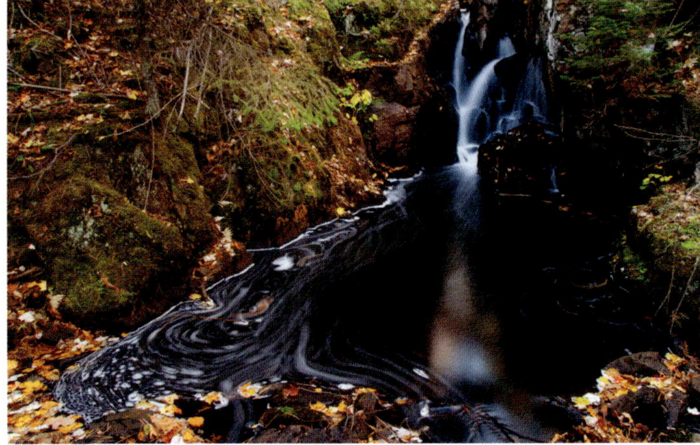

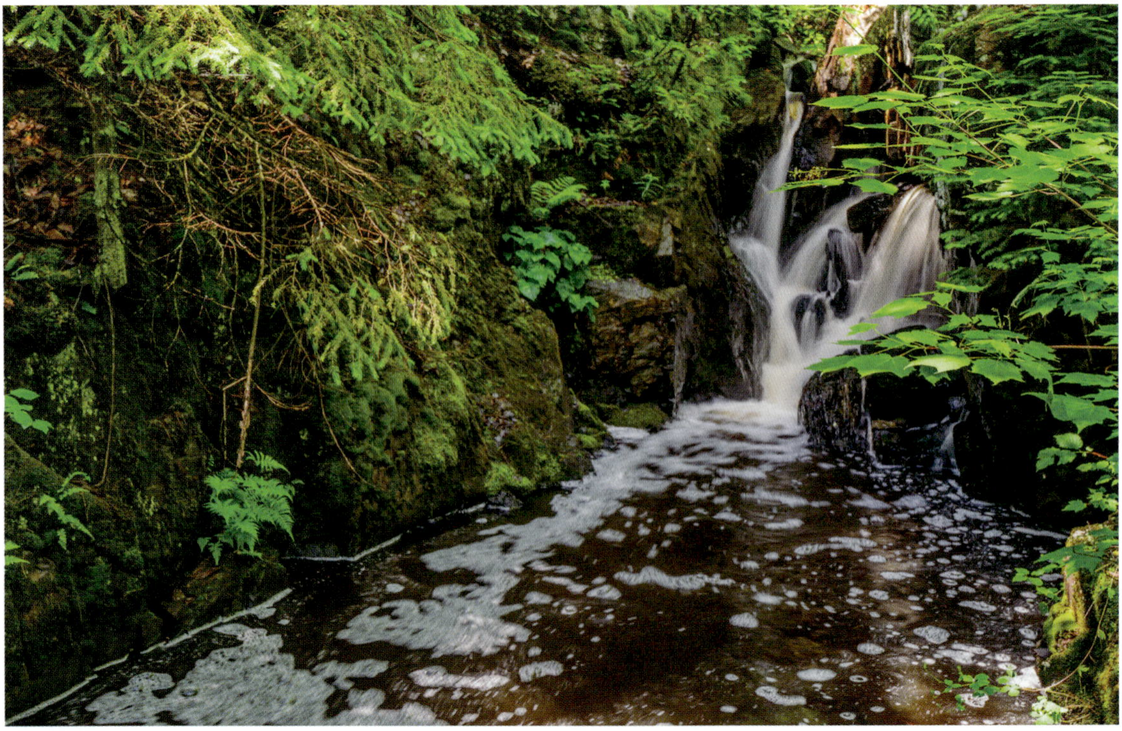

Schweitzer Falls Hike

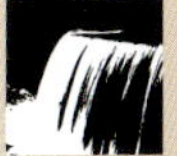

It is not a long hike from the small parking area next to the bridge through the pine trees, down the hill and around (or through) the marshy area and undergrowth to the overgrown viewing area situated on high banks above Schweitzer Creek. For as short as the hike is, it is equally difficult! The thick undergrowth, the cedars boughs, something makes it easy to get turned around on this hike. For that reason, I highly recommend using a GPS or at least marking your path for a safe return trip.

Directions: Take CR-565 west and south from Palmer off of M-35. In 2.8 miles park on the right (northwest) side of the road just past the bridge over Schweitzer Creek. Hike to the GPS coordinates for the falls. Warning! This is through thick brush, boughs and undergrowth.

SCHWEITZER FALLS (SCHWEITZER CREEK)

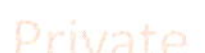

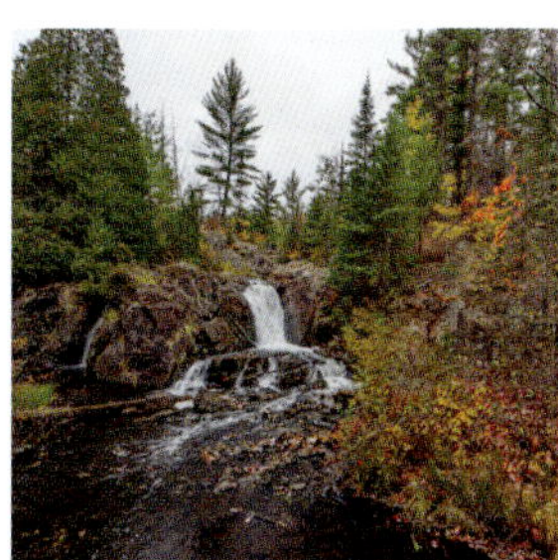

Must See:	6	GPS:	N46 24.442 W87 35.780
Height:	18 feet		
Time:	30-45 minutes	Hiking Information	
		Path:	None
Driving Information		Length:	200 yards
Signs:	None	Elev. Change:	Moderate
Road:	Secondary	GPS:	Required
Access:	Somewhat easy	Danger:	Moderate
4WD:	N/A	WP Boots:	Required (to cross creek)

There is thick undergrowth and downed trees making this short walk difficult to navigate. Use a GPS, a compass, or mark your trail. You don't want to get turned around in these woods! Schweitzer Creek and Warner Creek join 3 miles downstream to create the East Branch of the Escanaba River. Some 60 miles later the Escanaba River empties into Lake Michigan.

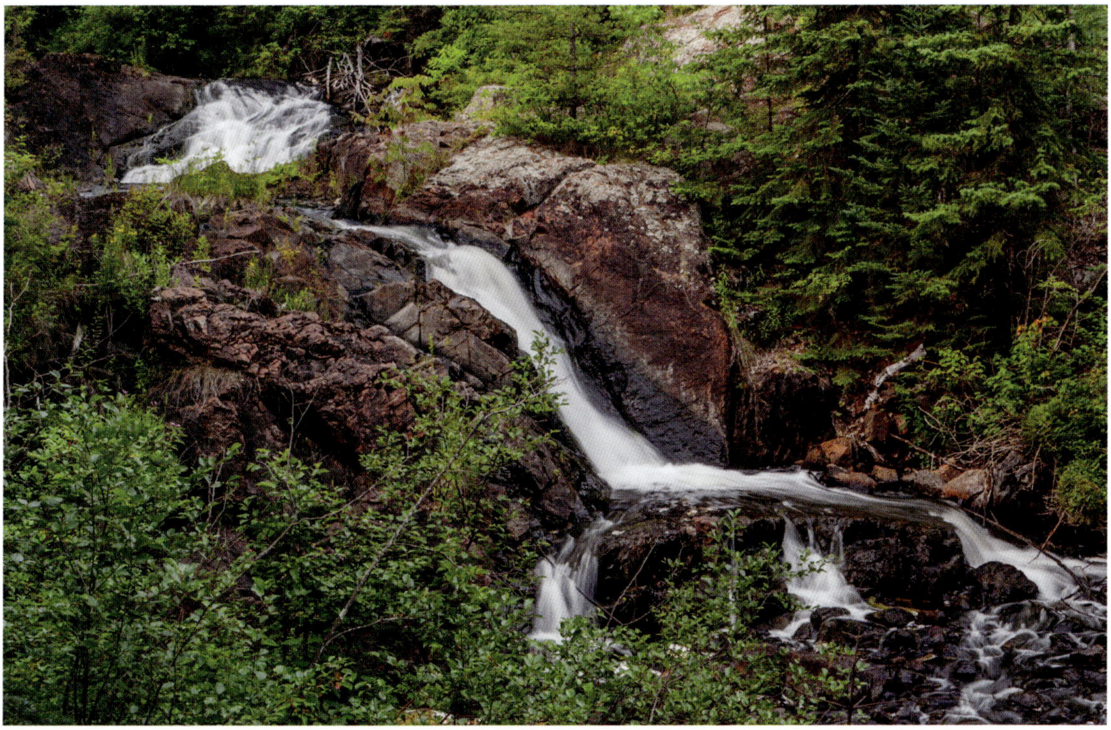

Tiger Falls Hike

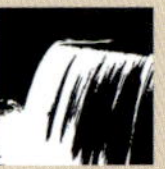

The land on the northern side of Schweitzer Creek at Tiger Falls is privately owned. I think I have found a way to the falls, but I haven't had a chance to verify it yet.

Directions: Take CR-565 west and south from Palmer off of M-35 for 2.5 miles. Turn to the southeast onto CR-MWC and drive to the end (.7 miles). (It may be possible to drive closer to the falls. Check out the 2-track heading east before attempting to drive down it.) Park. Hike down the 2-track just described to the east. There may be several heading the same general direction. Hike to the GPS coordinates for the waterfall. (It's about .3 miles from the end of CR-MWC.)

TIGER FALLS (SCHWEITZER CREEK)

Private

Must See:	?	GPS:	N46 24.203 W87 34.493
Height:	? feet		
Time:	? minutes	Hiking Information	
		Path:	?
Driving Information		Length:	.3 miles
Signs:	None	Elev. Change:	?
Road:	Dirt	GPS:	Required
Access:	Somewhat difficult	Danger:	?
4WD:	?	WP Boots:	?

I haven't been on this hike. It is possible that CR-MWC is passable, or gated, or posted as off limits. This area is owned by the Tilden Mining Company and I am not sure of their stance on hiking on their property.

Warner Falls Hike

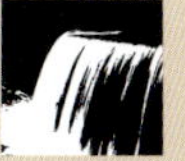

There are not a large number of waterfalls in Michigan that can be seen from a vehicle. Warner Falls is one of those elite few! The waterfall presents itself beautifully as seen from the road. It cascades down in a widening fan shape as it tumbles over a steep face to the marshy spill pool at the base. The creek then slowly moves through swampy land until it runs right next to M-35 for several miles.

Directions: Drive just south of Palmer on M-35. The waterfall will be seen on the right (west), down in a valley. Park just past the bridge off the side of the road. Walk back along the road to view the falls closer. I like to walk on the "dirt" side of the guard rail as the shoulder of the road is not very wide and there can be some traffic in this area. At the north end of the guard rail there is a trail of sorts that heads down the steep hillside over a bed of loose shale to the falls at the bottom.

WARNER FALLS (WARNER CREEK)

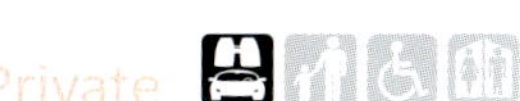

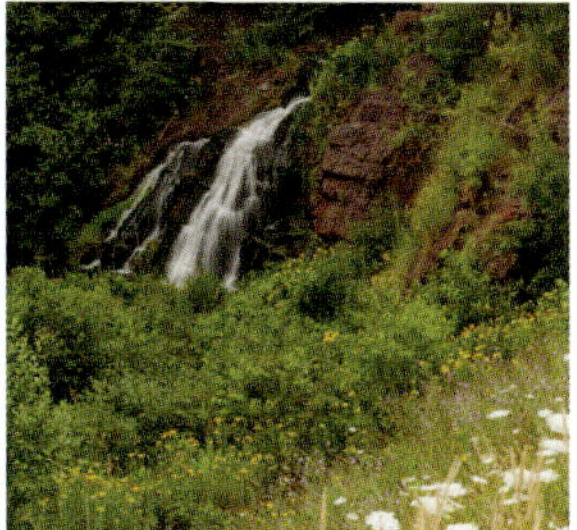

Must See:	7	GPS:	N46 25.999 W87 35.930
Height:	20 feet		
Time:	5-20 minutes	Hiking Information	
		Path:	N/A
Driving Information		Length:	N/A
Signs:	None	Elev. Change:	N/A
Road:	Main	GPS:	N/A
Access:	Easy	Danger:	N/A
4WD:	N/A	WP Boots:	N/A

This very nice waterfall can be viewed from the bridge area or up close if you carefully pick your way down the loose shale and follow the dirt path to the bottom of the falls.

It's a steep climb down to the waterfall itself. Staying up at the road, however, still offers a great view!

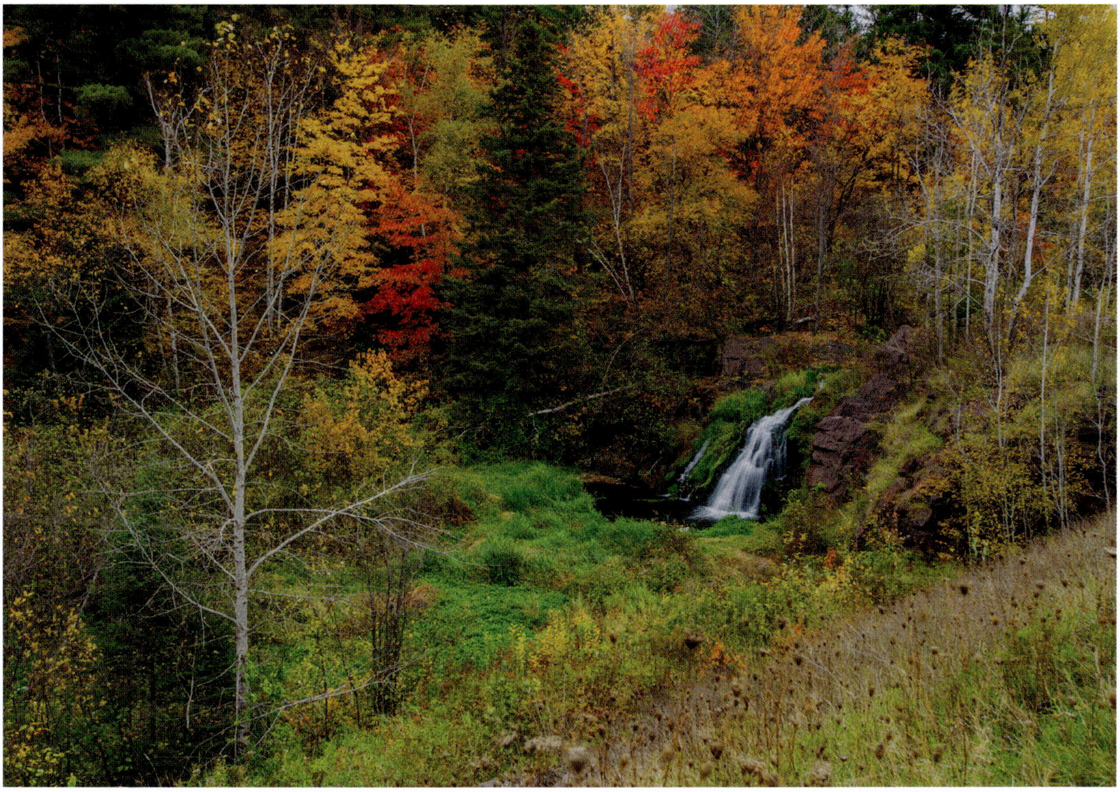

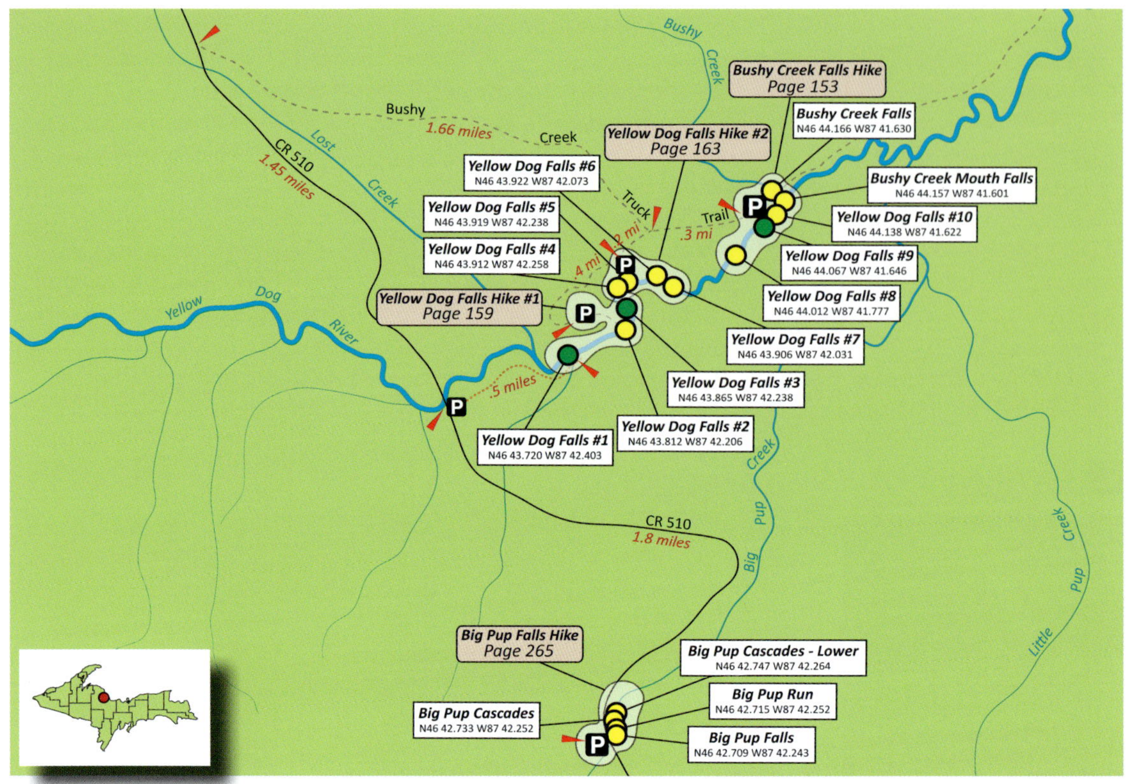

Big Pup Falls Hike

Although I've been told that a family of otters lives near the falls, I have never had the pleasure of watching them at play. Big Pup Creek starts dropping just after it passes beneath CR-510. Big Pup Falls comes first. Then the narrow creek runs down into a gorge in a weaving pattern. Several drops are prominent amongst the rapids that continue near the base of the ravine. These make up the rest of the Big Pup Falls.

Directions: On CR-510, 1.8 miles south of the Yellow Dog River Bridge is a bridge over the Big Pup Creek. Park on the northwest side of the bridge. Big Pup Falls is a short 100 feet from the road. Climb down into the somewhat steep ravine to the falls further downstream.

BIG PUP FALLS (BIG PUP CREEK)

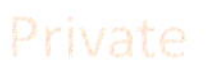

Private

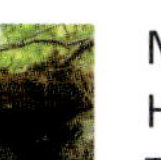

Must See:	6	GPS:	N46 42.709 W87 42.243
Height:	4 feet		
Time:	5-15 minutes	**Hiking Information**	
		Path:	Unimproved footpath
Driving Information		Length:	100 feet
Signs:	None	Elev. Change:	Slight
Road:	Dirt	GPS:	Helpful
Access:	Somewhat easy	Danger:	Moderate
4WD:	N/A	WP Boots:	N/A

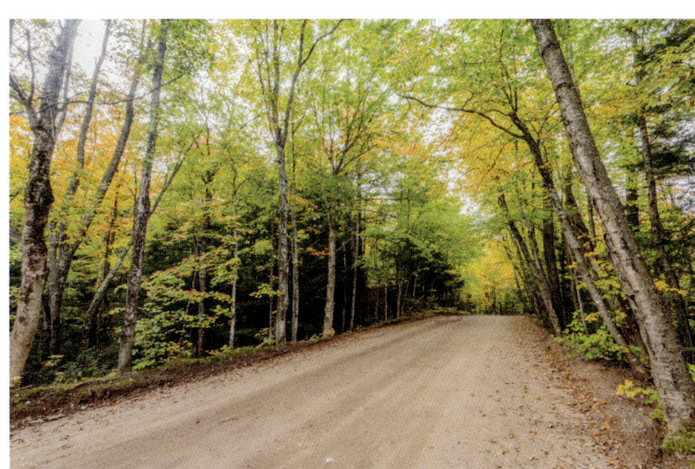

Big Pup Falls is a long, cascading waterfall starting with a nearly shear fall into a roundish splash pool. The waterfall continues as it churns down a long twisting channel, descending into a rock strewn ravine. This almost qualifies as a "Kid Friendly" waterfall. There is a nice place up near the top drop for playing among large trees. The ground is mostly undergrowth free. The concern I have is that the ravine drops off quickly and small children should be closely supervised in this area.

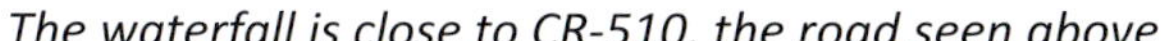

Fractured bedrock creates a nicely cascading waterfall with 6 foot moss covered walls immediately below the falls. Towering evergreens overshadow the creek and eliminate most ground cover. Therefore, there are lovely, clear viewing areas along both banks.

The waterfall is close to CR-510, the road seen above

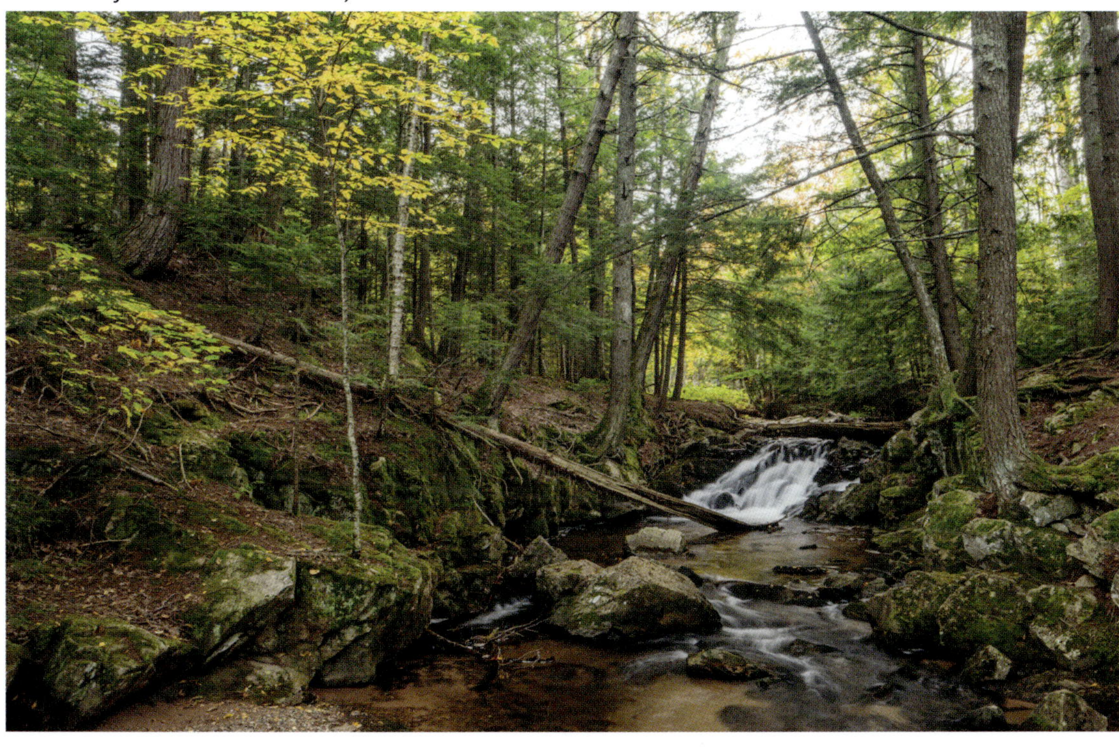

BIG PUP RUN (BIG PUP CREEK)

Private 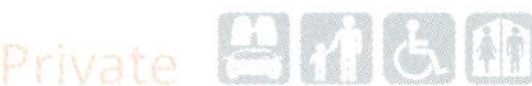

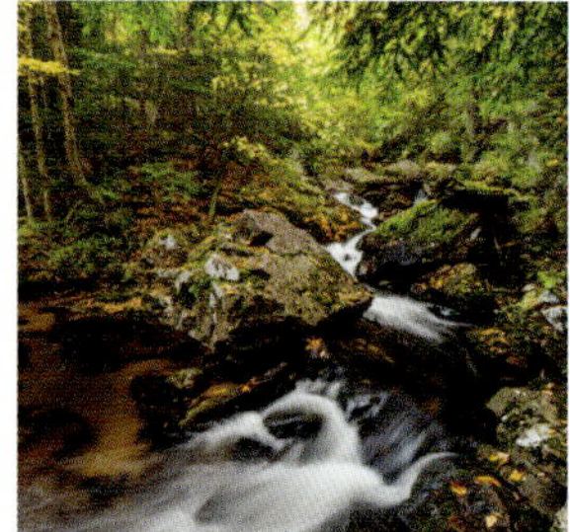

Must See:	5	GPS:	N46 42.715 W87 42.252
Height:	20 feet		
Time:	10-25 minutes	**Hiking Information**	
		Path:	None
Driving Information		Length:	200 feet
Signs:	None	Elev. Change:	Moderate
Road:	Dirt	GPS:	Helpful
Access:	Somewhat easy	Danger:	Moderate
4WD:	N/A	WP Boots:	N/A

About 25 yards below Big Pup Falls, the drop into the ravine gets serious. The creek descends over a number of small cascades, with the largest drop toward the bottom of the large "C" shaped run. There, with large chunks of bedrock fallen from the steep ravine walls looking on, the creek makes a zigzagging final burst before leveling out for a bit. It's a steep climb down the 10 foot rock wall at the base of the run to get down to the river's edge.

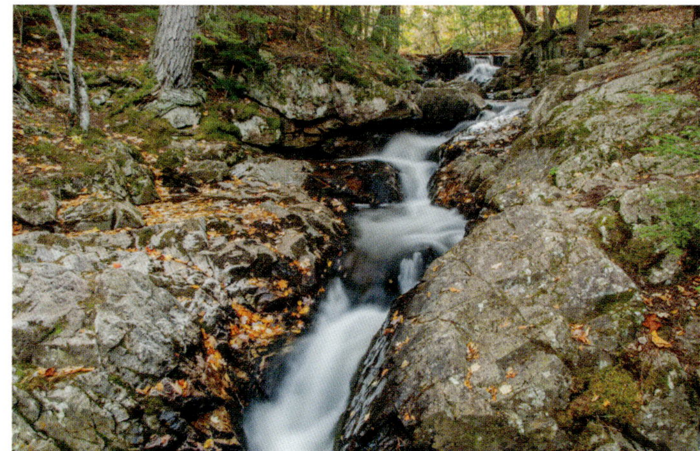

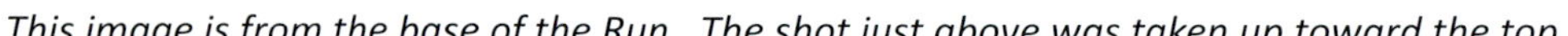

This image is from the base of the Run. The shot just above was taken up toward the top.

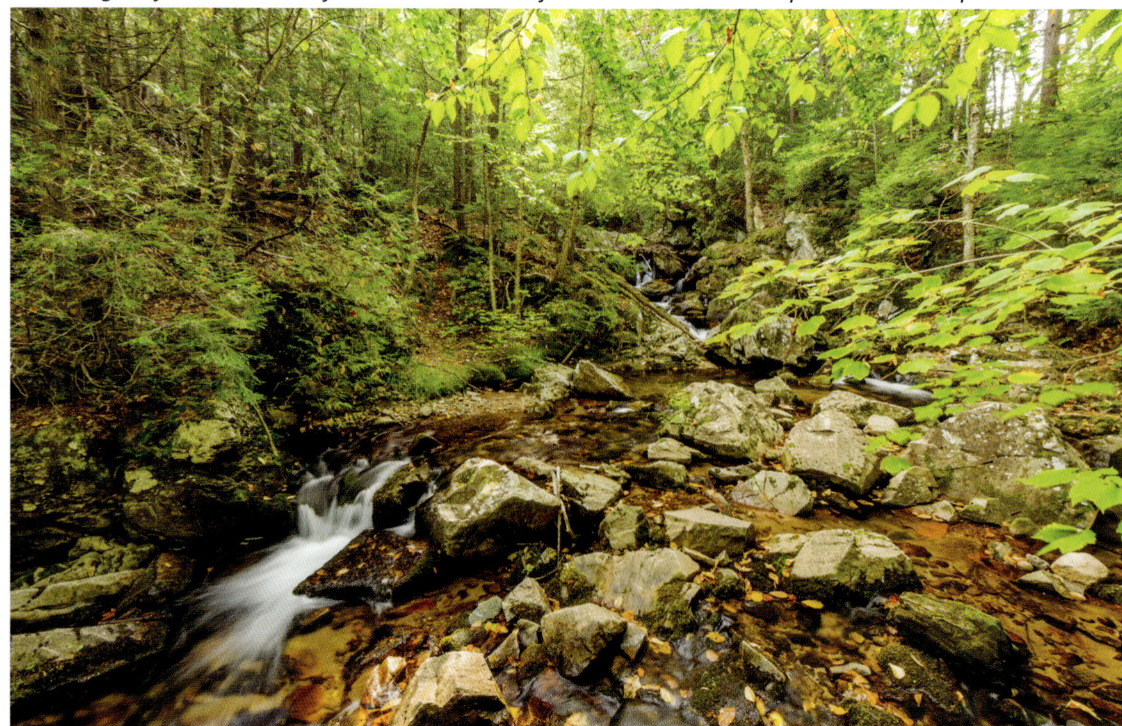

BIG PUP CASCADES (BIG PUP CREEK)

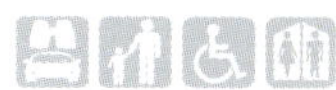

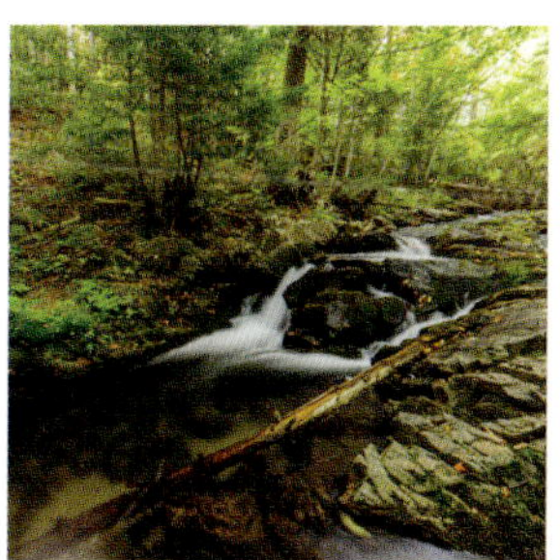

Must See:	5
Height:	5 feet
Time:	15-30 minutes
Driving Information	
Signs:	None
Road:	Dirt
Access:	Somewhat easy
4WD:	N/A

GPS:	N46 42.733 W87 42.252
Hiking Information	
Path:	None
Length:	125 yards
Elev. Change:	Moderate
GPS:	Helpful
Danger:	Moderate
WP Boots:	N/A

After the "Run", the creek takes a little breather and then starts down a short 75 feet of rapids, culminating in a nice split double cascading waterfall. Wedge shaped rocks form the base of the waterfall. Evergreens, more dominant up at Big Pup Falls, give way to a good sized stand of birch and maple down here. This ravine turns a wonderful golden yellow in autumn. What a beautiful hike it is on a crisp October morning!

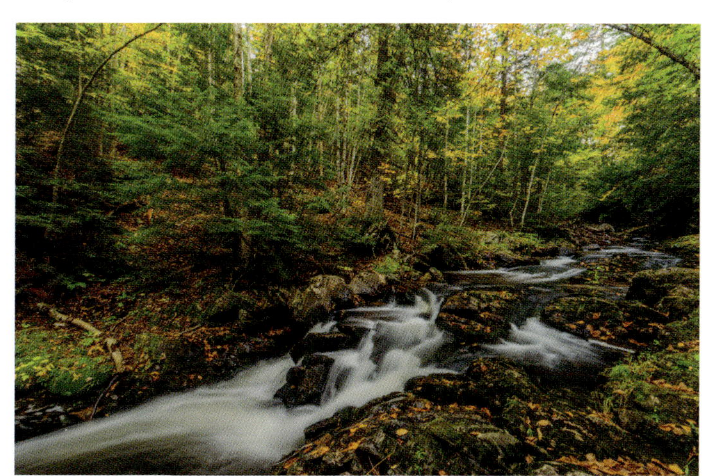

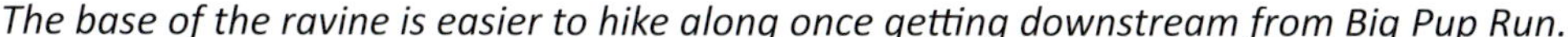

The base of the ravine is easier to hike along once getting downstream from Big Pup Run.

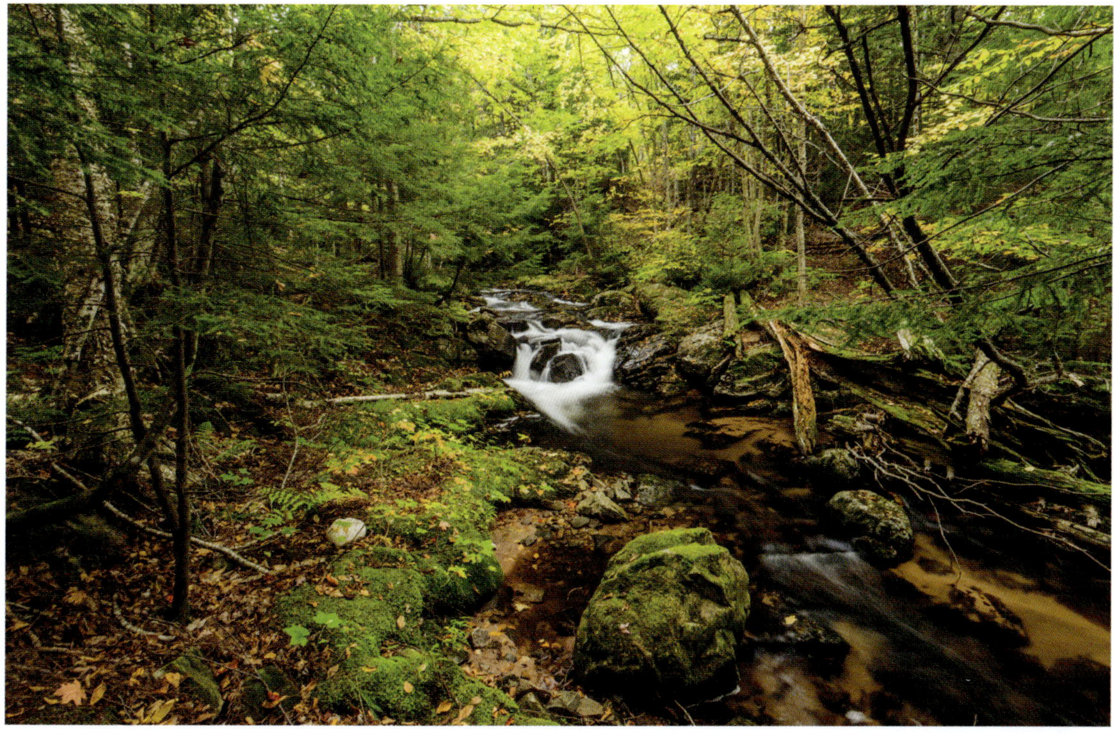

BIG PUP CASCADES - LOWER (BIG PUP CREEK)

Private 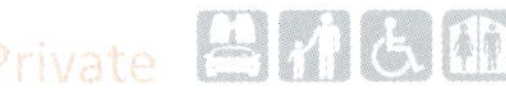

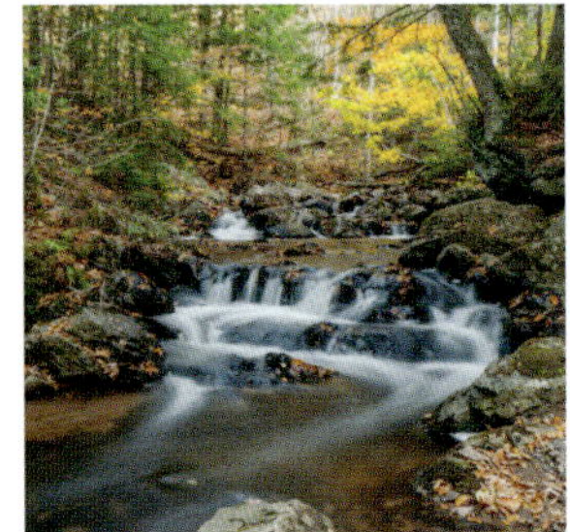

Must See:	4	GPS:	N46 42.747 W87 42.264
Height:	4 feet		
Time:	20-40 minutes	**Hiking Information**	
		Path:	None
Driving Information		Length:	150 yards
Signs:	None	Elev. Change:	Moderate
Road:	Dirt	GPS:	Helpful
Access:	Somewhat easy	Danger:	Moderate
4WD:	N/A	WP Boots:	N/A

Below the "Cascades", the creek turns a sharp corner. Here, another short set of small cascades is found in the medium width creek. The cascades end in a 2 foot drop with good sized boulders once again lining the edge of the creek. They're like parade goers watching a "watery float".

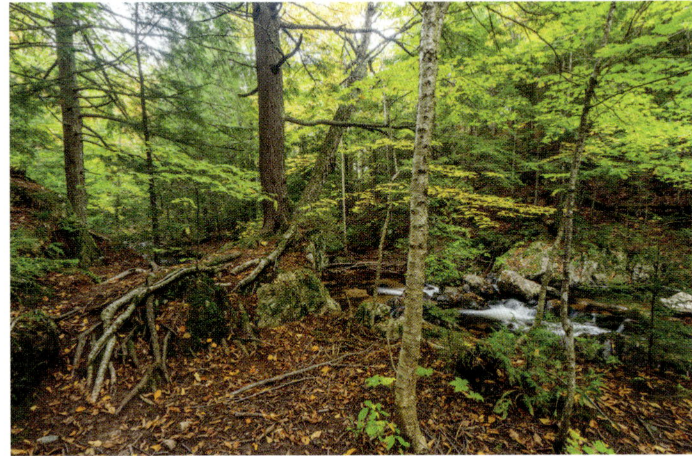

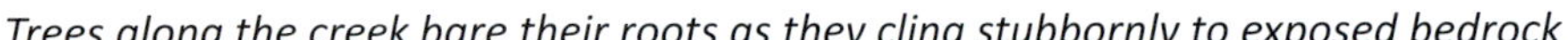

Trees along the creek bare their roots as they cling stubbornly to exposed bedrock

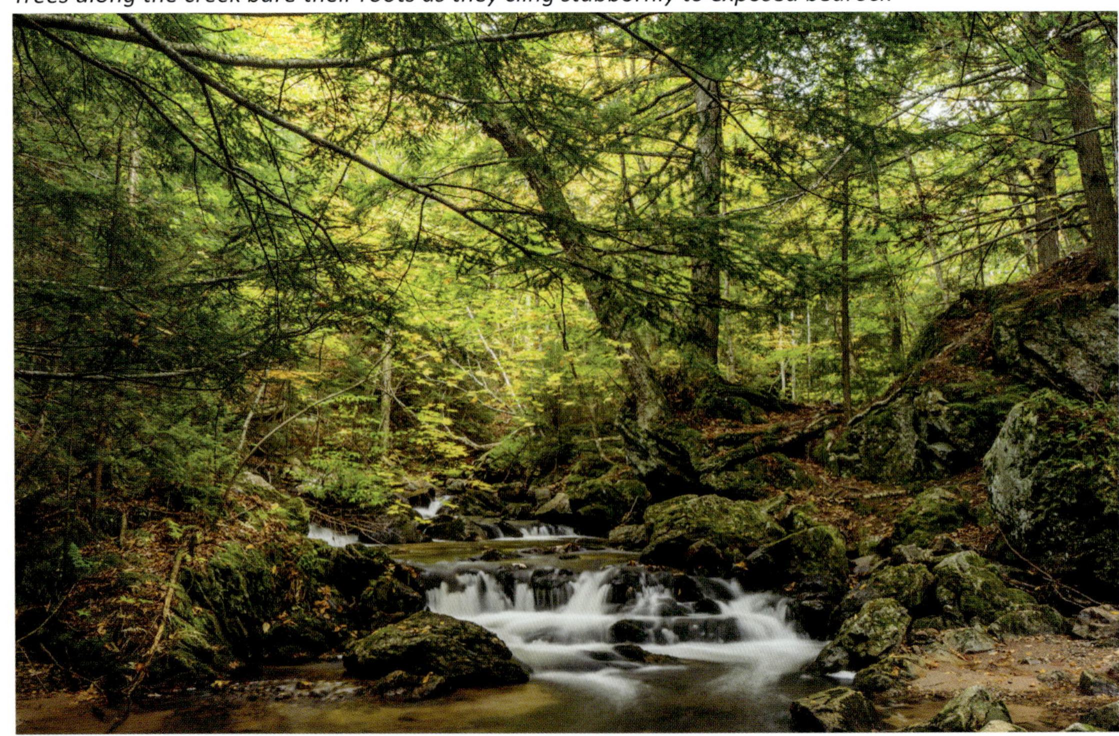

Bushy Creek Falls Hike

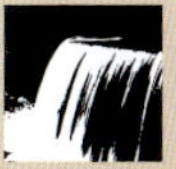

Bushy Creek flows through hardwoods with a scattering of conifers here and there. Rolling hills are topped with the canopy of a mature forest overhead and the crunch of fallen leaves beneath. As the creek nears the Yellow Dog River ravine it starts cutting its own smaller ravine. Near the start of this ravine is Bushy Creek Falls. And at the end of the ravine, where Bushy Creek meets the Yellow Dog River, Bushy Creek Mouth Falls finishes bringing the creek down to the river's level.

Directions: Turn onto CR-510 from CR-550 just south of Big Bay. In 2.6 miles, turn left (southeast) to stay on CR-510. In 2.6 miles, turn left (east) onto a 2-track at N46 44.555 W87 43.849. A 4WD is recommended. Drive 1.9 miles. Park on the left where a private drive turns off to the right. Walk down the 2-track straight ahead to the creek (the 2-track drops off sharply down into the Bushy Creek Ravine after the parking spot). Bushy Creek Falls are just upstream, and visible from here. Downstream, at the end of the creek, is Bushy Creek Mouth Falls. Follow the Yellow Dog River upstream to Yellow Dog Falls #10, #9, and #8 over the next .29 miles.

BUSHY CREEK FALLS (BUSHY CREEK)

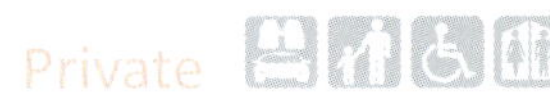

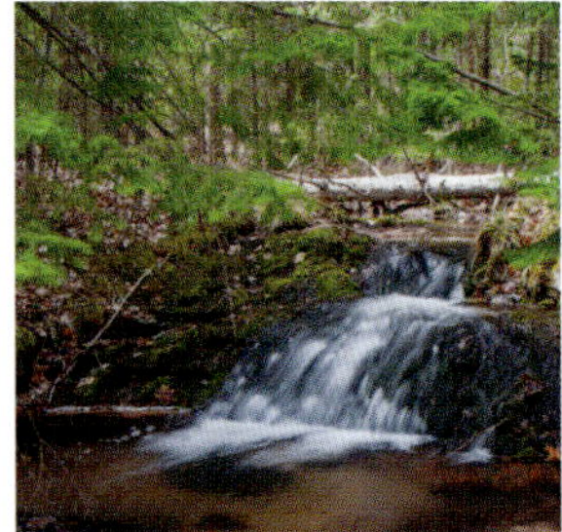

Must See:	4	GPS:	N46 44.166 W87 41.630
Height:	3 feet		
Time:	5-15 minutes		

Driving Information		Hiking Information	
		Path:	None
		Length:	100 feet
Signs:	None	Elev. Change:	Moderate
Road:	2-track	GPS:	None
Access:	Difficult	Danger:	Slight
4WD:	Recommended	WP Boots:	Recommended

Just feet upstream from Bushy Creek Truck Trail's crossing of Bushy Creek is a small, secluded waterfall. The 3 foot drop fans out to 10 feet wide as it enters the spill pool. Maple, birch and tamarack trees shroud the waterfall in dark shadows.

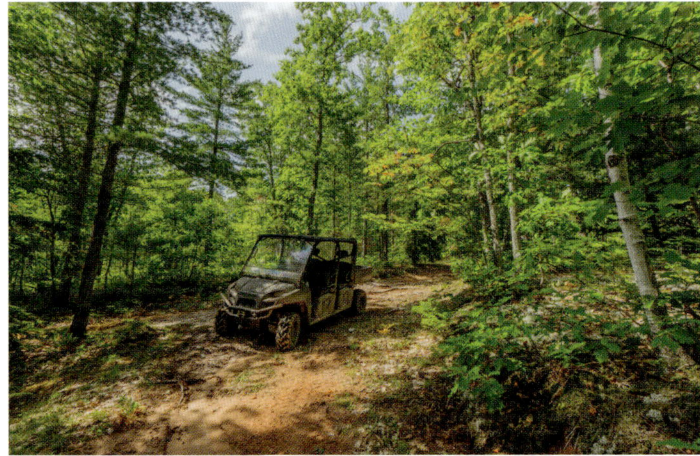

The "trail" drops into the steep ravine at such an angle that a very high clearance 4WD will be needed to attempt to continue down the trail. Head downstream 100 feet to see the taller waterfall as the creek enters the Yellow Dog River.

Park at the top of the steep 2-track (above) that crosses the creek just downstream from the waterfall.

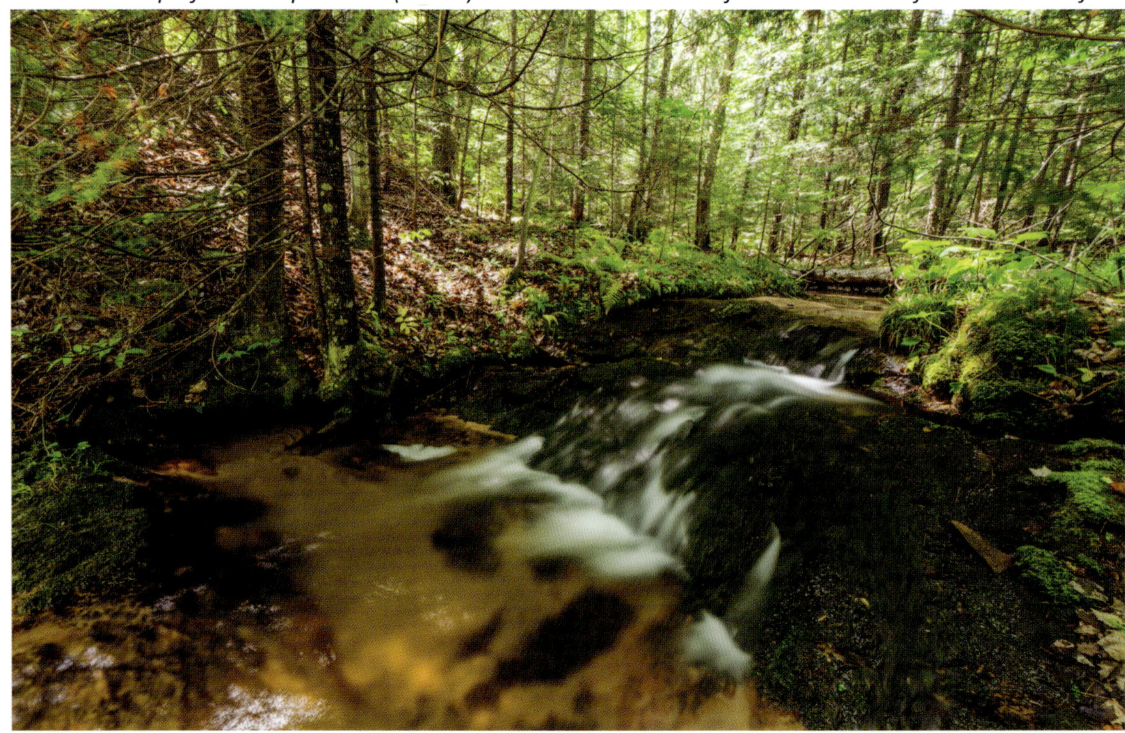

BUSHY CREEK MOUTH FALLS (BUSHY CREEK)

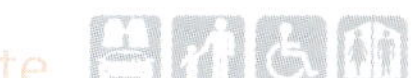

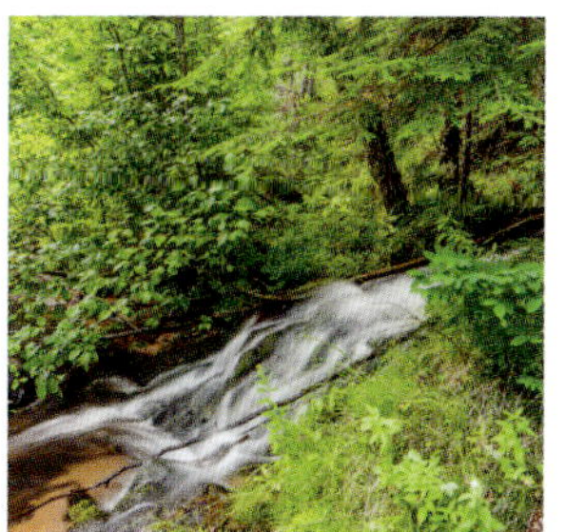

Must See:	5	GPS:	N46 44.157 W87 41.601
Height:	20 feet		
Time:	10-20 minutes	**Hiking Information**	
		Path:	None
Driving Information		Length:	150 feet
Signs:	None	Elev. Change:	Moderate
Road:	2-track	GPS:	None
Access:	Difficult	Danger:	Slight
4WD:	Recommended	WP Boots:	Recommended

The closer that Bushy Creek gets to the Yellow Dog River the quicker it runs downhill until it fans out over moss covered rocks in a final burst for the nicest looking portion of this drop. Since the waterfall ends right at the river's edge, it is not easy to view. It may view nicely from the other side of the Yellow Dog River. However, the river normally runs quite swiftly, so take caution if trying to cross.

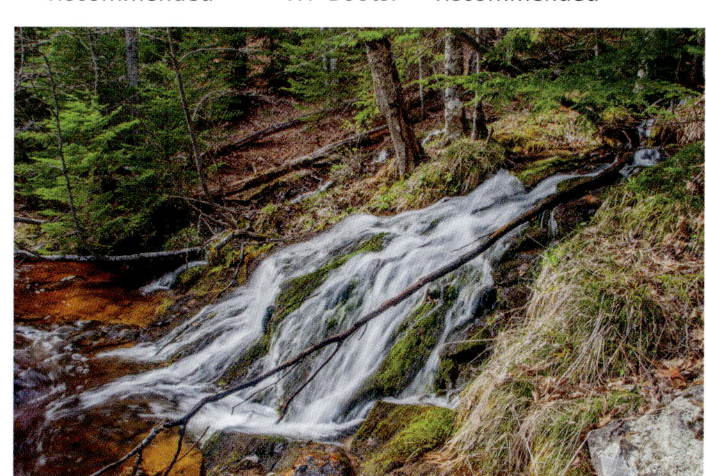

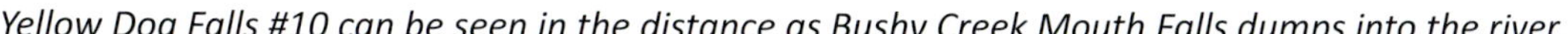

Yellow Dog Falls #10 can be seen in the distance as Bushy Creek Mouth Falls dumps into the river.

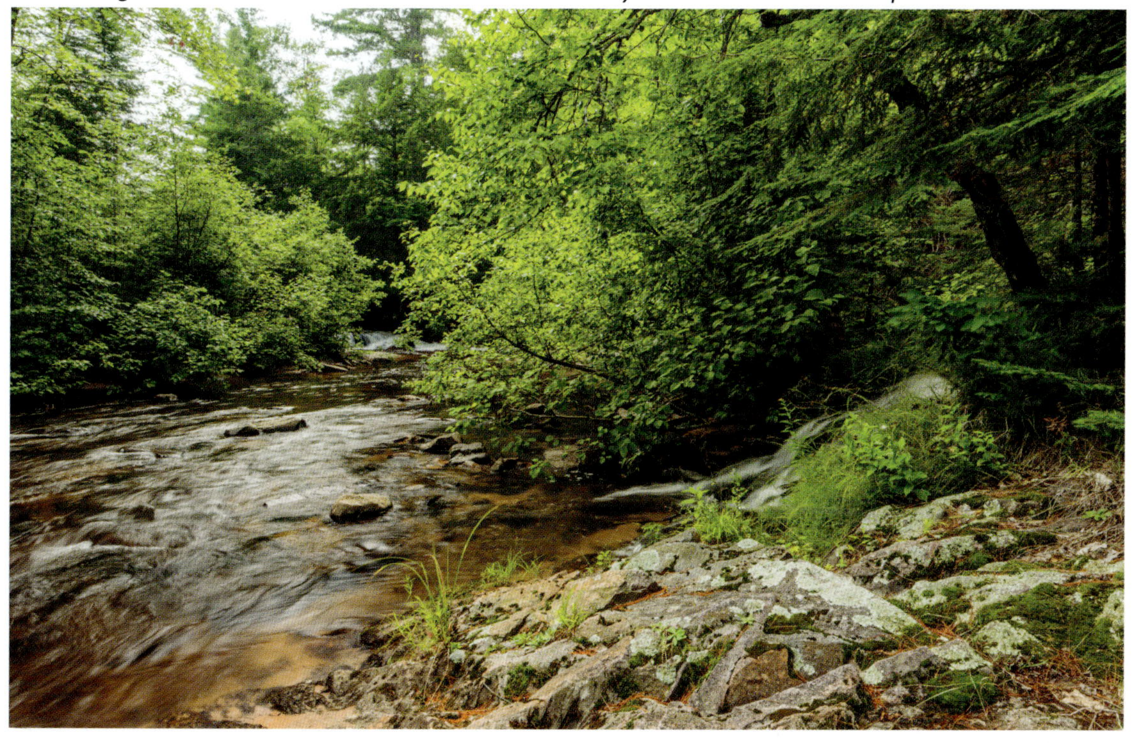

YELLOW DOG FALLS #10 (YELLOW DOG RIVER)

Private 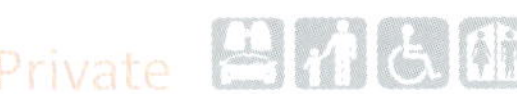

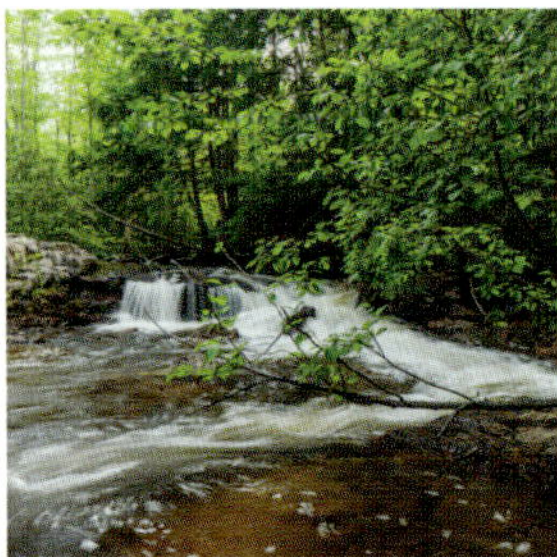

Must See:	6	GPS:	N46 44.138 W87 41.622
Height:	4 feet		
Time:	10-20 minutes	Hiking Information	
		Path:	Slight footpath
Driving Information		Length:	110 yards
Signs:	None	Elev. Change:	Moderate
Road:	2-track	GPS:	Recommended
Access:	Difficult	Danger:	Moderate
4WD:	Helpful	WP Boots:	Recommended

Yellow Dog Falls #10 can be seen from the river's edge while viewing Bushy Creek Mouth Falls. The river rushes down over a knobby outcropping. The bedrock tapers down as it reaches the base of a ravine wall on the near side of the river. The river then turns and the resulting waterfall is taller on the far side, while the stronger current is on the near side.

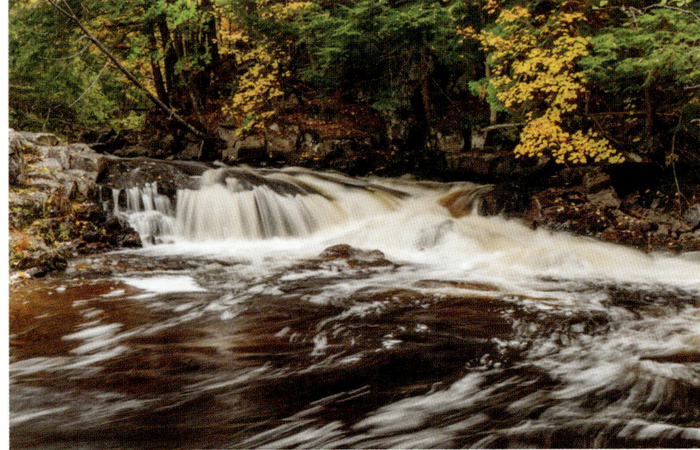

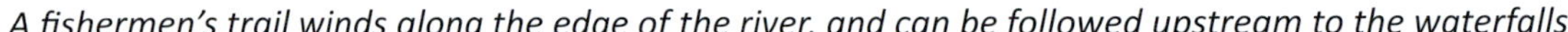

A fishermen's trail winds along the edge of the river, and can be followed upstream to the waterfalls

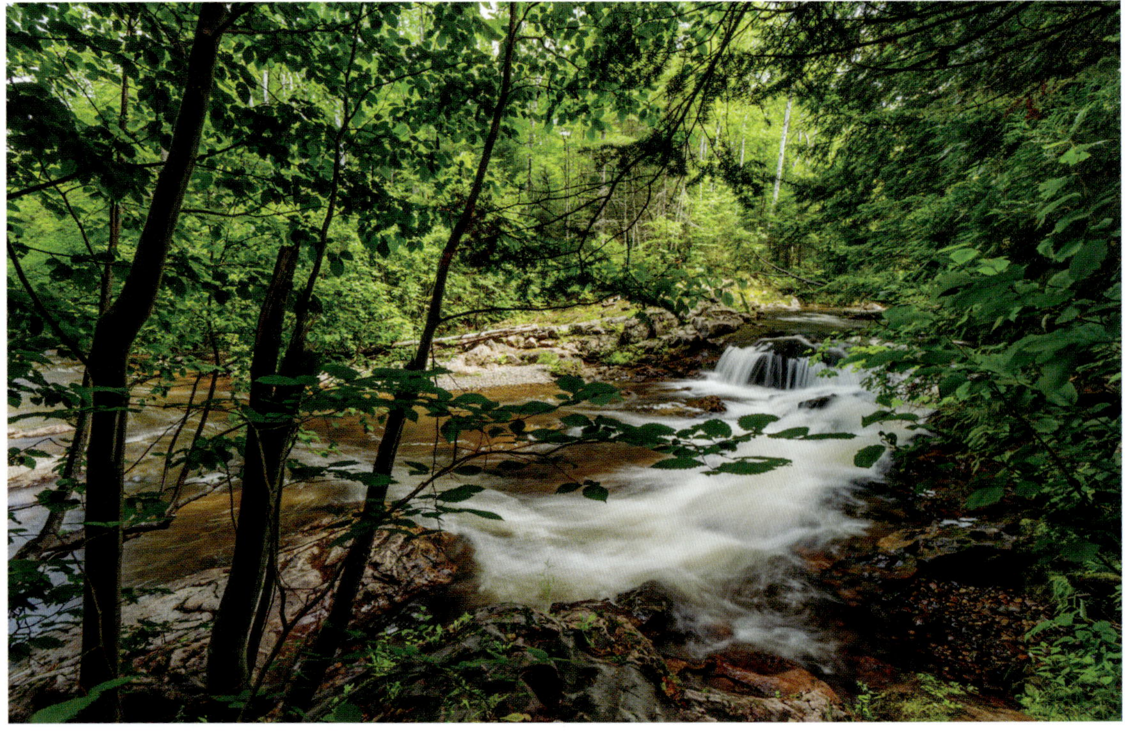

YELLOW DOG FALLS #9 (YELLOW DOG RIVER)

Private 

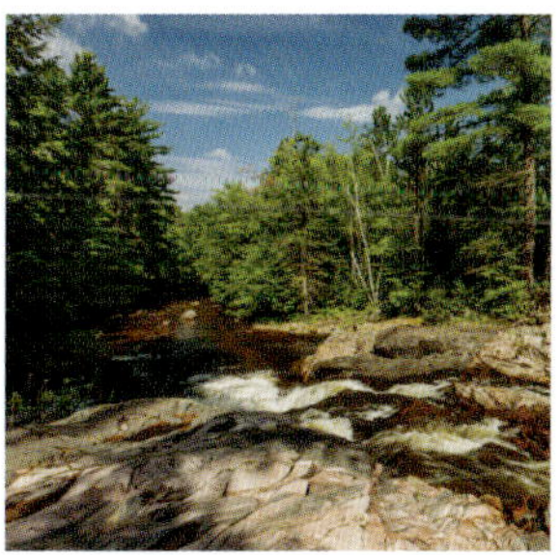

Must See:	7	GPS:	N46 44.067 W87 41.646
Height:	15 feet		
Time:	20-30 minutes	**Hiking Information**	
		Path:	Slight footpath
Driving Information		Length:	.14 miles
Signs:	None	Elev. Change:	Moderate
Road:	2-track	GPS:	Recommended
Access:	Difficult	Danger:	Moderate
4WD:	Helpful	WP Boots:	Recommended

Follow the fishermen's trail along the river from #10. The river surrounds a craggy island. Cedar, maple, moss and ferns dominate the sparsely soiled mass. On either side, the river begins the waterfall with numerous cascades. The river then gathers itself together again with both branches cascading into a circular spill pool at the base of the island. Flowing 30 feet further through a channel in the bedrock, the now 20 foot wide river cascades a final 10 feet. There is exposed bedrock on both sides of the river.

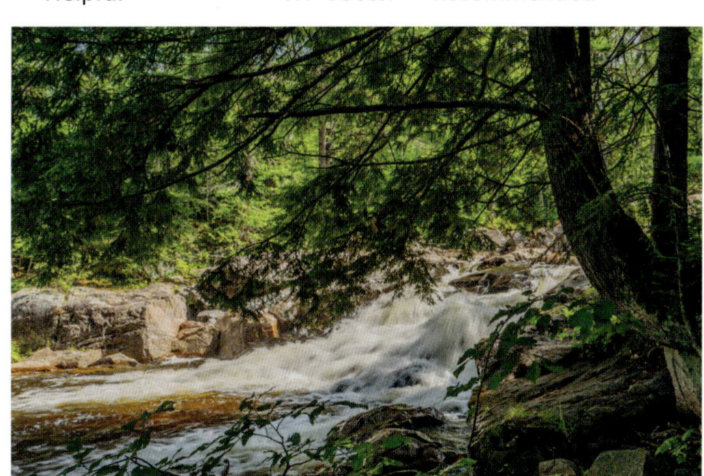

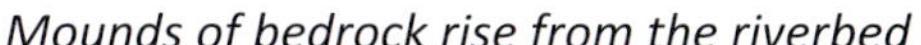

Mounds of bedrock rise from the riverbed

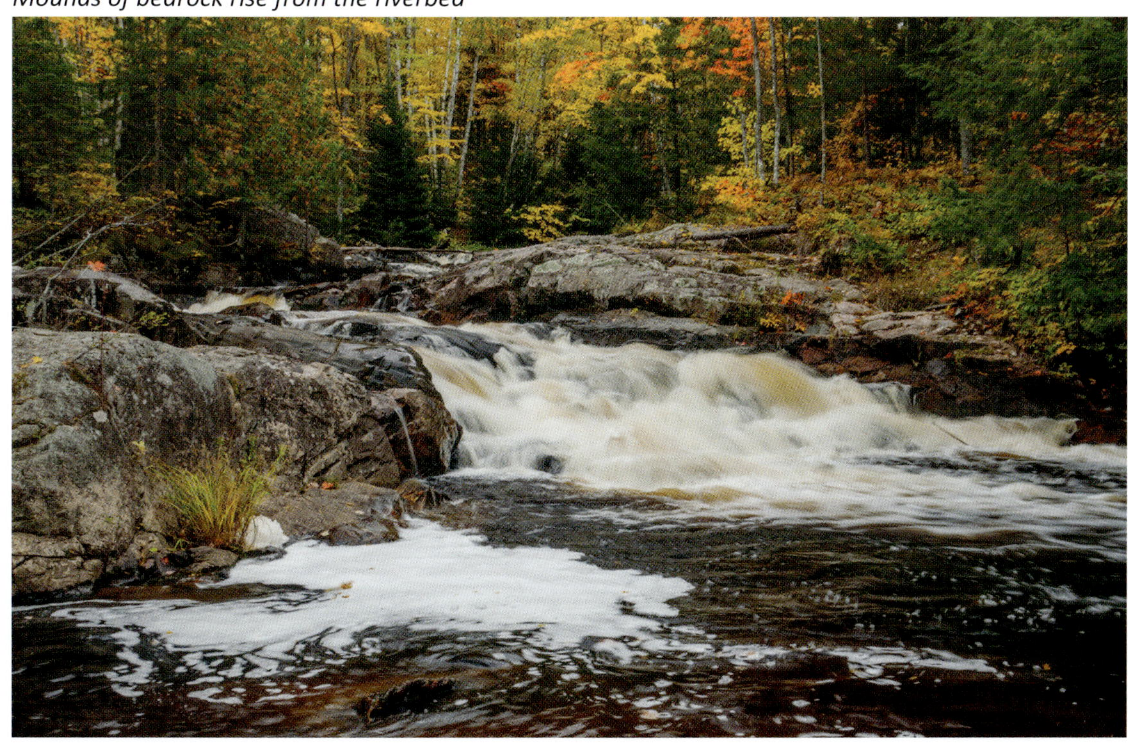

YELLOW DOG FALLS #8 (YELLOW DOG RIVER)

Private 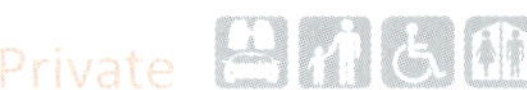

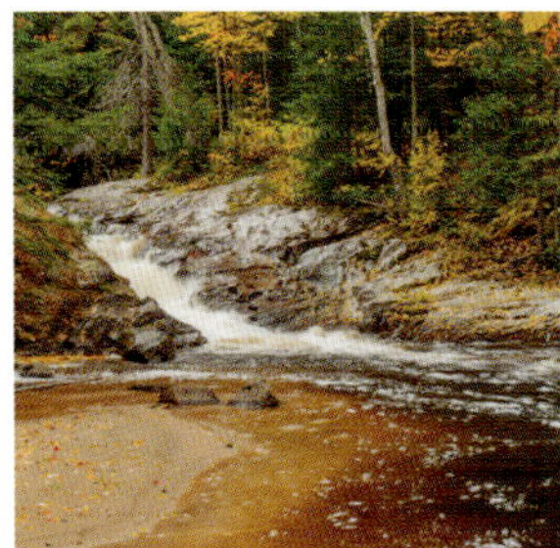

Must See:	5	GPS:	N46 44.012 W87 41.777
Height:	10 feet		
Time:	35-50 minutes	**Hiking Information**	
		Path:	Fishermen's trail
Driving Information		Length:	.29 miles
Signs:	None	Elev. Change:	Moderate
Road:	2-track	GPS:	Recommended
Access:	Difficult	Danger:	Moderate
4WD:	Helpful	WP Boots:	Recommended

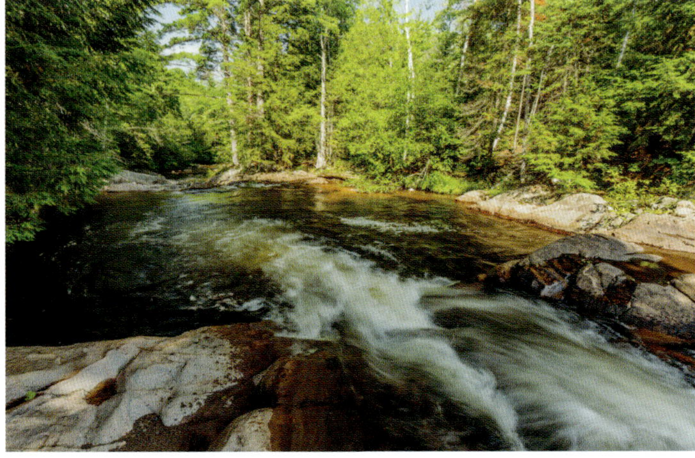

Continue from #9 down the fishermen's trail. A great view of the waterfall opens up as the trail rounds a bend in the river about 50 yards below the falls. A channel has been cut through the solid bedrock, forcing the river through the narrow passageway. As if to protest, the river throws up a "rooster tail" halfway down the channel. Dusty brown-gray bedrock lies exposed along the channel. Up above the falls, the Yellow Dog River is backed up by a natural dam. A ridge of basalt slows the river down, widening it out into a playful pool. A narrow, 10 foot wide section of this "dam" has eroded over the years, allowing the river to continue out into another large pool before it drastically narrows again as it enters the channel at the top of the waterfall.

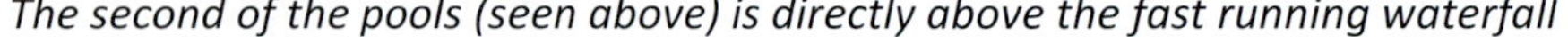

The second of the pools (seen above) is directly above the fast running waterfall

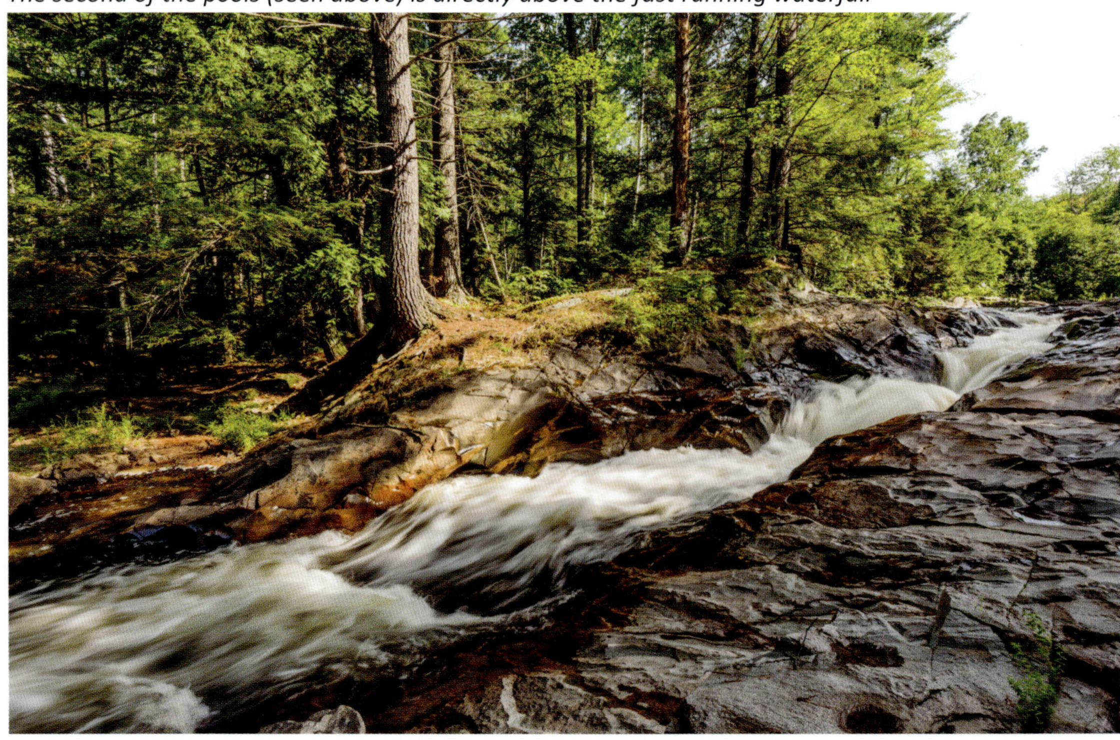

Yellow Dog Falls Hike #1

The Yellow Dog River is over 31 miles in length and by the time it flows below CR-510 it is about 7 miles from Lake Independence. The first 4 miles of the river are designated as a "wild river" by the US Fish and Wildlife Service. The rugged river has its start in Bulldog Lake, within the confines of the McCormick Tract. It then flows over the Bulldog Falls, through the Yellow Dog Plains, over Wylie Dam Falls, Pinnacle Falls, then over the Yellow Dog Falls and on to Lake Independence.

The most popular of the Yellow Dog Falls and most associated with that name is the #1 falls. It is the first waterfall found down river from CR-510. Most hike in from CR-510 to this waterfall, but I recommend an alternate route, especially if you have a 4WD.

Directions: There are two main ways to access the Yellow Dog Falls.

Easiest Driving (Southern Route)
The first and most popular is to drive down CR-510 to the bridge over the Yellow Dog River. On the far side of the bridge (south) is a parking area on the east side of the road. An obvious trail heads down river, crosses a couple of wet areas (waterproof boots are recommended) and ends at Yellow Dog Falls #1. This is about 1/2 mile hike to this point. The trail does continue along the river, but rapidly deteriorates. I have hiked this side of the river down to the #10 falls and back and I really don't recommend it! The undergrowth is thick and there are many cedars with low dead branches to hinder progress. This route approaches the river from the south.

Easiest Hiking (Northern Route)
The second idea is to drive down Bushy Creek Truck Trail, the same 2-track that is used to get to Bushy Creek. Turn onto CR-510 from CR-550 just south of Big Bay. In 2.6 miles, turn left (southeast) to stay on CR-510. In 2.6 miles, turn left (east) onto a 2-track at N46 44.555 W87 43.849. A 4WD is recommended. (This is the same 2-track for driving to the Bushy Creek Falls.) Stay on the "main" 2-track for 1.66 miles. Turn right. Drive .6 miles. Park at an obvious parking spot (N46 43.832 W87 42.336). Hike down to the river along the good footpath. It ends at the river at Yellow Dog Falls #2. Hike along a fishermen's path upstream to #1, or downstream along the river to #3. The rest of the falls (#4 to #10) are more easily accessed via the hikes further downstream.

YELLOW DOG FALLS #1 (YELLOW DOG RIVER)

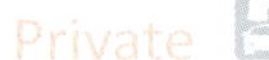

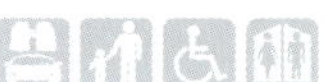

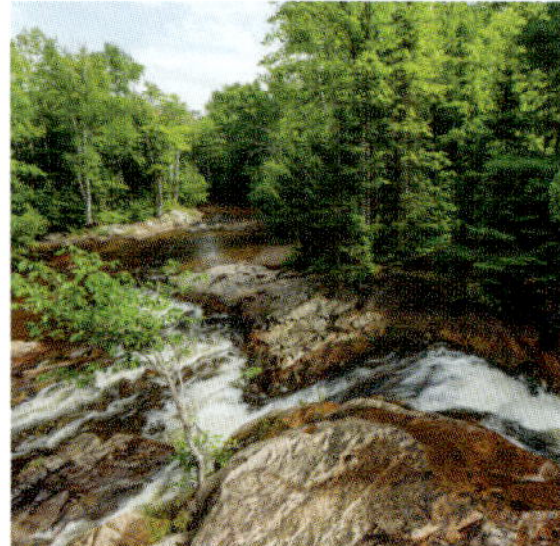

Must See:	8	GPS:	N46 43.720 W87 42.403
Height:	11 feet		
Time:	*30-40 or 45-60 minutes	Hiking Information	
Driving Information		Path:	Footpath
		Length:	*.45 miles or .35 miles
Signs:	None	Elev. Change:	Moderate
Road:	*Dirt or 2-track	GPS:	Recommended
Access:	*Easy or Difficult	Danger:	Moderate
4WD:	*N/A or Helpful	WP Boots:	Recommended

*The first piece of information refers to the Southern Route and the second, the Northern Route. (See page 159)

Known traditionally as "Yellow Dog Falls", the #1 falls can be easily accessed from both the north and south sides.

Smooth, wildly curved bedrock below the falls makes for a great viewing or picnicking platform when the river is low. A large rock outcropping juts forward in the middle of the falls, forcing the river to split around it, cascading down either side. A secondary drop of 3 feet is below the irregularly shaped spill pool.

The same volume of water flows over all of the waterfalls in this stretch of the Yellow Dog River, but this waterfall displays itself in such a way as to feel more powerful. Ferns and even a hardwood tree grow on the bulwark of rock in the center of the waterfall. It splits wide (about 75 feet), a white frothy cascade on both sides rushing down to a second level of pitted yellowish-brown bedrock. The waterfall then rushes back together in front of the exposed face, finishing the drop with a final 2 foot plunge into the river below.

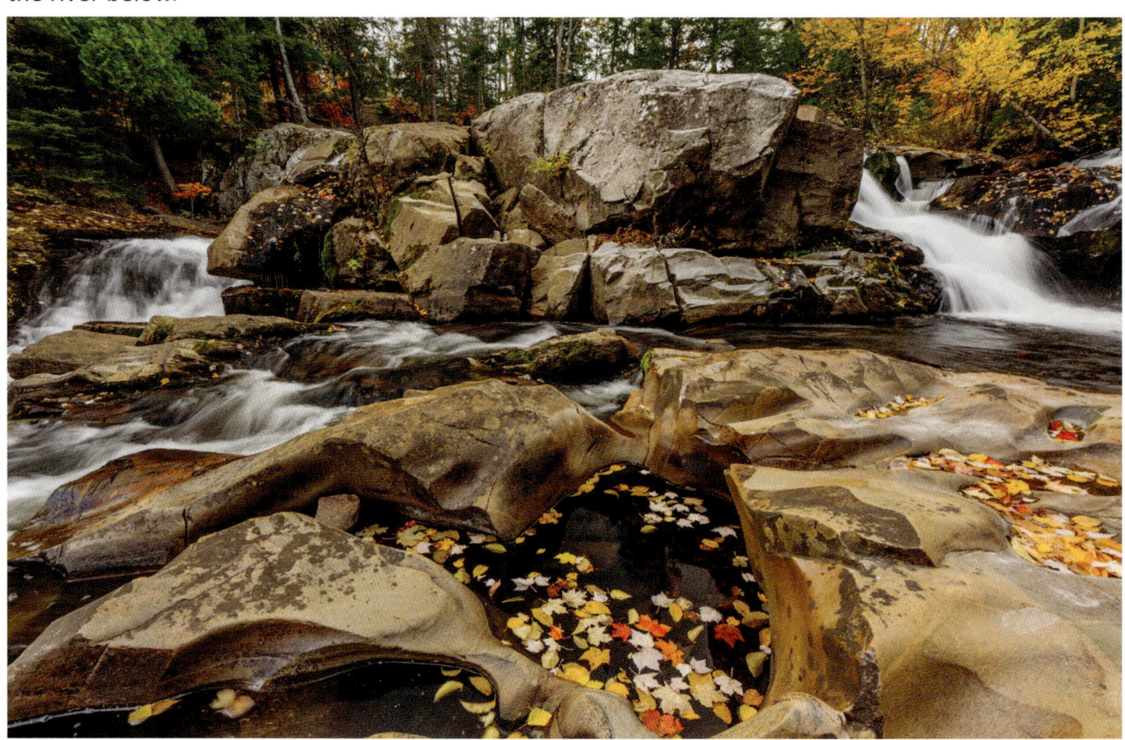

YELLOW DOG FALLS #2 (YELLOW DOG RIVER)

Private 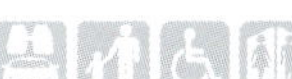

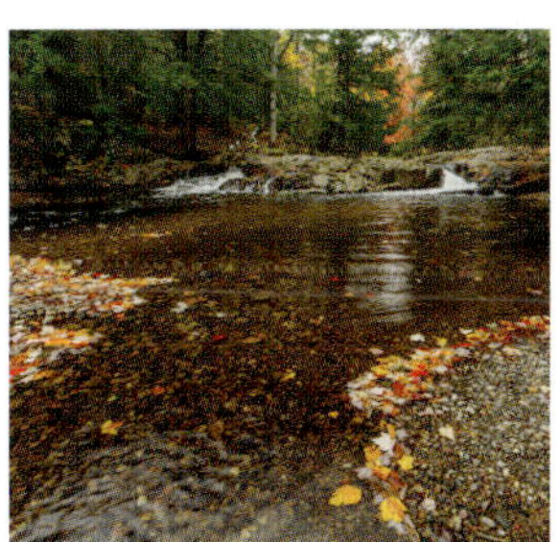

Must See:	4	GPS:	N46 43.812 W87 42.206
Height:	2 feet		
Time:	*40-60 or 15-20 minutes	Hiking Information	
		Path:	Footpath
Driving Information		Length:	*.65 miles or .13 miles
Signs:	None	Elev. Change:	Moderate
Road:	*Dirt or 2-track	GPS:	Recommended
Access:	*Easy or Difficult	Danger:	Moderate
4WD:	*N/A or Helpful	WP Boots:	Recommended

*The first piece of information refers to the Southern Route and the second, the Northern Route. (See page 159)

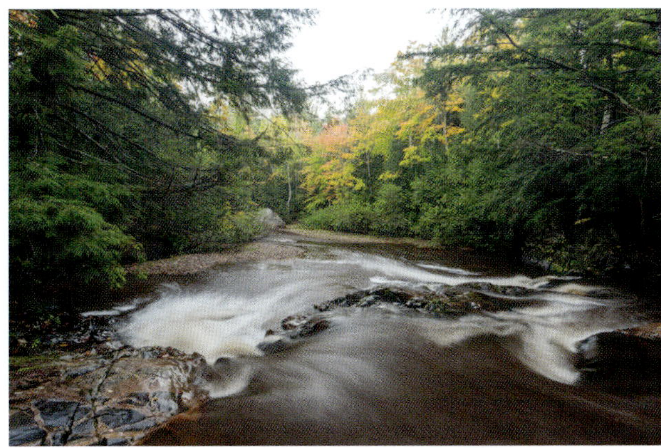

When the river is low it may be possible to wade through about 6 inches of water to a pebble-covered sandbar to get the best view of the falls. Large cedars overlook the rocky riverbed. The river winds and narrows above the falls. It then quickly widens back out from 8 feet to 40 feet as it passes by smooth, mounded reddish-gray bedrock. The river then suddenly plunges on both sides of the river at low points along a jagged face. An idyllic camping area is next to the river between the #2 and #3 falls.

Beautifully colored leaves are plentiful during autumn. Exotic golds and reds stand in stark contrast to the earthy tones in the river. The soft crunch underfoot mixed with the aroma of decaying leaves and chill in the air stimulate the senses!

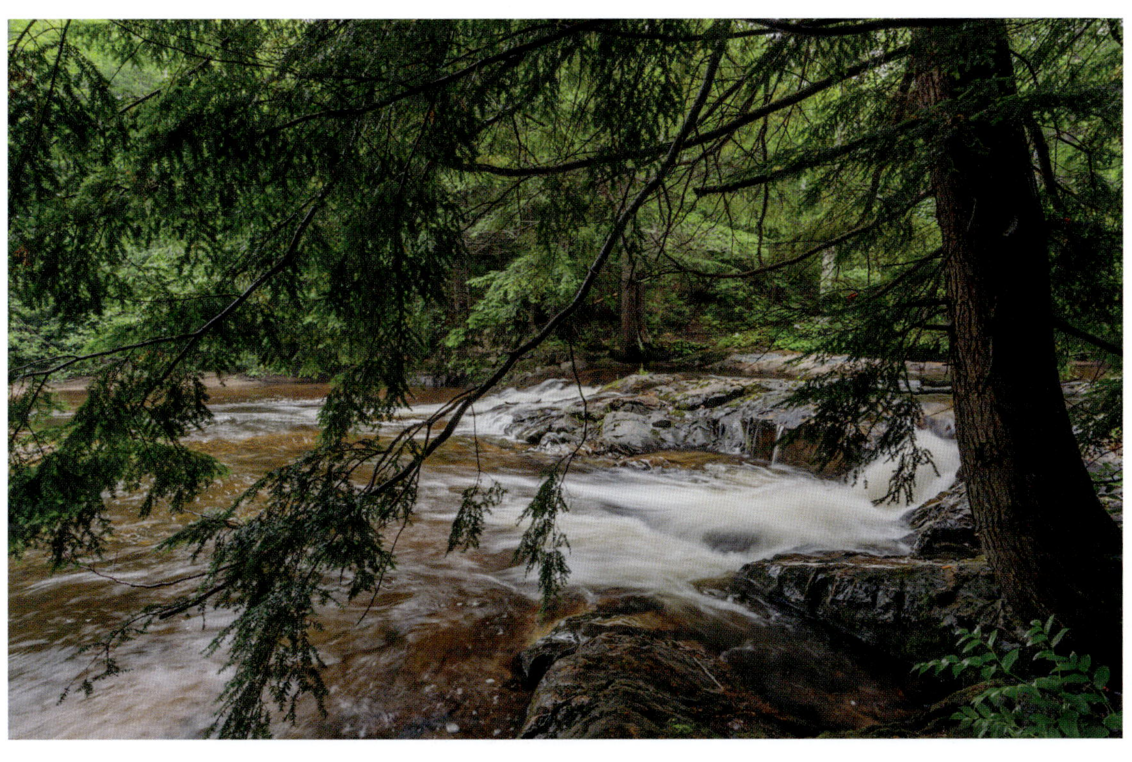

YELLOW DOG FALLS #3 (YELLOW DOG RIVER)

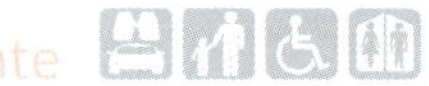

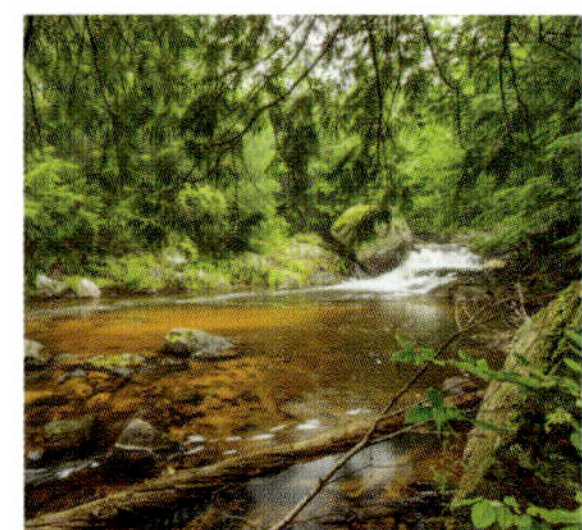

Must See:	7
Height:	10 feet
Time:	*45-65 or 25-40 minutes
Driving Information	
Signs:	None
Road:	*Dirt or 2-track
Access:	*Easy or Difficult
4WD:	*N/A or Helpful

GPS:	N46 43.865 W87 42.238
Hiking Information	
Path:	Footpath
Length:	*.72 miles or .21 miles
Elev. Change:	Moderate
GPS:	Recommended
Danger:	Moderate
WP Boots:	Recommended

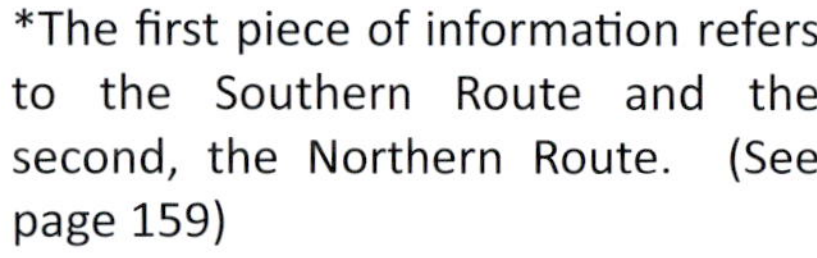

*The first piece of information refers to the Southern Route and the second, the Northern Route. (See page 159)

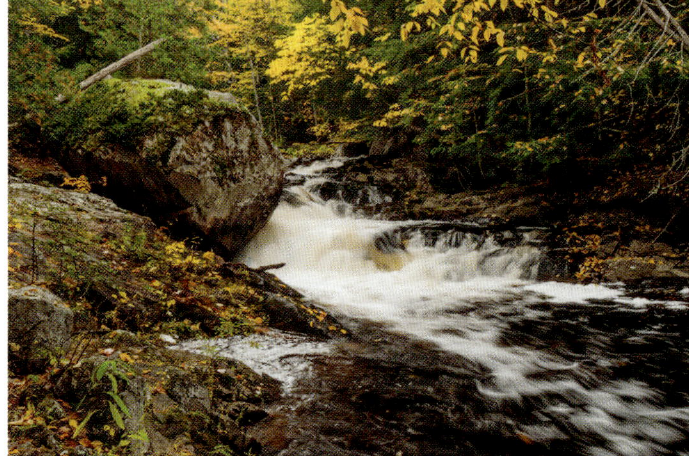

A 15 foot rounded rock sits alongside the waterfall in the river (I've heard this waterfall referred to as "Eyeball Falls"). The jagged bedrock in the riverbed is being carved smooth by the relentless force of water and time. Moss, lichen, and ferns hang on tight to the moist rocks along the river. A couple small cascades get the waterfalls started. Then the river falls at the large rock, shooting down about 4 feet before turning and dropping another 4 feet along the south side of the river.

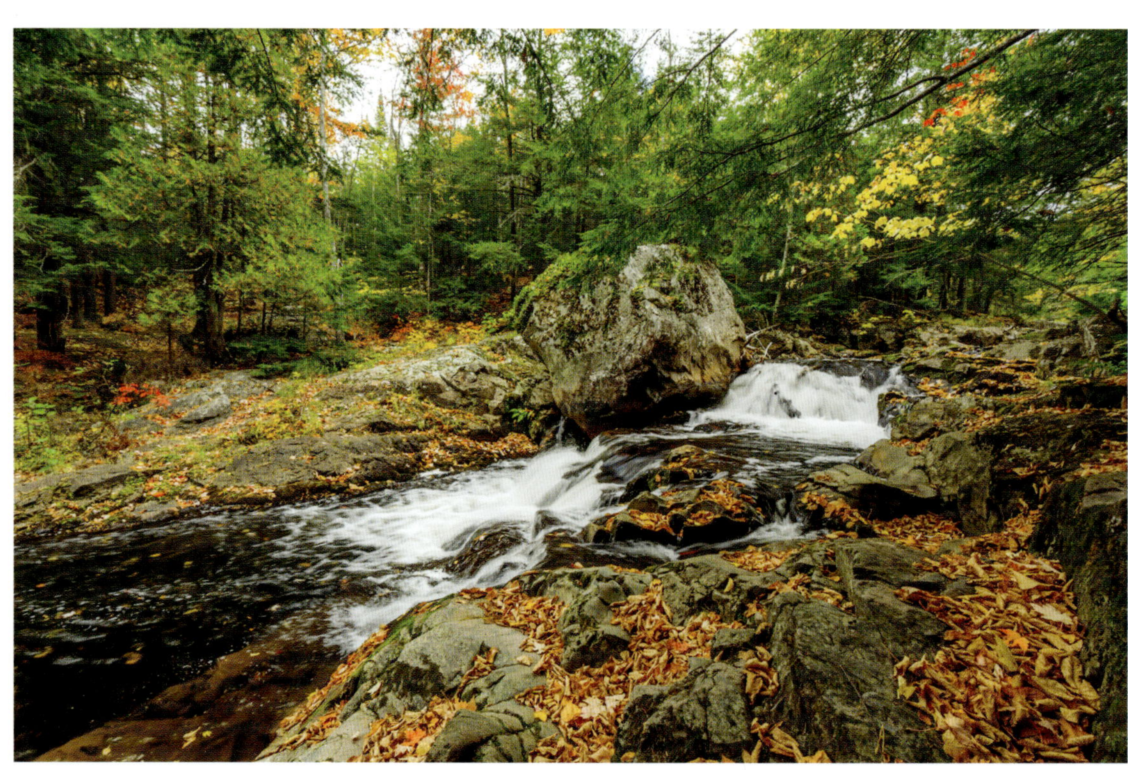

Yellow Dog Falls Hike #2

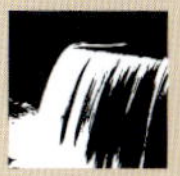

The middle section of the Yellow Dog Falls is most easily accessed from this particular parking spot that's found partway down the 2-track that parallels the northern side of the Yellow Dog River.

Directions: Turn onto CR-510 from CR-550 just south of Big Bay. In 2.6 miles, turn left (southeast) to stay on CR-510. In 2.6 miles, turn left (east) onto a 2-track at N46 44.555 W87 43.849. A 4WD is recommended. (This is the same 2-track for driving to the Bushy Creek Falls.) Stay on the "main" 2-track for 1.66 miles. Turn right. Drive .2 miles. Turn left (south) on a 2-track (just past a sandy pit). Park at the end of the short trail. (N46 43.946 W87 42.243). Hike down to the river along the good footpath. It ends at the river at Yellow Dog Falls #5. Hike just a couple dozen yards upstream to #4. The hike downstream to #6 and #7 is more difficult. Those two waterfalls are close together, so once getting to #6, #7 is nearby.

YELLOW DOG FALLS #4 (YELLOW DOG RIVER)

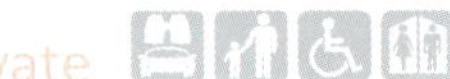

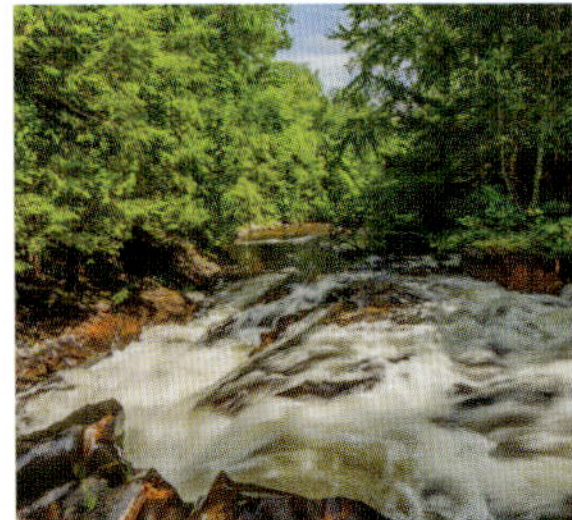

Must See:	5	GPS:	N46 43.912 W87 42.258
Height:	10 feet		
Time:	15-25 minutes	Hiking Information	
		Path:	Footpath
Driving Information		Length:	85 yards
Signs:	None	Elev. Change:	Moderate
Road:	2-track	GPS:	Recommended
Access:	Difficult	Danger:	Moderate
4WD:	Helpful	WP Boots:	Recommended

The trail from the vehicle will come out at #5. Hike the short distance upstream to #4.

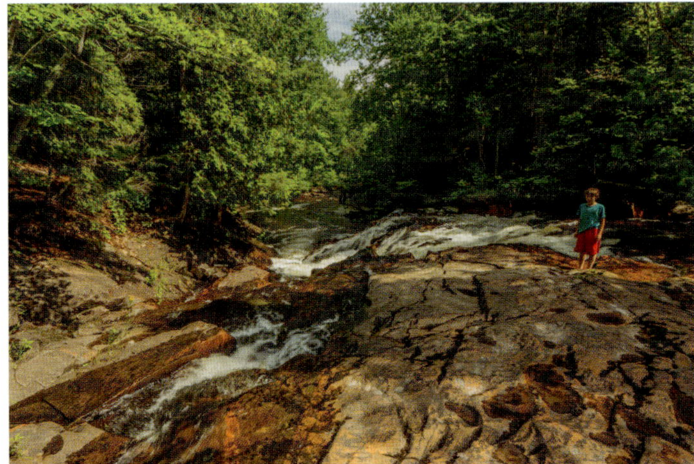

The bulk of the river runs toward the northern side of the river and cascades down into a horseshoe shaped cavity. After running a number of yards over a rocky riverbed there is a final drop, the river pouring over a rounded, short cascade.

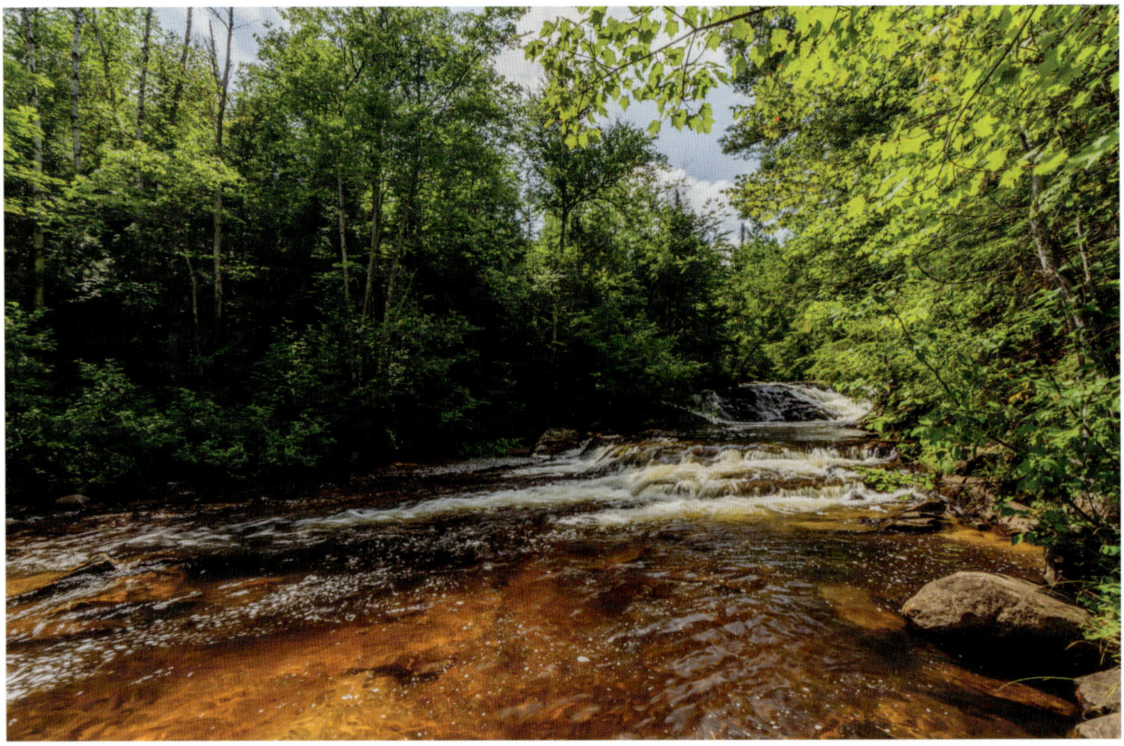

YELLOW DOG FALLS #5 (YELLOW DOG RIVER)

Private 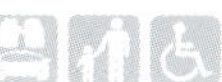 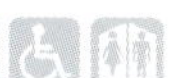

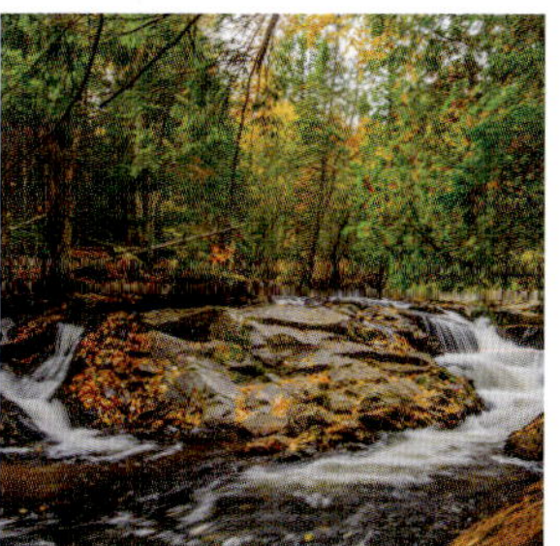

Must See:	4	GPS:	N46 43.919 W87 42.238
Height:	5 feet		
Time:	10-20 minutes	**Hiking Information**	
		Path:	Footpath
Driving Information		Length:	50 yards
Signs:	None	Elev. Change:	Moderate
Road:	2-track	GPS:	Recommended
Access:	Difficult	Danger:	Moderate
4WD:	Helpful	WP Boots:	Recommended

Hike a mere 50 yards down to the river and this waterfall. From here, follow the river just 35 yards upstream to the #4 falls. It's a longer hike (.15 miles) to the next waterfall downstream.

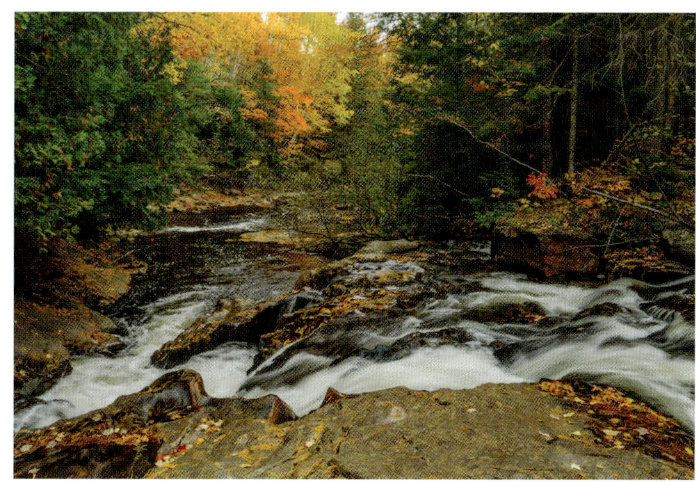

The river widens out at the waterfall, dividing around a short rocky island in the center of the waterfall. The two arms of the waterfall cascade down 5 feet. As the river rises, it creeps up the island, until it covers even the highest point during the spring melt.

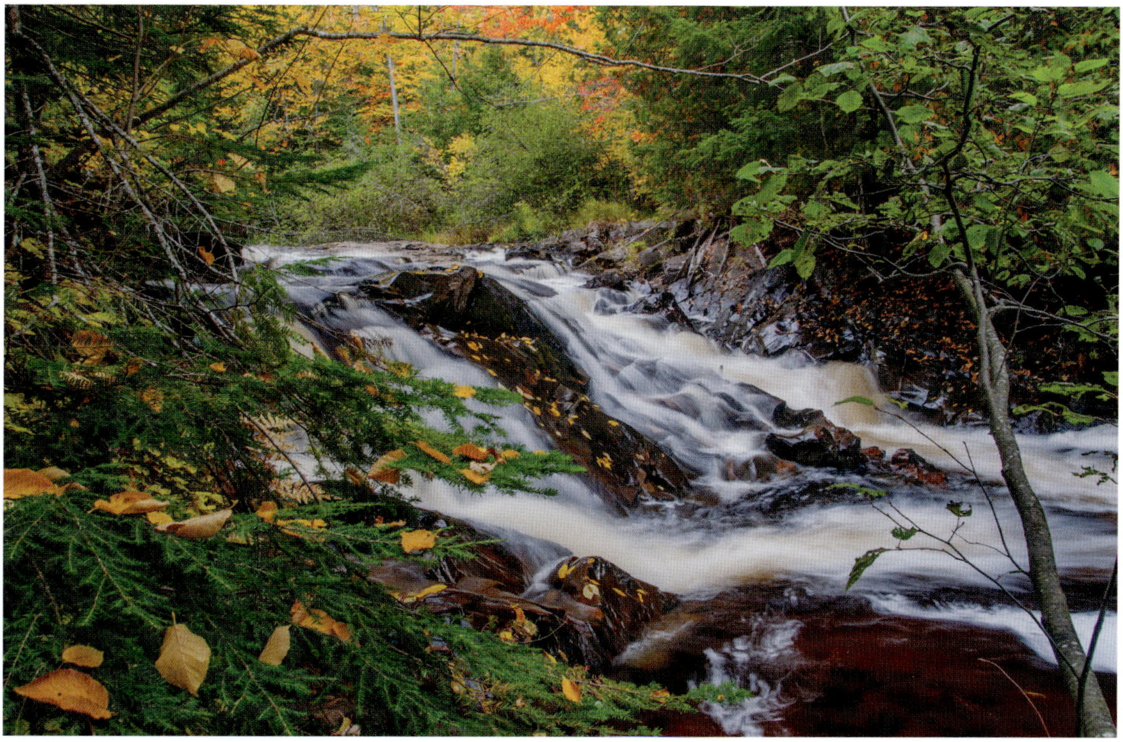

YELLOW DOG FALLS #6 (YELLOW DOG RIVER)

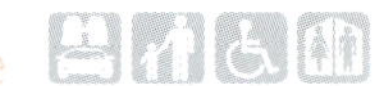

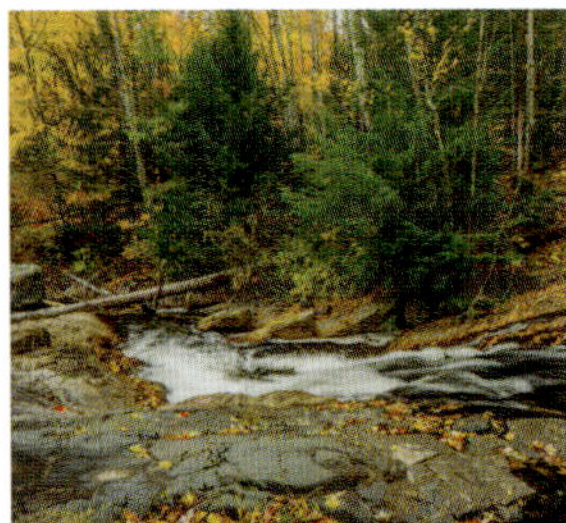

Must See: 5
Height: 6 feet
Time: 30-50 minutes

Driving Information
Signs: None
Road: 2-track
Access: Difficult
4WD: Helpful

GPS: N46 43.922 W87 42.073

Hiking Information
Path: None
Length: .18 miles
Elev. Change: Moderate
GPS: Recommended
Danger: Moderate
WP Boots: Recommended

Lichen, of various shades of green, grows in interesting patterns along the northern side of the river. Not only do I prefer the view from that side, but the hike is much easier as well! The "trail" on the southern side of the river becomes negligible. Tightly packed evergreens impede hiking. There stiff, dead lower branches snapping as you attempt to push through them. There is not much of a trail on the northern side in this area either, but hiking through this forest is much easier - and shorter!

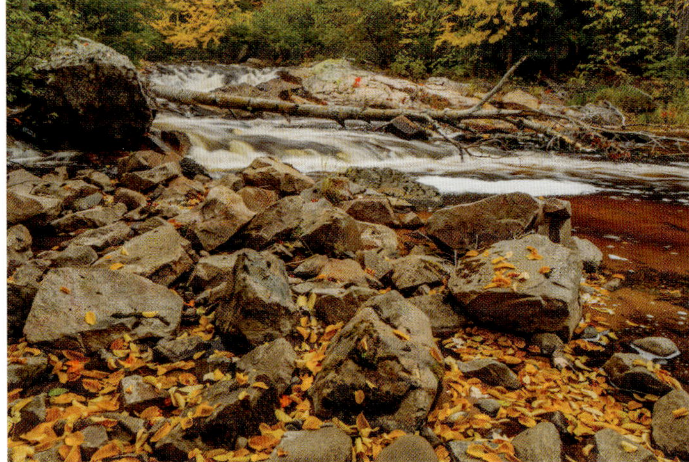

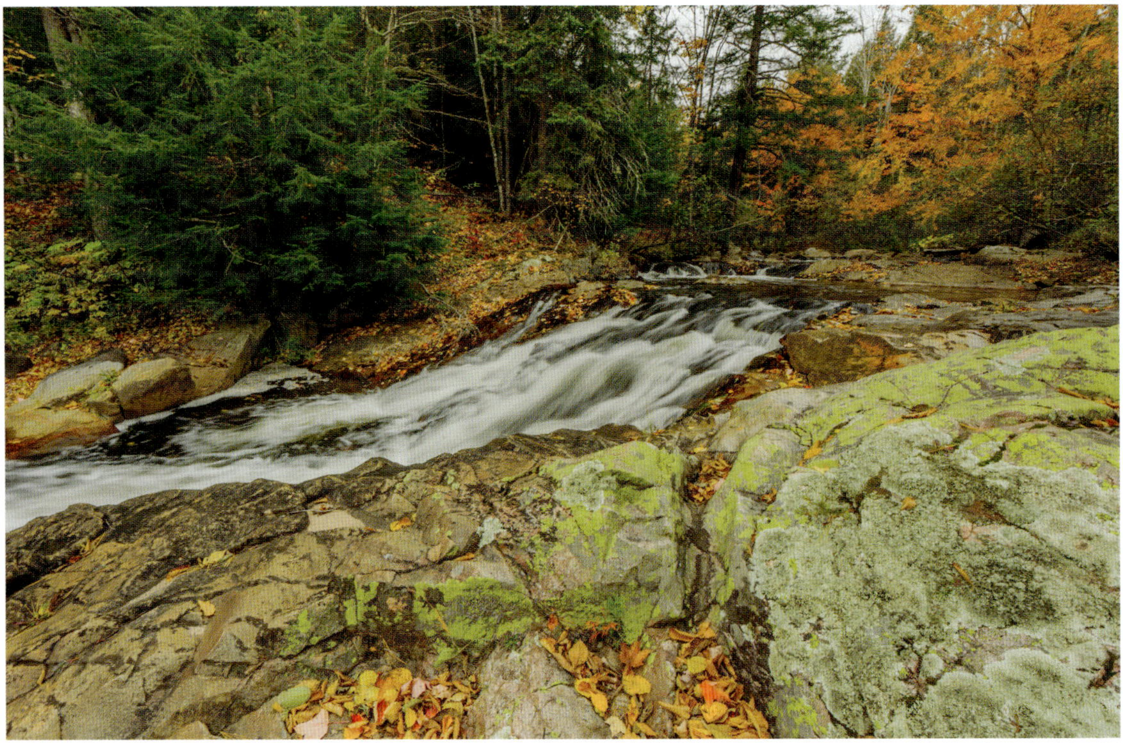

YELLOW DOG FALLS #7 (YELLOW DOG RIVER)

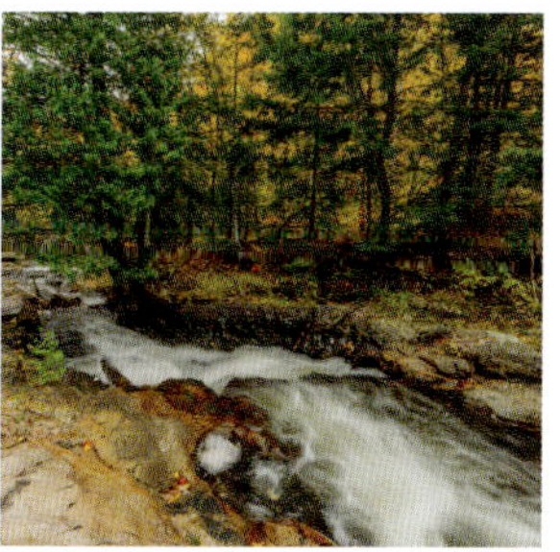

Must See:	5	GPS:	N46 43.906 W87 42.031
Height:	8 feet		
Time:	40-60 minutes		

Driving Information		Hiking Information	
		Path:	None
		Length:	.22 miles
Signs:	None	Elev. Change:	Moderate
Road:	2-track	GPS:	Recommended
Access:	Difficult	Danger:	Moderate
4WD:	Helpful	WP Boots:	Recommended

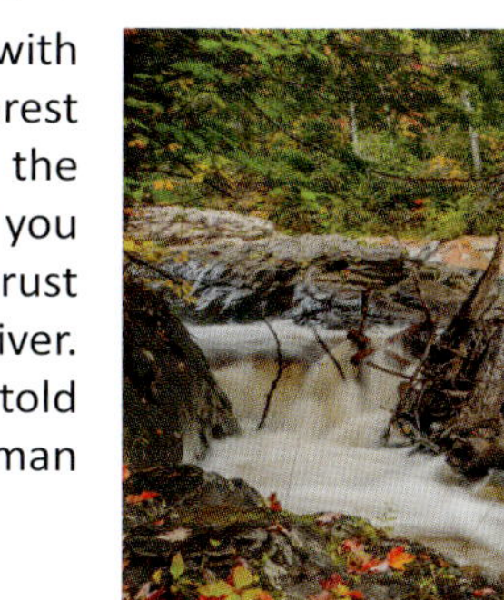

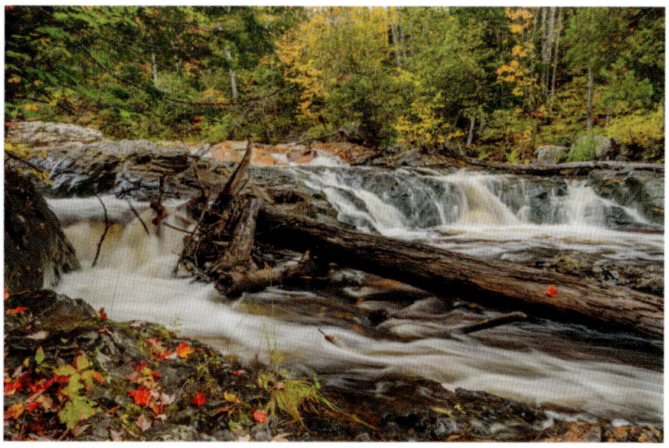

My first experience at this waterfall brought with it a surprise! After hiking a mile from the nearest road to get here I found a "cross" stuck in the waterfall. Look at the picture to the right and you may see it caught there between two upthrust roots from the large fallen tree lying in the river. Where did it come from? I have since been told that it was part of a memorial for a fisherman that was placed near a waterfall upstream.

Once again, I really recommend viewing this waterfall (as well as the rest of this series) from the north side. There is not really a trail on either side of the river in this area, but the shorter easier hike is from the northern side.

There is an interesting mixture of bedrock in the riverbed. It changes from ruddy to charcoal blue with a phosphorescent feel to it and in one area these colors are even intertwined. Get out and look around you! You never know what you will find!

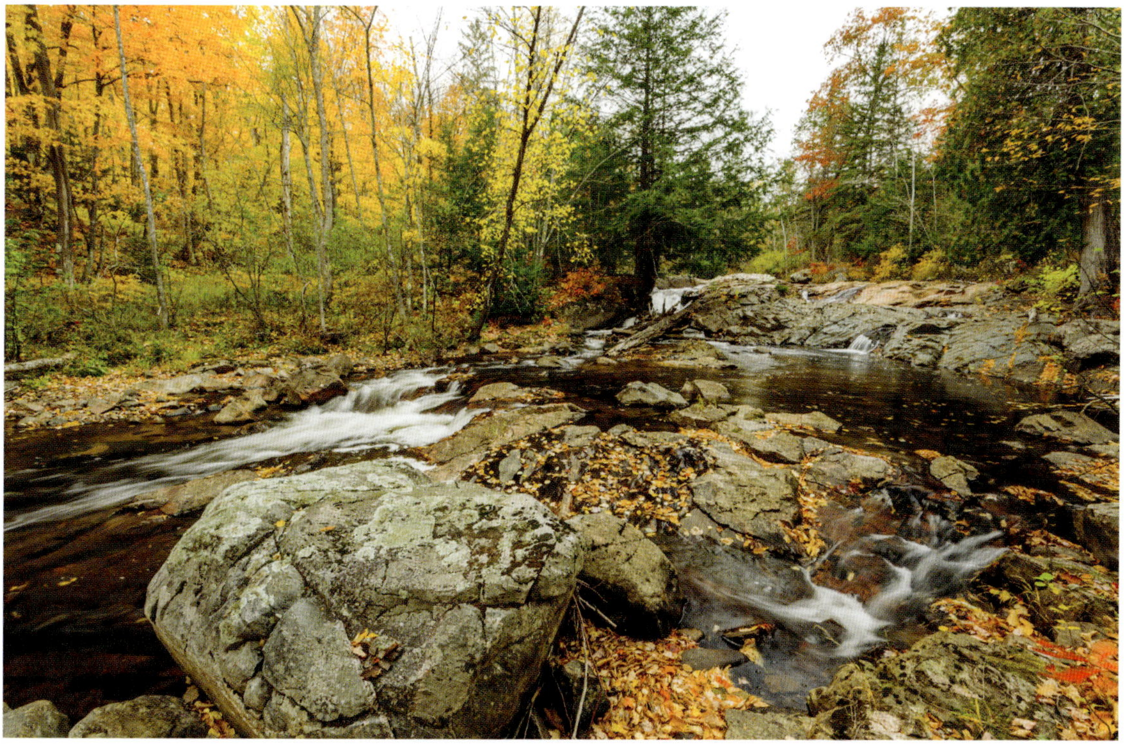

CHAPTER 3
MENOMINEE COUNTY

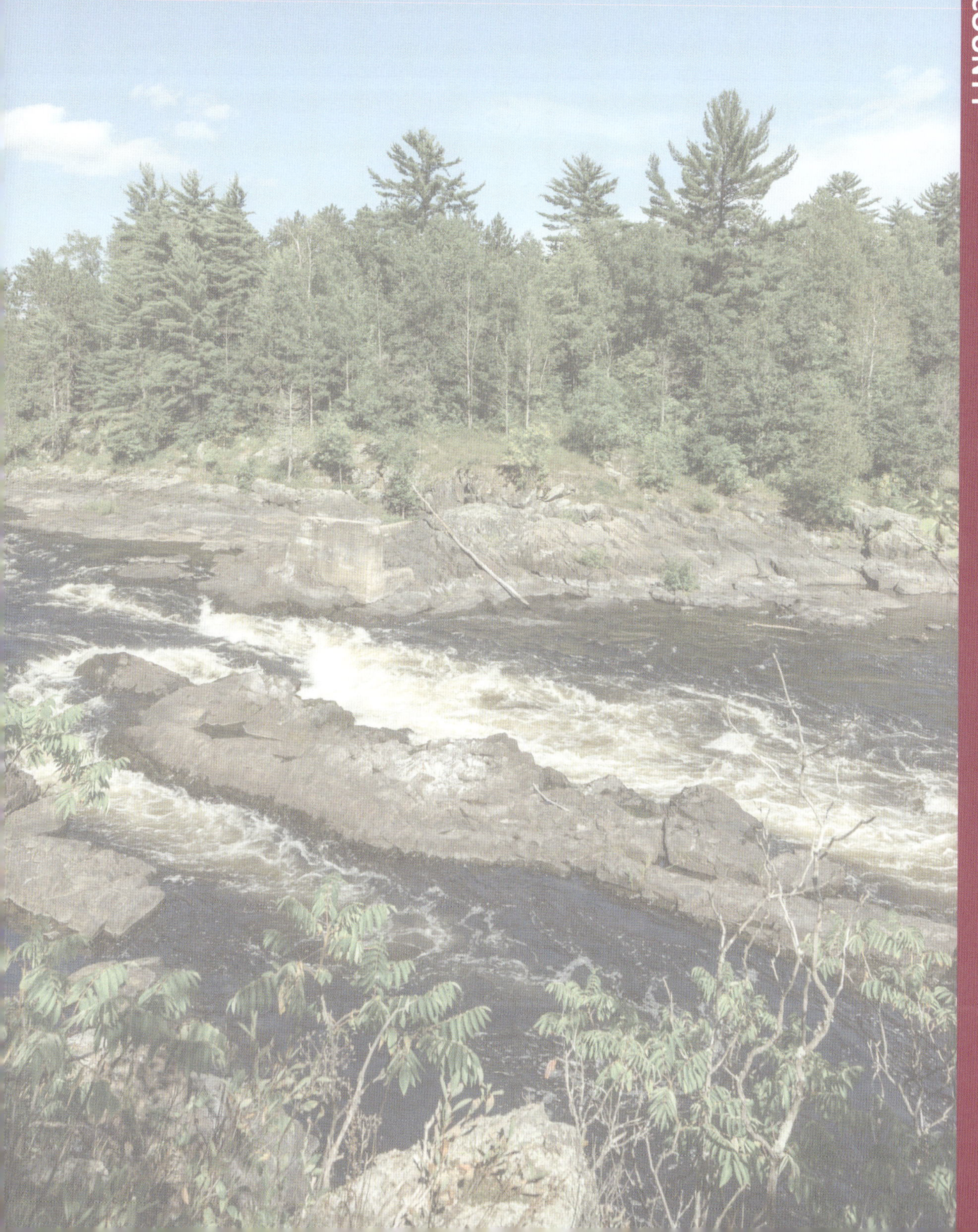

MENOMINEE COUNTY CONTENTS

MAPS..

HIKES..

WATERFALLS........................

TABLE OF CONTENT KEY

MENOMINEE COUNTY FACTS

Founded:	1861
Size:	1,044 square miles
Population (2010):	24,029
County Seat:	Menominee

Menominee County was named after the American Indian tribe "Mamaceqtaw" whose name means "The People". Europeans, however, referred to them as the "Manoominii". This was the Ojibwa name which meant "The Wild Rice Eaters". The Menominee, according to their oral history, have always lived here, and consider their origination to be the area where the Menominee River enters Green Bay.

The county was founded in 1861 as "Bleeker County". In 1863 it was incorporated and the name was changed to "Menominee County". The lumbering industry took off soon afterwards, and for awhile the city of Menominee was producing more lumber than any other city in the United States! The population of the county ballooned at that time as well. In 1870, there were only 1,791 residents in the county, but by 1890 that number had jumped to 33,639. By 1900, the lumbering heyday had subsided, and the population had dropped to 27,046 and it has never reached the 30,000 mark again.

As much of the county's eastern side is bordered by Lake Michigan's Green Bay, water activities are plentiful. Enjoy boating, fresh water and ice fishing, time on a sandy beach, or watching sailboat races out in the beautiful waters of the great lake. The Menominee North Pier Lighthouse is also a popular attraction. Spend time in the city of Menominee. It is the 4th largest city in the Upper Peninsula. Only Marquette, Sault St. Marie, and Escanaba are larger. Take time to check out the restored downtown as well as the sister city of Marinette, Wisconsin which is on the south side of Menominee River and is connected by three bridges to Menominee.

Up near Wallace, some 16 miles north of Menominee, is the DeYoung Family Zoo. It is a small but well run zoo with a good number of exotic animals. It is open seasonally. For schedule information and pricing, check out their website at *www.thedeyoungfamilyzoo.com*.

Menominee County Map

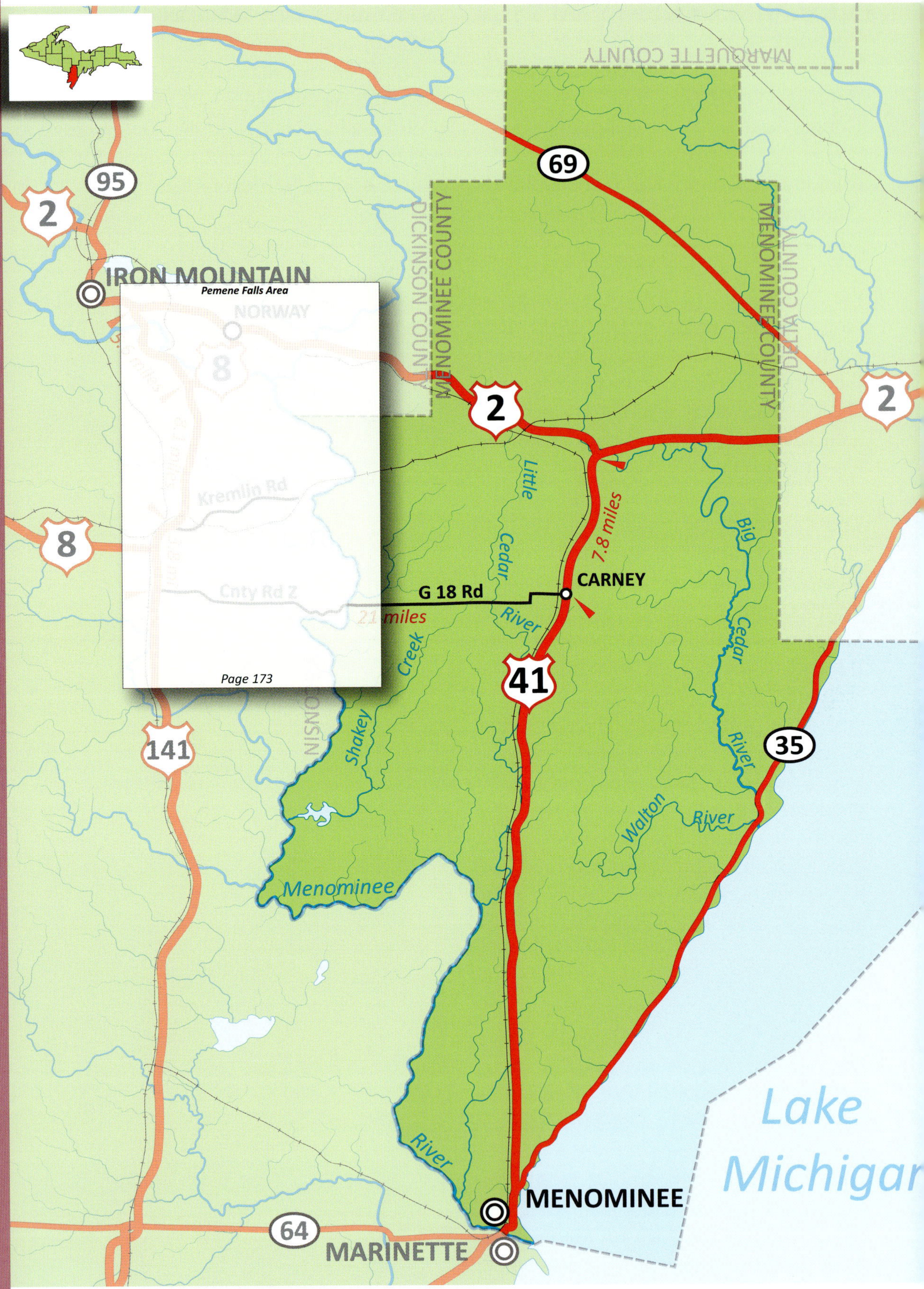

MARQUETTE COUNTY
69
95
2
IRON MOUNTAIN
Pemene Falls Area
NORWAY
8
Kremlin Rd
Cnty Rd Z
Page 173
DICKINSON COUNTY
MENOMINEE COUNTY
DELTA COUNTY
2
Little Cedar River
7.8 miles
Big Cedar River
8
CARNEY
G 18 Rd
21 miles
Creek
Shakey
41
141
WISCONSIN
35
Walton River
Menominee
River
Lake Michigan
MENOMINEE
64
MARINETTE

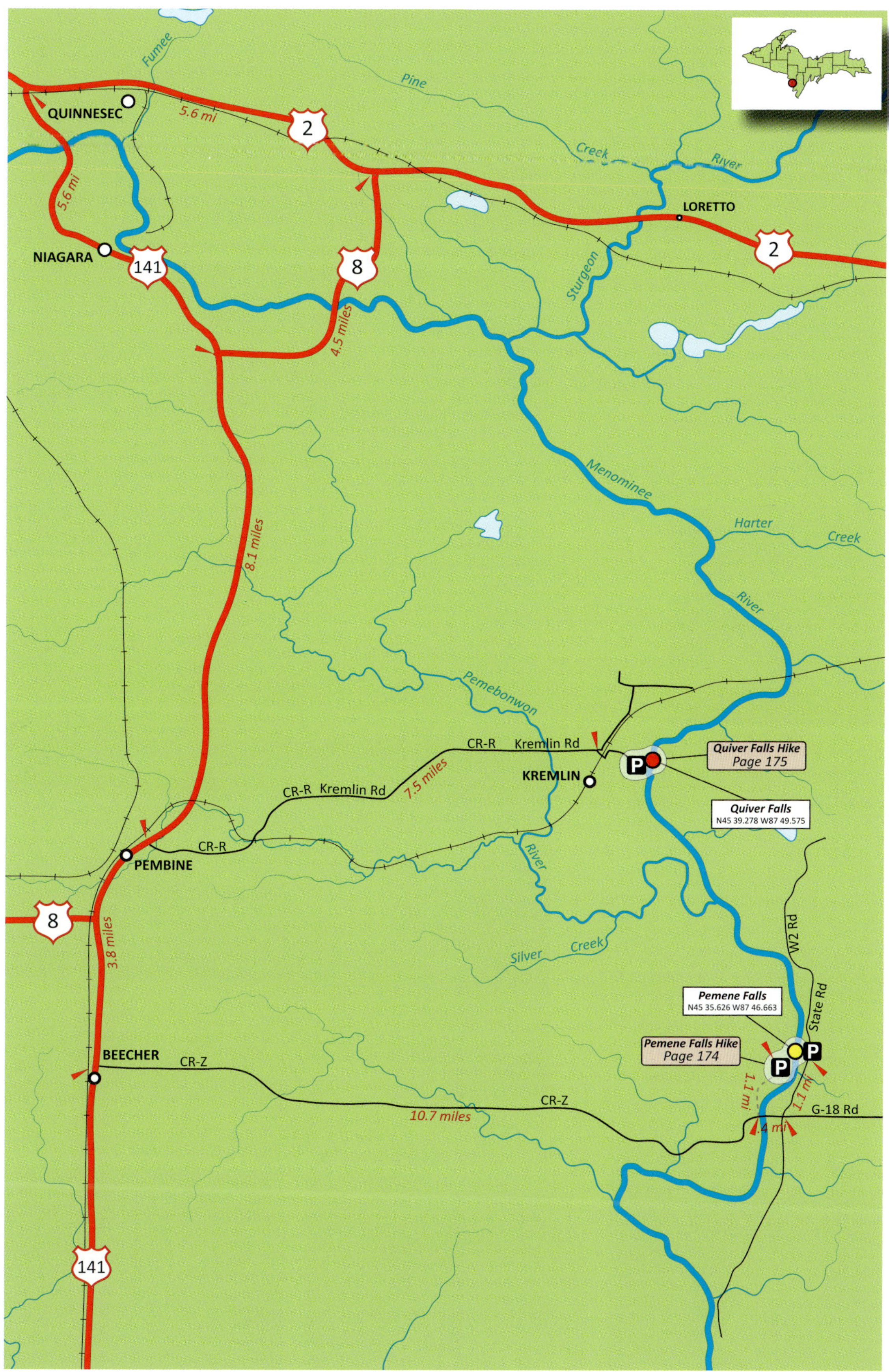

QUINNESEC
5.6 mi
2
Fumee
Pine
Creek
River
LORETTO
2
5.6 mi
NIAGARA
141
8
Sturgeon
4.5 miles
Menominee
River
Harter
Creek
8.1 miles
Pemebonwon
River
CR-R
Kremlin Rd
KREMLIN
7.5 miles
CR-R Kremlin Rd
CR-R
PEMBINE
Quiver Falls Hike
Page 175
Quiver Falls
N45 39.278 W87 49.575
8
3.8 miles
Silver
Creek
W2 Rd
State Rd
Pemene Falls
N45 35.626 W87 46.663
Pemene Falls Hike
Page 174
BEECHER
CR-Z
CR-Z
10.7 miles
1.1 mi
1.1 mi
.4 mi
G-18 Rd
141

Pemene Falls Hike

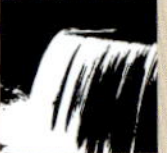

After having been to the Wisconsin side of the river, I have discovered that there is an easy looking access point on the Michigan side. I haven't verified it, so I will give you directions to the Wisconsin side. Use the area map on the previous page to see my directions on viewing from Michigan via State Road.

Directions: From US-2, head south into Wisconsin on US-141 to Beecher. Turn left (east) onto County Road Z. In 10.7 miles, just before getting to the Menominee River, turn left (north) on Verheyen Road. Travel about 1.1 miles on a deteriorating dirt road to the trailhead in the Wisconsin State Park. Some signage is there describing the area. The footpath begins at the shaded parking area with a narrow, but easily hiked trail. It heads straight to the river, turning quickly to the left once the river comes in view. Presently, it descends to the shore level and as the trail drops, the undergrowth increases. At several places, the trail is barely discernible, but since it follows the river, there is no fear of becoming lost. Two hundred yards before the rapids, an outcropping rises to offer a great initial view. Continue on the footpath around a small cove and up again to a higher bluff up above the rapids.

PEMENE FALLS (MENOMINEE RIVER)

Private 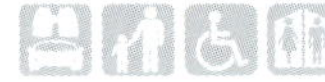

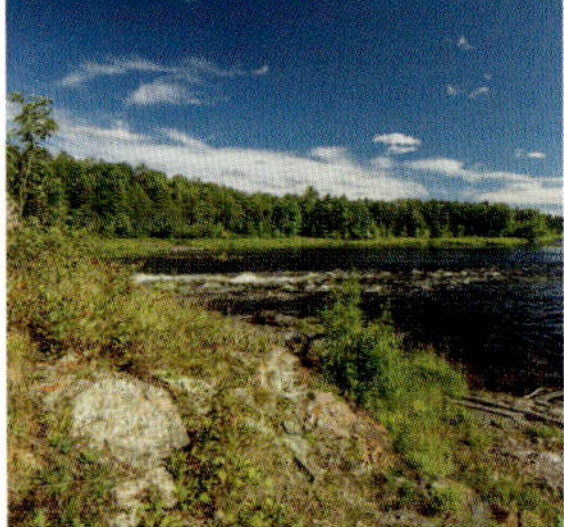

Must See:	5	GPS:	N45 35.626 W87 46.663
Height:	8 feet		
Time:	45-70 minutes	Hiking Information	
		Path:	Footpath - faint at times
Driving Information		Length:	.35 miles
Signs:	None	Elev. Change:	Minor
Road:	2-track	GPS:	Helpful
Access:	Somewhat difficult	Danger:	Minor
4WD:	N/A	WP Boots:	N/A

The river runs in a narrows, constricted between masses of rock. A rib of rock further splits the river. Concrete remains of an old bridge or dam are still in place, now billboards for graffiti. The river widens dramatically after the rapids, opening up in an expanse that is viewed generously from a 30 foot outcropping along the riverbed.

I'd like to check this out from the Michigan side. It looks like a short dirt road heads almost to the old concrete abutments at the river.

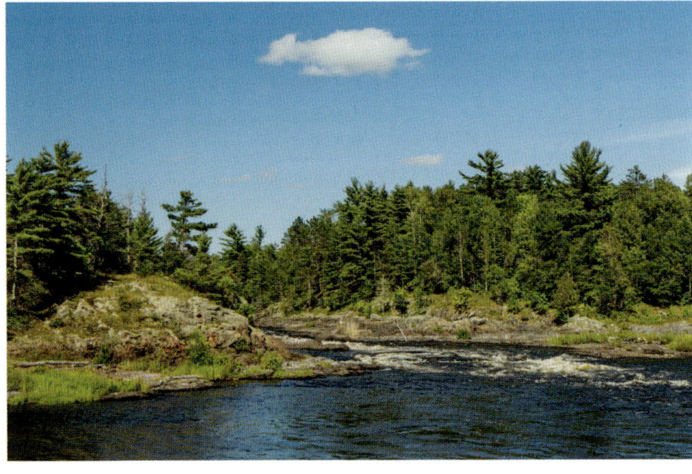

Part of the trail by the river

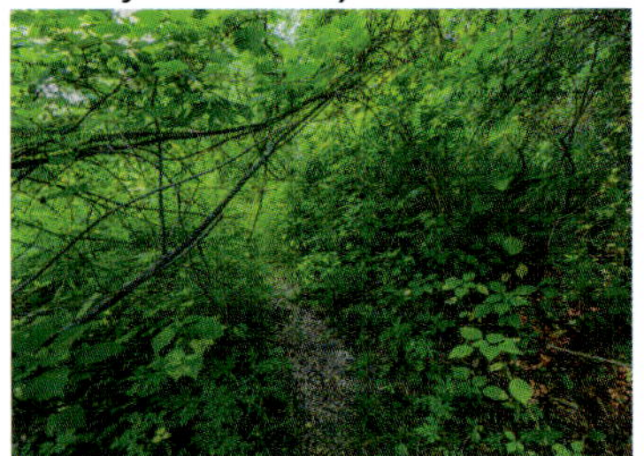

The better part of the footpath

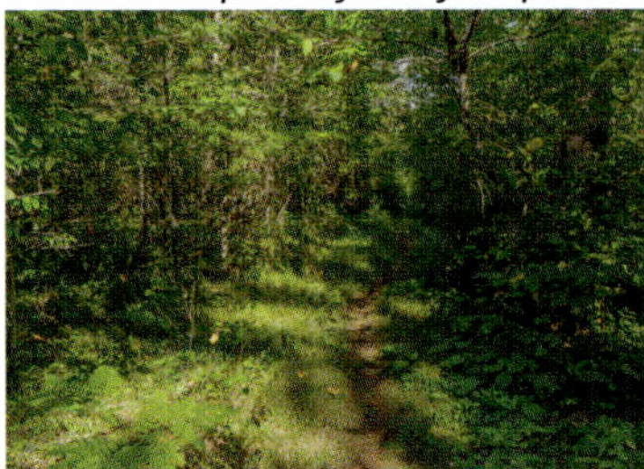

The 2-track to the trailhead

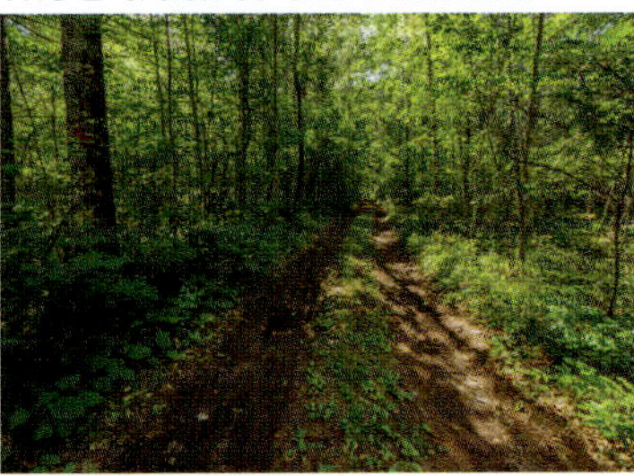

Quiver Falls Hike

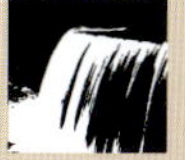

Quiver Falls is a short set of rapids on the Menominee River in a portion of the river that surrounds a good sized rocky island. The bulk of the river flows over toward the Michigan side, but there is no good access to that side. The rapids on the Michigan side of the river can't be viewed from the Wisconsin overlook, so the river looks very narrow, even though it really isn't.

Directions: Head south into Wisconsin from US-2. Off of US-141 just north of Pembine, turn left (east) onto County Road R (Kremlin Rd). Drive 7.5 miles on the winding road. Turn right (southeast) onto Pembine Dam Road. It immediately crosses a set of railroad tracks and turns to the left (north), following the tracks. It becomes a dirt road and turns hard to the right (east) into the woods. Upon entering the forest, drive .7 miles. Park. The rapids are just 50 yards to the south.

QUIVER FALLS (MENOMINEE RIVER)

Private 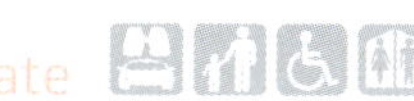

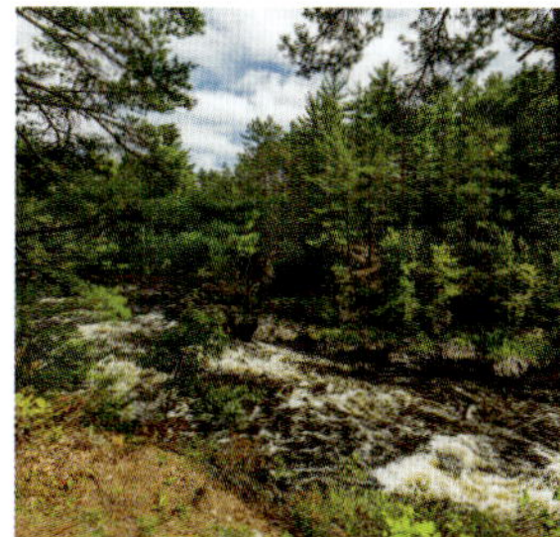

Must See:	2	GPS:	N45 39.278 W87 49.575
Height:	5 feet		
Time:	5-10 minutes	Hiking Information	
		Path:	N/A
Driving Information		Length:	50 Yards
Signs:	None	Elev. Change:	Slight
Road:	Gravel	GPS:	N/A
Access:	Somewhat Difficult	Danger:	Slight
4WD:	N/A	WP Boots:	N/A

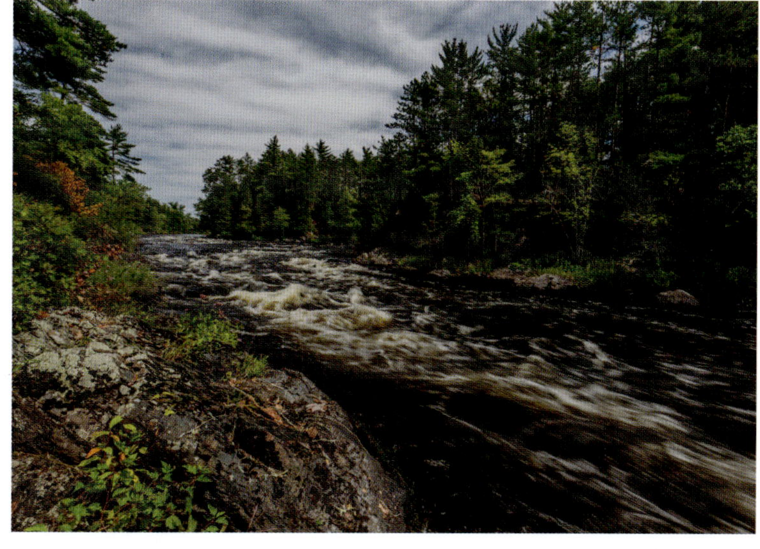

The Menominee River State Recreation Area encompasses a good sized portion of land in both Michigan and Wisconsin along the Menominee River. Features of note include Pemene Falls, Quiver Falls, and Piers Gorge further upstream. It is a collaborative effort between the Wisconsin DNR and Michigan DNR.

Quiver Falls (as seen from the Wisconsin side of the river) is a short set of rapids that runs in a relatively narrow channel between 20 foot high rock walls.

Would you care to seek out more amazing waterfalls in this great state? Then you'll want to check out the rest of the Waterfalls of Michigan Guidebook Series! These should be available at a store near you. If not, request them!

To order online, go to *www.mifalls.com*. That's where you'll also be able to browse through Phil's line of calendars, postcards, and other fine products, stocked in great retail locations around the state of Michigan.

Do you see an image you'd love to hang in your house or office space? The pictures in this book, and many more, are available as archival quality prints, ready to be framed. They can also be purchased, ready to be hung, as canvas wrapped or aluminum prints. Once again, head to *www.mifalls.com* for more information.

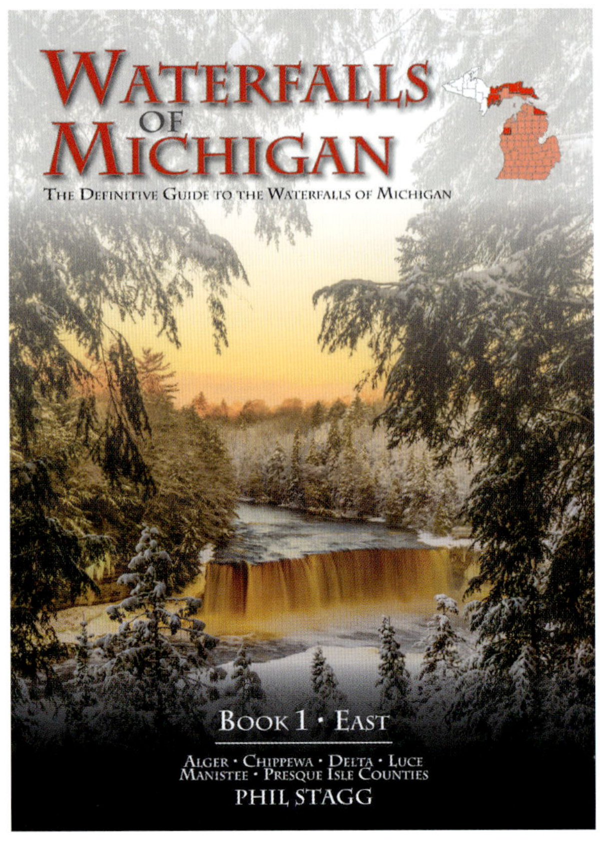

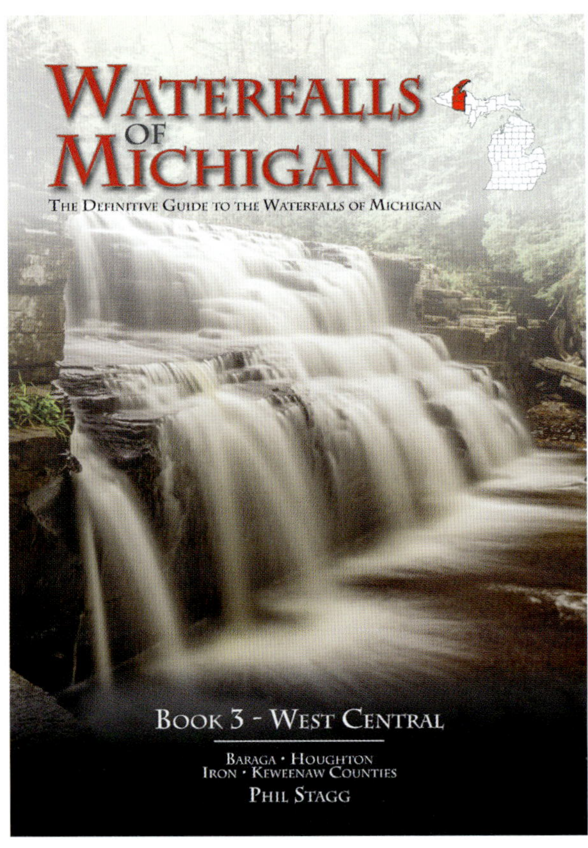

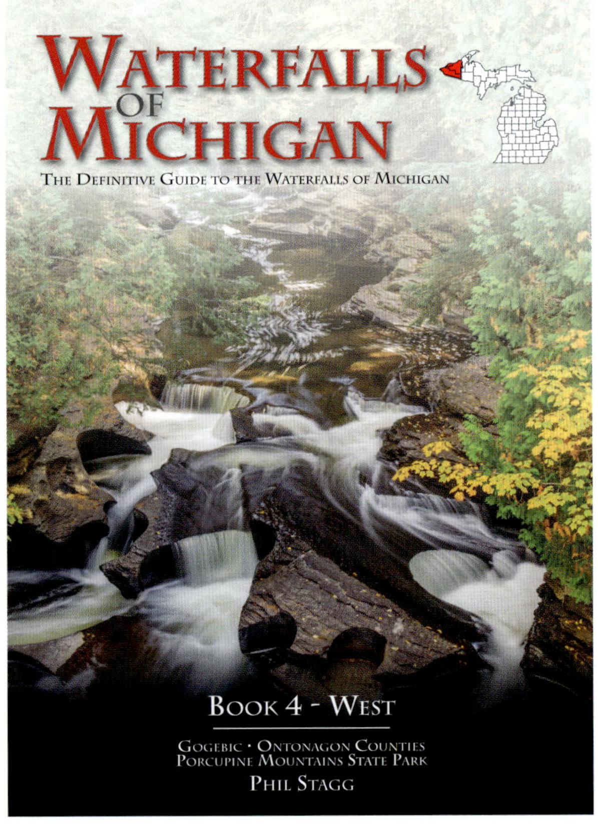

Index

Index